5600 JOKES
FOR ALL OCCASIONS

5600 JOKES
FOR ALL OCCASIONS

by
MILDRED MEIERS
and
JACK KNAPP

WINGS BOOKS

NEW YORK

201 East 50th Street, New York, New York 10022,

http://www.randomhouse.com/

Random House
New York • Toronto • London • Sydney • Auckland

Printed and bound in the United States of America

Library of Congress Cataloging-in-Publication Data

Meiers, Mildred.
  5600 jokes for all occasions.

  Earlier editions published under title: Thesaurus of humor.
  Includes index.
  1. Wit and humor. I. Knapp, joint author. II. Title.
PN6151.M4 1980   808.87   80-20984
ISBN 0-517-32091-6

30 29 28 27 26 25

INTRODUCTION

WHATEVER HUMOR you want is contained in this book. You will enjoy reading it purely for pleasure and laughter, but it is most valuable as a book of quick reference, a helpful guide to the writing and telling of jokes. For not only is this book a mine of material but it also makes it easy for you to select the material you want and shows you how to make the most of it. It is important therefore to read the following pages which tell you

    1. How to select your material
    2. How to write and tell jokes
    3. How to adapt jokes
    4. How to write sketches and continuities.

We suggest you read the entire introduction before proceeding with the selection and development of your material.

HOW TO SELECT YOUR MATERIAL

FIRST, glance through the table of contents to see the general plan of the book. Note that the humorous situations are broadly classified into I. INDIVIDUALS, II. INSTITUTIONS (Marriage, government, etc.) and these are so subdivided that every subject is related to the subjects before it and after it. For the association of ideas is a specially important factor in humor.

Many topics are related also to other subjects in other parts of the book. These are listed as RELATED SUBJECTS at the end of each section.

Now turn to any subject—Accidents, 615-709, for instance. Here are 95 jokes. Certainly you will be able to select enough for most needs. But if you require more material, look at

1. The previous topic (Health) which may apply, and proceed with the topics before that, as long as they apply.

2. The **RELATED SUBJECTS** (at the end of the section).

3. The following subjects (Explosion, Injury, Sickness, etc.) may apply.

This process may be continued until you have the jokes you want and as many as you need.

Since the Index is alphabetical and much more comprehensive and detailed than the Table of Contents, it is better to refer to the Index when looking up a topic. The numbers listed are joke numbers, not page numbers. In all probalility your topic will be listed. If by any chance it isn't, try a synonym or related word or a more general or more specific word. Thus, you will find Coffee, Tea, Caviar, etc. listed. However, you will not find Brussels Sprouts, though Food, Vegetables, etc., are listed.

HOW TO WRITE AND TELL JOKES

BEAR IN mind that the humorous situations contained in this book are basic. They are really outlines, not only funny as they are, but also capable of adaptation, expansion and development.

First, personalize the humor. Name the characters and the place. It is much better to use, instead of

HE AND SHE	Yourself and your wife *or*, Mr. & Mrs. Smith (people in your audience)
A WRITER	Mark Twain or Ernest Hemingway
A SALESMAN	Jack Robinson or some individual well-known to your audience
A WELL-KNOWN WOMAN	Betty Ford, Jackie Onassis, or the Mayor's wife, etc.
A HOTEL	The Waldorf-Astoria or the local hotel
WALKING DOWN THE STREET	Fifth Avenue, Wilshire Boulevard, etc.

Personalizing the story will make it warmer, more interesting and more appealing. When you choose the names to mention, take into consideration the reputations, the associations, fads and foibles of the various possible people. Thus you may be able to add special point, a ludicrous twist or recall a laughable occurrence that everyone will recognize. In this way the picture you make is clearer and more complete. And it is all-important to present a picture.

Compare

"A man and a girl were walking down the street" *with*
"Woody Allen was walking down Vine Street with Jane Fonda".

The first sentence is just words, the second makes a picture.

But personalizing the joke is only part of adaptation. Switching is another important device. Number 4568 is a simple example.

"Who called that master of ceremonies a monkey"?
"Who called that monkey a master of ceremonies?"

Substitute actor, salesman, manicurist or anything else that is apt and a good joke is made better. Likewise, the word "monkey" can be replaced by some other epithet.

A further example of this technique is number 4914:

"If I tear a piece of paper into four, what do I get?
Quarters.
And if I divide it into eight?
Eighths.
And if I divide it into eight thousand parts?
Confetti."

By substituting the word "steak" for paper you have "hamburger" for the final answer. By substituting the word "apple" for paper, you have "applesauce."

Now by using an entirely different approach, we have still another joke:

"If you see one Hollywood player with a mirror, what is it?
A love scene.
If you see two Hollywood players on the screen, what is it?
A crime scene — two people trying to steal the show.
If you see four Hollywood players on the screen, what is it?
An all star cast."

Thus, with a little imagination, one joke has become four.

Having selected a joke and made it your own, the next thing to consider is how to get it across, how to tell it or write it. This matter of delivery is chiefly a question of assurance, knowing your joke and knowing it is good. You must have the clear and definite picture in your mind. Then you will have no trouble in conveying that picture by voice or pen to your audience or readers. Tell it simply and without fumbling. The real skill will come with practice and growing assurance. For the art of humor, like every other art, requires constant exercise.

Before you tell your joke, consider where to pause, where to give your audience a chance to visualize the picture so clearly that when you introduce the unexpected or ludicrous "punch" the effect will be most laughable. This pause may be an actual pause or it may be some unimportant interjection, such as "Well, then" or "And do you know what." Some comedians giggle a moment, or waggle a cigar, or slap someone's back. But the purpose is the same, to let the audience grasp the situation.

A fact to bear in mind is that the first words of any speech almost never register in the minds of listeners. Every experienced speaker says a few unimportant words at the beginning to enable the audience to get into focus with him. No expert starts off with the meat of his message, story or joke. Therefore, start either with some attention-calling device or with a few words of generalities, such as "Everyone is interested in love. As a matter of fact, even I—" and then go on.

If you have planned your delivery properly, you may be certain that your joke will be successful.

Up to this point we have considered the single joke. Of course, for most purposes, several jokes or series of jokes are required. If the several jokes are to be used separately or interspersed in a speech or lecture, no additional principles are involved. But for a series or a continuity a special technique is required.

HOW TO WRITE SKETCHES, SKITS AND CONTINUITIES

DECIDE on a definite setting. As an example, we'll take a courtroom scene. Refer to the Index and you find Court Procedure listed with three sub-headings. The logical starting point is TRIAL 5251-5275. 5263 and 5264 present an opportunity for a good beginning.

> "What floor is this, your Honor?
> The fifth floor.
> I'm going upstairs.
> What for?
> I want to be tried in a higher court.'
>
> *Judge:* Order, order, order in the court!
> *Prisoner:* I'll take a ham sandwich on rye with beer."

Then number 5269 fits right in:

> "*To witness:* Take the chair!
> *Witness:* What for? I got plenty of furniture now."

And follow with 5271:

> "*Judge:* Have you a lawyer?
> *Prisoner:* No, but I have some good friends on the jury."

And possible 5258:

> "*Judge:* Do you want a lawyer to defend you?
> *Prisoner:* Not particularly, sir.
> *Judge:* Well, what do you propose to do about the case?
> *Prisoner:* Oh, I'm quite willing to drop it as far as I'm concerned."

By this time the suggestion will come to you that the cause of the trial should be determined. A divorce? Drunkeness? Robbery? Whatever it is, that particular topic presents an additional source of humor and it is important to select one with comic possibilities. Let's say it's a case of a stolen cow. Before you consult COW, look at the topics before and after TRIAL. JUDGE (before) offers possibilities, so does ATTORNEY, etc. Likewise FINES-SENTENCES, etc. (after). Consult the RELATED SUBJECTS that are mentioned and select the likely possibilities. In this way you will have a plentiful supply of jokes specifically covering a courtroom scene. Then by referring to COW you will have an additional source of humor.

Now, consider your picture and visualize it. In this particular case, we need additional characters besides Judge, Prisoner, Lawyer, etc. A Drunk might be a good source of humor. We can adapt No. 5264, mentioned above, to introduce the drunk who could be placed somewhere in the courtroom. The prisoner's sweetheart, buddy or boss, etc. might also be useful for comedy. Thus, DRUNK, SWEETHEART, etc. are additional topics that may be consulted.

By this time, we have ample material and we have developed our continuity. There still remains the process of adaptation. Some of this suggests itself almost automatically. For instance, we adapted No. 5264 from an exchange between Judge and Prisoner to an exchange between Judge and Drunk. But be sure also to personalize all the dialogue in accordance with the setting.

One other factor that will be effective in building up your sketch is *Off Shoots*. Take 5264 again: "Ham sandwich on rye with beer." This presents an opportunity to use jokes about Ham, Sandwich, Rye, Beer. And furthermore, the line can be adapted to "plum pie and a glass of milk" or "a plate of Jell-o with Sanka" and continue from there.

We have taken at random an ordinary setting and we have shown how about 1,000 jokes were marshalled for use. It is just as simple to assemble the humor on any topic.

A joke may also be "switched" by changing the punch line.

Example: Let us use number 2238:

"Let's sleep in the gutter.
Why?
Plenty of room with running water."

By "switching" the last line you may easily develop a number of different situations. Examples: "No danger of falling out of bed." — "I'm a fresh air fiend." — "We're here, why not go to sleep?" — "We'll wake up in the groove."

As you can readily see, the possibilites are endless.

The variations of jokes and continuities which may be derived from and suggested by this book are limited only by your own imagination. There is no reason why you may not use all the infinite subjects for mirth the world has to offer.

Unfortunately, there are probably many of you who realize the tremendous power that comedy possesses but cannot unleash it. Perhaps you run into difficulty when you begin to grope for the appropriate dash, the delicate *espirit*, or the direct "punch." Undoubtedly you have often wondered where to turn.

It is to fit your demand, to fill a need which has hitherto gone unfulfilled, that *5600 Jokes For All Occasions* has been created.

TABLE OF CONTENTS

NOTE: *In order to know how to use this book properly, it is important to read the introduction.*

(For alphabetical list of 4000 subjects, see *Index,* page 573)

Numbers in smaller type below are joke numbers, not page numbers.

INDIVIDUALS

INSTITUTIONS

5600 JOKES
FOR ALL OCCASIONS

I.–INDIVIDUALS

HUMAN BEINGS

EXISTENCE

LIFE

1 How long can a man live on his nerve?
Oh, I don't know. How old is your father?

2 Is it true that married men live longer than single men?
No, it only seems longer.

3 When a person is told he only has twelve months to live, he's got
to do something about it!
You told me yesterday your doctor only gave you one month to live.
I know, but I saw eleven other doctors.

4 Stop yawning.
I'm tired.
Then place your hand over your mouth.
What? And bite myself. I might get hydrophobia.
How could you get hydrophobia?
I have been leading a dog's life for three years.

5 What type of person lives longest?
A rich relative.

6 Do you know any reliable rule for estimating the cost of living?
Yes. Take your income, whatever that may be, and add 10 per cent.

7 Why do women live longer than men?
I don't know, unless it's because paint is a great preventive.

8 I have to fight another duel today.
Do you make a habit of dueling?
I lead a duel life.

9 I have written a book! I have put down my life in verse.
Your whole life?
How can I write my whole life? I'm not dead yet.

10 Today's tabloid biography: High chair, high school, high stool,
high finance, high hat—hi, warden!

RELATED SUBJECTS
Age 45-107
Death 124-145

BIRTH

11 Under what sign of the Zodiac was she born?
Under what?
Under what sign was she born?
ROOM FOR RENT.

12 On what day were you born?
Monday.
What day—what date in the month?
The date on which I was born.
I know, but when were you born?
The day after they took my mother to the hospital.

13 Where were you born?
I was born in Oregon, but I went to school in Chicago.
Gee—you had some way to go, didn't you?

14 Where were you born?
In New York. I wanted to be near my mother.
What's your parents' names?
Papa and mama.

15 I used to pout and fret and curse the day I was born. Did you ever do that?
No, I was three years old before I learned to swear.

16 I was born in New York.
Funny things happen in Chicago, too.

17 When I was born I weighed two pounds.
Did you live?
Sure — you ought to see me now!

18 I wonder where he was born?
He was born on a farm.
On a farm? Any more in the litter?

19 Born?
Yes, sir.
Where?
Russia.
What part?
All of me.
Why did you leave Russia?
I couldn't bring it with me.
Where were your forefathers born?
I only got one father.
Your business?
Rotten.

Where is Washington?
He's dead.
I mean, the capital of the United States?
They loaned it all to Europe.
Now, do you promise to support the Constitution?
Me? How can I? I've got a wife and six children to support.

20   How come you were born in Ireland?
     My mother wanted me near her.

21   Were you born out of wedlock?
     No—I was born in New York City.

22   Where were you born?
     In a hospital.

23   When were you born?
     April 2nd.
     A day too late.

24   I wish I had been born in the Dark Ages.
     So do I, you look terrible in the light.

25   My mother was terribly disappointed when I was born.
     Did she want a boy?
     No, she wanted a divorce.

26   I was born in vain.
     That's funny. I was born in Ohio.

27   I was born in Victoria, B. C.
     B.C.? You look it.

28   She was born on her parents' wooden anniversary so they called
     her "Peg."

29   So you're a Southerner? Where were you born?
     Southern Maine.

30   Where were you born?
     Where was I born? Say, I was only a little baby at the time. Do you
     remember where you were born?

31   He claims to have been born with a gold spoon in his mouth.
     If he was, I'll bet it had somebody else's initials on it.

32   When did you first see the light of day?
     Well, I was born in Pittsburgh, but it was three years later that I
     first saw the light of day when I moved to Philadelphia.

33   When was your son born?
     In March—he came the first of the month.
     Is that why you call him "Bill"?

34   I was born under an unlucky star. I have been cursed from the day
        I was born.
     How could being born under an unlucky star influence your life?
     I was born under the sign of the Big Bear—I was born with bare feet.

                              RELATED SUBJECTS
                              Age 45-107
                              Names of People 939-1017
                              Baby 3359-3389

STORK

35   How many children has your uncle got now?
     I haven't seen him since yesterday. He had 25 or 30 then.
     I guess the stork is familiar with his house?
     The stork was very careful at first. He'd fly over the house, land on
        the roof and bring them down the chimney. Now, he just yells
        down and says: "Come on and get 'em!"

36   The little girl in the zoological park tossed bread pieces to the
        stork, which bobbed its head toward her for more.
     What kind of bird is that, Momma?
     It's a stork.
     O-o-o-h! No wonder it recognized me!

37   An elderly woman was escorting two little girls around the Zoo.
        While they were looking at the stork, she told them the legend of
        the ungainly bird—how it was instrumental in bringing them to
        their mamas.
     The children looked at each other with sly glances, and presently
        one whispered to the other: "Don't you think we ought to tell the
        dear old thing the truth?"

38   Man: (To newsboy) Give me a Sun.
     Newsboy: Whaddya think I am, the stork?

39   It says here in the paper about a "Stoic"— what's them things?
     Gee, kid—yer dumb. A stoic is de boid that brings de babies.

40   What happened to that stork of yours?
     He's still kidding around.

41   Now, Jill, tell the class what a stork is.
     Why, Miss Jones! You know there's no such thing as the stork!

42   The day the baby was born, when the father saw how ugly the kid
        was the father ran down to the zoo and threw rocks at the stork.

43   He isn't any good—never was any good and never will be any good.
        In fact, when he was born his mother should have thrown him
        away and kept the stork.

44 The stork's getting lazy.
   Getting lazy?
   Yeah, he's bringing them six at a time now.
   RELATED SUBJECTS   Baby 3359-3389
   Marriage 2882-3051

AGE

45 (Silly girl) : How old do you think I am?
   Forty-four years old.
   (Silly girl) : How do you happen to make that out?
   I have a brother twenty-two and he is half nuts.

46 I'm very young.
   How young are you?
   In the neighborhood of sixteen.
   You had better move.

47 How old are you?
   Well, I'd be twenty in October, but for one thing.
   What is that?
   I was born in February.

48 I want to commit suicide.
   Why do that?
   I'm suffering from lumbago.
   Oh, give yourself another chance. How old are you?
   Eighteen.
   Oh . . you're also suffering from loss of memory.

49 How old is your girl?
   Petty Lovey is just eighteen years old. I saw it on the city record
      and you can't scratch that out.
   What do you mean, she's eighteen years old? Why, she's had the
      seven-year itch four times and you can't scratch that out.

50 How old is your new girl?
   She says she has lived 32 summers—but I heard afterwards she'd
      spent most of her life at the North Pole.

51 So you know Miss Trumpet, the famous actress?
   Oh yes—we lived next door when we were kids. Then we were the
      same age—but now I'm 35 and she's just 18.

52 I have two million dollars and I'm 85 years old—will you marry
      me or am I too old for you?
   You have two million dollars and you're 85 years old? I'll marry
      you. Why, I'd be satisfied if you were ten years older.

53 We did have a vacancy in the chorus but you're too late.
   Too late?
   Yeah, about ten years too late.

54   My fiance's birthday is next week and I want to give him a surprise.
        What would you suggest?
     Tell him your real age!

55   How old are you?
     That is a difficult question. The latest personal survey available
        shows my psychological age to be 12, my moral age, 4, my anatom-
        ical age 7, and my physiological age 6. I suppose, however, that
        you refer to my chronological age, which is 8. That is so old-
        fashioned that I seldom think of it any more.

56   How old are you?
     I'm just eighteen.
     Just eighteen! Time marches backwards.

57   I like that dress you're wearing.
     I got it for my 16th birthday.
     It certainly wore well, didn't it?

58   Gracious, it's been five years since I've seen you. You look lots older.
     Really, my dear, I don't think I would have recognized you if it
        weren't for the coat.

59   How old is she?
     I don't know how old she is, but a good cup of tea rests her. I know
        she has stopped patting herself on the back and is patting herself
        under the chin now.

60   How old are you?
     Twenty years old.
     Only twenty?
     You mean that it doesn't seem possible that I'm 20 years old.
     I can't imagine anyone being so dumb in such a short time.

61   I suppose I'll never get married.
     Why do you say that?
     Well, I'm not old enough for the young men, and I'm not young
        enough for the old men.

62   Wonder why we never had a woman for president?
     Sap! Don't you know the president has to be over 35 years of age?

63   A man is as old as he feels and a woman as old as she feels like
        admitting.

64   How old is she?
     Oh, I couldn't say—but she knew the Big Dipper when it was only
        a drinking cup.

65   How old is she?
     I don't know, but everybody was overcome by the heat from the
        candles at her last birthday party.

66 Doctor, I'm suffering from a pain in my right leg.
There's no cure, alas! It's because of old age.
You must be mistaken, Doctor. The left leg is as old as the right
and it doesn't hurt me at all.

67 My wife is just forty.
Why don't you change her for two twenties?

68 There's a chorus of seventy at the theatre.
They look it.

69 I used to be young once.
What a memory—what a memory!

70 How old are you?
Eighteen.
Eighteen, eh?
Yeah. How old are you?
Well, the way you figure, I'm not born yet.

71 How old are you?
I'm eighteen and I'm very shy.
Yeah, shy about ten years.

72 What's the dangerous age for a married man?
His wife's.

73 The seven ages of women are: The first age is a baby, then an infant,
then a miss, then she's a young woman, a young woman, a young
woman, and a young woman.

74 I always feel safe when there's a man around the house.
Well, you should at your age.

75 How old is your girl?
Twenty summers.
How many winters?
None—she lives in California.

76 How old is he?
Four years old.
He doesn't look it.
I know—he was born very young.

77 How old is she?
Thirty.
She looks older.
I know—she was born old.

78 The seven ages of women are: Her own and six guesses.

79 Are you married?
Yes—twice.

Your age?
Twenty.
Also twice.

80 He doesn't know how old he is?
No—he can't count up that high.

81 You're very beautiful.
Say, when I was sixteen years old the President of the United States
    presented me with a beauty prize.
Go on, you can't get me to believe Lincoln went in for that silly stuff.

82 A recent show advertised a chorus of seventy, but some of them
    didn't look to be a day over sixty-five.

83 Well, how old would you say I am?
Let's see—I don't know what to say.
Well, you must have some idea.
I have several ideas. The only trouble is that I hesitate whether to
    make you ten years younger on account of your looks or ten years
    older on account of your intelligence.

84 What do you think is a nice age for women?
Well, I think thirty is a nice age for women. Especially if she hap-
    pens to be forty.

85 Friend: You're too old for such things.
Judge: Too old! Why, I could give you twenty years.
Friend: Now, now, Judge. Don't start talking shop.

86 I don't intend to be married until I'm thirty.
I don't intend to be thirty until I'm married.

87 Oh, there's something very mysterious about her.
What is it?
It's a big secret.
Well, what is it? Tell me.
It's about her birth.
Well, what's so mysterious about that?
The date.

88 There are two ways of telling a woman's age when she's thirty. First,
    it shows on her face and then ten years later she shows it on her
    birthday cake.

89 When he asked me how old I was I couldn't remember whether I
    was twenty-four or twenty-five.
And what did you say?
Eighteen.

90 I wonder if I shall ever live to be a hundred?
Not if you remain twenty-two much longer.

91   What's the meanest thing you can do to a woman?
     Will her a fortune payable at the age of thirty-five.

92   When I flirted with you, I thought I was picking up a chicken.
     Well, I must have been a chicken 'cause when I flirted with you, I
     picked up a worm.

93   Man: (Selling medicine) Look at me—hale and hearty. I'm over
       300 years old.
     New Assistant: Is he really as old as that, Joe?
     Assistant: I can't say — I've only worked for him for 100 years.

94   Little boy, how old is your mother?
     Aw, she was forty-two but she's marked down to 27.

95   Have you known Phyllis long?
     Oh, yes. I've known her ever since we were the same age.

96   How old is your grandfather?
     I don't know, but we have had him a long time.

97   How old do you think I am?
     You don't look it.

98   To what do you attribute your great age?
     I can't say yit. They's several o' 'em testimonial fellers a-dickerin'
     with me.

99   I feel like a two year old.
     What?
     I feel like a two year old.
     A horse, or an egg?

100 Are you and your twin brother the oldest of your family?
     No, mother and daddy are quite a bit older.

101 Are you the oldest?
     No — my sister is older than me.
     And who comes after her?
     Nobody. If anybody does they can have her.

102 I'll let you know I come from a line of hale and hearty ancestors.
       Why, I had an uncle that drank and stayed up late every night
       and he died at the ripe old age of 94.
     Just goes to prove it'll get you in the end.

103 Old Man: Young man, you can put in your paper that my secret of
       health and long life is to eat some garlic every day.
     Reporter: Why do you refer to it as a secret?

104 My grandfather lived to be 90 years old.
     Ninety? What finally got him?
     Liquor and women.

That shows they'll get you in the end.
No—he couldn't get either one, so he just laid down and died.

105   My father's eighty years old and never uses glasses.
I notice that he prefers to drink out of a bottle.

106   This seems to be a healthy country. You say you are nearly 70 and
can still do a full day's work. That's pretty good.
Yes, but my old dad, who is 97, is even a harder worker than I am.
His health must be wonderfully good.
No, it ain't. For the last several years he ain't had quite his old-time
pep. Sometimes I kinda think farmin' don't agree with him.

107   How old are you?
Just passed 27.
Well, what detained you?

RELATED SUBJECTS   Old Maid 2568-2582
Birth 11-34   Wife 3111-3112
Female (the) 925-938

BIRTHDAY

108   My girl's birthday is tomorrow. What do you think she wants for
her birthday?
Not to be reminded of it.

109   It's cold in this room. We should have some more heat.
Why don't you light up the candles on your birthday cake? They
should heat up the whole house.

110   Boo! Boo! Boo!
What are you doing?
Tomorrow's my girl's birthday—and I want to surprise her—so
I'm practicing.

111   We're celebrating the anniversary of my sister's birthday.
The anniversary of your sister's birthday? You celebrate an anniversary or a birthday. They're different ideas entirely.
That's what you think. But we're celebrating the 15th anniversary
of my sister's eighteenth birthday.

112   I hate to think of my twenty-ninth birthday.
Why? What happened?

113   A kind lady, being duly impressed by a tramp calling at her back
door, gave him a whole cake. The tramp said: That's very nice,
lady; would you mind sticking forty candles in it? Today's my
birthday.

114   I'm going to have twenty candles on my birthday cake.
What are you going to do—burn the candles at both ends?

115 How did you get that black eye, Mrs. Higgins?
Well, me 'usband came out of jail on 'is birthday.
Yes?
And I wisht him many 'appy returns.

116 Have a look at the cake I decorated for my birthday party. Don't
you think my sense of design is wonderful?
Yes, but your arithmetic is terrible.

117 When you quarreled today, you let your husband have the last
word. That was not usual.
No, but I wanted to give him a little pleasure—it's his birthday.

118 John, I'm awfully disappointed. You haven't given me anything
for my 29th birthday.
Twenty-ninth? You've forgotten, darling. I gave it to you last year.

119 Birthstones:
For laundresses, the soapstone.
For architects, the cornerstone.
For cooks, the puddingstone.
For soldiers, the bloodstone.
For politicians, the blarneystone.
For borrowers, the touchstone.
For policemen, the pavingstone.
For stock brokers, the curbstone.
For burglars, the keystone.
For tourists, the Yellowstone.
For beauties, the peachstone.
For editors, the grindstone.
For motorists, the milestone.
For pedestrians, the tombstone.

120 So you're twenty-nine years old today? Isn't it terrible to celebrate
a birthday so close to your thirtieth one?
Oh, no, I'm getting used to it.

RELATED SUBJECTS
Astrology 1278-1285
Party 3575-3579
Gift 3943-3962

SECOND CHILDHOOD
121 I think you are in your second childhood.
Well, if I am, I'm having a lot better time than I had in my
first one.

122 I wish to goodness we could go home, mother, but dad wants to stay
for three more dances.
Yes, dear, your father is a trial, isn't he? But, after all, one can be
old only once.

123   A Scotchman: A fellow who saves all his playthings for his second childhood.

RELATED SUBJECTS
Age 45-107
Fresh People 2397-2408
Flirtation 2779-2784
Lady Killer 2792-2793

DEATH

124   It's no use worrying about life, old pal.
Why not?
Because you'll never get out of it alive.

125   My cousin has invented a new coffin. It just goes over the head.
What's the idea?
It's for people who are dead from the neck up. Do you want to buy one?

126   Do you believe it is possible to communicate with the dead?
Yes, I can hear you distinctly.

127   What is it that walks, talks, sleeps, eats and still is dead?
What?
You.

128   An Irishman saw, while passing through a graveyard, these words written on a tombstone: I still live.
Pat looked a moment and then said: Bejabbers, if I was dead, I'd own up to it.

129   So Jones is dead. Did he leave his wife much?
Oh, nearly every night.

130   (Stick up)
I've got to have money.
What for?
I gotta bury a friend.
That's too bad—when did he die?
Tomorrow—and you're next if you don't give me some money.

131   What must a man be to be buried with military honors?
A captain.
Oh, pshaw! Then I lose my bet.
What did you bet?
I bet that he must be dead.

132   What's the idea kicking my bucket of water over?
I just wanted to see how it felt to kick the bucket.

133   And poor Harry was killed by a revolving crane.
My word! What fierce birds you have in this country.

134　I have a posthumous book of an author who lived in my home town. Where does he live now?

135　Shaking your hand is like seeing the footprints on the sands of time.

136　Father, can my new boy friend replace your business partner that died this morning?
It's all right with me—if you can arrange it with the undertaker.

137　Didn't he leave you alone when he died?
Leave me a loan? As a matter of fact, he made a little loan off me just before he died.
His death touched me deeply.
Did he make a loan off of you, too?

138　I was grieved to hear your husband has gone at last.
Yes, and I only hope he's gone where I know he ain't.

139　If I should die would you visit my grave often?
Yes, I have to pass the graveyard to go to my hair dresser, anyway.

140　Whiskey kills more people than bullets.
That's because bullets don't drink.

141　My uncle was finally put to rest last week.
We didn't know he had passed away.
He didn't, but my aunt did.

142　You know, in Egypt they have a peculiar superstition. They're afraid of burying people alive, so when a man dies they bury him for sixty days and then dig him up, place him on a cold slab, and have twenty beautiful girls dance around him for two hours.
What good does that do?
Well, if he doesn't get up—he's sure to be dead.

143　Two things we're sure of—Death and taxes.
Yeah, but one thing about death, it doesn't get worse every time Congress meets.

144　Say, listen, I'm not dead.
No? Well, the doctor says you are.
But I tell you I'm not.
Lie down—do you want to make a liar out of the doctor?

145　Nell, after I die, I wish you'd marry Deacon Brown.
Why so, Hiram?
Well, the deacon trimmed me on a horse trade once.

RELATED SUBJECTS
Cemetery 173-176
Widow 188-192
Heaven 2555-2565
Murderer 5219-5224

SUICIDE

146 My girl has turned against me. I'm going to commit suicide. I've
        nothing to lose.
        Well, tighten your belt—you're losing your pants.

147 You picked a good day to end it all by drowning.
        Something is holding me back.
        What?
        I can't swim.

148 Why don't you get a rope and swing yourself up on a tree in front
        of her house and that will make her feel terrible.
        I would, but I can't do that.
        Why?
        Because if I were dead she wouldn't want me hanging around.

149 My father committed suicide.
        That wasn't very thoughtful of him.
        I'll say it wasn't—when he got through he didn't turn off the gas
        and our bill was terrible.

150 (Man sentenced to 90 years kills himself in court)
        Judge: That will be ten years more for contempt of court.

151 My boy friend said he was going to jump off a cliff 300 feet high
        if I didn't marry him.
        Sounds like a big bluff to me.

152 How do you know that the man who shot himself was insane?
        He had two teeth filled an hour before he did it.

153 My uncle jumped off a twenty story building today.
        Say, what are you talking about? There isn't a twenty story build-
        ing in this town.
        Well, he jumped off a ten story building twice.

154 Oh, sir, there's a Scotchman out here who wants to buy ten cents
        worth of poison to commit suicide. How can I save him?
        Tell him it'll cost twenty cents.

155 I'm going to commit suicide. Where is the best place to shoot
        myself?
        Well, shoot yourself in the chest. You're dead from the neck up
        anyway.

156 A man was shot, a knife was found by his side, and you're asking
        me who poisoned him? Well, who poisoned him?
        Nobody. He hanged himself.

157 You say he killed himself? What was the motive?
        I don't know, sir, he just jumped in front of the train.
        Ah—loco-motive.

158   If you refuse me I'll blow my brains out!
      Oh, how could you?

159   I heard one of the students in college took chloroform and died.
      Yeah, some of these courses are pretty tough.

160   I'm going to shoot the man who married my wife.
      But that's murder, isn't it?
      No, it's suicide.

161   Why did your uncle commit suicide?
      On account of his absentmindedness.
      What do you mean?
      He went to the citizens' training camp and shot himself one night
        when on guard duty. He forgot the password.

162   Statistics prove that marriage is a preventive of suicide.
      Yes, and statistics also prove that suicide is a preventive of marriage.

                              RELATED SUBJECTS
                              Heaven 2555-2565
                              Love 2595-2640

UNDERTAKER

163   My father always says he'll get them sooner or later.
      Sooner or later?
      Yeah—he's an undertaker.

164   You told me yesterday your uncle was a Southern Planter. Does
      he have a cotton plantation?
      No. He's a Southern Planter. He's an undertaker in New Orleans.

RELATED SUBJECTS   Cemetery 173-176
Death 124-145   Mourning 193-199

FUNERAL

165   My brother is a scientist. He crossed a peach with a plum, and
      got a nectarine.
      I don't think that's so good. My uncle crossed a locomotive with
      an automobile and got a funeral.

166   Are you going to your uncle's funeral?
      Oh, no, I'm working today and my motto is business before pleasure.

167   (Banker acting as pallbearer): I carried him so long, I might as
      well carry him in death.

168   What do you need with the money?
      I need it for railroad fare. My nephew died. I have to buy him a
      round trip ticket to Alabama.
      What are you talking about? You just said your nephew was dead.
      What's the idea of a round trip ticket to Alabama?
      Well, we got about forty relations in Alabama who would like to

take a last look at him, and I figured it was cheaper to send him back down there for them to see than to pay for all of them to come up here to see him.

169   Was the funeral nice?
Lovely. I put him in a swell spot. I paid twenty dollars for a tombstone.
How come you got it so cheaply?
That's because the man I bought it from at the tombstone place did a little chiseling.

170   A friend of mine is having a funeral from his house and I have to stand out on his porch at the front door.
What good could you do standing out on his porch at the front door?
I got to be the crepe.

171   Why don't you join the Navy?
Why?
Well, if you're fortunate enough to die while on active service, they give you a beautiful funeral, headed by a wonderful band.

172   There goes the funeral of a great polo player.
Yes, he rides just like he was part of the hearse.

RELATED SUBJECTS   Widow 188-192
Death 124-145   Friend 1037-1056

CEMETERY

173   Well, what do you think of our little city?
I'll tell you, brother, this is the first cemetery I ever saw with lights.

174   The place is so healthy they had to shoot a traveling salesman to start the cemetery.

175   A man died. He had been operated on so many times that they put the following notice on his tombstone: Gone to join his kidneys, his appendix, his tonsils and his adenoids.

176   When a preacher said to Mr. Jones that he should give a small donation for a fence around the cemetery, Mr. Jones said: I don't see any use in a fence around a cemetery. Those who are in there can't get out, and those who are out sure don't want to get in.

RELATED SUBJECTS
Death 124-145
Mourning 193-199

GHOST

177   I didn't believe in ghosts either, so I said I'd stay in the haunted house. I moved right in and the first night at three o'clock in the morning, a ghost came through the wall just as if there weren't no wall there at all.

What did you do?
I went through the opposite wall the same way.

178 I saw a ghost up there.
What did it look like?
It looked like a jackass.
Awww, don't be afraid of your own shadow.

179 When he dies, he's threatened to come back and haunt me.
He won't do that.
Why not?
Oh, 'cause he hasn't got a haunting license.

180 Listen, ghost, how much will you charge to haunt my girl's father?
For $10 I'll agree to scare him out of his wits.
Here's $5.
I said $10.
Yes, but he's only a half wit.

181 And my brother intends marrying a second wife who is so ugly that
he has to tell his children ghost stories for two weeks so that she
won't frighten the children when he brings her home.

182 I'm a ghost—I'm the ghost of Joe Doak the saxophone player.
Joe Doak, the saxophone player? You must have died suddenly.
Yes. I was playing a saxophone solo and for the first time I forgot
to put cotton in my ears.
What happened?
I dropped dead.

183 It's no use—you're as deaf as a post.
(Deaf man) No, sir, don't believe in 'em.
Don't believe in what?
(Deaf man) Ghosts—no, sir. Nothin' to be afraid of. A skeleton's
nothing but a stack of bones with the people scraped off.

RELATED SUBJECTS   Spiritualism 1276-1277
Death 124-145   Fear 2340-2347

REINCARNATION

184 Sure I believe in reincarnation.
You do?
I'll say, and when I come back to earth, I want to be a mattress.
A mattress? Why?
So I can lie in bed all day.

185 Do you believe in reincarnation?
Yes—because nobody could be as dumb as you are in one lifetime.

186 Do you believe in reincarnation?
Yeah, and that's what's worrying me.

Worrying you?

Yeah, if I die and make up my mind to come back as a dog, I'm afraid my wife will make up her mind to come back as a flea.

187   I hope in your next life you're a centipede and have ingrown toe-nails.

RELATED SUBJECTS
Death 124-145
Mind Reader 1259-1285

WIDOW

188   Did you hear about the pretty girl, the young widow and the old maid?

No, I haven't heard about them. What happened?

They all lived in the same house, and each agreed to come down in the morning and repeat the word "morning" for each kiss they had received the night before.

For every kiss they were to say "morning"?

Yes. The pretty girl came down and said: Good morning! It's a pretty morning this morning. Then the young widow came down and said: Good morning! It's a pretty morning this morning. If tomorrow morning is as pretty a morning as this morning, it will be a pretty morning tomorrow morning. Then the old maid came down.

And what did she say?

Howdee!

189   I'm going to marry a widow.

I wouldn't want to be the second husband of a widow.

I'd rather be the second than the first.

190   Where did you get that black eye?

You know that pretty little woman who said she was a widow?

Yes.

Well, she isn't.

191   Don't you know the difference between grass widows and grass-hoppers?

Don't be silly—my uncle says there isn't any difference—they both hop at the first chance they get.

192   Didn't your husband die and leave you a widow?

I wouldn't know what to do with a widow if I had one.

RELATED SUBJECTS   Funeral 165-172
Death 124-145   Marriage 2882-3051

MOURNING

193   What's the matter—you look mournful?

That's just it—I've just finished a big dinner and I am more'n full.

194 Hi, Harry! What's the matter? You look like you just got back
from a funeral.

Well, Joe, my wife got hit by a truck.

Oh, that's too bad. You look pretty busted up.

If you think *I* look bad, you should have seen my *wife!*

195 Please play the piano for us?

I don't think I can—My aunt passed away last week.

That's all right—just play on the black keys.

196 What are you crying about?

My little dog—I lost him—he died today.

Well, my mother-in-law died this morning. You don't see me
crying out like you are.

You didn't raise your mother-in-law from a pup.

197 Why does she wear mourning?

For her husband.

She never had a husband.

That's why she is mourning.

198 Well, I see you're wearing a black tie in mourning for me. Why
not a black suit, too?

Because you're only dead from the neck up.

199 I saw your uncle, the flag pole sitter, this morning, but he was
sitting at half mast.

Yeah, he's in mourning for his wife who died yesterday.

> RELATED SUBJECTS
> Death 124-145
> Flowers 3768-3771

LAST WILL AND TESTAMENT

200 My uncle's very kindhearted. He made out his will and he left
my father $10,000; my mother $5,000, and my brother and I
each $5,000.

Your uncle hasn't a red cent to his name.

Yeah, but it just goes to show what a kind-hearted man he is. He'd
leave it to us if he did have it.

201 "Well," said the dying business man, "you better put in a clause
about my employees. To each man who has worked for me 20
years I give and bequeath $50,000."

"But," said the lawyer, "you haven't been in business twenty years."

"I know it, man, but it's good advertising."

202 Pat O'Brien lay at death's door and he sent for a lawyer to make
his last will. O'Brien's wife remained in the room while the
lawyer was there.

Lawyer: State your affairs briefly.

Pat: Timothy Duggan owes me $5.
Mrs. Pat: Good, sensible to the last.
Pat: Patrick Kelly owes me $15.
Mrs. Pat: Sensible to the last.
Pat: To Michael McKay I owe one hundred dollars.
Mrs. Pat: My soul, listen to him rave.

203   Did that millionaire grandfather of yours remember you when he
        made his will?
        He must have—he left me out.

204   To my girl's father, I will leave the house.
        Whose house?
        His house.
        Why, you can't leave his own house to him.
        Well, he came in and told me the other night: I'm sick of seeing
        you around here. Leave my house!

205   And to my mother I'll leave the Brooklyn Bridge.
        Do you own it?
        No.
        Then how can you give it to her?
        I can't take it with me, can I?

206   The will has some provisions.
        You mean, he left me some groceries.

207   When my grandfather died he left me $10,000.
        That's nothing. When my grandfather died he left the earth.

RELATED SUBJECTS   Heaven 2555-2565
Death 124-145   Attorney 5235-5244
Widow 188-192   Money 5457-5479

INSURANCE
208   Look here, woman, you know that you married me just for my
        government insurance!
        I know that honey, but aren't I willing to let you die a natural
        death?

209   Suppose I took out insurance on my husband's life today and to-
        morrow he dies. What do I get?
        Life.

210   Well, I must run along. I've got a date with nine insurance men.
        What's the idea—nine insurance men?
        I'm going to insure Oscar.
        Who is Oscar?
        My cat.

211   Does your uncle carry life insurance?
        No, he just carries fire insurance. He knows where he is going.

212   What happens to the money?
      Mr. Fisher gets that.
      Who is Mr. Fisher?
      Bennie Fisher. (Beneficiary)

213   The premium is very small. For $20 we insure your house for a
      period of three years.
      You mean you'll pay me $2000 if my house burns down during
      that time?
      Exactly. Of course, we made a careful investigation first.
      That's what I thought. I might have known there'd be a catch in
      it somewhere.

214   Did you ever take out an insurance policy?
      Yeah.
      Accident?
      No, I took it out on purpose.

215   I should get your lowest rate on this life insurance policy I'm
      taking out, said the hardened criminal.
      How so?
      Don't you remember — "The good die young"?

216   Mother, may I go in to swim?
      Certainly not—my dear—it's far too deep.
      But daddy is swimming.
      Yes, dear, but he's insured.

RELATED SUBJECTS   Marriage 2882-3051
Death 124-145   Attorney 5235-5244
Accident 615-709

ANATOMY

FACE

217   These marks on my nose were made by glasses.
      How many glasses?

218   I see strength, courage, kindness and despair in your face.
      But how can you see all that in my face?
      I can read between the lines.

219   I've put a fortune into my girl's face.
      Paying for her expensive beauty treatments?
      No—feeding her in expensive restaurants.

220   I'm looking for new faces.
      Well, don't look at me—I've had this one for years.

221   She thinks I've got a crazy cat. Someone told her I had a silly puss.

222   Every time my girl looks into my eyes, time stands still.
      No wonder.

What do you mean, no wonder?
Your face would stop any clock.

223   How much is this comical picture? This one in front of me — I'm
      looking right at it.
      That is a comical picture, but it isn't a picture. It's a looking glass.

224   You should enter the cat show.
      Why?
      You've got such a long puss this morning.

225   I entered a face making contest.
      Oh, you did — who won the second prize?

226   Smile that way again.
      (She blushed and dimpled and smiled).
      Just like I thought — you look like a chipmunk.

227   I'm a power in this community. I can go any place on my face.
      Kinda looks like you been using it plenty.

228   She has the kind of a map only Rand and McNally could love.

229   You have a drawn look.
      No — it's an over-drawn look. I just got notice from the bank.

230   Here's a picture of my sweetheart. Gee, is she wonderful. She's a
      wonderful girl. She fell from Heaven right into my arms.
      She looks like she fell on her face.

231   You shouldn't make fun of people's faces. Don't forget your face
      and her face came from the same mold.
      What?
      I said, don't forget your face and her face came from the same mold.
      Yes, but hers is moldier.

232   You know the girls all smile when they look at you. But they don't
      give me a glance.
      They're afraid to laugh out loud.

233   Have you a skillet down at your house that just died?
      Whoever heard of a skillet dying?
      Somebody told me you had a dead pan.

234   I heard you got arrested last week. What was the charge?
      I slapped a woman's face. Say, what are you laughing at?
      I was just looking at your face.
      I can't help it if I'm homely.
      I know, but you could stay in the house. Well, that certainly is a
      puzzle to me.
      What's puzzling you?
      How did you ever get close enough to a woman to slap her?

235   I once had a beard like yours, and when I saw how terrible I
       looked, I got it cut off.
       I used to have a face like yours, too, and when I saw how terrible
       it made me look, I grew a beard.

236   How do you feel?
       I feel just like I look.
       That's too bad.

237   Last Sunday that girl was standing in my uncle's corn field and the
       birds took her for a scarecrow. She frightened the crows so
       much they brought back the corn they had stolen three days
       before.

238   If I only made $2 a day, I'd be ashamed to show my face.
       If I had a face like yours, I'd be ashamed to show it, too.

239   Even when you went to the front, you carried my picture over
       your heart.
       Well, I figured if your face would stop a clock, it would stop a
       bullet.

240   He has such a long face, the barbers charge him twice for shaving it.

241   Who is that homely woman standing over there with the white hat?
       That's my wife.
       Pardon me — my mistake.
       No — my mistake.

242   I say, old deah, do you neck?
       If I don't, how do you suppose I came to this house party — on
       my face?
       Well, if you did, you sure came over a helluva rough road.

243   I can't seem to place your face, said the plastic surgeon, who was
       having difficulty with one patient's face-lifting operation.

       ────────

       The plastic surgeon's slogan: We maim to please.

244   Say, you baby-faced looking baboon . . .
       What are you trying to do — make a monkey out of me?
       Why should I take all the credit?

245   At an evening party the guests were asked to take part in a game
       in which everybody was to make a face, the one who made the
       worst face to win the prize. It seemed as if all did their worst.
       Then the judge went up to one woman who was sitting off in
       a corner.
       Judge: Madam, I think you've won the prize. Allow me to . . .
       Woman: Sir, excuse me — I wasn't playing.

246   He went to a masquerade party once and when they asked him to take off his mask he said he didn't have one on.

247   Be it ever so homely, there's no face like one's own.

248   Your face would stop a clock.
      And yours would make one run.

249   He's very kind to dumb animals.
      Then why doesn't he give that face back to the monkey?

250   He has such a sour face I'll bet he was raised on a pickle.

251   I want to see how long it takes to have your mustache grow.
      This mustache will improve my looks 50 per cent.
      Why don't you grow a beard?
      I would, but people told me I'd look like you.
      I won't take that from anybody. I got as good a looking face as there is in this place.
      I'll put my face up against yours any time.
      Not while I can run.

252   I saw your brother riding down the street and he had a pinched look.
      Yeah? I wonder why?
      He was riding in the patrol wagon.

253   Put your head back so I can get a good look at your face. You are not so handsome, but you'll do.
      Are you looking for someone to marry your daughter?
      No, I need a new scarecrow.

254   He is always fortunate at bumming rides.
      He ought to be. His face would stop a train.

255   Bootblack: Shine your shoes, mister?
      Bank President: No!
      Bootblack: Shine 'em so you can see your face in 'em?
      Bank President: No!
      Bootblack: Coward!

256   Her expression is so sour that when she puts face cream on it curdles.

257   There I was alone, but a fellow was making such terrible faces at me I fainted.
      If you were alone, how could anybody be making faces at you?
      I don't know, but I saw the face in the mirror.

258   Have you a cat with a sense of humor?
      What do you mean?
      Someone told me you had a funny puss.

259   Had such an ugly face — he rented himself out to frighten people with hiccups.

260   Look at that horrible picture over there.
      That's not a picture — you're looking in a mirror.

261   Fay says her face is her fortune.
      Well, I'm sick of hearing hard luck stories.

262   Why did you marry such a homely man?
      He asked me, dearie.

RELATED SUBJECTS		Eyes 459-490
Baby 338-340		Ears 498-505
Shape (Physical)	341-347	Nose 537-543
Feet 405-430		Mouth 546-547
Legs 433-439		Teeth 548-578

DESCRIPTIONS OF PEOPLE

263   He has sort of a bridge character — his honor's weak and he's simple.

264   She reminds you of the country. A cornfield in early spring. She looks like a scarecrow. She has arrived at the squirrel age of life. To her, a young man would be the nuts. She is a horsy old maid — in fact, if any man asked her to marry him, she wouldn't say "neigh."

265   From the hips up your girl looks like she's too fat. Her stomach looks like a beer keg.
      That's natural. That's all she uses it for.

266   A dame is as strong as her weakest wink.

267   She reminds me of an automobile because she has knock-kneed action and floating kidney power.

268   I have a new boy friend now.
      What's he like?
      Oh — whiskey — gin — anything.

269   She had a head like a doorknob.
      How come?
      Any man can turn it.

270   Mom, you said the baby had your eyes and Daddy's nose, didn't you?
      Yes, darling.
      Well, you'd better keep an eye on him — he's got Grandpop's teeth now.

271   She's got a couple of double chins. Ripples on the ocean. Every time she talks she broadcasts over short waves.

272   Ursulla says fie's like a book — always turned down at the corners.

273   I want a girl who is good, clever and beautiful.
      Say, you don't want one, you want three.

274   You are beautiful. You are adorable. You are sweet, fine, wonder-
      ful. You are everything that's good.
      Oh, you flatterer, how you exaggerate.
      Well, that's my story, and I'll stick to it.

275   Is she beautiful?
      No, but she's consistent.

276   Sometime in her life she must have been a telephone operator.
      Why?
      She never answers you.

277   You mean the girl with blue eyes, sweet dimple in her chin —
      blonde hair — blue dress — no stockings?
      Yes.
      I never noticed her.

278   He has good points.
      So have pins, but they stick you.

279   Her hair is so red when she goes out nights the chickens think it's
      sunrise and start to crow.

280   She's a bright girl — she has brains enough for two.
      Then she's just the girl for you.

281   You remind me of an airplane.
      Why?
      You're no good on earth!

282   Is she pretty?
      Well, she always gets a seat in the subway.

283   I've often thought you were an angel.
      Because I am such a nice fellow?
      No, because you are no good on earth.

284   Please, just one kiss?
      Nay, nay, sir!
      Please!
      Nay, nay.
      For cripe's sake, was your mother scared by a horse?

285   I knew him when he had only one stomach.

286   There goes Irys, the human dynamo.
      Dynamo?
      Yes, everything on her is charged.

287   She reminds me of a house — painted in front, shingled in back and no attic.

288   She had a beautiful pair of eyes, her skin had the glow of a peach, her cheeks were like apples, and her lips like cherries — that's my girl!
No — that's a fruit salad.

289   Your wife looks very healthy.
She's big and fat.
Does she have a double chin?
Yes, but it don't show. Her lip hides it!

290   He was such a tough fighter they called him Ace-in-the-hole — because he was always face down. He was sort of a canary guy. He couldn't sing, but he was a little yellow.

291   Do I look like a beer?
No — beer has got a head on it.

292   My wife has a heart of gold and teeth to match.

293   Listen, I know a girl that's dying to meet you — she's beautiful — she's rich — she's a honey — she's . . .
Then, why don't you want her?

294   His lower jaw receded so much he had to use his Adam's apple for a chin.

295   How can you look so clean and laugh so dirty?

296   He's the kind of fellow that would spend his time in a Nudist Colony trying to get subscriptions to a fashion magazine.

297   Why did you engage that man as cashier? He squints, has a crooked nose and outstanding ears.
Of course. He will·be so easy to identify if he ever absconds.

298   What kinda woman did you marry?
She's an angel — that's what she is.
Boy, you sure are lucky. Mine's still livin'.

299   She certainly is polished, doncha think so?
Yeah. Everything she says casts a reflection on someone.

300   You're a low-down, spineless jellyfish and do you know what I'm going to do to you?
What?
I'm going to break every bone in your body.

301   You say he is a man of parts?
He certainly is. Half the time he plays the part of a philanthropist, and the other half of the time a public robber.

302   So you're looking for a wife. Well, there is one lady I can offer
      you — but I will be honest with you and tell you in advance that
      she squints and has false teeth.
      False teeth! Are they gold?

303   I've never met your wife; she's a blonde, isn't she?
      I'm not sure. She's visiting a beauty shop this afternoon.

RELATED SUBJECTS
Body 338-340
Shape (Physical) 341-347
Feet 405-430
Legs 433-439
Eyes 459-490
Ears 498-505
Nose 537-543
Mouth 546-547
Teeth 548-578
Left-Handed 602-604
Compliment 2420-2439
Not Myself 2485-2487
Dishonesty 2500-2502
Cleanliness 3351-3358
Clothing 3391-3502

RESEMBLANCE

304   Those girls look exactly alike. Are they twins?
      Oh, no. They merely went to the same plastic surgeon.

305   That boy of ours gets more like you every day.
      What's he been up to now?

306   Do you know that homely fellow sitting on the other side of the
      room?
      Certainly. He is my brother.
      Pardon me. I hadn't noticed the resemblance.

307   Well, now that you've seen my son, which side of the house do
      you think he resembles?
      Of course, his full beauty is not yet developed, but surely you don't
      suggest he looks like the side of a house.

308   John is knock-kneed and his wife is bowlegged. Who do you
      suppose their boy will take after when he is older?
      Probably after some girl.

309   She's a perfect photograph of her father.
      And a pretty good phonograph of her mother.

310   He's the living image of me.
      What do you care, so long as he's healthy?

311 She's got a dash of her grandmother; a dash of her grandfather;
a dash of her mother and a dash of me . . .
And I've gotta dash, too. Dash to the nearest stree. car.

312 Man: Get ready to die. I'm going to shoot you.
Victim: Why?
Man: I've always said I'd shoot anyone who looked like me.
Victim: Do I look like you?
Man: Yes.
Victim: Then shoot.

313 Every time I look at you I think of a great man.
You flatter me. Who is it?
Darwin.

314 You remind me of Moses because every time you open your mouth
the bull rushes.

315 They both liked and disliked the same things — they both liked to
fight and they both disliked each other.

316 You remind me of my mother . . .
No!
Yes. She told me not to be seen with you.

317 I have a head like Lincoln's.
Well, Lincoln's head was long like yours — but not so thick.

PLASTIC SURGEON

318 What will the operation of lifting my face cost, doctor?
Five thousand dollars, madame.
That's robbery. Isn't there something less expensive I could try?
You might try wearing a veil.

319 I had my face lifted.
What happened?
My face slipped out of the doctor's hand.
I'd hardly know you.
How do you like my new face?
If it had splinters in your skin, you'd look like the face on the bar-
room floor.

320 She had her face lifted so many times the doctor ran out of skin, so
he took some skin off of her right thumb and grafted it on to

her nose. Now, everytime she goes hitch hiking, her nose shoves to the right.

321   What's the matter with her?
Just had her face lifted.
Wasn't the operation successful?
Yes, the operation was all right, but she had it lifted so many times, her face is out of focus.

322   Yes, this is a beauty shop. You want your face lifted? Well, you can get one day service, or if you want to leave your face, we'll deliver it free of charge.

323   It isn't necessary for a man to have his face lifted. If he is patient it will grow up through his hair.

324   My uncle had his face lifted.
How did they do it?
With a piece of rope around his neck.

RELATED SUBJECTS
Face 217-262
Hospital 831-834
Doctor 838-860
Operation 883-860
Beauty 4725-4735

PICTURE

325   How much do you charge for taking children's photographs?
Five dollars a dozen.
You'll have to give me more time, I have only ten now.

326   She showed him a picture of her father holding her on his knee when she was a baby and he asked her, "Who is the ventriloquist?"

327   So you and your wife had your picture taken together, did you?
I'll bet that was sweet. How did the photographer pose you?
The photographer said he wanted us to look natural, so he posed my wife with her hand in my pocket.

328   Whose picture was that you were looking at a little while ago?
That was my very dear little wife.
I didn't recognize her. She didn't look natural.
Well, in the picture she's got her mouth shut.

329   I'd like to see your girl.
I'll send you three pictures of her.
Why three?
She ain't all in one picture.

330   So you've been in jail?

Yeah. I took my camera and went down to the Art Gallery and they arrested me for snapping those pictures.
They couldn't arrest you for snapping pictures.
They could when you snap them off the wall.

331 I had the picture in my hand, and one of the officers busted the picture over my head.
And you still think you were double-crossed?
Sure — I was framed.

322 Why did they hang that picture?
Because they couldn't find the artist.

333 One of the exhibitors' wives was out at the studio today and a cameraman offered to take her picture. But she refused. She said: When he looks through that camera he sees me upside down. And I haven't any underskirt on.

334 Gee, these artist folks is funny. When I'm going to have my picture took I put on all my best clothes. When they's going to paint it, they takes 'em all off.

335 Whose picture is that?
Oh, that's a picture of me when I was a baby.
Gee, but you were a nice baldheaded baby.
Wait a minute — you're looking at that picture upside down.

336 Kid: I'm making a picture of father — where's the red ink?
Mother: What do you want with the red ink?
Kid: I'm up to his nose.

337 Do you make life-size enlargements from snapshots?
Certainly, miss. That's our specialty.
Well, let's see what you can do with this picture of the Grand Canyon.

RELATED SUBJECTS
Descriptions of People 263-303
Shape (Physical) 341-347
Artist 1653-1677
Beauty 4725-4735

BODY
338 Tell me how many ribs a woman has.
I tried to count them once, but it was kinda dark so I couldn't see very well.

339 The human anatomy is a wonderful bit of mechanism.
Yes. Pat a man on the back and you'll make his head swell.

340 Do you file your nails?
No, I cut them off and throw them away.

RELATED SUBJECTS
Description of People 263-303

SHAPE (Physical)

341   Did you know that running is good for the figure?
I should say I does. Once it kept a charge of buckshot out of mine.

342   She has an Income Tax Figure — that is, she should be arrested for not filling out her form.

343   That's a pretty dress you have on, and you wear it well, too. How do you keep your figure so beautiful?
I swim a lot.
Swim? Is that good for the figure?
Yes.
Did you ever take a look at a duck?

344   How do I look?
Where did you get that bathing suit?
I got it for a ridiculous figure.
I see you have.

345   How do you like this girdle I'm wearing?
That's a great girdle you have.
See how it straightens me in the front?
But look how it pushes you out in the back.

346   What well developed arms you have.
Yes, I play a lot of tennis.
You ride horseback, too, don't you?

347   I saw you in a bathing suit and I could hang my hat on a half dozen places.

RELATED SUBJECTS
Face 217-262
Description of People 263-303
Picture 325-337
Bathing Suit 4281-4283
Beauty 4725-4735

FAT PEOPLE

348   My uncle bought my aunt a violin.
I didn't know your aunt played the violin.
She doesn't. He just wanted a place to rest her chin.

349   Fat Man: (In a movie to little boy sitting behind him) Can't you see, little fellow?
Little Boy: Not a thing.
Fat Man: Then keep your eye on me and laugh when I do.

350   Is he really so very fat?
      Fat! Well, I'll tell you just how fat he is. Last winter he had the
      mumps for three weeks before he found out about it.

351   What makes you so heavy, Herman?
      My dad says I have an iron constitution.

352   How do you account for that fat woman getting out of that crowd
         so fast?
      I don't know — unless it was the survival of the fattest.

353   He's so fat he can't tell where to bend over and where to sit down.
      So he has someone hit him with a board and if it knocks the
      wind out of him, he knows that side is his stomach.

354   I saw you being introduced to that big fat man. What's his name?
      I don't know — I couldn't get near enough to him to catch it.

355   She's so fat that when she falls down she rocks herself to sleep try-
      ing to get up.

356   I had a funny experience with a fat girl last night. We were sitting
      in the dark and I thought we were necking, but all the time I
      only had hold of her arm.

357   I sure have to laugh at the man across the street.
      Which one?
      The man with the woman weighing three hundred pounds.
      Why laugh at him?
      Twenty years ago she broke my heart by refusing to marry me.

358   He's so fat he can't play golf.
      Why is that?
      Because if he puts the ball where he can hit it, he can't see it, and
      if he puts the ball where he can see it, he can't hit it.

359   Yes, travel broadens one.
      She must have been around the world.

360   (Big fat woman) : I'm afraid of my shadow.
      You ought to be — you look like a crowd is following you.

361   We were walking down the street the other day — my wife and
      me — and when we came to a mud puddle I didn't carry her
      across.
      What did she say to that?
      She said I wasn't as gallant as I was when she was a gal.
      What did you say?
      I told her she wasn't as bouyant as she was when I was a boy.

362   Who is that fat party getting on the car?
      Party? She's an excursion.

363   Look at the big woman over there. I'm going to ask her to dance.
      (To woman) Pardon me, madam, may I have the honor of the
      fourteenth dance?
      But, my man, there are only thirteen dances to be played.
      I know it.

364   Her hair looks terrible and she's too fat. She should diet.
      She's going to, but can't make up her mind what color.

365   The stout lady on the scale was eagerly watched by two small boys.
      The lady dropped in her cent, but the machine was out of order
      — only registered 75 pounds.
      "Good night, Bill," gasped one of the kids in amazement. "She's
      hollow."

366   He is so fat in shorts he looks like a chiffonier.
      What is that?
      A big thing with drawers.

367   He's so fat he had the mumps two weeks before he knew it.

368   So fat he was arrested three times for jay-walking and all the time
      he was waiting on the corner for the signal to change.

369   Going to have an operation to remove excess fat.
      What are you going to do — have yourself beheaded?

370   Davis certainly married a big woman, didn't he?
      Yes, but you ought to see the one he got away from.

                              RELATED SUBJECTS
                              Description of People 263-303
                              Thin People 401-404
                              Humor 2365-2380
                              Food 4825-4878

DIET

371   I'm on an "A" diet.
      An "A" diet? You mean you can only eat things that begin with
      "A"?
      No, I can only eat a bowl of soup, a chicken, a salad, etc.

372   Been on an 18 day diet for four weeks. I don't eat potatoes and
      I'm never going to eat bread any more.
      You mean, you're never going to eat bread again?
      No — not me.
      Then how you gonna pick up your gravy?

373   I'm sick and tired of trying to reduce. I've been bending and twist-
      ing for two hours.
      That's nothing. My brother just finished a 4-year stretch.

374   What are you doing?
      I'm trying to keep slim.
      What's the matter with Slim? Can't he keep himself?

375   I lost one hundred and seventy pounds since I last saw you.
      How so?
      My husband left me.

376   You ought to go on a diet.
      Yeah, but I can't decide whether to go on a Milwaukee diet, or an
          Italian diet.
      A Milwaukee diet, or an Italian diet? What kind of a diet is that?
      Well, if I go on a Milwaukee diet I just drink beer. If I go on the
          Italian diet I'll just drink the best wine and eat ordinary bread.
      Go on the Italian diet and I'll go on it with you and I'll bring the
          bread.

377   Will you have a peanut?
      No, they're fattening.
      What makes you think peanuts are fattening?
      Did you ever see an elephant?

378   How are you coming along with your reducing?
      I guess I must be one of those poor losers.

379   Are you on a diet?
      No — on commission.

380   You're on the wrong diet — you eat too much soldier food.
      What do you mean soldier food?
      Everything you eat goes to the front.

381   Have you a very large piece of pork?
      Yes, ma'am.
      Well, I want you to cut off twenty pounds all in one piece.
      There you are, ma'am. Shall I wrap it up?
      Oh, no. I don't want to buy it. I've been reducing. I've lost twenty
          pounds, and I want to see how much that is.

                              RELATED SUBJECTS
                              Shape (Physical) 341-347
                              Food 4825-4878

EXERCISE

382   I'm putting on weight, Doctor. What should I do?
      Regular exercise. Push yourself away from the table three times
          a day.

383   Weight put on by over indulgence in malted liquors can be taken
          off by a series of reducing exercises. No. 1 — Move the head
          firmly from side to side when somebody suggests another half-
          pint.

384   If your grandmother saw you doing that, she'd turn over in her
      grave.
      Oh, well, she needs the exercise.

385   Exercise will kill all germs.
      Yeah, but how am I to get the germs to exercise?

386   What made you join the police force?
      My doctor told me I should get more exercise.
      What has getting more exercise got to do with being a policeman?
      Why should I walk on my own time when I can be a policeman and
      get paid for it?

387   How does he manage to keep himself in condition like that?
      Every morning at 7:30 he gets up and turns on the exercises over
      the radio.
      That's wonderful. Does he take those exercises?
      No — but the girl across the street does.

388   Do you ever take long walks before breakfast?
      That all depends on whose car I've been out in.

389   What you need is exercise. You should have a little sun and air.
      Why, I'm not even married.

390   When I was a boy I thought nothing of a ten mile walk.
      Well, I don't think so much of it myself.

391   Every morning I bend forward and draw my hands up like this.
      Why on earth do you make such motions?
      How on earth is a man going to put on his overcoat?

392   Do you know — every time I bend over and put my hands down
      to my knees and pull them up again, I get terrible pains in my
      back?
      Why do you do it then?
      Do you know of any other way to put your pants on?

393   I'm tired. You do my callisthenics for me, will you?
      Okay. One, two, three, four, five, six, seven . . .
      That's enough . . . I'm getting too tired.

394   Doctor: Same old story, my friend, men can't live without air. No
      use trying it. I could make myself a corpse, like you are, doing
      the things you do — sitting in an office. You must get fresh air.
      You must take long walks, and brace up by staying out-doors.
      I advise you to take long walks . . .
      Patient: But, Doctor . . .
      Doctor: That's right, argue the question — that's my reward.
      Now, will you take my advice? Take long walks every day.
      Several times a day . . .
      Patient: I do walk, Doctor, I . . .

Doctor: Of course, you walk. I know that, but walk ten times as much as you do now. That will cure you.

Patient: But my business . . .

Doctor: Of course, your business prevents it. Change your business, so that you'll have to walk more. What is your business?

Patient: I'm a letter carrier.

Doctor: My friend, let me examine your tongue again.

395   How is your father?
Father walks in his sleep so he can get his rest and exercise at the same time.

396   My mother, when she was a girl, used to walk ten miles every morning.
Don't kid me — they didn't have automobiles in those days.

397   All these exercises must be taken in front of an open window.
That makes it rather awkward.
Well, why so?
I need the increased strength first so that I can open the window in my new house.

398   Why do you eat in the cafeteria and not in the grill?
Oh, the doctor said 1 should take a long walk before meals.

399   Tom and I have arranged our holiday. We're going to hike.
It's wonderful how popular that place has become. Everybody's going there nowadays.

400   What do you do for exercise?
Oh, I let my flesh creep.

RELATED SUBJECTS
Shape (Physical) 341-347
Sickness 741-801
Swimming 4289-4297
Sports 4319-4505
Prizefight 4495-4499

THIN PEOPLE

401   She was so skinny that once when she was swimming — a man on the beach was throwing sticks out into the ocean so his dog could bring them back. And she was so skinny, the dog brought her back three times.

402   He used to be fat, but he's sure skinny now. Remember that watermelon he had tattooed on his chest?
Yeah — why?
You ought to see it now. It looks like an olive.

403   I'm worried about dad. He is so thin.
Well, just how thin is he?

You know how thin you are, and you know how thin I am. Well, he's thinner than both of us put together.

404 No wonder that horse is so thin.
Sure she's thin — why, she's so thin I has to put a blanket over her to keep the wind from blowing the hay out.

RELATED SUBJECTS
Description of People 263-303
Shape (Physical) 341-347

FEET

405 I have a terrible corn on the bottom of my foot.
That's a foine place to have it. Nobody can step on it but you.

406 I should have been a song writer — I have squeaking shoes.
What has squeaking shoes got to do with being a songwriter?
I've got music in my soles.

407 Keep your feet where they belong.
Don't tempt me.

408 Who invented high heels?
A pretty girl who was continually being kissed on the forehead.

409 You're stepping on my foot. Why don't you put your foot where it belongs?
If I did, you'd go through the door.

410 That's a nice bathing suit.
Do you like it?
Get out of that row boat until I look at you.
That's no row boat — that's my feet.
Your feet?
Yeah. When the sun is out I sit down and stick my feet up and people pay me to lay in the shade.

411 I've got a brother with three feet.
What do you mean?
Well, my mother got a letter from my brother and he said: You would hardly know me — I've grown three feet.

412 What's the matter with your foot? You're limping.
I guess it's on account of my new police shoes.
Police shoes?
Yeah. Everytime I put them on, they pinch my feet.

413 What size shoe do you wear?
Four is my size, but I wear sevens because fours hurt my feet so.

414 I'm going to try to get a date with that beautiful girl.
She wouldn't even wipe her feet on you.
She couldn't — I'm too small.

415　What attracted you to me in the first place?
　　　Your shoes. I was always taught that the greatest lovers in the
　　　　world had the largest feet, and you have the largest shoes I've
　　　　ever seen.
　　　You flatter me.
　　　But tell me, whose shoes are you wearing?

416　I'll never forget when I started working for Greta Garbo. I was
　　　　her footman.
　　　Why did you leave the glamorous star?
　　　I was discharged. I accidentally stepped on her feet as she entered
　　　　the car.
　　　What did she say?
　　　She said to get off her feet.
　　　Was it much of a walk?

418　Why don't you take off your derby?
　　　I can't take my hat off — I'm a detective.
　　　What size shoes do you wear?
　　　Eleven and a half. Why?
　　　That proves you're a detective.

419　What size shoes do you wear?
　　　Well, I take size six, but seven feels so good — I buy eights.

420　Does he really have big feet?
　　　Well, all I know is that when we were on the train together, he
　　　　needed a shine, and the porter shined one of his shoes and a suit-
　　　　case.

421　You're always talking about my big feet — well, let me tell you
　　　　I'm glad I've got big feet.
　　　Why?
　　　Well, when I was hunting lions in Africa, I ran out of ammuni-
　　　　tion and there was a lion following me. It started to rain and
　　　　I started to run so the lion wouldn't kill me — well, it rained
　　　　and rained and the lion kept following me, but he finally fell
　　　　into one of my footprints and before he could scramble out,
　　　　he was drowned.

422　My aunt always had a lot of dogs and cats, but now she only
　　　　keeps a cat, but she still has trouble with her dogs.

423　If I had only two things, I could have kicked from goal to goal.
　　　What were they?
　　　Greta Garbo's feet.

424　Peg wears awfully tight shoes, doesn't she?
　　　Sure; it's the only chance she has to be squeezed.

425　Look at your feet. They're so wide. I'll bet when you take off your
　　　　shoes your toes spread out like the spokes in a wagon wheel.

426   What's the idea of throwing that pair of shoes away?
      They bane no gude. I try them on six fellows and they don't fit
      anyone.

427   She has such big feet when she takes off her shoes and stockings,
      she's half undressed.

428   You should put your best foot forward.
      Well, the last time I put my foot forward it landed in the wrong
      place.
      What happened?
      My foot landed on a man's stomach when his back was turned.

429   His shoes squeak just like little mice. They squeak so much, cats
      follow him around.

430   He's got fallen arches.
      Why doesn't he pick them up?

                              RELATED SUBJECTS
                              Anatomy 217-604
                              Shoe Store 5454-5456

CHIROPODIST

431   How did you happen to become a chiropodist?
      Oh, I always was at the foot of my class at school, so I just naturally
      drifted into this profession.

432   I think married life is like a chiropodist's hand.
      What do you mean?
      If the shoe pinches you, you put your foot in it.
      Into what?
      The chiropodist's hand.

                              RELATED SUBJECTS
                              Shoe Store 5454-5456

LEGS

433   He wouldn't rent you that flat, eh?
      No, he said that I was so bowlegged that I would be continually
      rubbing the paper off the walls.

434   You've got the prettiest legs in captivity.
      They're not in captivity; I'm single.

435   So you bought that car with pin money?
      Yes, last week I won a prize for having the prettiest legs in town.

436   Walk this way.
      I can't.
      Why not?
      You're bowlegged.

437   She's bowlegged.
      That's right, she is. Legs like hers are few and far between.

438   She was so knock-kneed that when she was walking I heard one
      knee say to the other: I let you pass last time, now give me a
      chance.

439   My sister was very bowlegged. You know what bowlegged is?
      Well, she went to the doctor and he broke her legs and reset
      them straight and now she's suing the doctor.
      Suing the doctor? Why?
      Because she's not what she's cracked up to be.

RELATED SUBJECTS
Anatomy 217-604
Chorus Girl 4563-4565

WOODEN LEG

440   I've got an uncle with a wooden leg that drinks.
      Is that so?
      Yeah.
      Does it injure the finish?

441   My uncle will have to limp the rest of his life.
      What happened?
      My brother wanted to take him down a peg, so he cut a piece off
      his wooden leg.

442   I've got to buy a bottle of liniment and a bottle of furniture polish
      for my uncle's rheumatism.
      I can understand why you're buying the liniment for his rheuma-
      tism, but what is the furniture polish for?
      He has rheumatism in his legs and one of them is wooden.

443   Your dog bit me and I'm going to sue you.
      Never mind! I'll give you $50 to settle out of court.
      Okay. I'll take the money. Say, what are you laughing at?
      That's a counterfeit bill. What are you laughing at?
      I've got a wooden leg.

444   I married because I had cold feet.
      And you're not troubled any more?
      I still have cold feet — the man I married has wooden legs.

445   My uncle has a wooden leg.
      That's too bad.
      Yeah, and it pains him just awful.
      How could a wooden leg pain him?
      His wife hit him over the head with it.

446   I've got a cedar chest.
      Wonderful! I've only got a wooden leg.

447   My nephew burned my uncle's leg and now he's crippled.
      Your little nephew burned your uncle's leg and he's crippled?
      Yeah.
      Well, how did it happen?
      He started the fire in the furnace with my uncle's wooden leg.

                        RELATED SUBJECTS
                        Anatomy 217-604

CRIPPLE

448   If you don't watch out, you'll be crippled for life — maybe longer.

449   This patient here limps because one foot is shorter than the other.
         Now what would you do in such a case?
      I imagine I would limp, too.

450   Curious Old Lady: Why, you've lost your leg, haven't you?
      Cripple: Well, damned if I ain't.

451   Would you rather be lame or blind?
      I'd rather be lame.
      Why?
      Because when I was blind people were always giving me counter-
         feit money.

452   My physical condition isn't good — I'm an invalid.
      Whatever happened to you to make you an invalid?
      I was gassed four times in a dentist chair.

453   I was an invalid once.
      You were? When was that?
      When I was a baby. I couldn't walk until I was a year old.

454   Here, poor fellow, is a quarter for you. It must be terrible to be
         lame, but I think it must be worse to be blind.
      You're right, ma'am. When I was blind, people was always steal-
         ing money outta my cup.

455   He's really a man of parts. Before he goes to bed, he takes out his
         false teeth, takes out his glass eye, takes off his toupee and takes
         off his wooden leg.

456   Have you any scars?
      No, only the one I'm smoking.

457   He removed his left arm below the elbow; his right leg below the
         knee, took out two sets of pearly teeth and dropped them in a
         glass of water, took out his right eye and placed it in the glass
         to watch the teeth; reached up and removed all his glossy black
         hair; but when he reached around with his remaining arm to
         take out his collar button, his newlywed wife ran out of the
         room and yelled: "Come quick — come quick! He's going to
         take off his head!"

458   So you think you would be a suitable valet for me. I must remind
      you that I'm pretty much of a wreck. I have a glass eye, a cork
      leg, an artificial arm that needs looking after, not to mention a
      wig and false teeth.
         That would be all right, sir. I've had plenty of practice. You see
      I once worked in the assembly room of a big motor concern.

                              RELATED SUBJECTS
                              Description of People 263-303
                              Accident 615-709
                              Injury 716-740

EYES

459   Doctor, will I be able to read after I get my glasses?
         Indeed, you will.
         Well, that'll be great. I never could read before.

460   Optician: How many lines can you read on that chart?
         Patient: What chart?

461   Will you permit me to paint your portrait in profile? There is a
      certain shyness about one of your eyes which is as difficult in
      art as it is fascinating in nature.

462   I had trouble with my eyes — I saw spots in front of my eyes.
         Do your glasses help?
         Yeh — now I can see the spots much better.

463   She has watchman eyes. They both keep watching her nose.

464   He has restaurant eyes.
         What do you mean?
         When he eats in a restaurant, one eye can watch his food and the
      other eye watches his hat and coat.

465   He gave her a ring to match her eyes.
         What color was the stone?
         Her eyes are generally bloodshot — so he gave her a ruby.

466   You'd think they'd let your uncle in for half price — he only has
      one eye.
         Yeah — well, we have to pay double for him. It takes him twice
      as long to see the show.

467   Where is the Green Room?
         I don't know.
         Don't you work here?
         Yes, sir.
         Then why can't you tell me where the Green Room is?
         I'm color blind.

468   My brother had to give up his job with the Zoo.

Why?
He was always seeing spots in front of his eyes.
What did he do at the Zoo?
Washed leopards.

469   It was pitch dark and you sat down to read the paper?
That's right.
Don't tell me you read in the dark.
It rests my eyes.
How can you see the print?
I can't. That's how it rests my eyes.

470   You have two beautiful eyes.
Oh thank you!
Too bad they're not mates.

471   Why do you wear dark glasses?
Because I can't bear to see my wife work so hard.

472   What are spectacles?
Spectacles are glasses that people look through.
If you looked through a window would you call it a spectacle?
It's according to what you saw.

473   Honey, your eyes make me dizzy.
Say, don't blame my eyes.

474   You mean I can't see so good?
That's it.
Well, the doctor told me if I'd quit drinking I'd regain my eyesight.
Did you quit?
Yeah, I quit, but things didn't look so good to me as when I was
   drinking, so I started drinking again.

475   They arrested my brother for stealing money out of a blindman's
   cup.
That's terrible — stealing money.
Oh, it wasn't stealing money that made me ashamed of him, it's
   the fact that he took the money while the blindman wasn't
   looking.

476   Where are you going with that cane and tin cup? We've got a date.
I know. You said it's a blind date, and I thought I might as well
   cash in on it.

477   Where'd you get those big eyes?
They came with the face.

478   Do you see that barn over there on the horizon?
Yes.
Can you see that fly walking around on the roof of the barn?
No, but I can hear the shingles crack when he steps on them.

479 Well, John, did you give the Judge my note?
Yes, but there isn't any use writing to that man.
Why do you say that, John?
'Cause he's blind—blind as a bat. Do you know he asked me
twice where my hat was—and all the time it was on my head?

480 Cross examining a man who had witnessed an accident:
Did you see the man on the train?
Yes, sir.
Where was he?
About thirty cars back from the engine.
Where were you?
I was back of the tender of the engine.
About what time of night was it?
Eleven o'clock.
Do you mean to tell me that you saw that man thirty cars away at
eleven o'clock at night?
Yes, sir.
How far do you think you can see at night?
'Bout a million miles, I reckon — how far is it to the moon?

481 I think the judge was cross-eyed.
Why?
Because he gave the Prosecuting Attorney thirty days.

482 He went blind from drinking coffee.
Whoever heard of such a thing? How did it happen?
He left his spoon in the coffee.

483 What's the idea of that cross-eyed man for a store detective?
Well, look at him! Can you tell who he is watching?

484 Say, do your eyes bother you?
No — why?
Well, they bother me.

485 Last week a grain of sand got into my wife's eye and she had to
go to the doctor. It cost me three dollars.
That's nothing. Last week a fur coat got in my wife's eye and it
cost me three hundred dollars.

486 That boy you were riding with has trouble with his vision, you say?
Yeah, he sees parking spots before his eyes.

487 I have lost my glasses.
Well, why don't you look for them?
How can I look for them until I find them?

488 He's cross-eyed, but he likes it, because in a restaurant when the
waiter puts the check on the table he reaches for the mashed
potatoes.

489   Do your new spectacles help your eyes?
       Yes. I never have my eyes blackened now like I used to before I
         wore 'em.

490   Don't drink that stuff, Joe. The wood alcohol will make you
         blind.
       Oh, that's all right—I've seen everything.

                              RELATED SUBJECTS
                              Anatomy 217-604

NEARSIGHTEDNESS

491   So your brother lost his job with the fire department.
       Yeah — it was on account of his nearsightedness.
       What happened?
       He spent a whole afternoon squirting water on a red-headed woman
         before he discovered it wasn't a fire.

492   My porcupine is in the hospital on account of his nearsightedness.
       What happened?
       He's so nearsighted, he mistook a cactus plant for his sweetheart.

493   I'm looking for some ostrich eggs.
       What for?
       My grandfather's nearsighted and I want to color him some ostrich
         eggs for Easter.

494   I'm so nearsighted I nearly worked myself to death.
       What's being nearsighted got to do with working yourself to death?
       I couldn't tell whether the boss was watching me or not, so I had
         to work all the time.

495   (Nearsighted grandma): Look, June, there's a real old-fashioned
         girl. Her dress buttons all the way up the back.
       June: Nonsense! That's her spine.

496   My mother is so nearsighted she got on a train and when the train
         pulled out she said: Conductor, let me off at the first stop — I
         thought this was a lunch wagon.

497   Yesterday I went to the top of the Empire State Building to look
         at the city.
       Did they charge you $1?
       No, they only charged me 50 cents because I'm nearsighted.

                              RELATED SUBJECTS
                              Description of People 206-303

EARS

498   She has ears like steam shovels — they're always picking up dirt.

499   Don't holler in my ear.
       Excuse me — I thought it was the microphone.

500   I'm getting worried. Last night I heard the worse noise in my ears.
      Where did you expect to hear them?

501   The doctors operated on a friend of mine for a constant ringing
      in his ears before they found out he was a bellhop.

502   You took the words right out of my ear.
      No, that's not right. It's you took the words right out of my mouth.
      But I heard it before I said it.

503   Everything she says goes in one ear and out the other.
      Yeah — there's nothing to block traffic.

504   I won't stand for any more of this. Are you listening?
      Yes, I'm all ears.
      So is a donkey.

505   Small thin ears are a sign of weak character.
      Yeah, and large, thick ones are a sign of weak defense.

                           RELATED SUBJECTS
                           Anatomy 217-604
                           Prizefight 4495-4499

DEAFNESS

506   Have you seen the new doctor that just came to town?
      (Deaf) Hey?
      Doc Hammersmith — (LOUD) Hammersmith — HAMMERSMITH!
      (Deaf) Sorry, son, but I can't make a thing out of it but Hammer-
        smith.

507   (Deaf) Last night I got held up.
      When was this catastrophe?
      (Deaf) They wasn't no cats after me, I just got held up.

508   (Deaf) Dog my buttons, but them younguns can sing, eh?
      Right you are, Grandad.
      (Deaf) Hey? What's that ye say?
      I said — you're right . . . CORRECT — You're CORRECT!
      (Deaf) Cracked? Who's cracked, ye young fool?

509   How's your cousin Ed?
      (Deaf) Eh?
      How's your cousin Ed?
      (Deaf) My cousin's head? Oh, it's got a bump on it. His wife hit
        him with a picture.
      Did she? Was it a picture of him?
      (Deaf) Well, he says it was a strikin' likeness.

510   (Deaf) Say, did you know my cousin ain't had his hair cut in forty
        years? (LOUD) I say, HE AIN'T HAD HIS HAIR CUT IN FORTY
        YEARS.

I hear you. He must be eccentric.
(Deaf) No, his name ain't Cedric, it's Ed.
No — No. I say HE MUST BE PECULIAR NOT TO HAVE HIS HAIR
   CUT IN FORTY YEARS. HE MUST BE ECCENTRIC.
(Deaf) Nope, he's bald.

511   Well, are you having a good time?
(Deaf) Eh?
Having a good time . . . good time?
(Deaf) Ye say ye haven't got a dime? Well, don't come to me.
I didn't say that . . . I said ARE YOU HAVING A GOOD TIME? GOOD
   TIME!
(Deaf) Oh, well — it's a little after eight o'clock, I reckon.

512   You're getting all mixed up. I'll have to elucidate.
(Deaf) Got a date with Lucy, eh? That's fine. She got a friend?

513   Hello, you old night owl.
(Deaf) Oh, so it's your night to howl.

514   So you took your girl out and spent a lot of money on her?
(Deaf) Spilt a lot of honey on her?
No, I said you spent a lot of money on her?
(Deaf) No — I only spent $8 on her.
Only $8?
(Deaf) Yeah, that's all she had.

515   Is Rosie a good dancer?
(Deaf) Well, she ain't any denser than anybody else.
No, I said is she a good dancer?
(Deaf) Oh, yeah, I'll say. I call her Mustard because she's always
   on my dogs.

516   Was there much of a crowd?
(Deaf) Am I proud?
No, was there much of a crowd there?
Yeah — I'll say. My gal fainted and I had to dance around the
   floor three times before I could find a place to sit her down.

517   Your ears are sure red.
(Deaf) Who's dead?
No — I said your ears are red.
(Deaf) Oh, Rose did that. When I tried to kiss her she said "No,"
   but I thought she said "more" . . . (southern accent)

518   Well, how's the gad-about?
(Deaf) What yer mad about?

519   Haven't you ever wished you were married?
(Deaf) No — I've never fished for herring — but I've fished for
   baracuddie.

520   (Deaf) We had a big fight.
Did you and your wife have some words?
(Deaf) No — no, not in the woods — on the front stoop.

521   Was she speechless with rage?
(Deaf) Did she ever speak on the stage?
No — WAS SHE SPEECHLESS WITH RAGE?
(Deaf) Only time she'll be speechless with rage is when rigor mortis sets in.

522   It was so hot I nearly smothered.
(Deaf) You say you'd like to meet her mother?

523   Can you tell me how to get to Bryant Street?
What's that, stranger? I'm a little deaf.
I beg your pardon?
I said, I'm a little deaf. I didn't hear you.
You don't say! I'm deaf, too.
That's too bad. Now, what was it you wanted?
Can you tell me how to get to Bryant Street?
Sure, you go this way four blocks and then turn to your right. It's the third street down.
That's Bryant Street, is it?
Oh, no. Excuse me, old man. I thought you said Bryant Street.
Never heard of it. Sorry, stranger.

524   Three men, all slightly deaf, were motoring to London in a noisy old car. As they were nearing the metropolis, one asked, "Is this Wembley?" "No," replied the second, "This is Thursday." "So am I," chirped the third one. "Let's stop and have one."

525   Man calling on telephone: Hello, this is Joe.
Deaf man answering: Eh?
Man: This is Joe! J for John, O for Otto and E for Eddie.
Deaf man: I know all you guys, but which one is talking now?

526   Your father spends a lot of time in talking picture theatres. Why is that?
On account of his deafness.
They can't cure him.
On account of being deaf they don't bother him much.

527   When they tried him the judge let him go free.
Why?
The robber was deaf.
What has that got to do with it?
Well, don't you know that you can't convict a man without a hearing?

528　Poor old Perkins has completely lost his hearing. I'm afraid he'll lose his job.
Nonsense! He's been transferred to the Complaint Department.

529　(Deaf) Ye say she's going to hang? Who's going to hang and what for?
Well, nobody's going to hang.
(Deaf) What's that?
I said no one's going to hang. HANG! HANG!
(Deaf) Go hang yourself — ye fresh whippersnapper.

530　I forgot you were a little deaf. How have you been feeling lately — had any of your spells?
(Deaf) Hey?
I said have you had any of your spells. HAD ANY SPELLS?
(Deaf) What smells?

RELATED SUBJECTS
Description of People 263-303

DEAF AND DUMB

532　Deaf and dumb guy wears boxing gloves to bed so he won't talk in his sleep.

533　She talks so much she was married three years before she found out her husband was deaf and dumb.

534　That girl on the bench has been snapping her fingers under her boy friend's nose all evening. Wonder why he doesn't say something back?
They're deaf and dumb — I guess the poor guy can't get a finger in edgewise.

535　Who is that man over there snapping his fingers?
That's a deaf-mute with the hiccoughs.

536　What do you mean by telling your boy friend that I was deaf and dumb?
I didn't say deaf.

RELATED SUBJECTS
Talk 1432-1481

NOSE

537　So you had an operation on your nose?
Yes, it was getting so I could hardly talk through it.

538　There's a fly on the end of your nose.
Brush it off.
Why should I?
Well, you're closer to it than I am.

539 I hear they're going to run Jimmy Durante for president.
     That's impossible. They will never be able to get his nose on a three cent stamp.

540 Do you know I've had my nose to the grindstone for a year?
     You had your nose to a grindstone for a year?
     Of course. Why are you laughing?
     I'll bet it was a beauty when you first started!

541 You've got a very good nose as noses run.

542 His nose is so big — while walking in France he caught a cold in England.

543 You must think my head is soft.
     No, but I know why your nose isn't soft.
     How do you know my nose isn't soft?
     Because when you stick it in my buisness, it won't break off.

                    RELATED SUBJECTS
                    Anatomy 217-604

SNEEZE

544 What was the station the conductor called?
     He didn't announce any station. He just put his head in the door and sneezed.
     Get the bundles together quickly, this is Oshkosh.

545 Chocolate sneeze: Hershey! Hershey!
     Suspicious sneeze: Whoisshe! Whoisshe!

MOUTH

546 You've got an awful big mouth, haven't you, mama?
     Whatever do you mean?
     Well, papa told nursey last night that you swallowed everything he told you.

547 Her mouth is so small she uses a shoe horn to take aspirin.

                    RELATED SUBJECTS
                    Anatomy 217-604
                    Talk 1432-1481
                    Kiss 2720-2774

TEETH

548 What's making that awful racket?
     Grandma ain't used to her new teeth yet, and she's bustin' up all the saucers drinkin' her tea.

549 Darling, in the moonlight your teeth are like pearls.
     Oh, indeed! And when were you in the moonlight with Pearl?

550   Look, that man is coming to pieces.
      People don't come to pieces.
      No? Well, I just saw his teeth fall out.

551   Please ma'am, do you wear false teeth?
      Sir!
      Oh, I don't mean to be curious. Only this road is a leetle rough,
         and ef your teeth ain't good and fast you'd better put 'em in
         your pocket.

552   (Child crying) Boooooo!
      What seems to be the matter?
      I've got a new tooth but it's just a plain white one — and I wanted
         a nice gold one.

553   I took my Aunt over to my girl's house for dinner and when my
         girl said: Pass your plate, my aunt took out her teeth and said:
         Which one — my upper or lower?

554   Where are my false teeth?
      I borrowed them for a minute. I wanted to bite off the end of
         my cigar.

555   Your teeth are chattering. Stop it. We don't want people to get
         a false impression of us.
      I can't help it — they're false teeth.

556   She had teeth like the Ten Commandments.
      What do you mean?
      They were all broken.

557   Is the steak tender?
      I can't tell, I'm using my father's false teeth.

558   I have a toothache.
      If I were you I'd let the dentist pull it out.
      If it were your tooth I would have it taken out.

559   They tied my feet together but I freed myself with my teeth.
      How could you free yourself with your teeth when your feet were
         tied together? You couldn't reach them with your mouth.
      No, but I took my teeth out and they bit the rope in two.

560   What happened to you?
      Three thousand people bit me.
      Three thousand people?
      Yeah — I was in a fight and somebody bit me — I knew I'd know
         those teeth marks, so I made everybody in town bite me.

561   He shows all of his teeth when he smiles — his false teeth are
         the pride of his life. The other day he got in a fight and got
         smacked in the jaw — and swallowed his false pride.

562 Our baby just cut two teeth. I told my wife she should be ashamed of herself letting the baby play with a knife.

563 She has an upper plate though.
How did you find that out?
Well, it just came out in the conversation.

564 He only has two teeth and one of those he got when he joined the Elks.

565 Are you the fresh young feller that sold me this stuff yesterday and said it was toothpaste?
Yes, sir.
Well, I tried fer half an hour this morning, and I'll be derned if it would make my teeth stick in.

566 How old is she?
I don't know — but she's had three sets of teeth.
What do you mean — three sets of teeth? You only have two sets of teeth — your baby teeth and your adult teeth.
Yeah? Well, how about the ones grandfather willed her?

567 It's a false woman who doesn't know her own teeth.

568 He had false teeth. Bought them back in 1930. He was so mad he gnashed his teeth. It really was a 1930 gnash.

569 She had very big teeth.
She had buck teeth?
I don't know what she paid for them, but they stuck out.

570 What are you saving that tooth you had pulled for? A bookmark?
No.
A paper weight?
No.
A door stop?
No. I'm going to take it home, play some sad music, draw up an easy chair, put it on the table and laugh and laugh.
Why?
I'm going to sprinkle some sugar on it and watch it ache.

571 The baby is crying because he is getting his first teeth.
Because he's getting teeth he is crying? What's the matter, doesn't he want them?

572 I've got to find my piece of carmel candy that I dropped.
Never mind — let it go — have another piece.
No, I've got to find my piece of candy.
Why do you have to find that particular piece?
Because my teeth are in it.

573   She kissed him on the bridge at midnight but she'll never do it again.
      Why not?
      Because she broke his bridge.

574   You don't wear any medals or pins, do you?
      No — why?
      Well, I thought from the looks of your teeth you must belong to
      the Elks.

575   The other day my brother took his wife into a restaurant and he
      ordered sandwiches for both of them. When the waitress brought
      the sandwiches my brother started to eat, but his wife just sat
      there and finally the waitress asked if there was something wrong
      with the sandwich. And my brother said: There's nothing wrong
      with the sandwich. She's waiting for her teeth. I'm using them.

576   Excuse me, my tongue got around my eye tooth and I couldn't
      see to talk.

577   A male movie star, always thinking of his public, had an X-ray
      of his teeth retouched before showing it to his dentist.

578   Do you use tooth powder?
      Naw! I don't believe in cosmetics for men.

                          RELATED SUBJECTS
                          Age 45-107
                          Description of People 263-303
                          Food 4825-4878

DENTIST

579   Got your teeth filled, eh? Did the dentist do a good job?
      Well, I can honestly say he spared no pains.

580   Man: Hey, that wasn't the tooth I wanted pulled.
      Dentist: Calm yourself, I'm coming to it!

581   Did you have a good time at the dentist's?
      I was bored to tears.

582   Dentist: What's your business?
      Patient: I'm a gag writer.
      Dentist: Well, I'll try and live up to your idea of my profession.

583   I'm learning to be a dentist by mail.
      How interesting.
      Yes, but it's very discouraging at times. I have a man in my office
      now — I've had him under ether for six months. He has an
      abscess. And I won't have my abscess lesson until next July.

584   Now, open your mouth! Not too wide. I just want to look in. I
      don't want to jump in. Mmmmm, that tooth will have to come
      out. I'll make you a bridge.
      Will you make a good bridge?
      Will I? I'll make you a bridge that will go up and down with
      the tide.

585   This tooth keeps me awake at night. What can I do for it?
      You could get a job as night watchman.

586   Can you give me gas?
      Where have I heard that word before? Gas!
      You must have gas.
      And how!
      What do you use for gas?
      Bicarbonate of soda.

587   I want to get two teeth pulled out; how much do you charge?
      Sit down and let me see where they are.
      You can't see them — they're in my girl's neck.

588   Doctor, I came here to get my tooth pulled. Will it take long?
      It won't be long now. Hold still. Take it easy. There, I got it.
      The joke is on you.
      How is that?
      You pulled the wrong tooth.

589   Did he find anything wrong with you?
      My teeth. They were all good except one bridge which was put in
      by a dentist in London.
      I get it. London bridge is falling down.

590   I see you have acute pyorrhea.
      I'm glad you like it.

591   Absentminded dentist fixing his car — takes out a wrench and
      says: Now, this is going to hurt a little.

592   The dentist had been trying to collect a bill for a set of false teeth.
      Did he pay you?
      Pay me! Not only did he refuse to pay me, but he actually had the
      effrontery to gnash at me with my teeth.

593   Dentist: Have you seen any small boys ring my bell and run away?
      Policeman: They weren't small boys — they were grownups.

594   You say you've never had a tooth filled, yet I find flakes of metal
      on my drill.
      That was my collar button.

595   Absentminded Judge to dentist: Do you swear that you will pull
      the tooth, the whole tooth and nothing but the tooth?

596   I'd like to go to a woman dentist.
      Why do you want to go to a woman dentist?
      Because it would be a pleasure to have a woman say open your
         mouth instead of shut up.

597   A gangster went into a dentist's office and said to the dentist: Pull
         my tooth.
      The dentist said: Which tooth is it?
      And the Gangster said: Find it yourself — I'm no stool pigeon.

598   Which tooth do you want extracted?
      Pullman Porter: Lower seven.

599   I've just been having a tussle with the dentist.
      Which beat?
      It ended in a draw.

600   That dentist wasn't painless.
      Why, did he hurt you?
      No, but he yelled when I bit his finger.

601   I had to go down to the dentist and I sure enjoyed it.
      You mean to say you enjoy going to the dentist?
      Sure, I had to take my grandfather's teeth down there to be fixed.

RELATED SUBJECTS
Mouth 546-547
Gas 907-909

LEFT-HANDED

602   If you really want work — Farmer Gray wants a right-hand man.
      Jus' my luck, lidy — I'm left-'anded.

603   What are you holding your side for?
      I have to hold my side — I think I have appendicitis.
      But you're holding your left side. Your appendix is on your right
         side.
      I told you I was left-handed.

604   You've entered this debit item under credit.
      Sorry, sir, you see I'm left-handed.

RELATED SUBJECTS
Anatomy 217-604

PHYSICAL CONDITION

HEALTH (Good)

605   This place isn't fit for a dog.
      Yes it is — come in.

606   Are rosy cheeks a sign of good health?
      Yes. Why?
      She is more healthy on one side than the other.

607   I like that country — it's very healthy. All the time I was out there
         I never paid a doctor bill.
      I know that. I met the doctor and he told me.

608   And, Doctor, do you think cranberries are healthy?
      I've never heard one complain.

609   I drank his health so often I ruined my own.

610   Hello, Bill, how's your health?
      Not so good — it hasn't been drunk lately.

611   How do you feel?
      I can't kick.
      Rheumatism, eh?

612   So your wife has gone to Palm Beach for her health. What did
         she have?
      Eight hundred dollars her father gave her.

613   You're looking very good this morning. Have you had good news?
      Wonderful! My husband has broken down and we're going to
         Palm Beach for the winter.

614   I feel fit as a fiddle.
      You look like a saxophone.

                              RELATED SUBJECTS
                              Death 124-145
                              Exercise 382-400
                              Sickness 741-801
                              Athlete 4319-4323

HEALTH (Ill)

ACCIDENTS

615   Our gas range exploded and blew mother and father out of the
         house together.
      That's terrible.
      Yeah, but it made mother very happy.
      Made your mother very happy?
      Yeah — that was the first time they'd left the house together in
         twenty years.

616   My brother swallowed a box of firecrackers.
      Is he all right now?
      I don't know. I haven't heard the last report.

617   My cousin swallowed a frog.
      Did it make him sick?
      Yes, he's liable to croak any minute.

618   My sister's baby swallowed a bottle of **ink!**
      Incredible!
      No. Indelible.

619   What happened to you?
      You know that deep hole in front of the studio?
      Oh, yes — I meant to tell you about it.
      Don't bother — I found out all about it.

620   A man dropped off the eaves of this building and was killed.
      That's what he deserves for eavesdropping.

621   My brother fell down two flights of stairs with two pints of gin.
      Did he spill the gin?
      No, he kept his mouth closed.

622   I fell off the roof of our house.
      Did you get hurt?
      No, I bounced and bounced.
      What made you bounce?
      I had on my new spring pants.

623   This morning the waiter tripped over the carpet and spilled the
         coffee over my lap, but I didn't get mad. I didn't say anything.
      Why not?
      It was Chase and Sanborn coffee, and *You* can't complain about
         that.

624   My brother's in the hospital. He got run over by a street car.
      I'll bet you feel badly.
      I would feel badly if he were my REAL brother.
      Don't be silly! Isn't he your real brother?
      Since he's been run over by the street car, he is only my HALF
         brother.

625   My little brother swallowed a button.
      What did you do?
      I gave him a button hook to play with.

626   I just saw a man jump off a ten story building.
      That's nothing — jump back up — that's the trick.

627   I was almost killed twice in an airplane.
      Once would have been enough.

628   My uncle and another man fell from a 10 story building the other
         day and neither one was injured.
      How did that happen?
      They were both killed.

629   Was your uncle killed in the fall?
No, but he would have been except for one thing.
What was that?
He fell into an open man hole and was drowned.

630   That was a terrible accident. I suppose it knocked you out?
No — but the doctor said if it had been anyone else, it would have caused concussion of the brain.

631   While you were gone, Ma'am, your little Willie swallowed a bug, but don't worry, I had him take some insect powder.

632   Did you hear the stepladder fall, mama?
Yes. I hope your father didn't fall.
He hasn't yet. He's hanging to the picture moulding.

633   So your uncle fell down the stairs?
Yeah, but it was all the same, he had to come down anyway.

634   I fell over a cliff and landed in the water up to my knees. A fellow pulled me out or I would have drowned.
You couldn't drown when you were up to your knees in water.
Is that so? It happens I went in head first.

635   My brother fell off a building and went through the sidewalk.
Did he get hurt?
He surely was lucky. The sidewalk must have broken his fall.

636   A steam roller ran over my uncle.
What did you do?
I just took him home and slipped him under the door.

637   I just got a telephone call from a friend of mine. He has offices on the top floor of the Gray Building and he dropped ten stories — luckily he wasn't injured.
How could he drop ten stories and not get injured?
Well, you see he is a scenario writer, and he dropped them into the waste basket.

638   Bill can't come. He's in the hospital. Someone stepped on his pipe during the game.
I don't see how that would make him have to go to the hospital.
It was his windpipe.

639   Where is your brother?
He's in the hospital — his girl threw him over.
That shouldn't have made him go to a hospital.
This girl threw him over a cliff.

640   How'd you get that burn on your face?
Had my suit pressed.
What's that got to do with it?
I was in a hurry and didn't take my suit off.

641 I fell off a sixty-five foot ladder today.
It's a miracle you weren't killed.
Oh, I only fell off the first rung.

642 My little daughter has swallowed a gold piece and has got to be
operated on. I wonder if Dr. Robertson is to be trusted?
Without a doubt. He's absolutely honest.

643 I was looking around and was surprised to see a terrible railroad
accident.
Did you get a picture of the terrible wreck?
Sure— she had it taken the first day we were married.

644 My uncle fell off a ten story building.
Was he hurt?
I don't know — he hasn't stopped bouncing yet.

645 The baby swallowed your wedding band.
I thought his voice had a brassy ring.

646 Lucky we weren't all killed.
Well, better luck next time.

647 My sister's little baby ate a whole newspaper up.
What did you do — send for a doctor?
No, we just fed him a Literary Digest.

648 Man swallowed an egg and he's afraid to move — afraid it will
break; and afraid to sit still because he's afraid it will hatch.

649 (A robust woman lost her thumb in a trolley accident)
But why do you think that your thumb was worth $20,000?
Because it was the thumb I kept my husband under.

650 I swallowed a pan only yesterday and it hoits something terrible.
Vat kind of a pan — a dish pan maybe or a frying pan perhaps?
No — no — a fountain pan.

651 Have you ever been in a railway accident?
Yes, once when I was in a train and we were going through a
tunnel I kissed the father instead of the daughter.

652 Quick, Doctor, do something! I was playing a mouth organ an'
swallowed it!
Keep calm, sir, and be thankful you were not playing the piano.

653 (Man killed in accident; stranger runs up as it happens)
Stranger: Sorry, old man. But be sure and give my regards to my
first wife.

654 (Man prostrated on sidewalk)
Lady: And so this is the work of rum, is it?
Man: No, ma'am; this is the work of a banana skin.

655   I saw a man fall out of a window, and the remarkable thing is
      that he lives.
That's nothing. I saw a man run over by a train and engine.
And he lived?
Of course not, he died.

656   Pat, the Irish hod-carrier, had just fallen two stories and covered
      himself with mortar. Solicitous friend asks: Pat, are you hurt?
Pat: Nope, but I sure feel mortified.

657   Here, I'll help carry the trunk.
Okay.
(Trunk falls)
Better pick that trunk up quick.
Leave it stay there — we'll get someone to help us.
Better pick that trunk up — because Mr. Doakes wouldn't like it
      left there.
But where is Mr. Doakes?
He's under the trunk.

658   My gosh, boy, what happened to you?
I threw a horseshoe over my shoulder.
And what happened?
There was a horse nailed on it.

659   Did you hear about Pete? He drank some sulphuric acid by mistake.
Hurt him?
No, he said the only thing he noticed was that he made holes in his
      handkerchief every time he blew his nose.

660   I've just swallowed a great big worm.
Hadn't you better take something for it?
No — I'll let the thing starve.

661   Hey, it's pretty fortunate for you this accident happened in front
      of a doctor's house.
Yeah — but I'm the doctor.

662   Old Jonas Hardscrabble fell plumb off the roof of his house while
      he was shingling it.
Didn't his wife feel awful?
Awful is no name for it — he fell right into her bed of sweetpeas.

663   Jones expects 100% disability on his accident insurance policy.
      He says he is completely incapacitated by the loss of a thumb.
What's his vocation?
He's a professional hitch-hiker.

664   Oh John, the baby has swallowed the yeast.
Umph, you were always predicting he was bound to rise.

665　My uncle fell off a scaffolding and was killed.
　　　What was he doing up on the scaffolding?
　　　Getting hanged.

666　Come quick, Cy. The hired man just fell down the well.
　　　Drat his shiftless hide! Always schemin' ways ter dodge work.

667　I'm always having automobile accidents.
　　　Is that so? Well, you should stay on your side of the road. That's
　　　　what the white line is for.
　　　It is? I thought the white line on the road was for bicycles.

668　If you hugged the curve, you should have been safe.
　　　I know, but it wasn't that kind of a curve.

669　How did you happen to hit that telephone pole?
　　　(Drunk) I only hit it in self defense.

670　How did the accident happen?
　　　My wife fell asleep in the back seat.

671　I've got a flat tire. I ran over a bottle about a mile back.
　　　Couldn't you see it and drive around it?
　　　No, the fool had it in his hip pocket.

672　Do you want damages?
　　　I have all the damages I want. I need repairs.

673　Right here in this one city a man is knocked down by a car every
　　　　five minutes.
　　　I should think he would be worn out.

674　Why did you run down this man in broad daylight on a perfectly
　　　　straight stretch of road?
　　　My windshield was almost totally obscured with Safety First
　　　　stickers.

675　I was driving and the cars were tearing by at sixty miles an hour.
　　　I saw a car coming toward me and I turned out to let it pass.
　　　Then I saw another car coming and I turned out to let it pass.
　　　Then I saw a bridge coming toward me — I turned out to let
　　　　it pass, and that's all I remember.

676　I saw a man run over himself today.
　　　That's impossible.
　　　I did. This man drove up to a drugstore and asked the clerk for a
　　　　cigar, and the clerk said they didn't have any but they had some
　　　　across the street. He asked the clerk to get him one but the clerk
　　　　said he couldn't leave the store, so the man ran over himself.

677　A wild driver in a stolen car, no license, no lights, came down on
　　　　the wrong side of the street and went right through the red

lights, and smashed into my car and held the right front bumper in the left hand and the rear bumper in his right hand . . .

And what?

He started to play it — he thought it was an accordion. A cop came along and arrested me. I told the cop it wasn't my fault and he said it was my fault and I said: Why is it my fault? And the cop said: His father is the Mayor, and his uncle is the Chief of Police and I'm courting his daughter.

678 You must have had a terrible accident last night. The front of your car is all smashed in. What did you hit?

Last night I was driving and hit a cow . . .

A Jersey cow?

I don't know — I didn't see the license plate.

679 Joe says he has never had a wreck since he got his car.

I believe it— but he had an awful wreck when he got it.

680 I had an accident in my car — my car went from one side of the street to the other.

The tires were loose?

No, I was tight.

681 Did you meet with any disasters?

In one town I met my mother-in-law.

How is she?

She's fair to meddling.

682 (A man was being examined for an insurance policy.)

Have you ever had a serious illness? asked the doctor.

No, never.

Ever have a serious accident?

No.

You mean you've *never* had an accident in your life?

Never, except when the bull tossed me over the fence.

And you don't call that an accident?

No, sir! He did it on purpose!

683 What's all the commotion over there — a fire?

No — a fellow started to cross the bridge.

Well?

There wasn't no bridge.

684 Is this the garage?

Yes.

Well, send help as I've turned turtle.

You don't want a garage, you need an aquarium.

685 When that auto accident happened, I fell right out of the car.

It's a wonder your neck wasn't broken.

Well, it was interrupted.

686   How did you happen to have an accident with that used car I
      sold you?
      I couldn't put out my hand while I was pushing it around the
      corner.

687   I tried to turn the corner.
      Well, what happened?
      I was in the middle of the block.

688   A musician with a trombone under his arm was walking across the
      street and a man in an automobile hit him. The man yelled: You
      have a horn — why didn't you toot it?

689   I meant to stop and buy a book on etiquette on the way up here
      this evening.
      What is it you would like to know?
      In case of an accident, I would like to know should the lady precede
      the gentleman through the windshield?

690   Yesterday something didn't turn out right for him.
      What was that?
      The car in front of him.

691   What part of the car causes the most accidents?
      The nut that holds the wheel.

692   Now, Miss, what gear were you in at the time of the accident?
      Oh, I had on a black beret, tan shoes, a tweed sport dress . . .

693   I wonder why there are so many more auto wrecks than railway
      accidents?
      That's easy — did you ever hear of the fireman hugging the en-
      gineer?

694   Had a terrible automobile accident.
      What happened?
      I fell out of a patrol wagon.

695   Do you know more women are hit by woman automobile drivers?
      I suppose it's human.
      Why do you think that's human?
      I suppose it's because one woman always likes to run down another
      woman.

696   Did you have complete control of yourself at the time?
      No, my wife was with me.

697   What I can't understand is why you ran into the policeman.
      It was the best way I knew to sober up.

698   (Two pedestrians knocked down by auto)
      Didja get her number?

How could I get her number when she was going so fast?
Nice looking girl, wasn't she?
Yeah, didja see her beautiful brown eyes?

699   What was the cause of the collision at that corner today?
Two motorists after the same pedestrian.

700   In New York there is a man run over every ten minutes.
What a man!

701   Listen, mister, I had the right-of-way, didn't I?
Yeah, but the other fellow had a truck.

702   (There had been a motor wreck. One of the drivers climbed out in
a fit of temper and strode up to a man standing on the sidewalk,
thinking him to be the driver.)
Driver: Say, where is your tail light?
Stranger: Wot do you think I am — a bloomin' lightning bug?

703   Why don't you buy a car — it will make you a better man.
It would probably — it made my uncle a better man. The town
thinks he's great. Last week he donated six new patients to the
hospital.

704   Were you ever wrecked?
Yeah — three times by liquor and three times by women.

705   How did he happen to lose control of his car at the railroad crossing?
He's the kind of a man who always drops everything when the
whistle blows.

706   What was the boy whom you hit doing in the street?
I don't know, sir; I didn't think to ask him before he was struck
down and afterwards there wasn't any use.

707   Two women driving down a steep hill when the driver suddenly
screams: I've lost control of the car.
Oh, you say you can't stop the car. Good Heavens! What'll we do?
It doesn't matter anyway, I guess, there wasn't any room to park
along here.

708   Cop: Who was driving when this accident happened?
Drunk: No one. We were all sitting in the back seat.

709   Have an accident?
No, thanks — just had one.

RELATED SUBJECTS
Insurance 208-216
Hospital 831-834
Automobile 4042-4146
Train 4218-4242
Attorney 5235-5244

EXPLOSION

710   We had an accident over at our place yesterday. A terrific explosion.
      What happened?
      Well, I gave one of our chickens "lay or bust" feed and it turned out to be a rooster.

711   Where is Atoms?
      Atoms? You mean Athens, don't you?
      No — Atoms — the place where everything is blown to.

712   The walls of this room are all covered with spots.
      The last man who lived in this room was an inventor — he invented some sort of an explosive.
      Oh, the spots on the walls are explosive?
      No, the inventor.

713   Many a bad explosion is caused by the fermentation of a batch of mash notes.

714   Man was blown through the roof: As he was going up he sang that song: Pardon my sudden assent.

715   What caused the explosion at your house?
      Powder on my coat sleeve.

RELATED SUBJECTS
Death 124-145
Insurance 208-216

INJURY

716   Oh, Gerald, I've been stung by a wasp!
      Quick, put some ammonia on it.
      I can't, it's gone.

717   Did yer notice that Mrs. Binks 'as got a black eye?
      Yuh, it ain't respectable, 'er with 'er 'usband not out of prison for another week yet.

718   My brother fell off a ten story building.
      Was he injured?
      No. He fell through a man hole into the subway and was killed by an underground train.

719   Ouch! I burned my finger in the hot water.
      Why didn't you feel the water before you put your hand in it?

720   What are you doing with that bandage around your arm?
      I fell on my face.
      If you fell on your face, why bandage your arm?
      Because a fellow would look silly with his face tied up.

721   What's the trouble — are you hurt?
      No — gotta nail in my boot.
      Why don't you take it out?
      What! On my dinner hour.

722   I'm choking.
      Can't I help you?

723   My brother's going to the hospital tonight with a broken nose.
      Why doesn't he go this morning?
      Because my father isn't going to break it until he comes home from
      work tonight.

724   How did you get your hand full of splinters?
      I was out hunting — and caught a timber wolf barehanded.

725   My uncle had an accident with his car. It was a terrible accident
      but he had a good doctor. The doctor told him he would have
      him walking in a month.
      And did he?
      Yes. When the doctor sent his bill, my uncle had to sell his car.

726   How did you break your leg?
      I threw a cigarette in a man hole and stepped on it.

727   What's the matter with your finger?
      I hit the wrong nail.

728   I stood beneath my girl's window singing and serenading her, and
      she threw me a flower.
      What made the bump on your head?
      She forgot to take the flower out of the pot.

729   Why didn't your cousin fight last night?
      He couldn't.
      Why not?
      The rubber rubbed his back with alcohol, and he sprained his neck
      trying to lick it off.

730   I was shot in the head during the World War and only yesterday
      I coughed the bullet up.
      It certainly takes a long time to get anything through your head.

731   I was injured on the football team.
      How?
      I fell off the bench.

732   Brown of U.S.C. breaks his leg in the third quarter.
      What part of the leg is that?

733   When you fell off the scaffold and your wife got word that you
      were gravely injured, how was she taking it when they took

you home?

Very hard, indeed! She was sitting out on the front porch with my life insurance policy in her hands.

734   My mother got a black eye last night.

She should put a piece of steak on it.

If we'd had steak in the house, my father wouldn't have blacked her eye.

735   How did you get that black eye?

The door knob hit me when she opened the door.

736   Why all the black eyes, old man?

You see, it was this way: I came home drunk the other night and sat down to read a while before retiring and my wife came downstairs and saw me reading and beat me up.

What were you reading?

The checkerboard.

737   My brother fell out of the third story window and broke his nose.

What did the doctor do?

He prescribed bleeding and bled him out of $17.

738   How did your uncle break his ribs?

Leaning over the back of the seat of a street car to read the newspaper.

739   (Two men were getting ready for a dip in a swimming pool.)

Your shins are in pretty bad shape — hockey player?

Oh, no — I just led back my wife's weak suit in bridge.

740   How did Jack get that sore jaw?

A girl cracked a smile.

Well?

It was his smile.

RELATED SUBJECTS
Death 124-145
Insurance 208-216
Accident 615-709
Hospital 831-834

SICKNESS

741   Did you take my advice and sleep with the window open to cure your cold?

Yes.

Did you lose your cold?

No, I lost my watch and my pocketbook.

742 Doctor: Yes, it is some chronic evil which has deprived you of health and happiness.
Patient: Shhh! For heaven's sake, speak softly — she's sitting in the next room.

743 Your husband must be absolutely quiet. Here is a sleeping draught.
When do I give it to him?
You don't, you take it yourself.

744 And then I got clothing sickness.
Clothing sickness? What's that?
My tongue got a coat and my breath came in short pants.

745 Last night I caught a cold in my head and today my wife tried to break it up.
Well, that's nice of her.
Yeah, but she tried to break it up with a hammer.

746 She always has a stiff neck. Can't find anything to help it.
Try a little flattery — it usually turns their heads.

747 Just think, Jane has gone back to Arizona for her heart.
Poor dear, she's so absentminded that she is always forgetting something.

748 Oh, man, I'll never be a well man again. It happened sudden like this morning. I can't straighten up — I can't lift my head. I feel all drawn up!
Do you feel any pain?
No, there ain't no pain — I must be paralyzed. Get a doctor.
Here, let me examine you. Well, it'll be a great help if you'll unbutton the third buttonhole of your blouse from the top button of your trousers.

749 Was your husband nice to you during your illness?
Yes, indeed. He was more like a neighbor than a husband.

750 He's sick from eating cherries.
Eating cherries? Where'd he get them?
In the bottom of his cocktail glasses.

751 I've got a headache.
You know what's good for a headache?
No, what?
My brother had a headache once. I gave him half a glass of eyewash and half a glass of paregoric. Why don't you try it?
That would kill me.
I know. It killed my brother, too.

752 My aunt is very sick.
Sickness is just a mental condition — entirely in her mind.
She had a relapse.

She just thinks she had a relapse.
Well, she's dead now and she'd better not change her mind, because
she was buried yesterday.

753   He is very sick. He should be tapped.
He'll die.
What makes you think he'll die if I tap him?
Well, all I know is if anything is tapped in this house, it doesn't
last any longer than a week.

754   My aunt is sick in bed. She was such a healthy woman — weighed
200 pounds. I wonder how I'll get her on her feet again.
Why don't you try a derrick?

755   Oh, Doctor, when I get well will I be able to play the piano?
Of course.
That's marvelous. I never played it before.

756   Why, I'll have you cured of the measles in a week.
Now, Doctor, no rash promises.

757   Doctor: You've been working too hard. What you need is recreation. If I were you, I'd go home and take my wife to a show.
Patient: Thanks, Doc, thanks a lot. By the way, what's your
address?

758   I have laryngitis.
Oh, something wrong with your pipes?
What?
I said, you have something wrong with your pipes.
Pipes?
Yeah — you know what runs from the bathroom to the kitchen?
Cockroaches.

759   My uncle has a terrible cold. He can hardly speak.
Has he tried whiskey?
Yeah, that's why he can hardly speak.

760   Did the doctor take your temperature?
I don't know. All I've missed so far is my wrist watch.

761   Why do you keep looking down all the time?
The doctor told me to watch my stomach.

762   My brother was very sick so we called Doctor Smith. My brother
took his medicine and got worse. Then we called Doctor Jones
and my brother took his medicine and he got still worse. We
thought he was going to die, so we called Doctor Gray and he
was too busy, and finally my brother got well.

763   My wife's been very ill and the doctor told me I should take her to
the seashore, but I didn't have the money to do that.

What are you going to do about it?
Oh, I've found a way to bring the sea breezes to her.
How?
I fan her with a herring.

764 Well, all this sickness of hers has just been in her imagination.
How do you know?
Well, the doctor said all she needed was a little sunshine. I couldn't send her no place. I didn't have enough money, so I painted a sun on top of the ceiling of her room.
Did it help her any?
It liked to ruin her. When I came back I found her all doubled up with the sunburn.

765 You know my father has influenza all the time.
Doesn't your father know that whiskey is good for influenza?
Yeah — that's why he has it all the time.

766 My family is one of the first, but most of them have died from throat trouble.
Yes, hanged perhaps.

767 How's your husband getting on, Mrs. Malone?
Well, sometimes he's better, and sometimes he's worse, but from the way he growls and goes on when he's better, I think he's better when he's worse.

768 Well, you'll get along okay. Your left leg is swollen but I wouldn't worry about it.
No, and if your left leg was swollen I wouldn't worry about it, either.

769 My father has rheumatism.
Well, he's so careful — I'll bet it's in your mother's name.

770 He's in a bad state. Should I call a doctor?
No, call a statesman.

771 I had a bad case of the flu. I didn't know whether to feed a cold or starve it.
What did you do?
I flooded it.

772 Your pulse is as steady as a clock.
You've got your hand on my wrist watch.

773 I had an awful headache last night.
Yes, I saw you with her.

774 The doctor told me he'd be all right — just take a bath before retiring.
Well, the way business is now, he won't retire for 30 years.

775   I've been pushing you in this wheel chair all over the place until
        I have callouses all over me.
        And what you haven't got, I've got sitting.

776   I have a bad cold. What would you suggest for a man a little
        hoarse?
        A buggy.

777   That's a pretty flimsy excuse for coming late.
        How can I help it? I got a cold.
        They say feed a cold and starve a fever.
        I was just wondering . . .
        Wondering what?
        Why all the girls I have have colds and none have fevers.

778   His wife is sick — the doctor said she needed some fresh mountain
        air. He stayed home every night and fanned her with a picture
        of the alps.

779   Doctor, will you give me something for my head?
        My dear man, I already have one.

780   My, how my heart beats.
        What did you expect it to do?

781   Your stomach rumbles like a motor.
        Well, if it does it's from eating that truck.

782   Ah, Mrs. Higgens, and how is your husband today?
        Gettin' along grand, doctor. Why, 'e tried to 'it me this morning.

783   Hello, Smith, old man, haven't seen you for some time.
        Been in bed seven weeks.
        Oh, that's too bad. Flu, I suppose?
        Yes, and crashed!

784   I have told your wife that she must go to the mountains.
        That's all right, doctor; now tell me I must go to the seashore.

785   Doctor: (To man crying because he's sick) Cheer up, my good
        man — you'll pull through.
        Man: It isn't that, Doctor — but just think of all the money I've
        spent for apples to keep you away.

786   Troubled with your throat, eh? Ever gargled with salt water?
        Yes. I was nearly drowned while swimming last summer.

787   How are you?
        I can't kick.
        What?
        I can't kick.
        What's the matter — have you got rheumatism?

788 I think he's regaining consciousness, doctor, he tried to blow the foam off his medicine.

789 The doctor says your illness is all due to drink and that you must not take a drop more.
Yes, I didn't know it was such a serious illness. I thought it would just mean an operation.

790 How long have you been going about like this?
Two weeks.
Why, man, your ankle is broken! How you managed to get around is a marvel. Why didn't you come to me at first?
Why, doctor, every time I say something is wrong with me, my wife declares I'll have to stop drinking 'n smoking.

791 I'm afraid the mountain air would disagree with me.
My dear, it wouldn't dare.

792 Yes, my husband's laid up, a victim of football.
But I didn't know he even played the game.
He doesn't. He sprained his larynx at the match last Saturday.

793 I'm a little hoarse.
I knew you wasn't a lady.

794 She hasn't been sick a day in her life.
Gracious! Whatever does she talk about?

795 Wife: The doctor looked at my tongue and said it didn't look the same as usual.
Husband: Well, probably you held it still while he looked at it.

796 What's the matter?
I have a cold in my head.
That's something.
Sure, that's more than you have in your head.

797 I've got a headache.
It must be the damp weather — it gets in the bones.

798 My brother was sick and he went to the doctor.
Is he feeling better now?
No, he has a broken arm.
How did he break it?
Well, the doctor gave him a prescription and told him no matter what happened, to follow that prescription. And the prescription blew out of the window.
How did he break his arm?
He fell out of the window trying to follow the prescription.

799 Doctor, I have a cold or something in my head.
It must be a cold.

800   I've got a headache.
Don't tell me it's from thinking?
It's from that party I gave last week — I just got the bill.

801   Man: Send your nurse over.
Doctor: She's got the measles.
Man: I kissed her and I'll have the measles.
Doctor: I kissed her, too.
Man: Then you'll have the measles, and what's worse I've been kissing my wife.
Friend: (overhearing conversation) In that case, I'm going to have the measles, too.

> RELATED SUBJECTS
> Health (Good) 605-614
> Health (Ill)
>   a. Causes 615-830
>   b. Remedies 831-911

DISEASES

802   What would be the first thing you'd do if you had hydrofobby?
I'd ask for a pencil and some paper.
To make your last will?
No, to make a list of the people I want to bite.

803   Are you ever troubled with diphtheria?
Only when I try to spell it.

804   I bought my uncle some of that patent medicine.
Is he getting cured?
He was getting better until he read the wrapper around the bottle and now he's got two more diseases.

805   Famous writer to his doctor: Doc, I'm having trouble with my appendix.
Well, use footnotes instead.

806   I treat all kinds of love ailments. Just cured a man of matrimonial dyspepsia. He said when he came home his wife had a cold shoulder and a hot tongue for him.
What seemed to be the matter with him?
Domestic biliousness. Bills make husbands bilious.

807   The doctor told him he had a floating kidney so he went out and had an anchor tattooed on his back.

808   What are you taking for your dyspepsia?
Make me an offer.

RELATED SUBJECTS
Health (Good) 605-614
Germs 817-821
Fever 822-830
Hospital 3564-3660

HAY FEVER

809   I want to marry your daughter.
Can you give her what she's been accustomed to having?
Oh, yeah, I have had hay fever for years.

810   Let me kiss those tears away, sweetheart.
(She fell into his arms, but the tears flowed on.)
Will nothing stop those tears?
No. It's hay fever, but go on with the treatment.

811   What did you think of the Hula Hula dancers in Hawaii?
I had a tough break in Hawaii — I couldn't watch those Hula Hula
dancers; because they wore grass skirts and I had hay fever.

812   I had hay fever.
You did? Did you have it in the affirmative or the negative?
What do you mean?
Well, there are both kinds. Sometimes the ayes (eyes) have it and
sometimes the noes (nose) have it.

LOCOMOTAR-ATAXIA

813   My uncle had locomotar-ataxia once. He had it so bad he used to
whistle at crossings.

SEVEN-YEAR-ITCH

814   My uncle Joe had hard luck for twenty-one years. He had the
seven-year-itch three times.

815   Why are you buying two dozen scratch pads?
I've got the seven-year-itch.

816   He's so lazy he has the seven-year-itch and he's nine months behind
in his scratching.

GERMS

817   It says that thousands of germs can live on the point of a needle.
What a strange diet!

818   Cigar smoke kills germs.
Yes, but it's hard to get 'em to smoke.

819   Breathe deeply. Germs are killed by deep breathing.
       Yes, but how are you going to teach the germs to breathe?

820   Don't put that money in your mouth — there's germs on it.
       Don't be silly — even a germ can't live on the money you earn.

821   You see that old boy over there? He thinks in terms of millions.
       He doesn't look like a financier.
       He isn't. He's a bacteriologist.

RELATED SUBJECTS
Health (Ill) 615-911
Cleanliness 3351-3358
Drug Store 5430-5437

FEVER

822   Athlete: How high is my temperature, doctor?
       Doctor: A hundred and one.
       Athlete: What's the world's record?

823   Good morning, Mrs. Kelly, did you take your husband's tempera-
       ture as I told you?
       Yes, doctor, I borrowed a barometer and placed it on his chest; it
       said 'very dry,' so I bought him a pint of beer an' he's gone back
       to work.

824   The glass eater from the circus was in the hospital. The nurse,
       wanting to take his temperature, put a thermometer in his mouth.
       Two minutes later he said: That was delicious. I'd like some
       more of that.

825   The doctor said your wife is in the hospital with a temperature up
       to 104. What shall he do?
       Tell him to wait until it reaches 105 — and then sell.

826   You have a fever of 103.
       When it gets to 105 I'll sell.

827   He had a fever, so we put him in the cellar to heat the house.

828   Weren't you in the hospital last week?
       Yeah, I had a terrible high fever.
       What did they give you to slow down your heart action?
       An elderly nurse.

829   I'm an educated man. I graduated with the degree of Bachelor of
       Arts and other degrees.
       I graduated from college with 103 degrees.
       What do you mean, one hundred and three degrees?
       I had a fever.

830   Have you taken his temperature?
       No — is it missing?

> RELATED SUBJECTS
> Sickness 741-801

HOSPITAL

831   How's your brother who was in the hospital?
       Oh, he's all right, but I don't think he'll be home for quite awhile.
       Why, did you see his doctor?
       No, but I saw his nurse.

832   How is the best way to get to the emergency hospital?
       Just stand out there in the middle of the street.

833   My brother is a pan handler.
       That so?
       Yeah, he's an interne in a hospital.

834   Hospital jokes: Without any appendix.

> RELATED SUBJECTS
> Accident 615-709
> Sickness 741-801
> Operation 883-911

NURSE

835   A doctor was treating a man who had imbibed too much alcoholic
       beverage. He said to the nurse: If the patient sees green snakes
       again, give him some of this medicine.
       Later on he came back and the man was raving but the medicine
       hadn't been given him. The doctor said: Didn't I tell you to
       give him this medicine if he saw green snakes again?
       Nurse: But he didn't see green snakes. He's been seeing pink
       elephants.

> RELATED SUBJECTS
> Health (Ill) 615-911
> Doctor 838-860
> Operation 883-911

VISITOR

836   My brother's sick in the hospital. He's been pretty sick.
       I hope you went to see him and cheered him up.
       I did. I took him a lot of magazines, but I told him not to start
       any serials.

837   Your brother is pretty sick, isn't he?
       He's in bed and I was just up to see him.
       I hope you kept the conversation very cheerful, while you were
       there.

I kept it very pleasant. I told him I thought they had better get a carpenter over there to make the bedroom door wider. Couldn't get a coffin through it.

RELATED SUBJECTS
Hospitality 3564-3660

DOCTOR

838   Doctor: There goes the only woman I ever loved.
Nurse: Why don't you marry her?
Doctor: I can't afford to. She's my best patient.

839   Have you any aches or pains this morning?
Yes, Doctor, it hurts me to breathe. In fact, the only trouble now seems to be with my breathing.
All right. I'll give you something that will stop that.

840   My sister married one of the biggest doctors in town.
Does he have any money?
Sure, he has. Do you think she married him for her health?

841   What does he do for a living?
He used to be a surgeon, but he had to quit.
Too hard on his nerves?
No, too much inside work.

842   Just do as I say and you'll be another man.
Okay and, Doctor, don't forget to send your bill to the other man.

843   You've got chronic bronchitis, but don't worry, you'll be all right in no time.
You're so sure, I suppose you've had a great deal of experience with this sickness.
My dear, miss, I've had bronchitis myself for more than 15 years.

844   Doctor, I want a little wart removed.
You're in the wrong office, madam, the divorce lawyer is in the next office.

845   Why is a physician who doesn't drink like a shipyard?
Because he is a dry doc.

846   Why don't you go out with Gus? He's an M.D.
That's just it — Mentally delinquent.

847   Say, Doctor, what's this bill for?
Five hundred and fifty dollars—five hundred for twenty calls at $25 a call, and $50 for medicine.
All right, Doctor, here's fifty for the medicine. I'll pay the visits back.

848   Doctor: Stick out your tongue.
Man: What for? I'm not mad at you.

849 Is the doctor in?
     Yes, but the doctor is practicing.
     Well, I'll come back when he is perfect.

850 The doctor I consult tells you to play golf for your health.
     And if you already play golf, then what?
     He tells you to stop.

851 Doctor: My man, yours is a case which will enrich medical science.
     Patient: Oh, dear, and I thought I wouldn't have to pay more than
        five or ten dollars.

852 He's a very famous doctor — in fact, he's a bone specialist. He
     carries his own dice.

853 I'll never go back to that doctor again; he's old fashioned.
     What makes you say that?
     Well, he put something on my chest and listened to me with ear
        phones.
     He examined you with a stethoscope.
     Well, nowadays everybody uses a loud speaker and he still uses
        earphones.

854 Hello, old man. What's the matter? You're looking glum.
     No wonder. I'm attending that wealthy Mr. Golddig, you know,
        and I've sent him the wrong medicine.
     Indeed! Is it a serious blunder?
     Very serious. The medicine I've sent him will cure him in two days.

855 Is the doctor in?
     No, he stepped out for lunch.
     Will he be in after lunch?
     Why no, that's what he went out after . . .

856 Why did you break your engagement to Tom?
     He deceived me. He told me he was a liver and kidney specialist,
        and I found out that he only worked in the butcher's shop.

857 Why did you tear the back part out of that new book?
     Excuse me, dear, the part you speak of was labelled "appendix"
        and I took it out without thinking.

858 A little bird told me what kind of lawyer your uncle is.
     What did he say?
     Cheep! Cheep!
     Oh, yeh. Well, a duck just told me what kind of a doctor your
        pa is.

859 An invitation to dinner had been sent to the newly settled doctor.
        In reply the hostess received an absolutely illegible letter.
     Woman: I must know if he accepts or refuses.

Husband: If I were you, I should take it to the chemist. Chemists can always read a doctor's writing no matter how badly it is written.

The chemist looked at the slip of notepaper, went into his dispensary, and returned a few minutes later with a bottle, which he handed over the counter.

Chemist: There you are, madam. That will cost $1.

860   Doctor: It's most essential that you should refrain from doing head work during the next few weeks.
Patient: Yes, doctor, but it's my living.
Doctor: Oh, are you a scholar?
Patient: No, I'm a barber.

RELATED SUBJECTS
Health (Ill) 615-911
Advice 1978-1989
Drug Store 5430-5437

PHYSICAL EXAMINATION

861   I will examine you for $10.
Go ahead. If you find it I'll give you half.

862   Before he sent me out on this dangerous mission, he examined me to see if I was physically fit. He went all over me looking for my heart — he couldn't find it.
How was that?
Because it was in my throat.

863   Did you take an examination?
First they gave me a mental test to see what I knew.
Well, that only took a second — then what?
The doctor put tubes in his ears and a steel business on my chest. What was he doing that for?
He was tuning in on you.

RELATED SUBJECTS
Shape (Physical) 341-347
Feet 405-430
Legs 433-439
Eyes 459-490
Ears 498-505
Nose 537-543
Mouth 546-547

X-RAY

864   I'm learning to be an x-ray photographer. I took a picture of myself — showing the lungs, liver and kidneys. Yet I didn't pass my examination. Can you tell me why?
As the picture only shows your lungs, liver and kidneys — the reason you failed was because you didn't have your heart in your work.

865   (Looking at x-ray picture)
Here are the backbones and liver.
He must have swallowed a picket fence.
Those are his ribs.

866   Did they take an x-ray of your wife's jaw at the hospital?
They tried to, but they got a moving picture.

867   We had an x-ray picture taken of our dog.
Did the x-ray show anything?
I'll say it did. It showed me the seat of his pants.

868   I'll have to take an x-ray picture.
Fine, I'll comb my hair first.

869   Did you hear Erica is marrying her x-ray specialist?
Well, she's lucky. Nobody else could ever see anything in her.

RELATED SUBJECTS
Dentist 579-601
Sickness 741-801

MEDICINE

870   Are you taking the medicine regularly?
I tasted it and decided that I'd rather have the cough.

871   Now, be sure and write plain on them bottles which is for the horse and which is for my husband. I don't want nothin' to happen to that horse before the spring plowin'.

872   Why are you bouncing up and down like that?
I just took some medicine and I forgot to shake up the bottle.

873   I heard you were awful sick. Couldn't the doctor do you any good?
No. He told me to drink a gallon of whiskey after a hot bath.
And did you do it?
I couldn't finish drinking the hot bath.

874   Your new medicine has helped me wonderfully! A month ago I could not spank the baby and now I'm able to thrash my husband.

875   You said to take two aspirins and follow with a hot bath. I took the aspirins, but that bath! I drank so much water, my stomach goes in and out with the tide.

876 Why didn't you take your medicine?
I couldn't. One bottle was marked: Keep bottle tightly corked, and so I couldn't get any medicine out of it. The other bottle said: For adults only — and I never had the adults in all my life.

877 That medicine you gave me for corns is no good.
No?
I ate three cans of it, and it hasn't helped my corns a bit.

878 I can fix castor oil with orange juice so you won't taste it.
Good, I don't like the taste of orange juice.

879 I'll take another bottle of that cough syrup.
Someone sick at your house?
No.
Then what on earth do you buy all this cough syrup for?
I like it on my pancakes.

> RELATED SUBJECTS
> Health (Good) 605-614
> Health (Ill) 615-911

DIRECTIONS FOR TAKING MEDICINE

880 Speak up!
I can't talk any louder.
You can't talk any louder than that?
It's my throat.
You must have strained it. Why don't you see a doctor?
He didn't do me no good. He told me to wear these glasses on my neck. He told me to goggle my throat.

881 My Brother's in jail charged with murder.
Say, that's serious. How did it happen?
My father was sick and the doctor told my brother to give him a shot in the arm to relieve his pain — and my brother thought if one shot would help — why not empty the six shooter into him?

882 The doctor gave me twelve pills and said to take three a day.
But I took them all at once.
Why did you take them all at once?
Now, I won't have to take any for four days.

> RELATED SUBJECTS
> Sickness 741-801
> Diseases 802-816
> Nurse 835
> Doctor 838-860

OPERATION

883   (Tattooed sailor has operation)
Doctor: Sorry, son, but I had to sink three battleships before I could get to your appendix.

884   My brother's an officer in the army.
What makes you think he's an officer?
Because he's going to have a major operation.

885   I hear the surgeons have operated on you again.
Yes.
How many times does this make?
Five. They're going to put on a swinging door next time.

886   Could you pay for an operation if I thought one was necessary?
Would you find one necessary if I couldn't pay for it?

887   My sister's upset — she's all over the place.
What happened?
She was operated on and when they removed the stitches, she went to pieces.

888   My uncle was in a fire and burned all the skin off his leg.
What did he do for it?
He had to have some skin grafted from his scalp and put on his leg.
How did it work?
Swell — every time he walks down the street and meets a lady, he tips his knee cap.

889   I must operate on you.
Well, doctor, before you operate, I insist on having an inventory taken of everything I've got.

890   So the operation on the man was just in the nick of time?
Yes, in another twenty-four hours he would have recovered.

891   Last Friday he had his tonsils removed.
Was it a terribly bad operation?
No operation at all. It was the brand of liquor he'd been drinking.

892   What an odd scar you have! It runs the wrong way.
The doctor that operated on me was cockeyed and he cut me on the bias.

893   What kind of an operation did you have?
A cafeteria operation. The doctors just helped themselves.

894   Only yesterday they took my poor brother off to the hospital.
What are they going to do for him?
They're going to operate.
What for?

Four hundred dollars.
What did he have?
Four hundred dollars.
What was the complaint?
No complaint. Everybody was satisfied.

895 I once laughed all through an operation.
Is that so?
Yeah, the doctor had me in stitches.

896 Was this man ever operated on before?
Yes.
What for?
Three hundred dollars.
What did he have?
Two hundred and fifty.
No, I mean, what was the complaint?
That the bill was too high.
No, that isn't what I mean — what was he sick of?
Operations.

897 Lady: (After operation for appendicitis) Oh, doctor, will the
scar show?
Doctor: Not if you are careful.

898 Doctor, could you cut off a finger without chloroform?
Yes.
Pete, show him your finger.

899 They cured my father of drinking by an operation.
That so?
Yeah, they removed a brass rail that had been pressing against
his foot for years.

900 Man married a girl and she had to have her tonsils out. He sent
her father the bill because she should have had them out years
ago.

901 I've had five operations and the doctor wanted to operate on me
again and I refused.
Why?
Well, things are picking up and I refused to take another cut.

902 They're going to remove your father's appendix.
Good Heavens, has dad got that on the installment plan, too?

903 I've taken out his appendix, tonsils, and his adenoids, and that's
about all you can get out of him.

904   How is your Aunt Sarah?
      She had her appendix taken out the other day.
      Did they give her anything for it?
      No, it wasn't worth anything.

905   Doctor, will you operate on me?
      What for?
      Oh, anything you like. You see, I attend a lot of women's bridge
      parties, and never having had an operation, I simply can't take
      part in the conversation.

906   Doctor, when I go to the hospital to have my adenoids taken out
      will I lose my Southern accent?

                              RELATED SUBJECTS
                              Plastic Surgeon 318-324
                              Accident 615-709
                              Sickness 741-801
                              Hospital 831-834

GAS

907   We're going to operate on you. What will you have — gas,
      chloroform, or ether?
      I always believe in patronizing home industry. Give me a local
      anaesthetic.

908   Dentist: Will you take gas?
      Patient: (Absentminded) Yeah, and you'd better look at the
      oil, too.

909   Shall I give her a local anaesthetic?
      No. I'm rich — give her the best. Give her something imported.

                              RELATED SUBJECTS
                              Dentist 579-601

BLOOD TRANSFUSION

910   Three blood transfusions were necessary to save a lady patient's
      life at a hospital. A brawny young Scotchman offered his blood.
      The patient gave him $50 for the first pint; $25 for the second
      pint; but the third time she had so much Scotch blood in her
      she only thanked him.

911   I've got Spanish blood in me.
      By your mother?
      No — by transfusion.

                              RELATED SUBJECTS
                              Nationalities 1059-1101

MALE (THE)

912   Men may have their failings, but they don't kiss when they meet
      on the street.

913   What is the greatest invention in the world?
      Man is the greatest invention in the world.
      Yes, but woman is an improvement on that invention.
      That's what keeps men out late nights looking for improvements.

914   He's a man about town.
      Yes, and a fool about women.

915   You really have to marry a man to find him out.
      You said it! After I married him, I found him out every night
      with the lady next door.

916   Men are all alike, aren't they?
      Yes. Every one you meet is different.

917   Man's life: School tablets — aspirin tablets — stone tablets.

918   I'm a man — I've got hair on my chest.
      So has Rin-Tin-Tin.

919   Woman is nothing but a rag, a bone and a hank of hair.
      Man is nothing but a brag, a groan and a tank of air.

920   Do you really believe girls like conceited men better than the
      other kind?
      What other kind?

921   My dear, this book is a remarkable work. Nature is marvelous.
      Stupendous! When I read a book like this it makes me think
      how lowly, how insignificant is man.
      Do you have to wade through four hundred pages to discover
      that?

922   Men of my type are not running loose.
      Of course not, that is what the police department is for.

923   Men are all alike.
      Yeah — men are all I like, too.

924   (Switching woman-man situation around)
      Business woman: Well, I must hurry home to dinner. I love a
      good home cooked meal, don't you?
      Second woman: Yes, but I'm beginning to suspect my husband's
      spending his afternoons in the matinees. I'm positive that pud-
      ding we had last night came from the delicatessen.

                                       RELATED SUBJECTS
                                       Second Childhood 121-123

FEMALE (THE)

925 Do men like talkative women or the other kind?
What other kind?

926 You should be careful. You know what Kipling said: A woman
is just a rag, a bone and a hank of hair.
Well, that's fine. I'm in the junk business.

927 Do you believe in clubs for women?
When kindness fails — I do.

928 A woman's physical charms are her chief weapons in the battle
of love.
Well, one thing's sure. You'll never be arrested for carrying
concealed weapons.

929 Women are rivals when it comes to clothes.
Yeah, they all try to out-strip each other.

930 You shouldn't argue with a woman. Don't you know a woman
always has the last word?
I'm not so sure of that.
When doesn't a woman have the last word?
When she's talking to another woman.

931 Women are fools to marry.
Yes, but what else can a man marry?

933 When a girl is sixteen, she's good looking. When she's twenty-
five she has wrinkles. When she's thirty, she has gray hair.
When she's thirty-five, she turns blonde and starts all over again.

934 Look at that youngster — the one with cropped hair, the cigarette
and breeches, holding two pups. Is it a boy or a girl?
A girl! She's my daughter.
My dear, sir! Do forgive me. I would never have been so out-
spoken had I known you were her father.
I'm not — I'm her mother.

935 I wonder why they don't ever have a woman for president?
A president has to be over forty years of age and a great leader
of men, and you know as well as I do that no man would follow
a woman after she's forty years old.

936 What's your impression of women?

Gosh — we should love women.
Why do you say that?
Aren't half of our parents women?

937   The time will come when women will get men's wages.
You're right — next Saturday night.

938   Now, you pride yourself on being able to judge a woman's character by her clothes. What would be your verdict on my sister
over there?
Insufficient evidence.

RELATED SUBJECTS
Age 45-107
Description of People 263-303
Names of People 939-1017
Gossip 1518-1537
Adam and Eve 2534-2538
Girl 2588-2594
Flirtation 2779-2784
Marriage 2882-3051
Mouse 3902-3907
Beauty 4725-4735

NAMES OF PEOPLE

939   His name is Joe, but we call him Flannel.
His name is Joe, but you call him Flannel. I suppose you call him
Flannel for short?
No, because he shrinks from washing.

940   His friends call him "Choo-Choo" because he goes on a little toot.

941   What's your girl's name?
It's June.
I thought it was Lilly.
It was, but she married so often they call her June.

942   His name's Pete, but we call him Bottletop.
His name's Pete, but you call him Bottletop? I suppose you call
him Bottletop for short?
No, we call him Bottletop because he has a cork top and is screwy.

943   We named our new baby "Surrender."
Surrender? What made you call him that?
Mother and dad took one look at him and gave up.

944   I'm suspicious of that man. Said his name was Smith. It's an
assumed name. Why did he say Smith?
He wanted more descendants than anybody else.

945 My cousin's name is Waldorf Astoria. But that's not his name
     — really.
     You mean he's going under an assumed name?
     Oh, no, he took that name so he would have the same name as
     the name on his towels.

946 Who was that boy I saw you with?
     That's John P. Astor's son Archibald. But I always call him John.
     The son's name is Archibald but you always call him John? Why?
     Because he takes after his father.

947 I told you the name was Lummox. Just think of your stomach.
     That's what's wrong. I kept thinking of Kelly.

948 That's my girl Easter Egg.
     Why call her Easter Egg?
     Because she's hand painted on the outside and hardboiled in the
     inside.

949 I call my girl Cinderella.
     Why, because she's been abused?
     No, because I have to slipper ten and slipper five.

950 If my brother was here, I wouldn't need your signature. He can
     sign anybody's name to a check.
     What's his name?
     3-5-7-9-1.
     3-5-7-9-1?
     Yeah, that's his pen name.

951 Do you know I think you should have been named Maple Syrup.
     Maple Syrup? Why, that's a sap.
     You're telling me.

952 They call their little boy "Prescription."
     What's that for?
     Because it's so hard to get him filled.

953 Traffic Cop: What's your name?
     Truck Driver: It's on the side of me wagon.
     Traffic Cop: It's obliterated.
     Truck Driver: Yer a liar, it's O'Brien.

954 People should call you "Amazon."
     Why?
     Because you're so wide at the mouth.

955 He calls his sweetheart Tomato 'cause no one loves him like his
     Tomato can.

956   My name is Daniel Q. Baker.
      What's the "Q" for?
      When I was born, my father took one look at me and said to
      my mother: Mom, call it Quits.

957   They call him "Sardine" because they're always taking him to
      the can.

958   She said he was an Irish lad.
      Oh, really!
      No — O'Reilly.

959   Where do you find all the names of these children?
      We used to name all the children after characters in the Bible,
      but they all ran out. The last time I heard, we were on page
      64 of Sears-Roebuck catalogue.

960   Who gave her the car?
      A fellow who works in the garage.
      Oh, a mechanic?
      No, McCarty.

961   They named me Oscar after Irving.
      Named you Oscar after Irving? How could they name you Oscar
      after Irving?
      They named my brother Irving and when I was born they named
      me Oscar after Irving.

962   A man that couldn't read or write signed his checks with two X's.
      He prospered and one day the cashier of the bank noticed a check
      with three X's signed to it. Not being sure whether he should
      honor the check, he called the man and said: I have a check
      here signed with three X's — it looks like your check, but I
      wasn't sure.
      Yes, it's my check. You can honor it.
      But tell me, what's the idea signing three X's?
      Well, I'm doing pretty good and my wife thought I should take
      a middle name.

963   In Massachusetts they named a town after you.
      What is it?
      Marblehead.

964   Your first name is Jack, isn't it?
      Why, how did you guess it?
      Oh, I knew what your last name ought to be.

965   Even a dog likes a certain amount of petting.
      Perhaps that's why the girls call you a teahound.

966   Your cousin is quite a football player, isn't he?
Yes, they nicknamed him "Judge."
Why?
Because he was always on the bench.

967   My name is Ware.
Oh, Mr. Ware. I have some furniture stored in one of your houses.

968   They call him Luke because he's not so hot.

969   But Alice is not a German name.
Well, there were twelve in the family and when father saw me
he said: Das is alles.

970   Her friends call her "Liberty Bell" because she is half cracked.

971   Was she a good dancer?
I call her my little mustard.
Why?
She's always on my dogs.

972   What's your name?
Igiveup Whatisit.
What are you talking about — your father's name is Brown —
how can your last name be Whatisit?
Well, when I was born my father came in and took one look at
me and said: I give up — what is it?

973   What's your new girl's name?
Marcelle.
Think she'll be permanent?

974   (Over telephone)
Are you there?
Who are you, please?
Watt.
What's your name?
Watt's my name.
Yeah, what's your name?
My name is John Watt.
John what?
Yes.
I'll be around to see you this afternoon.
All right. Are you Jones?
No. I'm Knott.
Will you tell me your name then?
Will Knott.
Why not?
My name is Knott.
Not what?

975 Who is that man?
   I don't know.
   But I heard you call him "darling."
   I called him darling because I do not know his name.

976 I'm named after my parents. My dad's name was Ferdinand and
     my mother's name was Liza.
   What's your name, then?
   Ferdiliza.

977 They call him Sears Roebuck.
   Why Sears Roebuck?
   Because he is of the mail order.

978 They called her the "Village Bell" — everybody wanted to wring
   her neck.

979 He called his wife "Flo" because she talked in a steady stream.

980 What's your sister's name?
   Do you want to know what her name is or what we call her?

981 By the way, isn't your name Ivan Petrovitch?
   No.
   Aren't you glad?

982 They call him "Jack" because he's always giving flat tires a lift.

983 Called her "Seven and Eleven" because she was so thin when she
   walked you could hear her bones rattle.

984 Why do you call your girl "Bungalow"?
   Because she's painted in front, shingled in back, and nobody home
     upstairs.

985 What are they going to name the baby?
   They can't name the baby until one of the dogs dies.
   What's the idea?
   They gave all the good names to the dogs.

986 Why did they name your brother Archibald?
   Dad wanted him to be a prizefighter when he grew up and anyone
     with a name like that will get lots of practice.

987 They call him "Jig-Saw" — every time a girl looks at him he goes
   to pieces.

988 He always calls his wife "Fair Lady."
   How romantic! Why does he call her "Fair Lady"?
   It's habit — he used to be a street car conductor.

989   I call my girl "Cream of Wheat."
      Why?
      Because she's so mushy.

990   What do you call your sister?
      Pop calls her "Dusty" because she's been on the shelf so long.

991   I call her "Laryngitis" because she's a pain in the neck.

992   How do you spell your name?
      A-l-e-d-a-s-n-a-d-i-e-d-o-e-s-c-h-e-d.
      How do you pronounce it?
      Joe.

993   My girl's name is Rose — she has a name like a flower and a face
      like a weed.

994   We call him "Stag."
      Why?
      He is a dear with no dough.

995   They called him "Sliver" because he was always getting under
      everybody's skin.

996   What's your name?
      Mary.
      No, I mean your full name.
      It's Mary — empty or full.

997   I call her "Democracy" — I think the world is safe for her.

998   Why do you sign your name R. R. Robert C. C. Carr?
      I was baptized by a stuttering minister and he gave me that name.

999   His mother called him Louis; he was the fourteenth.

1000 What are your parents' names?
      Mama and papa.

1001 My name is T-t-t-tom.
      Okay — I'll call you Tom for short.

1002 What's his name?
      Druff — Dan Druff — Kind of a fellow never could get
      ahead; always in your hair.

1003 I always call my sheik Paul Revere.
      Because it's a midnight call to arms?
      No, because he is always horsing around.

1004 Why do you always call your wife "Honey"?
      Well, honey has always disagreed with me.

1005   Named him Milk Bottle because they found him on the doorstep.

1006   Shay, ish my name Heinz?
       No.
       Well, it oughter be 'cause I'm pickled.

1007   I call her my "Baseball" girl.
       Your baseball girl? Why do you call her that?
       Because she was throwed out at home.

1008   But why are you so anxious to take this young man into our firm?
       Well, if we took young Aabdt into the firm we could have first
       place in the 'phone book.

1009   What's your name?
       Gallop.
       What?
       Gallop. G like in grapefruit, A like in apple, 2 L's like in lemon,
       O like in orange and P like in peaches. Now, do you know what
       that spells?
       Sure — fruit salad.

1010   What's your name?
       Fred.
       Fred? Oh, baby talk—my muvver sews my clothes with fred.

1011   Ruth, what is your father's name?
       It's Daddy.
       Yes, dear, but what name does your mother call him?
       She don't call him any names. She likes him.

1012   Telegram for Mr. Neidspondiavanic — Telegram for Mr.
       Neidspondiavanic.
       Mr. Neidspondiavanic: What initial, please?

1013   I suppose you named your baby Homer because he is your favorite
       poet?
       Poet? — No, sir — I keep pigeons.

1014   They call her Flo because she has water on the knee and a creak
       in her back.

1015   How do you do, Mr. Right.
       My name's Brown.
       That's funny, I've always heard the customer was right.

1016   They call me Alexander the Great!
       Alexander the Great?
       Yeah, when the furnace gets low, they holler — Alexander — the
       grate!

1017 What's your girl's name?
I don't remember.
You don't remember what your gal's name is?
No — I think it begins with "M."
Margaret? Mildred? Mary? Martha? All those names begin with "M" . . .
No, I've thought of it now — Emma.

RELATED SUBJECTS
Description of People 263-303
Famous People 5029-5042

ACQUAINTANCE

1018 What is the difference between an acquaintance and a friend?
Well, when a friend wants to borrow money, he's an acquaintance.

1019 I understand you have a speaking acquaintance with her.
Merely a listening acquaintance.

1020 Remember, dear, if we should happen to meet my husband, you're only a nodding acquaintance.
Yeah — nodding doing.

1021 Do you know her to speak to?
No. Only to talk about.

1022 I met a young lady in the revolving door of a department store recently, but I couldn't make her acquaintance. What should I have done?
You should have started to go around with her.

1023 Does he know her well?
He must. I overheard him tell her she's getting fat.

RELATED SUBJECTS
Conversation 1501-1502
Gossip 1518-1537

INTRODUCTION

1024 (Man being introduced to ex-fiancee—she gives him the high-hat)
Sorry, but I did not get your name.
He: I know you didn't, but that is not your fault. Your tried hard enough.

1025   Have we met before?
Yes, I met you under the table at the Ritz.

1026   My brother is a window washer.
I never met him.
Stand near the window, he'll go by any minute and I'll introduce you.

1027   Did you meet Lord Upperbottom when you were in England?
Meet him? I shot at his country seat.
Did you hit it?

1028   Allow me to present my wife to you.
Thanks, but I have one.

> Conversation 1501-1502
> Fresh People 2397-2408
> Party 3575-3579

GOLDDIGGER

1029   I got a pearl out of an old oyster.
My sister got a real diamond out of an old crab.

1030   In the olden days an old man would take a pick and a donkey and go out into the wilds and dig for gold. The modern golddigger takes her pick and goes wild with a jackass.

1031   1st Golddigger: I've listened to so many hard luck stories today that I could cry.
2nd Golddigger: Yeah, they're getting me down, too.

1032   Where'd you get the mean blonde you had last night?
Oh, I just opened my pocket book and there she was.

1033   What is more beautiful than to have three little words whispered in your ear?
Having them in writing, dearie.

1034   One thousand francs bought me this ring in Paris.
One John bought me this car in New York.

1035   Golddigger's motto: Every man for myself.

1036   Why are you so nervous?
I'm awfully nervous. I just came from the Golddiggers of 1938.
The moving picture?
No, the Income Tax office.

RELATED SUBJECTS
Drinking 2055-2140
Flirtation 2779-2784
Clothing 3391-3502

Furs 3505-3515
Party 3575-3579
Chorus Girl 4563-4565
Money 5457-5479

FRIEND

1037   Jack hasn't come home. Am worried. Is he spending the night
        with you? Thus wired Smith's wife to five of his friends.
        Soon after the husband arrived home, and before long a messenger
        boy came in with five replies to the wires his wife had sent:
        They all read: Yes, Jack is spending the night with me.

1038   If you were always very kind and polite to all your friends
        what would they think of you?
        Some of them would think they could wipe their feet on me.

1039   I'll never forget the time we were ice skating on the lake. Sud-
        denly the ice broke, I plunged into the water. You threw off
        your coat, and your shoes, and jumped in after me. What a
        pal!
        What do you mean a pal; why wouldn't I jump in after you?
        You had my skates on.

1040   Yesterday you told me you'd be a friend to me to the end.
        That's right. I like you and I meant it, too. I'm your friend to
        the end.
        That's great — will you lend me $2?
        This is the end.

1041   Could you loan me $50?
        I hate to do it, because when a fellow lends money it always
        breaks up a friendship.
        But after all, we haven't been such good friends.

1042   My friends can't stand to see me starve.
        So what do they do?
        They talk to me with their eyes closed.

1043   Believe me, I pick my friends.
        Yes — to pieces.

1044   So your wife eloped with your best friend? Who was he?
        I don't know. I never met the fellow.

1045   We've been friends so long I couldn't forget you. If you died
        before me, I would go to your grave every week and put gifts
        to show I had not forgotten. I would put a box of your favor-
        ite cigars on your grave.
        Would you bring matches, too?
        Don't be silly! Where you're going, you won't need them.

1046   He said you were not fit to sleep with the pigs. I stuck up for
        you — I said you were.

1047 (Man making speech — one person claps)
To that one man who applauded, I am happy to be among friends.
I wasn't applauding. I was slapping my face to keep awake.

1048 I'm your friend and I have always wished you well.
I know that.
I hope you live to be as old as your jokes.

1049 The horse, like the dog, is man's best friend.
What?
I said, the horse, like the dog, is man's best friend.
Oh, that's silly. Because who wants to come home and have a
horse jump in his lap?

1050 The poor fellow has lost all his friends — all he has left are
his relatives.

1051 Time separates the best of friends.
So does money.
And don't forget marriage!

1052 Why so sad?
My best friend just got run over by a train.
Gee, that's tough!
You said it! He was wearing my best suit.

1053 Any friend of yours is — is a friend of yours.

1054 He said you weren't fit to sleep with the pigs.
And I suppose you pulled the old gag and said I was?
No, I stuck up for the pigs.

1055 Bill is your sidekick, isn't he?
Yes — we sleep together.

1056 Yes, it was a sad case about Hayes. Since he lost all his money
half his friends don't know him any more.
What about the other half?
They don't know yet that he has lost it.

RELATED SUBJECTS
Advice 1978-1989
Popularity 2383-2389
Hospitality 3564-3660
Neighbors 3661-3666

ENEMY

1057 He doesn't have an enemy. All his friends hate him.

1058 I be ninety-four and I haven't got an enemy in the world.
That is a beautiful thought.
Yes, indeed. Thank God they be all of 'em dead long ago.

RELATED SUBJECTS   Popularity 2383-2389
Fight 2145-2213   Revenge 2488-2489

NATIONALITIES

1059 (Man talking with foreign accent)
I didn't know you were a foreigner.
I'm not — I'm an American. My English teacher was a foreigner.

1060 Scientists claim that English will soon be the universal language, as it is now spoken almost everywhere but England and New York.

1061 An Englishman, visiting in New York City, invited an American friend to have a drink. The American said he couldn't because he was on the water-wagon. The Englishman did not get it at first, so the American explained it meant he wasn't drinking.
The Englishman, pleased with the phrase, planned to use it as soon as possible. A day later a friend invited him to have a drink. He laughed and shook his head, "I can't, I'm in the bathtub, you know."

1062 I often wondered why the English were such tea drinkers.
Yes?
Yes, but I know now. I had some of their coffee.

1063 America is a fool's paradise, said a European visitor. Maybe that's why so many of his fellow Europeans like to visit, too.

1064 McIntosh liked nothing better than to play his bagpipes.
Finally his wife said: Dearest, what an awful noise you are making!
Oh, am I? he said, and so he took off his heavy boots and went on playing in his stocking feet.

1065 An Irishman was always getting into fights, and his wife finally decided to put a stop to it the night he came home with a black eye, some bruises, and a few teeth missing.
Wife: Fighting again, Mike O'Brien? And who was it this time, if you don't mind my asking?
Husband: Oh, me and O'Leary had a few words, that's all.
Wife: O'Leary? You mean to stand there and tell me that a pipsqueak like O'Leary did that to you?
Husband: 'Tain't nice to speak ill of the dead, dearest!

1066 What is the difference between a French girl and an American girl?
The Atlantic ocean.

1067   My father was a Pole.
        North or South?

1068   I'm certainly disgusted with you.
        What's the matter?
        Last night when I asked you to drive my three Scandinavian
            cousins home, why did you come back three minutes later?
        They couldn't speak English, and they all went to different
            places.
        Well, I told you the one on the right lived on Forty-first
            street, the one on the left lived on Fifty-first street and the
            one in the middle lived on Eighty-fifth street.
        Yeah, I know, but the car hit a bump and they got mixed up
            and I had to have them sorted all over again.

1069   My grandfather was Irish, my other grandmother was Swedish,
            and I have an uncle who's Polish and an aunt on my mother's
            side who's French. Cousin Luis is Mexican, and my mother
            was born in Italy . . .
        Say, then, what are you?
        American.

1070   What nationality?
        Half Scotch — half seltzer.

1071   Pardon me, I'm a little deaf.
        That's all right; I'm a little Bohemian.

1072   Those who wish to abolish the eagle as the American standard
            have thought about substituting the bull in its place.

1073   Show me an Irishman and I'll show you a fool.
        I'm an Irishman!
        Er-r-r-r, that is — I'm the fool!

1074   Ireland must not be Heaven, for our traffic cops come from
            there.

1075   France is the only big nation that has no national sport. Gouging
            the tourists is strictly a business proposition.

        ───────

        The Scotchman was taking a drink of American liquor.
        And how much do they pay you for drinking this? he asked.

1076   That mansion belongs to the richest man in New York. He has
            a German cook, a French maid, a Jap valet, a Scotch garage
            mechanic, and an Irish chauffeur, a Swedish housekeeper,
            and an American secretary.
        That ain't a mansion. That's a world court.

1077   Wherever in the world you go, you'll always find the Jews are
         the leading people.
       How about Alaska?
       Vell, Icebergs ain't no Presbyterian name.

1078   Your neighbors are foreigners you say?
       Yeah, they must be—they never repay anything.

1079   What is meant by "typical American?"
       A "typical American" is a man who when he dies and goes to
         Heaven the first question he asks St. Peter is: "How much
         is the down payment on a harp?"

1080   Registered letter for Pat O'Hara!
       Hier ist mein. Here, it's mine.
       What? You're Pat O'Hara?
       Ja, dot's me. Und do I look like dis Pat O'Hara, mein Herr?
       No.
       Den vhy should I talk like I don't look? Vhy should I? So, gif me
         mein letter.

1081   She's a half caste.
       What?
       She's a half caste — a half caste!
       What happened to the other half?

1082   You know in Persia the men are so careless with their wives
         that it's no uncommon sight to see a woman and a donkey
         hitched up together.
       That's not so unusual—you often see it over here, too.

1083   Fred has no luck with women.
       Oh? I thought he was going to marry Miss Iceland.
       He was, but no more.
       What happened?
       She gave him the cold shoulder.

1084   How wonderful he looks! said Mrs. Kelly when she saw Mr.
         Cohen before he was taken to the cemetery for burial.
       And why shouldn't he? asked Mrs. Cohen. Didn't he just spend
         last winter in Palm Beach?

1085   I read an article that said: The French eat 200,000,000 snails
         a year.
       Maybe that's what makes them slow paying their debts.

1086   (Swedish farmer appearing for his naturalization papers)
       Examiner: Are you satisfied with the general conditions of this
         country, Mr. Olsen?

Olsen: Yah, sure.
Examiner: And does this government of ours suit you?
Olsen: Well, yah mostly—only I lak to see more rain.

1087   India has 43,000,000 untouchables — outcasts of Hindu society.
        That's nothing. Have you ever tried to make a touch in this
        country?

1088   America is the sort of nation in which a cigarette testimonial by a
        famous football player who has never smoked in his life is
        regarded as persuasive publicity.

1089   Where were you born?
        France.
        What part?
        Oh, all of me.

1090   Where yuh from?
        Ireland.
        Ireland?
        Yeah — Rhode Ireland.

1091   Do you know Nat Cohen?
        One of the cloak and suit Cohens?
        No, he's one of the ice cream Cohens.

1092   I killed my father. He was driving me nuts. I was hating him
        like anything.
        But why did you kill him?
        Because only for him — I wouldn't be born with this terrible
        no good dialect.

1093   The two great American classes include those who think they are
        as good as anybody, and those who think they are better.

1094   So you think you can fix up these windows? Do you know how to
        make a Venetian blind?
        Sure — I just stick my finger in his eye.

1095   They don't show comedies in the English movies on Saturday
        nights any more.
        Whyszat?
        They don't want any more laughing in church on Sundays.

1096   Dad, what branch of the family did we spring from?
        Son, the Murphys sprang from nobody; they spring at 'em.

1097   So you're an alien?
        No, I'm feeling fine.

1098 So, you've only been in this country a month?
Yeah, and already I have learned your two most important words — swell and lousy.

1099 I'd rather play to an English audience than an American audience.
What's the difference between an Englishman and an American?
Well, an Englishman first laughs out of courtesy, second, when the rest of the audience gets the joke, and, third, when he gets it himself.
What about an American?
Oh, he never laughs at all — he's heard it before.

1100 What's your birthplace?
Cairo.
Cairo? I didn't know you were Egyptian.
I'm not Egyptian.
Then where *are* you from?
Illinois.

1101 Do you know what the whale said when he swallowed a Frenchman?
No — what did he say?
I guess I've swallowed a frog.

> RELATED SUBJECTS
> Blood Transfusion 910-911
> Ancestry 3218-3247
> Foreign Languages 3990-3999
> English 4934-4954

SCOTCHMAN

1102 What's yon? asked the Scotchman when he first arrived in Canada.
That's a moose.
Well, if that's a moose, I'd hate to see your rats!

1103 We knew a Scotchman who would never smoke cigarettes when he had gloves on. He said he hated the smell of burning leather.

1104 Then there's the Scotchman who married the half-witted girl because she was 50 per cent off.

1105 At last we've discovered the reason for the yellow lights in the traffic signals — it gives the Scotch motorists a chance to start their engines.

1106 Is golf strictly a Scotch game?
No. It also can be played with rye and gin.

1107   Two Scotchmen bet each other to see who could stay under water longest. The police are still looking for the bodies.

1108   Then there is the Scotchman who took his children out of school because they had to pay attention.

1109   Then there's the Scotchman that's so tight he refuses to perspire freely.

1110   Then there's the Scotchman who gave his son a licking because he bought an all day sucker at four o'clock in the afternoon.

1111   Then there's the Scotchman who went on his honeymoon alone.

1112   Then there's the Scotchman who got kidnapped and went crazy thinking about the ransom his wife was trying to pay to free him.

1113   Sandy, the canny Scot, rose from his chair and gestured dramatically before his wife: To hell with the expense, give the canary another seed.

1114   And then there was the Scotchman who ordered asparagus and left the waiter the tips.

1115   Scotchman: Get behind your lover, you unfaithful wife. I'm going to shoot you both.

1116   Why, Mac, you've lost your stutter!
Ay, A've been doin' a lot of telephonin' tee America lately.

1117   When a Scotchman's baby cries for a peppermint stick, he takes the baby out and lets him lick a barber pole.

1118   I'll take an order of Scotch asparagus.
Scotch asparagus — did you say?
Yes — without tips.

1119   Doesn't that Scottish boy ever take you to the cinema?
No, I think he must have found a girl who can see pictures in the fire.

1120   "Two pennyworth of bicarbonate of soda for indigestion at this time of night," cried the infuriated druggist, who had been aroused at 2 A.M., "when a glass of hot water would have done just as well."
"Well, well," replied MacDougal, "I thank ye for the advice, and I'll no bother ye after all. Good night."

1121   There's been a smash and grab raid at the jeweler's.
Did they get away with it?
No! They were Scotch, and they were arrested when they came back for the brick.

1122 And then there's the Scotchman who is putting off buying an atlas until world affairs look a little more settled.

1123 Did you hear about Sandy McCulloch finding a box of corn plasters?
No, did he?
Yes, so he went and bought a pair of tight shoes.

1124 Is there any truth in the report that MacTavish has bought the gasoline station?
Well, I don't know for sure, but the Free Air signs have been taken down.

1125 So Anna married a Scotchman. How does he treat her?
Reluctantly.

1126 Then there is the Scotchman who dialed the wrong number on an automatic telephone and insisted on talking to the wrong party the full five minutes to get his money's worth.

1127 And there was the Scotchman who told his children that Christmas was on December 28th so he could take advantage of the after-Christmas clearance sales.

1128 They say Sandy MacPherson bought a suit on the pay-as-you-wear plan.
Yes, and it's hung in his closet for 20 years.

1129 Scotch jokes: They're so tight, they won't give the answers.

1130 Once there was a Scotchman who was so tight he put boric acid in his grapefruit in order to get a free eyewash.

1131 Two Scots were mountaineering in Switzerland when one of them slipped and fell into a crevasse. The other, peering over the edge, saw his companion holding on almost by his fingernails.
Are ye a'richt, MacPherson?
Not exactly that, but if ye run down to the village an' git a rope I'll try to hang on here till ye come back. Hurry, for heaven's sake!
His companion disappeared and was gone nearly an hour. Suddenly his face appeared again over the edge of the cliff.
Are ye still there, MacPherson?
Aye! Have ye got the rope?
Nay—the dirty dogs in the village wanted 2 pounds for it.

1132 (A Scot who was a bad sailor was crossing the Channel. He went to the Captain and asked him what he should do to prevent seasickness.)
Captain: Have you got a sixpence?
Scot: Aye.
Captain: Well, hold it between your teeth during the trip.

1133   A Scotchman holding an important job in the city was always
       being twitted by an English friend about his nationality. By
       a curious chance the two met on a holiday.
       "Hallo," said the Englishman, "how on earth is your office
       managing to get on without you?"
       "Fairly well," answered the Scot cautiously. "You see, I left
       two Englishmen and a Welshman in my place."

> RELATED SUBJECTS
> Spendthrift 1990-1996
> Economy 1997-2030
> Humor 2365-2380
> Money 5457-5479

NOBILITY
1134   I'm Percy Oswald, Knight of the Golden Fleece, Knight of
       the Garter and Knight of Columbus.
       That's nothing — I'm Joe Doakes, night before last, night
       before that and every night.

1135   What was the result of that terrific fight the Duchess had with
       her husband?
       She retains the title.

> RELATED SUBJECTS
> Ancestry 3218-3247
> Famous People 5029-5042

SOCIETY
1136   My uncle has his name in the social register.
       He has his name in the social register with the wolf at his door?
       The wolf can't read. Besides, he's interested in the wolf. He
       read Little Red Ridinghood and he thinks maybe the wolf
       might be somebody's grandmother.

1137   The ex-debutantes had a dance last night.
       What's an ex-debutante?
       A girl that came out last year and wishes she was back in again
       this year.

1138   He's as common as an old shoe.
       You mean, he's a heel.

1139   Professional model: How would the debutantes like it if we
       decided to muscle in on their racket and come out every year?

1140   Actually there is no distinct class trodden under foot except
       those who hold aisle seats.

1141 Another who may be said to have his ups and downs is the unfortunate chap who happens to get an aisle seat at a movie.

1142 He's very upset because they've taken his name out of Who's Who.
Well, I've been busy all my life trying to keep my name in the telephone directory.

1143 Do you actually have any hope of being accepted into that exclusive club?
Sure — they've got to have some one to snub.

1144 I hope all your children are acrobats!
You mean aristocrats?
No, I don't. I hope they won't give you a tumble.

RELATED SUBJECTS
Egotism 2305-2319
Snob 2357-2360
Ancestry 3218-3247
Hospitality 3564-3660

CAVEMAN

1145 What kind of a man is he?
He's a man eighty-nine years old — he's a caveman.
A caveman eighty-nine years old?
Yeah — every time I kiss him, he caves in.

RELATED SUBJECTS
Second-Childhood 121-123
Description of People 263-303

INDIAN

1146 What's the purpose of this?
What?
I said, what's the purpose of this? You know what purpose is?
Sure — a purpose is an Indian's baby.

1147 He was the cleanest Indian in the tribe. When it was time for him to die, he refused to bite the dust.

1148 Don't you know what a papoose is?
Sure, it's the last car on a freight train.

1149 He's a collector of Indian Relics.
Guess that's a pretty good business.
Yes. He has Minnehaha's original teehee.

1150 I'll never forget the time an Indian was scalping my grandfather and they discovered he had a toupee.

1151 I'm Chief Running Water. These are my sons, Hot and Cold.
Luke didn't come —·he ain't so hot.

1152 Those Indians have a bloodcurdling yell!
      Yes, ma'am; every one of 'em is a college graduate!

1153 Let's go on the warpath.
      We can't — it's bein' paved.

1154 Mills wants $600 for playing the part of an Indian in our new
      film.
      Offer him $300. Tell him it's only a half-breed.

                        RELATED SUBJECTS
                        Geography 5003-5014
                        History 5015-5026

HILL-BILLY

1155 Sam, ah jes' seen an alligator eatin' our younges' chile!
      Ummmm — sho' nuff? You know, ah thought sum'n been
      gettin' our chillun!

1156 A backwoods woman, the soles of whose feet had been toughened
      by a lifetime of shoelessness, was standing in front of her
      cabin fireplace one day when her husband addressed her:
      Husband: You'd better move your foot a mite, maw; you're
      standing on a live coal.
      Wife: Which foot, paw?

1157 Hill-Billy: Let's patch up this here feud, Lemmel, until I get
      more shells from the mail order house.

1158 The Hill-Billy hadn't taken a bath for a long, long time. The
      situation grew so bad that his family finally deputized a com-
      mittee to force him to take a bath.
      The Mountaineer objected strenuously. He kicked, and he
      squawked, but finally they succeeded in undressing him. After
      removing several garments he was down to his long flannel
      underwear. Under this, much to his surprise, was a sweater:
      "Can yer imagine that?" he drawled. "And here I've bin
      searchin' high and low fer thet sweater fer over two years!"

1159 Hill-Billy: (Calling grandfather who had gone into the woods
      hunting) Gettin' dark, Grandpap. Better be a comin' home.
      Grandpap: Yep.
      Hill-Billy: Suppertime, Grandpap.
      Grandpap: Yep.
      Hill-Billy: (After waiting for him to come home — calls)
      Airn't ye hungry?
      Grandpap: Yep.
      Hill-Billy: Wal, air ye comin' home?
      Grandpap: Nope.
      Hill-Billy: Why ain't ye?

Grandpap: Can't.

Hill-Billy: Why can't ye?

Grandpap: Cause I'm caught in a b'ar trap.

1160 **Zeke,** a hill-billy, went into a restaurant to eat. The waiter brought him a napkin and Zeke pulled his gun and threatened to shoot the waiter: You take that blamed thing away at once. I reckon I know when to use a handkerchief without having danged hints thrown out.

1161 Mister, I've — I've come hyar ter ask yer fer yer daughter's hand.

Can't allow no sech thing. Ither yer takes the whole gal, or nothing.

RELATED SUBJECTS
Stupidity 1337-1381
Illiteracy 1390-1398

SECTION II

INTELLECT

OPERATION OF INTELLECT

MIND

1162 How old were you when you graduated from grammar school?

Twenty. I could have graduated sooner, but I was too kind. My teacher was an old lady and I hated to leave her. I stayed with her eleven years. What do you think of that?

You surely deserve a lot of credit — you certainly do. You have a soft heart — and a soft head.

1163 I'm half a mind to get married myself.

A half mind is all you need.

1164 I was wrestling with my conscience.

A half-wit match, eh?

1165 My uncle has a lot of horse sense.

I'll say he has. You can lead him to water but you can't make him drink.

1166 Did you ever have your head examined?

Yeah, my folks had it examined. But it was a waste of money. Why?

The doctors told my folks there was nothing in my head to examine.

1167   Would you call your brother a donkey to his face?
       No, not if the donkey was standing near.
       Why not?
       He would kick my brains out.
       The donkey would kick your brains out?
       Yeah.
       Well, it wouldn't be much of a kick.

1168   I'm struck dumb.
       Don't be silly — you were born that way.

1169   Are you trying to make a monkey out of me?
       Why should I take the credit?

1170   So this is a battle of wits between you and me?
       No — I never pick on a man that's unarmed.

1171   I won't drink whiskey because I'm afraid of losing my mind.
       Don't worry, you can't lose what you haven't got.

1172   When I was a child I used to bite my finger nails; and the doctor
          told me if I didn't quit it I'd grow up to be an idiot.
       And you couldn't stop, huh?

1173   Your husband looks like a brilliant man. I suppose he knows
          everything.
       Don't fool yourself, he doesn't even suspect anything.

1174   It's wonderful how my hair parts exactly in the middle.
       Yes, on dead center, as it were.

1175   I've got a smart brother.
       You have?
       Yeah, he's been clear through Reform School and he's only 16.

1176   I'm hopelessly in love.
       On second thought, maybe you were right when you said you
          were hopeless.

1177   What do you think you're talking about?
       I don't think — I know.
       I don't think you know either.

1178   When I first met you, you were sweet, unaffected and simple,
          but you are no longer sweet and unaffected.

1179   Are you positive?
       Only fools are positive.
       Are you sure?
       I'm positive.

1180   I'm so unhappy — I'm so alone.
I'm here.
I'm still alone.

1181   Well, I'm falling in love and I think I should go to a palmist or
a mind reader. Which would you suggest?
You better go to a palmist — you KNOW you've got a palm.

1182   I've got a ringing in my head.
That's because it's empty. I've never had a ringing in MY head.
That's because it's cracked.

1183   I've got an idea.
Be kind to it. It's a long way from home.

1184   A fool and his money are soon parted.
I know that. Who got yours?

1185   I'm going to give up working and live by my wits.
Well, half a living is better than none.

1186   I manage to keep my head above water.
Well, wood floats.

1187   I won't stand for your insulting me. I've got lots of backbone.
Yeah, but the bone is all at the top.

1188   How does your head feel today?
Very well.
It should. It should feel as good as new — you have never used it.

1189   How long can a man live without brains?
I don't know. How old are YOU?

1190   Have you ever in your life seen anything like him?
Not since the circus left town.

1191   When I was twenty I made up my mind to get rich.
But you never became rich.
No. I decided it was easier to change my mind.

1192   I guess he didn't tell you he was getting a head fast.
Well, two heads are better than one.
In your case, one would be better than nothing.

1193   Remind me not to recognize any more people today.
I'll make a mental note of it.
That's right — make a note on something concrete.

1194   Well, here I am bright and early.
Anyway, you're early.

1195   Did you fall on your head when a baby?
       Yes, but they picked me up.
       Just my luck.

1196   Did anyone ever take you for a human being?
       Lots of times.
       Well, people will make mistakes.

1197   A half wit must have given you a piece of his mind.
       Yeah — and I still have it, too.

1198   Intelligence reigns supreme in my family.
       You must have been born during a dry spell.

1199   I have a new pocketbook, it just matches my shoes.
       What's in the pocketbook?
       Nothing — it's empty.
       Then it matches your head, too.

1200   Isn't it funny, when I stand on my head the blood rushes to my
          head, but when I stand on my feet the blood doesn't rush to
          my feet?
       Your feet aren't empty.

1201   How do you like San Francisco?
       Oh, all right, but I can't get used to walking around in the fog
          all the time.
       How can you tell the difference?

1202   I'm nobody's fool.
       Maybe you can get someone to adopt you.

1203   I'm not prejudiced at all. I'm going with a perfectly open and
          unbiased mind to listen to what I'm convinced is pure rubbish.

1204   Where is my hat?
       On the oven.
       On the oven? I wonder what ridiculous thing I shall find it on
          next.
       On your head, dear.

1205   No woman ever made a fool out of me.
       Who did then?

1206   I'm very smart.
       Yeah, you've got brains you've never used.

1207   Don't think you fooled me for a minute.
       No — well, you've fooled the public for years.

1208   I'm not myself tonight.
       I noticed the improvement.

1209   There goes Joe Doakes and his five gag men.
        Well, when you're making comedies, you have to have your wits
            about you all the time.

1210   I have no sense of humor.
        You're right — only you should have stopped with sense.

1211   A woman could make a monkey out of you in ten minutes.
        Maybe, but think of those ten minutes.

1212   Janet says she thinks I am a great wit.
        Well, she's half right.

1213   What does your father know about handling big bodies of people?
        He used to massage Minnesota Fats and Kate Smith.

1214   Noises in my head keep me awake.
        That's impossible.
        How's that?
        You can't transmit sound through a vacuum.

1215   Why don't you answer?
        I did.
        You didn't.
        I did, too — I shook my head.
        Well, I didn't hear it rattle.

1216   I've got an idea and it's a good one.
        It's beginner's luck.

1217   I don't know what to do for my weekend.
        Put your hat on it.

1218   Do you think I'm a fool?
        No, but what's my opinion against thousands of others?

1219   You fool!
        I'm not.
        Well, you'll do until a fool gets here.

1220   He got shell-shocked from eating peanuts in bed.

1221   Tell them all you know — it won't take long.
        It won't take any longer to tell them what we both know.

1222   It's as clear as mud.
        Well, that just about covers the ground, doesn't it?

1223   There's a man who is reputed to have a good head on his shoulders.
        Yes, and a different one every night.

1224   If all those people weren't out there, I'd be alone.
        But I'm here.
        I'd still be alone.

1225   I think we are intellectual opposites.
       What do you mean?
       I'm intellectual and you're just the opposite.

1226   I didn't say he was dumb — I said he was sixteen years old be-
       fore he could wave goodbye.

1227   He seems to be a single track man, doesn't he?
       You mean he only thinks of one thing at a time?
       Naw, he pushes a wheelbarrow.

1228   Most of the fire in the modern girl's eye is quenched by the water
       on her brain.

1229   A fool can ask questions that even wise men can't answer. That's
       why so many people flunk this course.

1230   I took an Intelligence Test one time, and I came out 100 in one
       thing.
       What was that?
       What does m-o-r-o-n spell?
       That spells "Moron."
       I passed 100 per cent in that one.

1231   You know I think association with brilliant companions is half
       one's college career.
       Well, well, I was just wondering why you have been hanging
       around me.

1232   You must think I'm a perfect idiot.
       You'll never be perfect but you're doing all right.

1233   I told her Joe called me a blinking idiot, and she said I should
       see an oculist.

1234   I've got an idea.
       Beginner's luck.

1235   Where are you going?
       My mind's wandering and I'm just going along.

1236   I'm a simple man of the people.
       Yeah, the simplest man in the community.

1237   You throw your tongue into high gear before your brain is turn-
       ing over.

1238   You've got a great future if you live long enough.
       Thanks, but how are you making out?
       Can't complain — still forging ahead.
       Still forging, huh?

1239   Do you know, dear, I just read an article that said: The cleverness of the father often proves a stumbling block to the son.
Well, thank goodness — our Bobby won't have anything to
fall over.

1240   Yes, I know fish is brain food, but I don't care so much for fish.
Ain't there some other brain food?
Well, there's noodle soup.

1241   Why was Solomon the wisest man in the world?
Because he had so many wives to advise him.

1242   An economist is a man who knows a great deal about a very
little; and who goes on knowing more and more about less,
until finally he knows practically everything about nothing;
whereas, a professor, on the othre hand, is a man who knows
a very little about a great deal and keeps on knowing less and
less about more until finally he knows practically nothing
about everything.

1243   The teacher told my mother I was a flathead and she went all
around to the neighbors and bragged about my being so level-
headed.

1244   You're going to drive me out of my mind!
That ain't no drive, my dear — that's a putt.

1245   And did she make a fool of me!
Isn't it funny what everlasting impressions some girls make on
men?

1246   I guess we all live and learn.
Yeah, but you just live.

1247   I live by my wits.
Now I know why you look so hungry.

1248   Father, I want to get married.
No, my boy, you are not wise enough.
When will I be wise enough?
When you get rid of the the idea that you want to get married.

1249   Can't you hear or haven't you got any brains?
I've got a lot of brains.
I suppose you invented them?
Maybe.
Well, don't worry about who invented brains. You'll never in-
fringe on the patent.

1250   My girl got mad and left me.
Why?

Without any reason.
Well, I knew somebody left you without it. I didn't know who.

1251   I'm going to give you a piece of my mind.
Just a small helping, please.

1252   Come on, a penny for your thoughts.
What do you think I am — a slot machine?

1253   Say, I went to college, stupid.
Yes, and you came back stupid.

1254   You don't know what's going on in the outside world.
I know, but it ain't my fault.
Why not?
I've got an inside room.

1255   You don't know what time it is.
What's the difference? I'm not going any place.

1256   I'll bet your wife is a woman of rare intelligence.
That's right. She rarely shows any of it.

1257   Gibbons is always bragging about his wife's wonderful mind.
Then you can guess how she looks without seeing her.

1258   They say Percy is wandering in his mind since he failed to pass
his final college examination.
Well, don't worry; he can't go far.

RELATED SUBJECTS
Smartness 1332-1336
Stupidity 1337-1381
Conversation 1501-1502
Memory 1576-1591
School 4885-4894
Definition of Words 4978-4991
College 5059-5096

MIND READER

1259   Fortune Teller: You have very peculiar lines.
Woman: Listen, I came here to have my fortune told, not to have
my lines criticized.

1260   Why, Bert, you're all excited — what's the matter?
I just came from a lady who told my fortune with numbers.
What's your lucky number?

It used to be Central 00000 but now she hangs up on me.
Who does?
My girl.

1261 I went to a fortune teller. She read my palm. She said I was going
to lose my automobile.
But you lost your automobile six months ago.
That's what I told her and she said: Can I help it if you don't
wash your hands for six months?

1262 Good evening. I'm a fortune teller.
What is my fortune?
Two dollars and a half.
Correct.

1263 I'm a crystal gazer.
Well, don't look at me. Go into the other room and look at my
wife — she's got a glass eye.

1264 Tell me what town I'll die in.
What good will that do you?
Then I won't go near it.

1265 I can tell by just looking in a girl's eyes, just what she thinks of me.
Gee! That must be embarrassing.

1266 I went to the mind reader, but she said she couldn't read me
very easily.
Yeah — it's very difficult to read blank pages.

1267 That's nothing — I went into a drug store, saw a man order a
chocolate sundae and immediately I knew he was a sailor.
How did you know?
He was wearing a sailor suit.

1268 Can I kiss you?
What am I — a mind reader?

1269 You have just come from dinner.
How did you know?
I know my onions.

1270 The Fortune Teller has had a very busy day today reading
minds. You should be a vacation for him.

1271 Do you wish me to read your mind?
How much would it cost me?
For a great mind — I charge $100; for an average mind — $50;
but a mind like yours I read for 50 cents.

1272   Do you wish to consult Woosung Pootung, the great Chinese
       Mystic?
       Aye, lass — tell 'im 'is mother's 'ere from Lancashire.

1273   Beware, my friend, of a tall, dark woman who will be con-
       stantly in your path. She's bad luck.
       Don't be silly! It's bad luck for her. I drive a steam engine.

1274   Did the palmist tell you the truth about yourself?
       Yes, but shucks! My wife has been doing that for years.

1275   You are about to be discovered by a big movie producer and
       will soon be a star.
       But that's the same thing you told my friend Rosa.
       I can't help it. You girls won't be satisfied with anything less
       nowadays.

                              RELATED SUBJECTS
                              Reincarnation 184-187
                              Curiosity 1323-1324
                              Dishonesty 2500-2502

SPIRITUALISM

1276   Ah, I hear the spirit of your late wife knocking.
       Who's she knocking now?

1277   I want to speak to my departed husband.
       Why?
       He died before I finished telling him what I thought of him.

                              RELATED SUBJECTS
                              Death 124-145
                              Ghost 177-183
                              Reincarnation 184-187

ASTROLOGY

1278   If you're an astrologer, tell me something about the astral regions.
       I know there is a woman in the moon.
       There's a man in the moon, but never a woman.
       If there wasn't a woman up in the moon, a man wouldn't stay
       up there that long.

1279   Do you know when Mars is in Virgo that means spots on the
       moon?
       I know when papa is in the barn, that means spots on the son.

1280   I'm studying astronomy.
       You are? Do you know what Mars is?
       Sure — everybody knows what mars is. Mars is a scratch you
       get on the furniture.

1281   That's a comet.
       A what?
       A comet. You know what a comet *is*?
       No.
       Don't you know what they call a star with a tail?
       Sure — Mickey Mouse.

1282   Now, boys, tell me the signs of the zodiac. You first, Ned.
       Taurus, the Bull.
       Right! Now, you Harold, another one.
       Cancer, the Crab.
       Right again! And now it's your turn, Albert.
       Mickey, the mouse.

1283   The light of the star I am going to show you takes four hours
         to reach the earth.
       Very interesting — but I'm afraid I can't stay so long.

1284   An astrologer tells me not to marry in January if I would
         avoid trouble.
       Well, the same advice is good for the other eleven months of the
         year, too.

1285   I was born in You-lie.
       Oh, you lie? You didn't need to tell me that — I knew it. Ac-
         cording to the zodiac you were born in Taurus, governing the
         bull.
       I was fooling — in April I was born.
       An April fool!
       I was born on the first day of May.
       I can believe that. May comes under the sign of Leo, meaning lion.
       Forward, that's when I was born. Forward March!
       It comes under the sign of Aries, the Ram. That's why you are
         always horning in. I thought you might be born in June, be-
         cause June comes under the sign of the Crab.
       I was born in September.
       Under the sign of Libra?
       Under the sign of Venus. I know him well — the Merchant of
         Venus.
       You give me a pain in the foot — I think you were born under
         the sign of Capricorn.

RELATED SUBJECTS
Age 45-107
Birthday 108-120
Luck 5588

IMAGINATION

1286   With a little thinking I managed to win $10 at bridge today.
       Beginner's luck.

Why, I began playing bridge years ago.
I know, but you've just begun thinking.

1287 The poor fellow, he's going crazy. Wherever he goes he sees
       beautiful girls following him.
       Oh, he only imagines it.
       Yeah, that's why he's going crazy.

1288 Excuse me — I was lost in thought.
       Yes, it's always easy to get lost where one is a stranger.

1289 That's funny.
       What?
       Oh, I was just thinking.
       Ha! Ha! That is funny.

1290 What are you thinking about?
       Thanks for the compliment.

1291 What are you thinking of?
       Nothing.
       Well, take your mind off yourself.

1292 Penny for your thoughts?
       No. I don't wanta turn pro.

1293 I thought of you all day yesterday.
       You did! How nice! Where were you?
       At the zoo.

1294 I bet I know what you're thinking about.
       Well, you don't act like it.

1295 My wife and I always think exactly alike, only she usually has
       first think.

1296 The thing for you to do is to stop thinking about yourself. Bury
       yourself in your work.
       Gosh — and me a concrete mixer.

RELATED SUBJECTS
Worry 2348-2355
Wish 2356

ABSENTMINDEDNESS

1297 He's so absentminded, he slammed his wife and kissed the door.

1298 He came here to see if he couldn't cure his absentmindedness.
       And how is he getting along — is he improving any?
       His wife took him downtown in a taxicab and he kissed the
       driver and gave his wife 60 cents.
       Improving, huh?

I don't know. At breakfast his back must have started itching. He poured the molasses down his back and scratched his pancakes.

1299 She's so absentminded, she has to read the Monday morning paper to see if she was in an automobile accident on Sunday.

1300 Your husband is simply wild about you, isn't he?
Yes, he raves about me all night in his sleep, but the poor absentminded fellow nearly always calls me by the wrong name.

1301 Why are you divorcing your husband?
Well, it's on account of his absentmindedness. The other night he was reading the paper and I slipped up and kissed him on his bald spot.
Yes?
And he said: Quit playing, honey, and get out those letters I dictated yesterday.

1302 Then there's the absentminded farmer who kissed his horse goodbye — and hitched his wife to the plow.

1303 Absentminded farmer discovers piece of rope in hand. "I've either found a piece of rope or lost a horse."

1304 (Drowning person): Help! Aid! Succor! I can't swim.
(Absentminded man): That's nothing. I can't play the bass viola.

1305 Nurse: Professor, a boy has arrived.
Professor: Ask him what he wants.

1306 The other night my uncle — the absentminded one — put out his wife, wound up the cat, and got in bed with the clock.

1307 Absentminded business man kissed his wife goodbye and slapped his secretary upon reaching his office.

1308 He was so absentminded he poured ketchup on his shoe laces and tied knots in his spaghetti.

1309 Servant: The doctor's here, sir.
Absentminded man: I can't see him; tell him I'm ill.

1310 Absentminded schoolmaster hands the waiter his dinner check: Take this back to your desk and work it out again.

1311 Nurse: You've just been presented with twins.
Father: Well, don't tell my wife, I want to surprise her.

1312 Did you say the professor was absentminded?
Absentminded! Why he read an erroneous account of his death in a newspaper and sent himself a wreath!

1313   Absentminded Professor: A collector at the door? Did you tell him I was out?

Maid: Yes, sir, but he doesn't believe me.

Professor: Well, then, I shall have to go and tell him myself.

1314   Absentminded business man finds himself in New York and wires his secretary to find out what he's there for. She replies: You're on your way to Princeton to deliver an address.

1315   He's so absentminded he stood in front of a mirror for two hours trying to remember where he'd seen himself before.

1316   He's a doctor but he's terribly absentminded. The day he got married, when the time came for him to place the ring on his wife's finger, he felt her pulse and asked her to stick out her tongue.

1317   Has anybody seen me vest?

Sure, Murphy, and ye've got it on.

Right, and I have, and it's a good thing ye seen it or I'd have gone home without it.

1318   Absentminded: Haircut, please.

Barber: Certainly, but if you really want a haircut would you mind taking your hat off first?

Absentminded: (Noticing girl sitting in next chair) Oh, I'm terribly sorry. I didn't know there was a lady present.

1319   I forgot my umbrella this morning.

How did you remember you forgot it?

Well, I missed it when I raised my hand to close it after it had stopped raining.

RELATED SUBJECTS
Mind 1162-1258
Forgetfulness 1609-1611

BROADMINDEDNESS

1320   Is your father working?

Yeah, but he expects to get fired.

Why?

He's a detective and he's too broadminded to make good.

1321   So your wife is very broadminded?

Yes, she believes there are always two sides to an argument — hers and her mother's.

RELATED SUBJECTS
Gossip 1518-1537

NARROWMINDEDNESS

1322   This room is a little narrow.
We'll give it to Uncle Emil. He is so narrowminded.

RELATED SUBJECTS
Gossip 1518-1537

CURIOSITY

1323   What other people do is none of my business.
That's very true.
Yeah — that's what they tell me — it's none of my business.

1324   He: I have been trying to discover why a woman is so much more curious than a man. Why do you suppose it is, Miss Winnie?
She: I don't know, I'm sure. I've never been curious enough to inquire.

RELATED SUBJECTS
Gossip 1518-1537

COMPARISON

1325   The town is so small they have "come again" painted on the back of the "Welcome" sign.

1326   You remind me of the horn on my uncle's car.
Why?
It doesn't give a hoot either.

1327   She has a head on her like the Statue of Liberty.
You mean, she has a big head?
No, it's empty.

1328   The town was so small, when the train stopped at the station, the engine was in the country.

1329   How did you get that lump on your head?
A kid hit me with a rock.
A rock? It must have been the size of an egg.
No.
Was it as big as my head?
A little longer, but not as thick.

1330   I hope the color of that blouse won't fade when it is washed.
Oh, it is as safe as the bloom on your cheeks.
Oh, well, then — won't you show me something else?

1331   As small as a night club dance floor.

RELATED SUBJECTS
Description of People 263-303

RESULTS OF REASONING

SMARTNESS

1332   My sister is very brilliant.
Oh, she picks up things fast?
Yeah, she's a shoplifter.

1333   He doesn't think you're educated.
I took up geography — what's he talking about?
And I suppose you took up Algebra?
I went through Algebra at night and I couldn't see a thing.

1334   Just to show you how good I am — if I can't answer your question
     I'll give you $20.
You'll give me $20 if you can't answer my question?
Yeah.
Okay, and just to make it interesting — I'll give you $10 if I can't
     answer your question.
You're first.
What is it that goes up in the air with a barrel and comes down
     with two legs and eye glasses?
You got me there — here's your $20.
Am I rich now!
All right — now tell me what is it that goes up in the air with a
     barrel and comes down with two legs and eye glasses?
I dunno — Here's your $10.

1335   So you think you know as much about it as the coach. How do
     you figure that?
Well, he just said himself that it was impossible for him to teach
     me anything.

1336   Will you ever get any sense?
Well, my brother and I know everything.
Yeah. Well, who was the first president of the United States?
Errrr . . . well, er, that's one my brother knows.

RELATED SUBJECTS
Mind 1162-1258
Egotism 2305-2319
School 4885-4894
College 5059-5096

STUPIDITY

1337   She is so dumb she thinks a Peeping Tom is a night watchman.

1338   She is so dumb when she heard of short wave reception she went
     out and bought a midget radio.

1339   No use playing those phonograph records — they're so scratched
     up you can't understand what they are.

They ain't as scratched up as they used to be. I sandpapered them down.

1340   And is that man dizzy?
Really?
He thinks that a football coach has four wheels.
Isn't that silly? How many wheels has it?

1341   Why are you hitting yourself on the head with that hammer?
I'm trying to make my head swell so my hat won't keep falling over my eyes.

1342   You sure are dumb — and you a daughter of Eve!
My mother's name is Flossie.

1343   Can I do something for you?
Well, you could, but you can't. My mother sent me down to buy some mouse velvet, but I can't match it.
Why not?
She forgot to give me the mouse.

1344   I was counting pigeons on the roof of the City Hall and a fellow came along and said: Say, Buddy, that's going to cost you $1 apiece for counting pigeons on the City Hall. I did some fast thinking and I gave him $14.
That's fast thinking all right.
Yeah, but the joke is on him — I'd already counted fifty pigeons.

1345   What's the idea of going around with a sun lamp?
My mother told me to spread a little sun wherever I go.

1346   Silly idea putting shoe polish in collapsible tubes.
How so?
You can't fool anyone that way. I knew the difference the minute I got the stuff in my mouth.

1347   I'll meet you at the golf course.
Okay. I'll be waiting there for you. How will I know when you get there?
I'll make a mark on the sidewalk.
All right, and if I get there first, I'll rub it out.

1348   She is so dumb she thinks a meadow lark is a party thrown in the country.

1349   I just adore Tuesdays.
Tuesdays? Why?
Because then I can tell myself that day after tomorrow I can say day after tomorrow will be Saturday.

1350   How does your wife like that new washing machine you gave her for Christmas?

No good. Every time she tries to get in it, the paddles knock her black and blue.

1351   I'm sorry I can't come to your party tonight. I have an engagement to see Romeo and Juliet.
That's all right. Bring them along, too.

1352   I had more fun last night. I went up to my room and hid in back of the door, and when I came in I went "boo" — and was I surprised!

1353   Last night I wrote myself a letter — I forgot to sign it, so I don't know who sent it to me.

1354   What are you doing with that lantern?
I found it.
You found it?
Yes, imagine — I found it right on the edge of a big ditch.

1355   Look out — you're rubbing all your powder off on my coat.
Oh, that's all right. I have more in my pocketbook.

1356   He is so dumb he can't count up to twenty without taking his shoes off.

1357   All of a sudden there was a big splash. Voices shouted: Man overboard — man overboard! And imagine my surprise when I discovered it was me splashing around in the water.

1358   Mr. Brown called about his account this morning.
And you told him I'd just left for California?
Yes, and that you wouldn't be back till late this evening.

1359   Get him dead or alive — the Sheriff has put $10,000 on his head.
Poor man — I don't see how he can stand up under it.

1360   Now, as you all know, the law of gravitation explains why we stay on earth.
But how did people stay on before the law was passed?

1362   What time is it?
Nine o'clock.
(Slaps face)
What's the idea?
I've been asking people all day what time it is and everybody tells me something different.

1363   Junior, don't ever again use such bad words.
But, Mother, Shakespeare uses them.
Well, don't play with him any more, then.

1364   He's so dumb he thinks the Kentucky Derby is a hat.

1365   Why is the bell ringing?
        Because I'm pulling the rope.

1366   I'm all tired out. My brother is making some cane seats for me
        and I had to look all over town to get some holes so he could
        wind the cane around them.

1367   He is so dumb — he planted a piece of dogwood and expected to
        raise a litter of puppies.

1368   June is sure dumb, isn't she?
        I hope to tell you! She thinks blackmail means letters of mourning.

1369   Do you know what they call lemons in Los Angeles?
        No, what?
        Lemons.

1370   She's so dumb — she thinks the "Forgotten Man" means the
        victim of last semester's love affair.

1371   How did you come to buy that new Lincoln. You just got a
        Cadillac.
        Well, I went into a Lincoln place to use their telephone and it
        didn't look nice to go away without buying something.

1372   The dumbest girl in the world is the one who thinks a hemlock
        is an attachment for a sewing machine.

1373   She's so dumb she thinks blood vessels are some kind of ships.

1374   Yesterday I went up to the stadium and cheered and hollered and
        yelled and had the best time. But I'm going to have more fun
        next time — next Saturday they'll be playing football.

1375   Why don't you wait and come home with me? We're having a
        Spanish Consul for dinner.
        No, I wouldn't come anyway now.
        Wouldn't you like a Spanish Consul?
        They're nice fish but they just won't fill me up.

1376   It's funny to see you here alone.
        What's funny about it? I came alone.

1377   This bill is terrific — $75 for a dress March 1st — March 2nd,
        ditto, March 15th, ditto.
        I don't know what it means, but I know I never bought the ditto.

1378   When I met you was I going down the street or up the street?
        You were going up the street.
        Fine — then I've had my lunch.

1379   She was so dumb she thought a buttress was a female goat.

1380   So dumb you don't know the civil war is over.
       I certainly do. I knew it two years ago.

1381   Is there anything you want to know?
       Yes, is it true that raisins are just worried grapes?

RELATED SUBJECTS
Mind 1162-1258

SUCKER

1382   I heard you've got a lollypop invention.
       What makes you think so?
       Well, my father says you made $500 on a sucker.

1383   He: (Bragging) Stop insulting me. Our candy company just
          named a big lollypop after me.
       She: Well, I made a sucker out of you first.

1384   There is a sucker born every minute.
       Yeah, but what good does it do you; nowadays they haven't any-
          thing to take away from them.

1385   My brother has a new invention — it's a sucker fountain pen.
       What do you mean — sucker fountain pen?
       It doesn't have a pen point — and you can't sign on the dotted line.

1386   What a sap to let a man sell you a dead horse for $20.
       Yeah? Well, I sold the horse for $100.
       How?
       I raffled him off. I sold a hundred tickets for a dollar apiece.
       What did the fellow say who won?
       Well, he made an awful fuss about it, so I gave him his dollar
          back.

1387   You got drunk last night and sold the Chrysler Building.
       Well, why are you so sad about it?
       I bought it.

1388   I suppose if someone came along and offered you the City Hall
          you'd buy it.
       No, I wouldn't.
       Why wouldn't you buy the City Hall?
       Because I bought it yesterday.
       How much did the man charge you for the City Hall?

(Laughs) He took all my life's savings.
And why are you laughing at it?
Because your wife gave me $600 for it this morning.

1389   What is that you're chewing?
It's called "Trick Gum" — the more you chew it, the smarter
you get. I'm going to chew this one second and have a lot of
swell ideas.
Got any more?
I've only got one stick left. I'll sell it to you for Ten Dollars.
Here's the Ten Dollars.
Here's the gum.
Boy, it's all right. It tastes good. Do you think I'll get smart from
this? Funny. I don't feel any different. I think it's a joke.
Say, you're smart already.

RELATED SUBJECTS
Dishonesty 2500-2502

ILLITERACY

1390   You say you can't read or write? How did that happen?
Well, you see it was this-a-way. I never went to school nohow only
one day, and that was at night, and we didn't have no light, and
the teacher didn't come.

1391   (A man with his ears stopped up is reading a letter to another)
What kind of nonsense are you two guys up to?
Well, he got this letter from his girlfriend, but he can't read, so
he asked me to read it for him, but then he stops up my ears so
I can't hear what she wrote to him.

1392   Cheeze, kid, dat last article you wrote for de paper wuz a pippin.
Dat's wot dey tell me. Y'know, buddy, sometimes I wisht I
could read.

1393   What are you doing with that paper?
I'm writing my girlfriend a letter.
Go on, you fool, you can't write.
That's all right, my girlfriend can't read.

1394   What are you going to do about this letter?
What letter?
This one. It has been laying around here over a year.
I don't know what to do with it.
Why don't you open it and see who it is from?
Don't be a fool! I don't even know who it is for.

1395   Don't you know who I am? I'm a radio announcer.
Well, ignorance is no excuse.

1396   That's a lovely ring.
Yes, it's an antickee.
You mean it's antique. And I thought you were smart.
You're not calling me ignorant, are you?
I merely said you are very illiterate.
Well, thanks!

1397   I'll bet you don't know how to write.
Yes I do — but I never write.
Why not?
I don't know how to read.

1398   Uncle Jack, in spite of his illiteracy, had built up quite a competency in his whitewashing and calcimining trade. During the course of some business with a notary, the latter produced a document, saying: Please sign this here.
Uncle Jack: Look here, sir. I don't ever sign my name. I'm a businessman, with no time for such trifles. I always dictate my name!

> RELATED SUBJECTS
> Hill-Billy 1155-1161
> Smartness 1332-1336
> Writer 1612-1642
> Athlete 4319-4323

INSANITY

1399   A farmer was driving past an insane asylum with a load of fertilizer. An inmate of the asylum saw him and called: What are you hauling?
Fertilizer.
What are you going to do with it?
Put it on strawberries.
You ought to live in here, we get sugar and cream on them.

1400   A nut was sitting in his cell, playing solitaire. Another nut was watching. Finally the kibitzer spoke up: Wait a minute. I just caught you cheating yourself.
Shhhh! Don't tell anybody — but, for years, I've been cheating myself at solitaire.
You don't say! Don't you ever catch yourself cheating?
Naw! I'm too clever.

1401   What made your brother go insane?
The rabbit on his chest drove him crazy.
How could a rabbit be on his chest?
Haven't you ever heard of anybody having a wild hair on their chest?

1402   Man (mumbling): Calling all limousines, coupes, roadsters,

sedans, calling all limousines, coupes, roadsters, sedans, etc.
What's the matter with that man?
Oh, he used to be a police report broadcaster — and he's lost his
memory, he can't remember the words: Calling all cars.

1403   He talks to himself — that shows he's insane.
Ridiculous. You wouldn't be insane just because you talked to
yourself.
No?
Of course not. I talk to myself. Do you think I'm insane?
I wouldn't say you're insane if you talked to yourself. But you
would be if you listened.

1404   I'm afraid you are crazy.
Well, are *you* all right?
Certainly, I'm all right.
Then I'm glad I'm crazy.

1405   Don't you know you have to be crazy to talk like that?
No, you don't *have* to be, but it helps.

1406   Being from Hollywood, maybe you can give us a few of the facts
regarding Lupe Velez and Johnny Weismuller. I understand
that Lupe says Johnny goes crazy every once in a while.
Well, that's easily explained — Johnny pulls this Tarzan stuff
and, after all, if you climb coco palms long enough, you're sure
to get nuts.

1407   The next scene is laid in an insane asylum. They are serving soup
to nuts.

1408   What's the idea of that Nudist standing on that dime all day
long?
He's cracked. He thinks he's Mr. Woolworth.
Mr. Woolworth?
Yeah — you know, nothing over ten cents.

1409   A doctor was showing a friend around a lunatic asylum. See
that man over there, he said.
Yes.
Well, he's the fellow who went mad on the night of his wedding
when his girl jilted him.
Too bad.
They passed on. Coming to a steel cell in which a man was banging
his head against the bars, the doctor said: Do you know who
that is?
No.
Well, that's the fellow who married the other fellow's girl.

1410   He went insane trying to find a place to put a cornerstone for a round house.

1411   Pleading guilty to deserting his wife and seven small children, and eloping with a grass widow and her ten children, a Buffalo man is held pending a mental examination.

1412   (Going through insane asylum)
1st Man: Don't take off your hat and don't act natural.
2nd Man: Why not?
1st Man: They'll never let you out.

1413   Where is your brother?
He is out ice skating on the lake.
There is no ice on the lake.
That wouldn't stop him.

1414   Do you know that statistics prove that over 11% more men than women are crazy?
Yeah, but who drives the men crazy?

1415   (Passenger and pilot way up in airplane when the pilot begins to laugh hysterically)
Passenger: What's the joke?
Pilot: I'm thinking of what they'll say at the asylum when they find out I have escaped.

1416   I feel like I'm going to die.
If you passed away, I would go crazy.
Yes, go crazy — you'd get married again.
I wouldn't go that crazy.

1417   Visitor: Why are you here?
Insane Patient: For no reason at all.

RELATED SUBJECTS
Description of People 263-303
Mind 1162-1258

SUSPICION

1418   My sister has a new boy friend but we're suspicious of him.
What makes you suspicious?
He always puts his derby over the keyhole when he sits in the parlor with sis.

1419   I have an idea that that fellow is a low-down snake in the grass.
What makes you think so?
He hisses when he speaks.

1420   Have you ever suspected your wife of leading a double life?
Continually — her own and mine.

1421   I'm setting a trap for my brother's wife.
       Whom do you suspect?
       A mouse in the pantry.

RELATED SUBJECTS
Curiosity 1323-1324
Jealousy 2775-2777
Marriage 2882-3051
Unfaithfulness 3057-3088

SUPERSTITION

1422   Do you think it's unlucky to postpone a wedding?
       Not if you keep on doing it.

1423   Do you believe it is seven years' bad luck if you break a mirror?
       No, indeed not. My brother broke one and he didn't have seven
            years' bad luck.
       He didn't?
       No, he was killed in an explosion the same day.

1424   They tell me the way to get rid of a wart is to bury a cat. Do you
            think that's true?
       Yes, if the wart is on the cat.

1425   I had a hunch today. I got up at seven, had seven dollars in my
            pocket, there were seven at lunch, and there were seven horses
            in the race — I picked the seventh.
       So he came in the winner?
       No, he came in seventh.

1426   There's a black cat in the dining room.
       Black cats are unlucky.
       This one isn't. She just ate your dinner.

1427   I knew I would have hard luck. We had dinner on the train and
            there were thirteen in the party.
       That's only superstition. What makes you think thirteen at dinner
            is unlucky?
       I had to pay the check.

1428   From now on I'm superstitious.
       What about?
       Black cats. I believe a black cat is hard luck.
       Just what makes you believe that?
       Last night my brother stepped on a cat and dropped the silverware
            and woke up the owner of the house.

1429   If your left hand itches that's the sign you're going to have some-
            thing and if your head itches that's the sign you've got some-
            thing.

1430   You're not scared, are you?
      No. As long as I have this rabbit's foot — I'm okay.
      Do you think a rabbit's foot lucky?
      It surely is. My wife came across it in my pants' pocket, and she
        thought it was a mouse.

1431   I think we'd better get going Friday.
      Not Friday. That's an unlucky day.
      I was born on Friday, and I don't think it's unlucky.
      Yeah — but what do your folks think?

RELATED SUBJECTS
Mind Reader 1162-1258
Luck 5583

COMMUNICATION OF IDEAS

TALKING

1432   You seem rather hoarse this morning, Mrs. Peck.
      Yes, my husband came home very late last night.

1433   They say her husband's words are sharp and to the point.
      Maybe that's the only way for him to get a word in edgeways,
      now and then.

1434   Have you noticed how a woman lowers her voice whenever she
      asks for anything?
      Oh, yes. But have you noticed how she raises it if she doesn't
      get it?

1435   Doctor, this is Mr. Henpeck. My wife just dislocated her jaw.
      If you're out this way next week or the week after, you might
      drop in and see her.

1436   Your report card shows you're very poor in deportment. It says
      you always talked out loud.
      I didn't talk. The guy in front of me talked — I only answered
      him.

1437   Calm yourself. In a minute you'll be on the platform making your
      speech and it will soon be over.
      And I'll be happy.
      So will everyone else.
      That sounds like liniment talk.
      What do you mean, liniment talk?
      You're rubbing it in.

1438   The only chance I get to open my mouth around my wife is when
      I yawn.

1439   Woman: (After a long, silly conversation about nothing): Well, I've enjoyed our little visit. I must be off.
You *must* be.

1440   Why didn't you hug her?
She talked my arm off.

1441   A pantomime is where people talk but say nothing, as usual.

1442   Silence is golden.
If silence is golden, you'll never be arrested for hoarding.

1443   I come from a very truthful family — a lie never passed my father's lips.
How do you know?
He talked through his nose.

1444   She talks so much I can hardly sleep at night.
Get some sleeping medicine.
That's a good idea — and take it.
No — give it to her.

1445   I'm having a hard time including that "nothing" in our conversation.
I don't know why. I have heard you talk for hours about nothing before.

1446   Don't you listen when a person talks? No one wants to be interrupted in the middle of a sentence.
Al Capone wouldn't mind.

1447   What did your father say about your wrecking the car?
Shall I leave out the swear words?
Certainly.
He didn't say anything.

1448   She is a marvelous conversationalist. She uses more meaningless words to say less about nothing.

1449   A cynic said recently of his wife: At the evening's end, she was so tired that she could barely keep her mouth open.

1450   He's a man of few words, isn't he?
Yes, so he was telling me all morning.

1451   Then there was the girl who remained an old maid because she never quit talking long enough for any man to kiss her.

1452   I'm speechless.
Good — just stay that way.

1453   The wife of a friend of mine doesn't speak to him any more.
What did he do?
Died.

1454   My wife can't even send a telegram without saying "stop" after
       every sentence.

1455   The police say that you and your wife had some words.
       I had some, sir, but I didn't get a chance to use them.

1456   Whatever I say goes!
       Then talk to yourself awhile.

1457   A woman who speaks twelve languages has married a man who
       speaks seventeen. That should be about the right handicap.

1458   Joe is the most optimistic person that I have ever seen.
       Howzat?
       He hasn't spoken to his wife for three years, but he believes that
       his turn will eventually come.

1459   She talks so much I'm hoarse listening to her.

1460   Money talks.
       Yes, but it doesn't give itself away.

1461   I called him everything I could lay my tongue to.
       What did he say?
       He was speechless.
       How come?
       I did all the talking.

1462   Why is Doddie Turner, that dizzy steno of yours, like a pants
       button?
       Dunno, unless it's because she's poppin off at the wrong time.

1463   They say that if a man's ears turn red then somebody's talking
       about him.
       Yeah, and you can bet that somebody's talking about him if his
       nose turns red.

1464   Stop! Stop!
       What do you think you are, a telegram?

1465   You're barking up the wrong tree.
       This is my natural voice.

1466   Jim has a terrible habit of talking to himself.
       That isn't so bad; just so he doesn't answer himself.

1467   Why did you give the gate to that new fellow you had the other
       night?
       Oh, he talked shop all the time.
       But most men do that.
       Yes, but this one worked for the weather bureau!

1468 Was your wife outspoken?
Not by anyone I know of.

1469 That last remark was in the dead letter office.
What do you mean?
It was uncalled for.

1470 Did your wife have much to say, when you got home last night?
No, but that didn't keep her from talking for two hours.

1471 She has a vocabulary of only one hundred words but she uses them over and over.

1472 But, my dear, you've been talking for half an hour, and I haven't said a word.
No, you haven't said anything, but you've been listening in a most aggravating manner, and I'm not going to stand for it.

1473 Doctor: And that habit of talking to yourself — there's nothing to worry about that.
Man: Perhaps not; but I'm such a damn bore.

1474 The traffic officer says you got sarcastic with him.
But I didn't intend to be. He talked to me like my wife does and I forgot myself and answered "Yes, dear."

1475 First Passenger: Hi! I'm sure glad you're here. I hate these intercontinental flights. I can't sleep on planes, and I've already seen the movie, and the last time I took this flight I didn't have anyone to talk to.
Second Passenger: Parlez-vous francais?

1476 Wife: Scientists claim that the average person speaks 10,000 words in a day.
Husband: Yes, dear, but remember, you are far above the average.

1477 I believe in saying it with flowers.
Yeah, but you only sent me one flower.
Well, you know I never talk much.

1478 I don't mind my wife growing a third set of teeth, but if she starts growing another tongue, I'm off to Reno.

1479 The wife of a friend of mine doesn't speak to him any more.
How come?
She's got lock-jaw.

1480 Your wife is a brilliant talker. I could listen to her all night.
I have.

1481 I'm a man of few words.
I know — I'm married, too.

BABY TALK

1482   I had to bawl out my husband for talking baby talk in the nursery today.
Oh, don't mind those child experts. It doesn't hurt to talk a little baby talk to a child.
But he wasn't talking it to the child — he was talking it to the nursemaid.

1483   Have you ever heard of Mark Twain?
Oh, baby talk! Mark Twain — is that something like the Sunset Limited twain?

1484   Did you see him winkin'?
Winkin'?
Yes. Winkin', winkin'.
Oh, baby talk. That's not him winkin', that's him Chevwolet.

1485   Drama? Don't you know what drama is?
Oh sure — baby talk — my drama lives in the country and we go to visit her every Christmas.

STUTTERING

1486   Did you make the debating team?
N-n-n-no. They s-s-said I w-w-w-wasn't t-t-tall enough.

1487   If a Hottentot tot taught a Hottentot tot to talk e'er the tot could totter, ought the Hottentot tot be taught to say aught or naught,

or what ought to be taught her? If to hoot and to toot a Hottentot tot be taught by a Hottentot tutor, should the tutor get hot
if the Hottentot tot hoot and toot at the Hottentot tutor?

1488   Will you please t-t-t-tell me — d-d-d-does t-t-t-this t-t-t-train
g-g-g-go t-t-t-to F-f-f-florida?
Yeah.
W-w-when d-d-d-d-does the t-t-t-train leave?
It left while you were talking.

1489   W-w-w-where do y-y-y-you g-g-g-get off at?
D-d-d-detroit.
W-w-w-w-what's taking you t-t-t-there?
I w-w-want to s-s-s-see pro-pro-professor Mac-Mac-MacEwen
to s-s-s-see if he can d-d-d-do a-a-anything for my s-s-stutter.
You w-w-w-will f-f-f-find he's a d-d-d-darned g-g-g-good m-m-m-
man — it w-w-w-was h-h-h-him that c-c-cured me.

1490   Two stuttering blacksmiths had finished heating a piece of pig
iron, and one placed it upon the anvil with a pair of tongs.
1st: H-h-h-hit it.
2nd: W-w-w-where?
1st: Aw, h-h-h-heck, we'll have to h-h-h-heat it again.

1491   He was dishonorably discharged.
How did it happen?
He was loading a bunch of soldiers on a boat, marching them on
to the dock. Four hundred of them went over the side and got
drowned before he could say: Halt. He stutters so.

1492   He's never spoken a hasty word to his wife since they married.
Remarkable!
Yeah — he stutters.

1493   K-k-k-k-kantcha s-s-s-see w-w-w-where you're g-g-g . . .
Going?
. . . g-g-going, ya b-b-b-big b-b-b-b . . .
Boob?
T-t-thank you.

1494   What makes you stutter?
I don't s-s-stutter — I j-j-just h-h-hesitate.

1495   You don't believe in freedom of speech?
G-g-go to the d-d-devil!

1496   I want some hot poppered butt corn — I mean cot buttered bop
corn — that is — corn buttered pop butt, or rather cuttered pot
born, I mean — oh well, gimme some peanuts.

1497   I want a pair of spec-rimmed hornicles — I mean spornrimmed
hectacles — confound it — I mean heck-rimmed spornacles.

I know what you mean, sir. Mr. Peck, show this gentleman a pair
of rimsproned hectacles. You've got me doing it.

RELATED SUBJECTS
Pronunciation 4992
Speech 5111-5123

SWEARING

1498   I swear I've never been kissed.
Well, I don't blame you for swearing.

1499   Lady: Doesn't that little boy swear terribly?
Another little boy: Yes, ma'am, he sure does. He doesn't put any
expression in it at all.

1500   Have you ever been to Amstergosh, New York?
Don't you mean, Amsterdam?
Yes, but I never swear over the radio.

RELATED SUBJECTS
Fight 2145-2213
Driving 4092-4127

CONVERSATION

1501   Have you any children?
No. Why?
Too bad. I was going to ask how they were.

1502   How do you find his conversation?
Like the waves of the sea.
You mean you find it rolling, irresistible, vital . . . ?
No — it makes me sick.

RELATED SUBJECTS
Talk 1432-1481
Gossip 1518-1537

INTERRUPTION

1503   The next person to interrupt the proceedings will be sent home.
Prisoner: Hurrah!

1504   This is going to be a real treat . . .
I know — I'm going to sing.
Will you please let me finish?
It would be a pleasure to see your finish.

RELATED SUBJECTS
Speech 5111-5123

EXPLANATION

1505   You follow me?
Sure, where're you going?
I mean, have you got the plot?
Yes, and I would like to bury you in it.

1506   And did I make myself plain?
No, God did that.

RELATED SUBJECTS
Talk 1432-1481
Speech 5111-5123

EXAGGERATION

1507   Where I come from they do things in a hurry. Why, they put up
buildings quicker than in any other city. They start a 20 story
building one day and in a week it's finished.
That's nothing — you should come down to our town. I was going
to work one morning and they were laying the cornerstone of a
building. When I came home from work that night, the landlord was putting tenants out for not paying their rent.

1508   It seems that a young man found himself stranded in the woods
with a gun and only one bullet. His story runs something like
this: When I found that my salvation depended upon my one
bullet, I decided to be careful. Suddenly, as I was walking
along the bank of a river, I saw eight ducks flying in a straight
line. Taking careful aim I fired, and the bullet passed through
the heads of all the ducks, killing them instantly. As the ducks
fell they broke a dead limb from a tree; this limb hit a moose on
the head and killed it; the moose in its death throes kicked a rabbit; the rabbit came sailing through the air, knocked me into the
stream and I came up with my pockets full of fish.

1509   There I was all alone — standing on the hill top — when in the
distance I saw ten thousand Indians coming . . .
How many Indians?
One thousand, and . . .
How many Indians?
Well, one Indian was coming in the distance.

1510   I tell you, sir, I have played in all the largest theatres in Europe.
Yes, sir. In America we have theatres so big that when a man in
the back seat throws an egg, it hatches out before it reaches the
stage.

1511   Those Kansas cyclones must be terrible.
G'wan, down in Florida the wind was so strong it blew out the
fuses.

1512   My girl is so tepid she held an egg in her hand and hatched two
        chicks from it.
        That's nothing. My girl walked up to a tree and kissed it. And it
        took thirty men to put out the forest fire!

1513   I've got a horse that's faster than any automobile.
        Faster than any automobile? Who was he sired by?
        What do you mean?
        What was his father's name?
        I told you he was *fast*. Why, he is so fast, he ran away before he
        found out what his father's name was.

1514   You should see my brother — is he fast? He can ring the front
        doorbell, go to the back door and run through to the front of
        the house in time to let himself in.

1515   I never saw such a season. My corn isn't an inch high.
        Your corn! Why, say, the sparrows have to kneel down to eat mine.

1516   They have such a large farm they send the young couples out to
        milk the cows and their grandchildren bring back the milk.

1517   Happily married for twenty years, we've been.
        How long?
        Ten years.
        How long?
        Well, all right, I don't even know if we're married or not.

RELATED SUBJECTS
Lying 1540-1564
Boast 2285-2304
Fishing 4380-4413

GOSSIP

1518   You know, I can't find anybody that knows anything about her
        past.
        All the people who know anything about her are dead.

1519   My wife bought a radio so she could turn it on and the neighbors
        couldn't hear us when we're talking.
        And did it work?
        That's just it. She found out that the radio kept her from hearing
        what the neighbors were saying.

1520   We are very angry at the way you have talked about our Samuel.
        This can't go on — even if he is a thief.

You say he is a thief?
Sure — and a murderer, too.
Wait a minute, you're talking about him yourself.
Well, I'm a relative and who knows better than me?

1521 I suppose you played bridge last night?
No — our bridge club broke up.
Why?
We had to break up because everybody attended every meeting,
and there was no one to talk about.

1522 I hope I can live up to all the things you've said about me.
That ought to be easy. I have had to live down all the things
you've said about me.

1523 Mr.: The iceman just told me that every woman in this block is
in love with him except one.
Mrs.: Hump! It must be that woman that moved in next door,
the stuckup thing!

1524 And they say the most terrible things about her — can any of
them be true?
I'm afraid not.

1525 Do you like that cake, Mrs. Brown?
Yes, my dear, very much.
That's funny. 'Cause mother said you haven't any taste.

1526 Are you worried because you think he'll tell lies about you?
I don't mind the lies, but if he ever tells the truth, I'll break
his neck.

1527 And anything you tell a woman goes in one ear and over the
back fence.

1528 You can't believe everything you hear.
No, but you can repeat it.

1529 She told me that you told her the secret I told you not to tell her.
The mean thing! I told her not to tell you I told her.
Well, don't tell her that I told you she told me.

1530 What do women talk about when they are together?
Just what the men talk about.
Aren't they terrible?

1531 Is it true, Miss Elderleigh, that you are going to be married soon?
Well, no, it isn't. But I am very grateful for the rumor.

1532 If you tell a man anything, it goes in one ear and out the other.
And if you tell a woman anything, it goes in both ears and out of
her mouth.

1533　Is she really married?
　　　Well, if she's not, I'm in a hell of a fix.
　　　How's that?
　　　I'm her husband.

1534　You say the nastiest things about people.
　　　Say, I say sweet things about people.
　　　When?
　　　When I send them flowers to their funeral.

1535　What do you call it when one woman is talking?
　　　Monologue.
　　　Right. What do you call it when two women are talking?
　　　Cat-alogue.

1536　1st Gossip: Why did they separate?
　　　2nd Gossip: Nobody knows.
　　　1st Gossip: Oh, how terrible.

1537　Have you heard the latest scandal?
　　　No, my wife's out of town.

　　　　　　　　　　　　RELATED SUBJECTS
　　　　　　　　　　　　Talk 1432-1481
　　　　　　　　　　　　Broadmindedness 1320-1321
　　　　　　　　　　　　Conversation 1501-1502
　　　　　　　　　　　　Hospitality 3564-3660

TWO-FACED

1538　Woman: (Talking to self) I tell you I did — I didn't — I did —
　　　I didn't — I did — I didn't . . .
　　　Who is that?
　　　A two-faced woman trying to have the last word with herself.

1539　She's two-faced. She has one face that has been lifted and the other
　　　one nobody would lift.

　　　　　　　　　　　　RELATED SUBJECTS
　　　　　　　　　　　　Description of People 263-303

LYING

1540　H'm! So you want a job, eh? Do you ever tell lies?
　　　No, sir; but I kin learn.

1541　At the hospital I seed one of these machines that tell if a man's
　　　lying.
　　　Pooh!
　　　Pooh? Did you see one?
　　　See one? I married one.

1542   Why was it that George Washington never told a lie, papa?
       Because nobody asked him when the economic depression would
       end.

1543   I think, dear, that you fib a little occasionally.
       Well, I think it's a wife's duty to speak well of her husband
       occasionally.

1544   (Being questioned on stand in court)
       Witness: I've been wedded to the truth from infancy.
       Prosecutor: Is the court to imply from this statement that you
       are now a widower?

1545   Can you tell by your husband's face if he's lying?
       Yes. If his lips are moving, he is.

1546   We found a dog, and whoever can tell the biggest lie, gets him.
       Well, I'm surprised at you boys. Don't you know it's wrong to
       tell lies? Why, I've never told a lie in my life.
       Here's the dog — you win.

1547   Nothing that is false ever does anybody any good.
       You're wrong, stranger. I have false teeth and they do me a lot
       of good.

1548   I tell you I don't tell fibs.
       I ought to make you eat those words.
       I can't — the capital letters get caught in my throat.

1549   There is only one thing that keeps you from being a bare-faced
       liar.
       What is that?
       Your mustache.

1550   Remember when they put you on the witness stand, you must
       not lie.
       I wouldn't lie — my uncle told a lie in court once.
       Your uncle told a lie? What happened to him?
       He won the case.

1551   I don't believe that.
       You don't think I'm lying, do you?
       No.
       Well, I am.

1552   He claims the country is getting along — progressing. He says
       George Washington couldn't tell a lie and now almost every-
       body can.

1553   How dare you tell my wife what time I got in this morning —
       especially when I told you not to tell?

I didn't tell her what time you came in. She asked me and I just said I was too busy getting breakfast to notice.

1554   I never told lies when a boy.
When did you begin, father?

1555   My accusers are right. I am a liar.
I don't believe you.

1556   Don't you think that Wordsworth was right when he said: Heaven lies about us in our infancy?
Sure, but he forgot to add that everybody lies about us in our maturity.

1557   I will lecture today on liars. How many of you have read the twenty-fifth chapter?
Nearly all raised their hands.
That's fine. You're the group to whom I wish to speak. There is no twenty-fifth chapter.

1558   How can you lie like that and look me in the face?
I'm getting used to your face.

1559   Frederick, when you came home last night you told me you had been to the Grand Hotel with Mr. Wilson, and Mrs. Wilson just called and said you were both at the Trocadero. Why did you lie to me?
When I came home last night I couldn't say "Trocadero."

1560   The first lie detector was made out of the rib of a man. No improvement has ever been made on the original machine.

1561   Mama, what is a "Second Story Man"?
Your father's one. If I don't believe his first story, he always has another one ready.

1562   The art in telling a story consists of knowing what to leave unsaid.
It doesn't make any difference, my boy. My experience is that she finds out anyway.

1563   She always presents the truth in such a way that nobody ever recognizes it.

1564   Does your husband lie awake at night?
Yes, and he lies in his sleep, too.

RELATED SUBJECTS
Exaggeration 1507-1517
Gossip 1518-1537
Boast 2285-2304
Dishonesty 2500-2502

SECRET

1565 Is it true that Mabel has a secret sorrow?
Certainly. Hasn't she told you about it yet?

1566 Can you keep a secret?
Sure.
I need to borrow some money.
Don't worry. It's just as if I never heard it.

1567 Can you keep a secret?
No, apartment rents are too high these days.

1568 Is your husband a member of any secret society?
He thinks so, but he talks in his sleep.

1569 I hear that John kissed you last night.
He didn't — and besides he promised not to tell.

1570 When you told her a secret you knew only two parties would
know about it: the Republicans and the Democrats.

1571 And they are keeping their engagement a secret, aren't they?
Well, that's what they're telling everybody.

1572 Did you tell anybody of your secret marriage?
No, I'm waiting for my husband to sober up — I want him to
be the first to know.

1573 Suppose you were writing a letter and you had a secret to write
and you didn't want to talk loud, you just wanted to whisper.
What would you do?
I don't know — what would you do?
You'd water the ink, wouldn't you?

1574 She told me that you told her the secret I told you not to tell her.
Hmmm! I told her not to tell you I told her.
Well, don't tell her that I told you she told me.

1575 We girls are getting up a secret society of our own.
Indeed! What's the object?
I don't know exactly yet, but will tell you all about it after I'm
initiated.

RELATED SUBJECTS
Gossip 1518-1537
Conduct 1802-1862
Club 3580

EXTENSION OF THOUGHT
MEMORY

1576   Come on — put on your gloves. Your fight's up next. What's the
       matter?
       I don't think I'm able to fight. When I left home I forgot some-
       thing.
       What did you forget?
       I forgot to stay there.

1577   Shall I forget to give you a ring, or shall I make a memo and let
       my secretary forget to give you a ring?

1578   What have you got a knot in your handkerchief for?
       My wife put it there to remind me to post a letter.
       And have you done so?
       She forgot to give it to me.

1579   Can you tell me what happened way back in 1776?
       I can't even remember what happened last night.

1580   Remember you had a date with me.
       I don't remember the date. I had the date in my book, but I lost it.

1581   People tie string around their finger to help them to remember.
       Yeah — and some people tie a rope around their neck to help
       them forget.

1582   I'm having a terrible time — I forget everything — my memory
       is gone.
       Well, just forget all about it.

1583   Well, you've got to go away and forget.
       I can't.
       Why not?
       My brother took my suitcase.

1584   There are three things I can't remember. I can't remember names
       — I can't remember faces — and — and . . .
       What's the third thing?
       I can't remember.

1585   The funniest thing happened to me on the way here to the studio
       tonight. It was very funny.
       Well, let me in on it. What happened?
       It sure was funny — I wish I could remember it.

1586   What's the string wrapped around your finger for?
       My wife put it there so I'll mail a letter she wrote.
       And what's the string on your index finger for?
       To remember to mail it air mail.

Did you mail the letter?
No, she forgot to write it.

1587 Oh, I always remember faces I never saw before.

1588 You got a good memory, but it's short.

1589 I have decided to train my memory.
What system will you use?
I don't know. I'm looking for one that will enable me, when I
am interviewed, to remember what to forget.

1590 Well, if it isn't John Corcoran, the man I met up in Maine one
rainy night six years ago at the Moose River Junction Railway
Station.
Good day, sir.
Aren't you going to try and sell me something?
No. I sell memory courses.

1591 My wife has the worst memory I ever heard of.
Forgets everything, eh?
No, remembers everything.

RELATED SUBJECTS
Mind 1162-1258
Absentmindedness 1297-1319
Recognition 1598-1608
Forgetfulness 1609-1611

REMINISCENCE

1592 Why, I knew you when you wore short pants.
That's nothing; I knew you when you wore three-cornered ones.

1593 Remember when girls bit their lips to make them red?
No.

1594 These people knew me when I was only a bum.
You haven't changed a bit.

1595 That takes me back to the good old days when I went to college.
Takes you back? What would it take to keep you there?

1596 Yes, I have had some terrible disappointments, but none stands
out over the years like one that came to me when I was a boy.
And what was it?
When I was a boy I crawled under a tent to see the circus, and
I discovered it was a revival meeting.

1597 Wife: Tom, it's just about a year since our honeymoon, when
we spent that glorious day on the sands.
Husband: We little thought then we'd be spending our first
anniversary on the rocks.

RECOGNITION

1598 Don't you know me?
Well, you do look familiar. What's your name?
I'm no stool pigeon — you'll have to find that out.

1599 Say, I remember you. Weren't we messmates in the navy?
Sure. You used to get into the same messes I did.

1600 It seems to me I've seen your face somewhere before.
How odd!
It certainly is.

1601 Man: Where in hell have I seen you before?
Bishop: I don't know. What part of hell are you from?

1602 Tell me, did any of your friends admire your engagement ring?
They did more than that. Two of them recognized it.

1603 You look familiar.
Well, I might be.

1604 Why didn't you answer the letter I sent you last week?
Because I didn't receive it.
You didn't receive it?
No, and besides I didn't like some of the things you wrote in it.

1605 Who is that tall, dark man on the eighth green?
Don't you remember him? He used to be your husband.
Oh, yes. I knew I'd met him somewhere.

1606 You recognize me, don't you?
I don't recall your face, but your language is certainly familiar.

1607 You remember me, don't you?
I can't place the name — but the breath is familiar.

1608 I saw that blonde girl friend of yours today, but she didn't see me.
Yeah, she told me.

FORGETFULNESS

1609 She: (Drunk) You are trying to forget me!
He: (Drunk) Noooo, I'm trying to remember you.

1610 He's very unhappy. He wants to go away from it all — so far away the June editions of magazines won't reach him until April first.

1611 My uncle wanted me to go out with some girls. I told him I wouldn't go out with girls. I'm forgetting girls.
Yeah, so am I. I'm for getting a couple right now.

RELATED SUBJECTS
Absentmindedness 1297-1319
Memory 1576-1591

CREATIVE THOUGHT

WRITER

1612 Is your book on "The Cultivation of Courage" finished?
Yes, but I can't get up nerve enough to take it to a publisher.

1613 How's the play you're writin' comin' along?
There's a little fillin' in to be done yet.
How much?
Well, I have the title completed an' the acts all numbered.

1614 Author: Well, sir, the upshot of it was that it took me ten years to discover that I had absolutely no talent for writing literature.
Friend: And you gave it up?
Author: Oh, no — by that time I was too famous.

1615 Don't you find writing a thankless job?
On the contrary, everything I write is returned to me with thanks.

1616 Have you read my new play?
Yes, but there are only two sheets to it.
That's all it needs — it's a bedroom farce.

1617 Friend: Which of your works of fiction do you consider the best?
Author: My last income tax return.

1618 Here's the manuscript I offered you last year.
Say, what's the idea of bringing that thing back here when I rejected it once?
You've had a year's experience since then.

1619 What's the name of your show?
Home Sweet Home — in two reels.
Home Sweet Home in two reels. Can't be done.

1620 I wrote that play like you told me to.

You did. What's the name of the play?
"Sore Throat — Hiccups — and Poor Eye-sight."
You call your play: Sore Throat — Hiccups — and Poor Eye-sight? Why?
You told me to put everything I had into it.

1621   What kind of stories do you write?
Oatmeal, Bran and Farina.
What kind are those?
Serials.

1622   I'm discouraged. I might as well tear up my play and I've worked on it for four long years.
That's the trouble — all work and no play.

1623   I'm putting everything I know into my next story.
I get it — a short story.

1624   A successful author is one who can make glaring mistakes in grammar and thereby cause them to come into good usage.

1625   Why did you call the hero of your story "Adam"?
You said to write it in the first person.

1626   I'm going to buy a plot for my brother.
Did he pass away?
Oh, no, he's writing a story.

1627   You know my brother is writing dime novels?
Yeah — well, that's one way to get rich.
Sure, when he has written ten of them, he'll have a dollar.

1628   I hope your recent marriage has turned out a great success.
Oh, quite; I've already made three plays out of my wife's successful past.

1629   Can't you suggest something to put a finishing touch to my story?
Yeah — a match.

1630   I've written a play — there are one hundred characters and everybody's name is Smith.
Why?
Why not?

1631   Do you think I should write and throw my stuff into a waste basket for a while?
No — just throw yourself into the waste basket and save time.

1632   What is the name of your new play?
The Broken Leg!
That's a funny name. Why are you calling it the Broken Leg?
Because it's got such a large cast.

1633   My uncle opened a show and he called it: "Night Shirt."
Why?
Because he put it on one night and took it off the next day.

1634   Yes, once I got ten dollars a word.
Hmmm! How was that?
I talked back to the judge.

1635   What happened to that writer you introduced me to last week?
     I never heard of him anymore.
He uses a nom-de-plume.
Is that as good as a Remington?

1636   You waste too much paper.
But how can I economize?
By writing on both sides.
But you won't accept stories written on both sides of the sheet.
I know, but you'd save a lot of paper just the same.

1637   I suppose you wrote that yourself?
Yes, sir.
You should be encouraged.
Yes, sir.
You should go to Hollywood.
Yes, sir.
And you should climb the highest mountain.
Yes, sir.
And drop off!

1638   I would like to write a novel.
Do you know how to write?
Oh, I shall use a typewriter.

1639   He's achieved quite a lot of success as a ghost writer.
How do you mean?
Well, he is able to hire another ghost writer to write his ghost
    writing for him.

1640   This is quite well written, but my firm only publishes work by
    writers with well-known names.
Splendid! My name's Smith.

1641   A pun is a joke at which everyone groans, because they didn't
    think of it first.

1642   Did you read the mystery story I wrote?
No, I haven't.
Boy, it's horrible.
If you wrote it, it would be horrible.
It's called: "The North Pole." It will give you the shivers.

POET

1643   Do you think the great outstanding poem of the century has yet
    been written?
    It has not only been written, but it has been rejected.

1644   I'm like the poet, I long for the wings of a dove.
    Huh! Right now I'd rather have the breast of a chicken, 'long
    with a couple of drumsticks.

1645   Nobody recites: "I Stood on the Bridge at Midnight" anymore.
    It's too old-fashioned. The bridge used to be where a boy
    stood at midnight, but now midnight is where he finds out
    where he stands at bridge.

1646   Say it with flowers,
    Say it with sweets,
    Say it with kisses,
    Say it with eats,
    Say it with jewelry,
    Say it with drink,
    But always be careful
    Not to say it with ink.

1647   Poet: My heart is in the ocean.
    Seasick Friend: You've got me beat.

1648   Stone walls do not a prison make, nor iron bars a cage . . .
    No, but they do help!

1649   Roses are red — violets are white . . .
    Violets are blue, you sap.
    Violets are white — I saw them on the line this morning.

1650   The only thing worse than spring poetry is winter, fall, and sum-
    mer poetry.

1651   I'll read you my latest poem — Thirty days has September, April,
    June and my uncle.
    How could your uncle have thirty days?
    The judge gave it to him.
    What for and when?

Two weeks ago when he was doing his Christmas shopping early.
How early?
Before the store opened.

1652 Do you think there is any chance of my getting this poem in your
        magazine?
      There may be. I'm not going to live always.

                        RELATED SUBJECTS
                        Love 2595-2640

ARTIST

1653 Ist: I'm an artist.
      2nd: I'm an artist, also.
      3rd: Oh, I see — a pair of drawers!

1654 Are you the great animal painter?
      Yes; did you wish to sit for a portrait?

1655 I paint a picture in five days and think nothing of it.
      Neither do I.

1656 This is my latest picture. Builders at work. It's very realistic.
      But they aren't at work.
      I know. That's the realism.

1657 They stole a Van Dyke — it was very valuable. It's very valu-
        able to posterity. Of course, you know what a Van Dyke is?
      Oh, sure, it's a pointed beard.

1658 Shall I paint you in a frock coat?
      Oh, don't make any fuss — just wear your smock.

1659 You say that I am the first model you ever kissed?
      Yes.
      And how many models have you had before me?
      Four — an apple, two oranges and a vase of flowers.

1660 Most famous artists die in poverty.
      Yeah, but I had to live in it.

1661 My brother's an artist.
      Don't be silly — he can't draw.
      Well, I heard my mother say he's the most realistic freak in the
        circus and he drew well.

1662 The most realistic drawing I ever drew was a sketch of a decayed
        apple.
      It must have been rotten.

1663 Here's a picture I just painted of the boys in the Senior class at
        college.
      Why, it looks like an empty room.
      Well, all the boys graduated.

1664   What are you drawing?
       I just drew a picture of a dog eating bones.
       That's interesting, but where are the bones?
       Oh, well, the dog ate all the bones.
       And where's the dog?
       You don't expect the dog to stay there after he'd eaten all the
          bones.

1665   My brother painted a picture of Santa Claus and it was so na-
          tural they had to take it down off the wall every month.
       Why?
       To give him a haircut.

1666   You look like an old Rembrandt.
       Is that so? Well, you don't look so snappy yourself.

1667   Do you think you can make a good portrait of my wife?
       My friend, I can make it so lifelike you'll jump every time you
          see it.

1668   Ah! What is this? It is superb? What soul! What expression!
          A step forward in art!
       Yeah! That's where I clean the paint off my brushes.

1669   We've just bought a Rembrandt.
       How many cylinders?

1670   I painted something for last year's academy.
       Was it hung?
       Yes, near the entrance where everybody could see it.
       Congratulations! What was it?
       A sign saying: Keep to the left.

1671   Here's the Mona Lisa.
       Aw, come on! That dame's smile reminds me of my wife's when
          she thinks I'm lying.

1672   How do you account for your success as a futuristic painter?
       I use a model with hiccups.

1673   What's this?
       A portrait of a lady.
       The guy that painted it must have been a woman hater.

1674   That's a fine portrait! Is it an old master?
       No, that's the old missus.

1675   An artist just drew my picture. Do you like it?
       It's beautiful, but it doesn't look like you.
       I know — I was busy, so my brother posed for it.

1676   My wife doesn't like the portrait you did of me at all—says it
          isn't natural.

I knew it! Didn't I tell you repeatedly, at each sitting, that you were not drinking enough?

1677 You should have a lot of money since you're an artist.
I ain't doing so good. I painted a picture of a lady and she said: The picture is terrible—I look just like a monkey.
I hope you were diplomatic about it.
Yes, I said to her: You should have thought about that before you had your picture painted.

> RELATED SUBJECTS
> Picture 325-337
> Sculptor 1681-1684
> Beauty 4725-4735

MODEL

1678 She's a model — models lingerie. Sort of a model of the undie world.
1679 I worked for a Steamship Builder.
Typist?
No, model.

1680 And do you like this model?
Yes, what's her name?

> RELATED SUBJECTS
> Beauty 4725-4735

SCULPTOR

1681 He said you were a sculptor but you should wash more often.
Are you sure that's what he said?
Well, he said you were a dirty chiseler.

1682 I wonder how long it took him to become a sculptor.
What makes you think he's a sculptor?
I heard my brother say: There goes Jim, the dirty chiseler.

1683 Sculptors run in my family.
Yeah, somebody told me your family was a bunch of chiselers.

1684 Why have you given the general such a peculiar pose?
You see, it was started as an equestrian statue, and the committee found they couldn't afford the horse.

> RELATED SUBJECTS　　　　　　　Artist 1653-1677
> Description of People 263-303　　Beauty 4725-4735

MUSICIAN

1685 I read the other day about a remarkable man who played the piano, and yet he had no hands.

That's wonderful, of course. And yet he has nothing on plenty of guys I hear on the radio every day. They sing — and yet they have no voices.

1686   I don't like that violinist. Something wrong with him. Something missing.
       Maybe it's a tin cup.

1687   She must be very musical.
       How can you tell?
       By the chords in her neck.

1688   Do you play any tunes?
       I play the piano some, but I just play to kill time.
       You certainly picked a marvelous weapon. I suppose you play by ear.
       I play by note.
       By note?
       I gave them $10 down and a note for the balance.

1689   How was your organ lesson?
       Fine, and my teacher is so religious.
       How's that?
       Every time I play, he cries, "Oh, my God! My God!"

1690   Why do you always cry when you play the violin.
       I don't know — but every time I play tears come to my eyes.
       Why not stuff cotton in your ears?

1691   My daughter's music lessons are a fortune to me.
       How is that?
       They enable me to buy the neighbors' houses at half price.

1692   What is your occupation?
       I used to be an organist.
       And why did you give it up?
       The monkey died.

1693   You play a mean violin. Where did you study?
       I studied with the same teacher Rubinoff studied with.
       Oh, you fiddled around together?

1694   I hear that you are a musician.
       No, but I own a saxophone.

1695   Why do you always play the same piece?
       It haunts me.
       It should, you've murdered it often enough.

1696   She put him on his feet. She was a piano player. She played the piano from morning until night and the only piece she knew was the Star Spangled Banner.

1697   I have an uncle that's conceited. He's seven feet tall and plays the flute.
      What makes you think he's conceited just because he's seven feet tall and plays the flute?
      Well, that's hi-flutin', isn't it?

1698   Been taking violin lessons for three years but can't play so good.
      Why not?
      Well, the first two years I didn't have a violin to practice on.

1699   (Musician playing cornet on Sunday)
      Clergyman: Do you know the Fourth Commandment, my good man?
      Musician: No, but if you will just whistle it over, I'll do my best.

1700   Musician: Well, all right, since you insist. What shall I play?
      Host: Anything you like. It is only to annoy the neighbors.

1701   He plays like he's possessed.
      He should—the piano was just re-possessed this morning.

1702   You say your son plays the piano like Paderewski?
      Yes. He uses both hands.

1703   I hope my husband wasn't rude when he asked you not to play.
      Oh, no, 'e ask me that I not play a certain tune.
      What did he say?
      'E say, don't play "For Ze Love Of Mike."

RELATED SUBJECTS
Music 1747-1752
Orchestra 1753-1758
Musical Instruments 1759-1783

SINGER

1704   Why is father singing to the baby so much tonight?
      He is trying to sing him to sleep.
      Well, if I was baby, I'd pretend I was asleep.

1705   She's a diva.
      A what?
      A diva!
      Why, she can't even swim.

1706   Whenever I sing I cry.
      Why do you sing?
      So I can cry.
      Why do you cry?
      Because I can't sing.

1707   I envy the man who sang the tenor solo.
       Really? I thought he had a very poor voice.
       So did I, but just think of his nerve.

1708   Yes, I'm continually breaking into song.
       If you'd ever get in key, you wouldn't have to break in.

1709   I'll have you understand my voice is very rich.
       Well, why don't you retire it?

1710   How about a song?
       Who, me?
       Yeah.
       Not me — I'll do my singing in the old bathtub.
       Don't sing very often, do you?

1711   After I'd sung my encore, I heard a gentleman from one of the
          newspapers call out: Fine! Fine!
       Dear me — and did you have to pay it?

1712   Can you sing opera?
       Of course!
       Do you sing Faust?
       I sing faust or slow — any kind you want.

1713   (Someone singing grand opera)
       What is that noise?
       That's Madame Sourpuss practicing her singing lesson.
       Oh, I thought somebody was being tortured.

1714   (After listening to a girl sing).
       I would call you a howling success.

1715   Can you carry a tune?
       Certainly.
       Well, carry the one you just finished out in the yard and bury it.

1716   What did you get the little medal for?
       For singing?
       What did you get the big medal for?
       For stopping.

1717   Shall I sing it with gusto?
       No—sing it alone.

1718   I once belonged to the fish quartette.
       What's that?
       The fish quartette is—First Tuna, Second Tuna, Third Barra-
          cuda and Fourth Bass.

1719   How did yodeling originate?
       Well, one must do something in Switzerland.

1720   A moment there, my sweet one. What flat are you singing in?
       This ain't no flat, it's a theatre.

1721   You're an outstanding singer, aren't you?
       Yeah, I'm outstanding, but Madame Priss is inside sitting.

1722   What is your range?
       Gas.

1723   They tell me that during this song there will be a chorus of
       mixed voices, but I hope they will get straightened out before
       they finish the song.

1724   How is your range?
       Full of gas.

1725   Mrs. Bottomsup, you'd better go up to the bathroom at once. I
       can't make out whether your husband is scalding to death or
       singing.

1726   Your voice surprises me.
       I studied and spent $1,000,000 to learn to sing.
       I would love to have you meet my brother.
       Is he a singer, too?
       No, he's a lawyer. He'll get your money back.

1727   My girl is a singer.
       Is she a finished soprano?
       No, but the neighbors almost finished her last night.

1728   She is a beautiful girl.
       Not bad. But she's a better singer.
       I should certainly like to marry her.
       She is a coloratura.
       I would like to marry her anyway.

1729   Where did you get the song you just sang?
       The composer of that number died when he was 25 years old.
       That was unfortunate — he should have died about twenty years
       sooner.

1730   What made you give up singing in the choir?
       I was absent one Sunday and someone asked if the organ had
       been fixed.

1731   I sang in a girl's trio once.
       Marvelous! What did you sing?
       A song.
       What voice?
       My own voice.
       No, what key did you sing in?
       I didn't sing in a key, silly—I sang in a night club.

1732   Why do you always go to the window and lean out when I start singing?
I want to let the neighbors know it isn't me that's singing.

1733   I'm going to take a bath.
Well, don't sing that long song you generally sing in the bathtub —we haven't much soap left.

1734   Can you imagine anything worse than that solo?
Yes, the quartette—it's four times as bad.

1735   When I sing people clap their hands.
Yeah, clap them over their ears.

1736   Yes, I'm a good singer.
Where did you learn to sing?
I graduated from a correspondence school.
Boy, you sure lost lots of your mail.

1737   I'm going away to study singing.
Good! How far away?

1738   It seems to me that I have seen you before.
You have, your honor. I gave your daughter singing lessons.
Thirty years.

1739   If you want to go over big, you must sing louder.
I'm singing as loud as I can.
Well, man, be enthusiastic. Open your mouth and throw yourself into it.

> RELATED SUBJECTS
> Music 1747-1752
> Orchestra 1753-1758
> Theatre 4506-4512
> Radio 4598-4610

SONG TITLES

1740   (Singing) Old Lady River . . . Old Lady River . . .
No — it's Old Man River — not old Lady River . . .
Never mind — I'm singing about Mississippi.

1741   Did you hear the new chump song?
What is it?
Everything I have is yours.

1742   Income Tax Song: Everything I have is yours.

1743   Do you know the Arthur song?
No, what is it?
Arthur any more at home like you?

1744   Repeal song: The return of the swallow by Gulp.

1745   How about your old friend, Chic Sale, the specialist?
He wasn't a specialist — he was a song writer.
What did he write?
"I Have to Pass Your House to Get to My House."

1746   Do you know *The Road to Mandalay?*
Yes, do you want me to sing it?
No — take it.

RELATED SUBJECTS
Musician 1685-1703

MUSIC

1747   I like Faust.
George Washington sang in Faust.
George Washington sang in Faust?
Yeah — Faust in War, Faust in Peace and Faust in the hearts
of his countrymen.

1748   I say, whatever key were you playing in?
Skeleton key.
Skeleton key — whatever do you mean?
Fits anything.

1749   When Jake's dog tipped over a table in the cafe, four waiters
dropped their trays at the same time, and two couples got up
to dance, thinking it was a new rock number.

1750   She: What is the name of that piece the orchestra is playing?
He: I don't know. Let's ask one of the boys in the orchestra.
She: (to man playing piano) What's that you're playing?
Player: A piano — lady — a piano.

1751   Can that orchestra play hot music?
Say and how! The last time they played they were so hot it started
the automatic sprinkler.

1752   Do you like Beethoven's works?
Never visited 'em. Wot does 'e manufacture?

RELATED SUBJECTS
Musician 1685-1703
Musical Instruments 1759-1783
Dancing 3584-3603
Theatre 4506-4512
Radio 4598-4610

ORCHESTRA

1753 Does your orchestra ever play by request?
A lot of times.
Ask them to play pinochle.

1754 I wonder what all those mummies over there are?
Don't be silly — those are the orchestra boys.

1755 Why did you pick the grocer to play the bass drum in your band?
Because he's an honest fellow and gives full weight to every pound.

1756 I can't keep my eyes off that man over there in the orchestra.
Which one?
The one with the big brass horn wound around his neck.
That's the tuba player. Why can't you keep your eyes off of him?
He sure is wrapped up in his work.

1757 (At concert)
What's that book the conductor keeps looking at?
That's the score of the overture.
Oh, really — who's winning?

1758 We were afraid someone would think of this new instrument — the combination of the violin and the saxophone.

> RELATED SUBJECTS
> Musician 1685-1703
> Dancing 3584-3603
> Chorus Girl 4563-4565
> Radio 4598-4610

MUSICAL INSTRUMENTS

1759 (Throws piano out window)
Why, you've thrown my piano out the window.
It was out of tune, anyway.

1760 My wife used to play the piano a lot, but since the children came she doesn't have time.
Children are a comfort, aren't they?

1761 Look at that cotton handkerchief on the violinist's shoulder. How can he get music out of a cotton handkerchief?
By blowing his nose.

1762 Would you donate five dollars to bury a saxophone player?
Here's thirty dollars, bury six of 'em.

1763 Don't you love the sweet moan of the saxophone player?
I'd rather hear his death rattle.

1764 Why don't you but a tiara for her — something for her head?

She doesn't have a headache.
How about a coronet?
That's like a saxophone?
No, it isn't a musical instrument.
Neither is a saxophone.

1765   What's the matter with the piccolo player?
He bent down to snipe a cigar butt and someone stepped on his
hand and broke two fingers and now he plays blue notes.

1766   There's one guy who is always up to his chin in music.
Who's he?
The violinist.

1767   I want to buy a hat for my brother.
What size?
It doesn't matter.
What do you mean—it doesn't matter?
I don't care what size it is—it's for his trombone.

1768   My aunt in Venice is sending me a gondola for Christmas. How
am I going to play it?
You don't play a gondola.
No?
No, you throw it over your shoulder like a shawl.

1769   A man offered $100 a string to me to stop playing the violin.
Did you stop?
Yeah—now I'm learning to play the harp.

1770   Your wife just eloped with the saxophone player who lives next
door?
Yes.
You take it rather calm—you don't seem to be surprised or
excited!
No, there's no reason to be. We stood the saxophone groaning
as long as we could. This morning the wife and I tossed to
see who should get rid of him. She lost.

1771   Your son is making good progress with his violin. He is beginning
to play quite nice tunes.
Do you really think so? We were afraid that we'd merely got
used to it.

1772   I've just got rid of my saxophone in part exchange for a new car.
I didn't think they accepted things like that for a car.
Well, this case was an exception. The dealer happened to be our
next door neighbor.

1773   I took up the accordion, but I got so fat it pinched my stomach and
I had to quit playing it.

1774   Before I learned to play the saxophone I used to be troubled with my neighbors, but now I haven't any neighbors.

1775   And he's dedicating this song to all the cats who gave up their lives to become fiddle strings.

1776   They laughed when he sat down to play the piano; when they saw how tight his pants were they nearly split.

1777   He's a saxophone player.
How did he get that bump on his head?
Playing a saxophone.
Oh, in front of someone's house?
No, in front of the trombone player.

1778   Whatever possessed a little man like you to learn to play the bass horn?
Well, on a cold night I find it much warmer than a cornet.

1779   I don't think the gentleman next door knows much about music.
Why?
Well, he told me this morning to cut my drum open and see what was inside it.

1780   I want a small place in an isolated position — somewhere at least five miles from any other house.
I see, sir — you want to practice the simple life.
Not at all. I want to practice the cornet.

1781   I see you advertised your saxophone for sale.
Yes, I saw my neighbor in the hardware store yesterday buying a gun.

1782   These expensive violins are worth one hundred dollars, but I'll take $10.
There must be a string attached to it.

1783   And then, of course, there's the musical carpenter. He plays on the two-b'four.

RELATED SUBJECTS
Musician 1685-1703
Music 1747-1752

INVENTOR

1784   Father, did Edison make the first talking machine?
No, my son, God made the first talking machine, but Edison made the first one that could be cut off.

1785 What do you think of my new invention?

I don't know what to say, professor. It's all right, except do you know that you have stuck a banana in your ear?

What? What did you say? I can't hear you when I have this banana stuck in my ear.

1786 My brother has discovered a new kind of cream—vanishing cream. It makes everything disappear.

Why doesn't he experiment with you?

1787 My brother has a new invention. A hollow piece of soap, so there won't be any useless little pieces left over after people have used it.

1788 What's your new invention like?

I'm making shoes out of old banana skins.

What kind of shoes could anyone make out of old banana skins?

Slippers.

1789 My uncle invented a machine where you put in a nickel and get a new wife.

Why doesn't he invent a machine where you put in a wife and get a new nickel?

1790 I'm working on a new invention, and this one will be very popular.

What is it?

Equipping the nozzle of a bottle with a zipper.

1791 He will make a fortune this Thanksgiving, too.

What's he doing?

He has invented a cranberry gun to shoot turkeys. You just aim the gun at the turkey, and when the turkey is shot, then it's ready to serve.

1792 What kind of an instrument is a rank?

I don't know what you're talking about.

Well, I was reading a book and it said: Edison was an inventor of the first rank.

1793 My brother is becoming quite an inventor, too. He's following Luther Burbank's footsteps.

How is that?

Grafting. He combines cucumbers with sweet potatoes so that the pickles won't be so sour.

1794 My brother invented a smokeless tobacco.

How does he make it smokeless?

He chews it.

1795 I have a new invention—it is shaped like a pistol, is the color of a pistol, and the same size as a pistol. Do you know what it is?

No—what?
A pistol.

1796 What's that you've got?
An invention I'm making for a radio set.
What is it?
A combination of nuts and wisecracks.

1797 I've got a new idea. Fortune in it.
What now?
It's an alarm clock that emits the delicious odors of frying bacon and fragrant coffee.

1798 I have a new sure fire invention. Mattresses with zippers.
Mattresses with zippers? What for?
So old maids won't have to get out of bed to see who's under it.

1799 They told me you are the man who invented spaghetti. Where did you ever get the idea of spaghetti?
Out of my noodle.

1800 My brother invented something to do away with insomnia.
It's a good idea, but think of all the sheep it will put out of work.

1801 My brother has a new invention and it's very practical, too.
What is it?
He makes chickens swim in hot water so they'll lay hard boiled eggs.

RELATED SUBJECTS
Cross-Breeding 3867-3871

ACTION

CONDUCT (IN GENERAL)

1802 When you arrive, give the Committee your name, give the doorman your card, the butler your coat and hat . . .
Yeah, I know — and the footman my shoes. I know my manners, I've been to those joints before.

1803 I kept regular hours for ten years.
What were you in for?

1804 He's a very nice man — he never goes any place without his wife, but his wife will go ANY place.

1805 Now, Junior, recite the poem Mama taught you — go ahead — recite the poem.

First give me a spanking.

Not now, Junior.

Hit me now and then I'll cry and then you'll give me a nickel to stop — then I'll recite the poem.

1806   He's never been known to steal a thing.

Fine.

He's been watched too close.

1807   Don't you smoke?

No, I don't smoke.

Do you drink?

No, I don't drink.

Do you kiss?

No, I don't kiss.

What do you do for fun?

Throw eggs into an electric fan.

1808   I see your father raised you properly.

Raised me? He used to raise me a foot off the floor when he raised me.

1809   I've been misbehaving and my conscience is troubling me.

I see, and since I'm a psychiatrist you want something to strengthen your will power?

No, something to weaken my conscience.

1810   He's always been a perfect gentleman with me.

He bores me, too.

1811   Joe, the gangster, is taking lessons in deportment.

How's he doing?

Fine. Two more weeks and he'll be deported.

1812   My brother certainly embarrassed me last evening.

Was he drinking?

No, he wasn't drinking. He did it without rum or reason.

1813   They are certainly nice people around here. When I first got here, the usher threw me out the side entrance for sitting in the wrong place. I said: See here, I come from an old aristocratic family. Then the usher came outside, picked me up, brought me back in and threw me out the front entrance.

1814   I saw a young man trying to kiss your daughter in the park last night!

Did he succeed?

No.

Then it wasn't my daughter.

1815   So you never let a man kiss you good night?

No, by the time he leaves me it's always morning.

1816   There were just two slices of cake left on the plate, and both Jim
        and Fred wanted one. Being courteous, Jim held both out to
        his companion, but to his surprise, Fred ignored good man-
        ners and chose the larger slice.
        Jim: Don't you have any manners? Why, if you had offered them
        to me, I'd have taken the smaller piece.
        Fred: So what's your problem? That's what you got, isn't it?

1817   May I sit on your right hand at dinner?
        I may need it to eat with, but you may hold it awhile.

1818   She: My lawyer told me to say "No" to everything.
        He: Do you mind if I hold your hand?
        She: No.
        He: Do you mind if I put my arm around you?
        She: N-n-no.
        He: We're going to have a lot of fun if you're on the level about
        this.

1819   Mother: Where do bad little girls go?
        Girl: Most everywhere.

1820   Stop reaching — haven't you got a tongue?
        Yes, but my arms are longer.

1821   Does your husband know any parlor tricks?
        No, he's house-broken.

1822   I went to a hotel — we had tea.
        Is that what they call it now?
        I paid for it. Then we went to dinner and I paid for that.
        I'll go out with you sometime myself.
        Then we went to a night club. I paid for that.
        And then I took her home. Should I have kissed her good night?
        No, you did enough for her.

1823   You should eat right.
        Eat right? The trick is to eat at all.

1824   Johnny, I wish you'd be a good little boy.
        I'll be good for a nickel.
        The idea! Why can't you be like your father, good for nothing?

1825   Who was that lady I seen you eating with last night?
        That was no lady, that was my knife.

1826   I'm so mad, I feel like going to the devil. How do you feel?
        I feel like the devil.

1827   My father said if I gave up all my bad habits he'd present me
        with $10,000.
        And you didn't do it?

Of course not. With no bad habits, what would I do with the money?

1828   He treats her like a dog.
       How do you mean?
       Lap dog.

1829   If you're not a good little girl you won't go to Heaven. Don't you
          want to go to Heaven?
       Well, I've been to the circus and the automobile show and to
          Europe. I can't expect to go everywhere.

1830   Did you ever have a romance in your life?
       I had a beautiful school teacher. Was she lovely? One day she
          asked me to stay after school.
       Did you do anything wrong?
       Yes. I didn't stay.

1831   She could dish it out—but she couldn't cook it.

1832   Never break your bread or roll in your soup.

1833   One more crack out of you and I'm going to give you a good
          spanking.
       It wouldn't be the first time I've been spanked.
       So you've been spanked before!
       Spanked *before!* Why, I've been spanked as far back as I can
          remember.

1834   You'll drive me to my grave.
       Well, you didn't expect to walk there, did you?

1835   He isn't any good — never was any good and never will be any
          good. In fact, when he was born his mother should have thrown
          him away and kept the stork.

1836   This is no time for flippancy.
       For what?
       Flippancy. Don't you know what flippancy is?
       You mean—when you take a coin and flippancy which one of you.

1837   Minister: And what does your mother do for you when you've
          been a good girl?
       Girl: She lets me stay home from church.

1838   Pop, how soon will I be old enough to do as I please?
       I don't know. Nobody has ever lived that long yet.

1839   The traffic officer says you got sarcastic with him.
       I didn't intend to be. He talked to me like my wife does and I
          forgot myself and answered: Yes, my dear.

1840   She treats her husband like a Grecian God.
       How's that?
       She places a burnt offering before him at every meal.

1841   I saw Brown the other day treating his wife the way I wouldn't
           treat a dog.
       Great Scott! What was he doing?
       Kissing her.

1842   Now, young man, before we drive any farther, I want to tell
           you that I don't flirt, so don't try to hold my hand or kiss me.
           Is that quite clear?
       Yes.
       Now, since that is settled and done with, where shall we go?
       Home.

1843   Do you lead a model life?
       No, I've done no posing.

1844   You made a jackass out of yourself at the party last night.
       How do you mean?
       By staying sober and acting your natural self.

1845   Could you pass the bread?
       I think I can. I moved pianos all summer.

1846   Say, your girl is a honey! Is she faithful?
       My girl is too good to be true.

1847   How did you get into the Vangergrit's party?
       Easy. I crashed the gate.
       You ought to watch where you're driving.

1848   Let's go and get drunk tonight.
       Can't. I'm minding the baby.
       What? Are you and Alice married?
       No, but she made me give up drinking and I'm minding her.

1849   A boy scout doesn't procrastinate.
       No, that's why I always do my good deed the first thing in the
           morning and get the darned thing over with.

1850   It is the duty of every one to make at least one person happy during
           the week. Have you done so, Freddy?
       Yes.
       That's right. What did you do?
       I went to see my aunt, and she was happy when I went home.

1851   I notice you're getting to be a gentleman. I noticed that you
           opened the barn door for your mother when she came in tonight.
       Shucks, that's nothing. I do the same thing for the cows every night.

1852   She bawled me out for eating with my fingers. But I've always said if food wasn't clean enough to pick up with your fingers, it wasn't fit to eat.

1853   (Making noises like animal)
What's the matter with you?
It's just the animal in me.

1854   So your new girl's a perfect lady?
Sure — she always makes me take off my hat before I kiss her.

1855   Dad, you are going to take me to the circus next week, aren't you?
Yes, my son. But only if you are very good.
Well, Dad, I'm going to try awfully hard, because if you can't take me you won't have any excuse for going yourself. I don't want to disappoint you.

1856   You promised me you would mend your ways this year — I can't see you've done it yet!
And have you never heard of invisible mendin'?

1857   My uncle died from politeness.
Died from politeness?
Yeah, he was a deep sea diver and he saw a mermaid and tipped his hat.

1858   Are you a man of settled habits?
Oh, yes; I've settled down to a constant round of drinking, smoking and carousing.

1859   Mother: You good-for-nothing! Why don't you take a pattern from your father?
Son: What has he done?
Mother: Why, he has just got two years off his sentence for good conduct.

1860   Father: D in work, D in effort, D in conduct. That settled it, Wilbur. From now on, you and I are through.
Son: Stop kiddin' yourself, pop. Just remember that I'm still an exemption on your income tax return.

1861   Go right down the hall, turn to the left and you'll see a sign that says: Gentlemen. Don't pay any attention to the sign — go right on in.

1862   That girl's a lady, I tell you.
Say, what makes you so doggone sure?
Look at the sign on that door she just went in.

RELATED SUBJECTS
Fight 2145-2213

Temper 2276-2284
Chivalry 2466-2474
Honesty 2490-2499
Right 2503-2507
Insult 2508-2518
Apology 2519-2520
Punishment 2521-2524
Unfaithfulness 3057-3088
Table Manners 4881-4883

IMPERSONATION

1863   Did you reprimand your little boy for mimicking me?
Yes, I told him not to act like a fool.

1864   Sure I can act! Look! (Imitates something)
You mean, you're a mimic.
Don't try to fool me — a mimic is sixty seconds.

1865   Imitation is the sincerest flattery.
Still, you wouldn't want me to step out with your best girl, would you?

1866   My uncle imitates worms for a living.
You mean he lies on the sidewalk in the rain?
No, he makes holes in antique furniture.

1867   I'm rather good at imitations. I imitate almost any bird you can name.
How about a homing pigeon?

1868   Stop acting like a fool!
I'm NOT acting!

RELATED SUBJECTS
Lying 1540-1564
Dishonesty 2500-2502
Actor 4514-4585
Radio 4598-4610

WILL POWER

1869   I thought you were a vegetarian.
I am.
Then why did you order steak?
I just wanted to test my will.

1870   I feel like whipping you, son.
Don't give in to your feelings, dad.

1871   Well, Constance, will you go for a ride with me tonight?
Sure — if you let your Constance be your guide.

1872 I hope she didn't weaken.
No, she didn't weaken. When I came back she was still kissing him.

1873 Resist the temptation.
I would, but it may never come again.

RELATED SUBJECTS
Mind 1162-1258
Conduct 1802-1862
Success 1945-1966

AMBITION

1874 I heard you refused a job of president of the company!
Yeah, there was no chance for advancement!

1875 You haven't any more ambition than a worm.
I don't know whether I have or not. I don't know any worms.

1876 I love to hear the alarm clock ring. I can't understand people who curse it as an interrupter of sweet repose. To me it seems the symbol of existence itself. It is the sign that the great city has awakened from its slumber, that a new day is beginning — that the streets and buildings will soon be filled with surging, progressive life. Faithful servant! I love to hear the alarm clock ring.
My, you're ambitious. What is your business?
I am a night watchman.

1877 (Two college presidents discussing what they'd like to do when they retire)
1st President: I'd like to be superintendent of an orphan asylum, so I'd never get any letters from parents.
2nd President: Well, I've a much better ambition. I want to be warden of a penitentiary. The alumni never come back to visit.

1878 I throw myself into everything I undertake.
Well, go out and dig a deep well.

1879 How old are you?
Twenty-seven.
Well, what do you expect to be in three years?
Thirty.

1880 Grass never grows under his feet.
A go-getter, eh?
No, a sailor.

1881 All you need to attain success is push — a little push will get you anywhere.

Oh yeah? Did you ever try to push on a door that was marked "pull"?

1882   And what, little girl, are you going to be when you grow up?
        I's donna be a blonde secretary so's my daddy will go out with
        me sometimes.

1883   Definition of a Go-Getter: A man who runs out of gas two
        miles from a station.

1884   You'll have to remember nobody ever layed down on the job and
        got results.
        What?
        Nobody ever layed down on the job and got results.
        Oh no? What about a hen?

1885   You know me — I throw myself into everything.
        I live over a lake — come over and see me sometime.

1886   Jack was the goal of my ambition, but alas!
        What happened, dear?
        Father kicked the goal.

1887   You should work hard and get ahead.
        I've got a head.

1888   What are you going to be when you grow up, daughter?
        I'm going to be either an artist or a dancer, because I don't think
        I'll be much good at this mother business.

1889   Why don't you get out and find a job? When I was your age
        I was working for $3 a week in a store and at the end of five
        years I owned the store.
        You can't do that nowadays. They have cash registers.

1890   I started out on the theory that the world had an opening for me.
        And you found it?
        Well, rather. I'm in the hole now.

1891   The secret of success is Pluck — all you need is PLUCK!
        Yes, but nowadays it's hard to find anyone to pluck.

1892   You know what a purpose is?
        Sure — a purpose is an Indian's baby.
        No — that's a papoose.
        A papoose? Why, that's the last car on a freight train.
        No — that's a caboose.
        A caboose? That's what you eat with corned beef. You know,
        corned beef and caboose.

1893   Dad, what was your great ambition when you were a kid?
        To wear long pants. And I've got my wish. If there's anybody

in this country that wears his pants longer than I do, I'd like
to see him.

RELATED SUBJECTS
Laziness 1967-1977
Opportunity 5585-5587

WORK

1894 Why do you work so hard?
I'm too nervous to steal.

1895 Wot excuse does he make fer not lookin' fer a job?
All of 'em.

1896 I guess my brother will be working now for a long time.
What makes you think so?
Well, he's working for a china warehouse and every time he
breaks a vase it is deducted from his pay check.

1897 Are you independent on your new job?
I should say so! I go to work at any time I want to before 7 and
quit any time I get ready after 5 o'clock.

1898 One of the workers on Riverside Drive was complaining because
he had no shovel. He finally told the foreman about it. Gee,
whiz, I haven't any shovel, he said.
Well, whaddaya kickin' about? You don't have to do any work if
you ain't got no shovel.
Well, I know, but I haven't got anything to lean on—like the
other guys.

1899 I just dreamed that I had a job.
I suppose that's why you're looking so tired.

1900 If you love work, why don't you find it?
Alas, lady, love is blind.

1901 Wife: Mrs. Terry's husband got a job yesterday.
Husband: Ain't it terrible, Molly, what some people will do
for money?

1902 Why doesn't your uncle go to work?
My uncle is a regular steam engine.
He's a good worker?
No, he's a good whistler.

1903 So your uncle didn't want to leave the prison?
No. He told the Warden it would be a pretty hard job to get
any work to do in his line nowadays.

What is his line?
He's a horse thief.

1904   You're in for a lot of hard work.
        I'll come out on top.
        How do you know you'll come out on top?
        Because my hair is falling out.

1905   It looks like I'll be looking for a job soon.
        Not worrying, are you?
        Seems somebody ought to be able to find work for me to do the
            little work I do. You don't know nobody that wants to hire
            nobody to do nothing, do you?

1906   If your wife made you go out and look for a job, what would
            you look for?
        A new wife.

1907   I'm leaving my work next week.
        Why are you leaving your work?
        Because I can't take it with me.

1908   I'm a steady worker.
        Yeah, and if you were any steadier, you would be motionless.

1909   Why did your brother quit his job?
        He said ·he didn't want to keep a horse out of work.

1910   I'll bet you're one of those people that drop their work and beat
            it as soon as the whistle blows.
        Not me. After I quit work I usually wait about five minutes for
            the whistle to blow.

1911   He is a pretty dependable fellow.
        Yeah — you can always depend on him not to work.

1912   Did your husband love you very much?
        Love me? He wouldn't even leave me to go to work.

1913   I know a place where you can get a job working for your meals.
        Oh, that wouldn't pay me — I eat so little.

1914   My father's very kind hearted.
        Kind hearted? Why, he'd rather see his family starve than work.
        Yeah — he looks out for his family. He sits in the window all
            day — says somebody has to look out for the family.

1915   My brother's in jail, but it isn't his fault.
        Oh, it isn't his fault?
        No, he went down to the Post Office to mail a letter — and you
            know he's been looking for work, so he was tickled to death
            when he saw a poster saying: MAN WANTED FOR ROBBERY IN

FRESNO. He told them he'd take the job — had had a lot of experience. Then they arrested him.

1916   Why are you wearing a harness?
If I work like a horse, I want to look like a horse.

1917   My father is still on strike.
How long has he been on strike?
Sixty-five years.

1918   What's the matter? You sure look worried.
Work — work — nothing but work from morning till night.
How long have you been at it?
Oh, I start tomorrow!

1919   He is the idol of the family.
Yes, idle for twenty years.

1920   How many people work here?
Oh, about one out of every ten.

1921   Occupation, lady?
I toil not, neither do I spin.
Lily of the field — scribbled the questioner.

1922   One reason why it is dangerous to go to sleep on the job is that you might fall off of it.

1923   Why aren't you working?
The boss and I had a fight and he won't take back what he said.
What'd he say?
He said: You're fired.

1924   I work nights. I go to work at eight o'clock in the mornings and work until 4 in the afternoon.
Wait a minute. You work nights, but you go to work at eight in the morning and work until 4 in the afternoon?
Yeah, I don't like night work, so I do it in the daytime.

1925   She is one of our fellow workers.
All girls are fellow workers.

1926   I'm working my way through Reform School and I wondered if you had any locks I could pick.

1927   I'm working my way through college — if you take five subscriptions for the . . .
No!
Take three and I'll go through high school . . .
No!
If you would only take one, I'll go through grammar school.
Here's a dime — come back when you get through kindergarten.

1928   Feminist: Isn't it horrible how women are exploited?
        Man: Yes, yes, it's horrible.
        Feminist: Well, don't you think wives should be paid wages?
        Man: Sure, I do! Why do you think I send my wife out to work!

1929   Foreman: Hey, Johnson, that man is doing twice as much as you.
        Johnson: Yeah, and I keep telling him, but you can't teach him
            anything.

1930   Just why do you want a married man to work for you, rather
            than a bachelor?
        Well, a married man don't get so upset if I yell at him.

1931   If the boss doesn't take back what he said to me I shall leave.
        What did he say?
        You're fired!

1932   She's a dairy maid in a candy factory.
        Dairy maid in a candy factory?
        Yeah — she's milking hershies.

1933   It's no disgrace to work.
        That's what I tell my wife.

1934   Why don't you work? Hard work never killed anyone.
        You're wrong, lady. I lost both of my wives that way.

1935   I left my last place because I was told to do something I didn't
            like.
        Really! What was that?
        Look for another job.

1936   I hear you have a new job.
        Yeah.
        From all I hear about it, you should be fired with enthusiasm.
        I was.

1937   How long have you been working here?
        Ever since the day the boss threatened to fire me.

1938   I wish I were like the rivers.
        What for?
        To follow my course without leaving my bed.

1939   The only things he ever made were mistakes and cigarette ashes.

1940   Why did you quit your last job?
        I got mad at the boss.
        What for?
        He said I stole ten dollars.

Why didn't you make him prove it?
He did — that's what made me mad.

1941   I wish every year had three hundred and sixty-five days of rest.
Are you mad! Then we would have to work a day every fourth year.

1942   You'll never do in my store — why, you hadn't been here a week until you had both of my stenographers and the bookkeeper out on dates!
Well, didn't you tell me to get familiar with the stock?

1943   I'll carve out a career for myself.
I heard you were a chiseler.

1944   We have come to the parting of the ways. I've found that a jackass and a horse can't work together.
Don't you call me a horse.

RELATED SUBJECTS
Success 1945-1966
Laziness 1967-1977
Honesty 2490-2499
Marriage 2882-3051
Salary 3271-3280
Businessman 5309-5321
Occupations 5362-5380
Interview 5382-5385
Reference 5386-5387
Lateness 5388-5392
Salesman 5403-5416
Beggar 5518-5537

SUCCESS

1945   I just read about this writer who started out poor, but died a millionaire. They say he acquired it through industry, economy, continuous effort, perseverance, a touch of genius, and an uncle who died and left him a million dollars.

1946   I'm a self-made man.
Well, that's what comes from hiring cheap labor.

1947   The man who counts in this world is the cashier.

1948   May I ask you the secret of success?
There is no easy street. You just jump at your opportunity.
But how can I tell when my opportunity comes?
You can't. You've got to keep on jumping.

1949   Why did she turn him down?
       He's a self-made man and she didn't want to marry a hero wor-
       shipper.

1950   Smith, you have been employed by me for five years. To mark
       my appreciation of this you will henceforth be addressed as
       Mr. Smith.

1951   How're you doing?
       Well, I manage to keep my neck above water.
       Well, I should judge so by the color of it.

1952   Everything he touches turns to gold. Everything I touch, they
       make me put back.

1953   Was that one of your prominent citizens? I noticed you were
       very respectful and attentive to him.
       Yes, he's one of our early settlers.
       Early settlers? Why, he's quite a young man yeu.
       True enough. I mean he pays his bills the first of every month.

1954   I hear your son is getting on.
       Rather. Two years ago he wore my old suits . . . now I wear his.

1955   What's she got that you haven't got?
       Room rent.

1956   When he speaks, a whole nation listens.
       A man of importance, he?
       No, only a radio announcer.

1957   I have the key to success.
       Throw it away.
       Why?
       You won't need it — you're a successful failure now.

1958   I'm a self-made man, that's what I am — a self-made man.
       You knocked off work too soon.

1959   I don't mind telling you, I'm a self-made man.
       Well, it's mighty nice of you to take all the blame that way.

1960   I'll have you understand, I'm a self-made man.
       Well, I wouldn't boast about it.
       Was that a nice thing to say? I always try to be a gentleman.
       Oh, you do imitations, too?

1961   Did he serve the public?
       Yes, he ran a saloon.

1962   He comes from a very prominent family. When his grandfather
       passed on, all the stores in town closed, and the day after his
       father went away, all the banks closed.

1963 I'll give you to understand my father is a big man. He's a Lion
— a Moose — and an Elk.
Gee — how much does it cost to see him?

1964 The suit you had on the other night was about three sizes too
big for you.
I know it doesn't fit me here, but when I'm home it fits just
right.
Why shouldn't it fit you here?
Well, you see, I'm a much bigger man in my home town.

1965 My boy, there are two things which are vitally necessary if you
are to succeed in business.
What are they, dad?
Honesty and sagacity.
What is honesty?
Always — no matter what happens or how adversely it may
affect you — always keep your word once you have given it.
And sagacity?
Never give it.

1966 They're very prominent. Their furniture goes back to Louis the
14th; their silverware to Henry the 8th . . .
And their automobile goes back to the finance company tomorrow.

RELATED SUBJECTS
Ambition 1874-1893
Egotism 2305-2319
Opportunity 5585-5587

LAZINESS

1967 I have my breakfast served in my bedroom every morning.
Well, you're sure getting lazy.
Oh, I don't know — I sleep in the breakfast room.

1968 I've come to the conclusion you're the champion lazy man.
How does it feel to be the ex-champion?

1969   Those are my brother's ashes on the mantel.
        So the poor fellow has passed to the great beyond?
        Heck, no. He's just too lazy to find an ash tray.

1970   The height of laziness — the man who will stand with a cocktail
        shaker in his hand waiting for an earthquake.

1971   What does he do?
        Photographs eclipses.
        Don't you know that a real eclipse only comes once in ten years?
        I know, and if he is lucky he might not have to be there.
        What do you mean he might not be there?
        Well, it might come on his day off.

1972   I just adore lying in my bed in the morning and ringing my bell
        for my valet.
        My goodness, have you a valet?
        No, but I have a bell.

1973   You're so lazy you'll never die.
        What makes you think I'm so lazy I'll never die?
        Even the Lord will get tired waiting for you.

1974   There's Jim carrying two ladders at a time, and you're only
        taking one.
        Sure, he must be too lazy to go back twice.

1975   You know he is the laziest man in the world. He is so lazy,
        he doesn't even bother to make coffee. He just puts coffee in
        his mustache and drinks hot water.

1976   He worries all the time. He can't figure out whether to lay
        in bed all morning or get up early so he'll have a longer day
        to loaf.

1977   He's been sitting there all day, doing nothing but wasting his
        time.
        How do you know?
        Because I've been watching him.

ADVICE

1978   What do you know about marriage?
Well, I don't know so much. I admit I haven't been married. I'm no hen either. But I'm a better judge of a good egg than any hen in this State.

1979   Just bide your time . . .
Can I bite my nails, too?

1980   How to be clever: When dancing always wear a feathered turban so your cleverness will be indicated to every one by the smiles of the young men when being tickled.

1981   Don't take your troubles to bed.
My wife won't sleep alone.

1982   Lawyer: Seventy-five dollars, please.
Client: What for?
Lawyer: My advice.
Client: I'm not taking it.

1983   You can catch more flies with sugar than vinegar.
Yes, but what do I want with flies?

1984   Do you think a father of 20 should marry again?
No, that's enough kids for anybody.

1985   Why don't you go to a lawyer?
My brother said any fool could advise me — so I came to you.

1986   Dear So and So: I love a homely girl with a sour disposition, but another girl who is beautiful and has a barrel of dough is nuts over me. Which one should I marry?
Dear Sir: By all means marry the one you love — and send me the other one's name and address.

1987   You know, Nora, our youngest daughter, is nearly seventeen years old, so today I had a frank discussion with her about the facts of life.
Ah! Did you learn anything new?

1988   What would you do if you were in my shoes?
I'd get a shine.

1989   Mrs. Lipsky: You never take any good advice.
Mr. Lipsky: No, if I did you'd be an old maid still.

RELATED SUBJECTS
Doctor 838-860
Friend 1037-1056
Mother 3262-3266
Father 3267-3270
Attorney 5235-5244

SPENDTHRIFT

1990   He's getting to be a spendthrift — he bought an all day sucker at six o'clock at night.

1991   You took her out and only spent five dollars on her?
Yeah, that's all she had.

1992   (Man arguing about price — stranger enters argument)
Man: You keep out of this. Whose money am I spending, yours or hers?

1993   Only yesterday I lit my cigar with a twenty dollar bill.
How extravagant!
It was a bill from my dentist, and I wasn't going to pay it anyway.

1994   You accuse me of reckless extravagance. When did I ever make a useless purchase?
Why, there's that fire extinguisher you bought a year ago. We've never used it once.

1995   Say, I spent $2 on my girl last night.
Only $2?
Yeah, that's all she had.

1996   I took my girl to dinner last night. Did I take her to a swell dinner!
That's rather nice of you taking her out — it costs money.
She's worth it. It cost a dime. I phoned her and went to her house for dinner.

RELATED SUBJECTS
Scotchman 1102-1133
Family 3209-3217
Money 5457-5479
Bank 5487-5494

ECONOMY

1997   I can tell you how to save money. You live in one room and let your girl live in the room next to you.
How will that save money?
Well, she will be living practically next to nothing.

1998   My cousin has found a way to cut his grocery bill in half.
You mean, he doesn't only eat half as much?
No, he eats the same amount, but his wife goes without her half.

1999   Are all your family as stingy as you are?
I'm not so stingy. You should know my uncle. One day my uncle walked down the street and he found a package of cough drops. That night he made his wife sleep out in the cold to catch a cold.

2000   That candy you're eating looks good.
It is good.
It makes my mouth water.
To show you what a good guy I am, here's a blotter.

2001   Are you going to give me a tip?
Not me.
Even the champion tightwad gives me a nickel.
Shake hands with the new champion!

2002   He's so economical, he puts glue in his mustache so his kisses will last longer.

2003   Don't tell me your boy friend is so tight you had to pay for your own dinner?
I had to pay for his, too.

2004   Ah, I see you have a dog. I thought you didn't like dogs.
Well, I don't. But my wife picked up a lot of dog soap at a bargain sale, so we had to get a dog.

2005   Your father is so stingy he looks over the tops of his glasses to keep from wearing them out.
He isn't stingy — he's just economical.
That must be a new name for being tight. He is closer than the next minute. He's so economical he hasn't spent eleven dollars in five years.
That's not so economical. My brother is more economical than that. He hasn't spent a cent in fifteen years.
Really?
But he'll be out next Thursday.

2006   The average man wouldn't worry about his wife wearing her skirts a little shorter, if only she'd wear her dresses a little longer.

2007   An "economy luncheon" menu begins with beef broth and ends with mince pie: it definitely makes both ends meat.

2008   We should get married, darling. Two can live as cheap as one.
Yeah, but it's worth the difference to me to stay single.

2009   Are you saving half the money you earn?
Naw, I don't earn that much.

2010   The stingiest man we know of is the one who gave his little girl a nickel not to eat any supper, who took the nickel away from her while she was asleep, and then refused to give her any breakfast because she lost it.

2011   He bites his nails.
Why, because he's nervous?
No — so he can't pick up cafe checks.

2012   He's the first to put his hand in his pocket.
       Yes, and keep it there.

2013   I'll give you a nice new shining penny.
       I'd rather have a nasty, dirty old dime.

2014   I'm going to give my uncle a check for $10,000 for his Christ-
       mas present.
       But you haven't got $10,000 in the bank.
       That doesn't matter. He wouldn't cash the check. He's so stingy,
       he'd save it.

2015   Mr. Househunter: I don't care for those apartments we looked at
       today. The rooms are too narrow, and the ceilings are too low.
       Mrs. Househunter: But they are cheap, dear; and you and I are
       neither very wide not very high.

2016   He's so cheap he never takes anything but a sponge bath.

2017   I got in a show last night scotfree.
       How's that?
       The other fellow paid.

2018   He should be clean — I hear he's always sponging.

2019   Have you got anything put away for a rainy day?
       Yeah — an umbrella.

2020   And another thing, following this budget you can cut living ex-
       penses in half.
       I have an idea how we can live on less than that.
       How?
       Live on two budgets.

2021   Well, I always keep my money in an old stocking at home.
       But you lose the interest that way.
       No I don't — I put a bit extra away for that.

2022   All the cheap skates are not on hockey players.

2023   I suppose your uncle takes your aunt out occasionally?
       No, he's so stingy the only thing he takes out is his teeth.

2024   He's so tight he keeps five dollar bills folded so long, Lincoln
       gets ingrowing whiskers.

2025   Why is your gown lemon color?
       Because I had such a hard time to squeeze it out of you.

2026   He is so stingy he heats the knives so his wife won't use too
       much butter.

2027   I wonder why it is we can't save anything.
It's the neighbors, dear; they're always doing something we can't afford.

2028   If you spend so much time at golf you won't have anything laid aside for a rainy day.
Won't I? My desk is loaded down with work that I've got put aside for a rainy day.

2029   My uncle's saving money.
Saving money? Why, he isn't even working, and yesterday he asked me for money to eat on.
I know, but he's saving money all the same.
How?
Well, he shaves himself and saves twenty-five cents, and he shines his own shoes and that's another ten cents he saves, and . . .
Listen, he isn't saving money. He doesn't have any money to spend.
Well, but you'll have to admit he's better off saving money he doesn't have than spending money he doesn't have.

2030   One way for a man to save money is to marry his second wife first.

RELATED SUBJECTS
Scotchman 1102-1133
Installment Plan 3171-3180
Budget 3315-3316
Finance 5457-5537

SMOKING

2031   Joe, can you loan me your good pipe and tobacco, pal?
Anything else?
No, I've got the match.

2032   How's your uncle's tobacco plantation coming?
Not so good. He finally gave it up. He couldn't make up his mind whether to plant cigarettes or cigars.

2033   Well, doc, what must I do?
You're not going to like it, but you will have to give up smoking for good.
Oh, that's easy! I've done that dozens of times!

2034   A great many men smoke "impromptu" cigarettes — they pick them up as they go along.

2035   Do you love to see a man smoke a pipe?
Yes, so why don't you give yours to one?

2036   How many cigarettes do you smoke a day?
Oh, any given amount.

2037   I never saw you smoke a cigar before.
No, I just picked it up recently.

2038   Where do you find tobacco?
Tobacco is found in North Carolina, South Carolina, Kentucky, and once in a while in a cigar.

2039   How come you're smoking a pipe?
My new girl says she likes to see a man smoke a pipe.
Yeah — but she said a man.

2040   Have a cigarette?
Not that kind. It's so strong, you have to knock the ashes off with a sledge hammer.
Have one of mine?
Oh no! They are TOO mild. You have to look in a mirror to see if you're smoking.

2041   Does your wife object to your smoking in the house?
Oh, she objects to my smoking anywhere; she says it's too expensive having both of us do it.

2042   We have all kinds of pipes — here's a new novel length pipe.
Oh, my husband never reads anything but short stories.

2043   Where did you get that cigar you're smoking?
Just a little thing I picked up on Broadway.
Yeah! You're telling me? I threw it away.

2044   Did you throw that cigarette butt on the floor?
What?
Did you throw that cigarette butt on the floor?
What?
Is that your cigarette butt on the floor?
No — go ahead — you saw it first.

2045   Gimme three cigars.
Strong ones or mild?
Gimme the strong ones. The weak ones is always busting in me pocket.

2046   Would it be possible to show me through the studio? I've never been through one before.
I'm sorry, but smoking isn't allowed in the other studios.
I'm not smoking.
But I am.

2047   Did you ever smoke a pipe?
I saw a man smoking a pipe once. I followed him three blocks and he wouldn't throw it away.

2048   This is the first cigar I have smoked in months.
      What's the matter?
      Times have been so tough everybody smokes their cigars down to
        the last puff.

2049   Have a cigar?
      No, thanks — sworn off smoking.
      Well, put one in your pocket for tomorrow.

2050   Do you mind if I smoke?
      I don't care if you burn.

2051   What kind of cigar are you smoking?
      Robinson Crusoe — a castaway.

2052   I want some cigarettes for my husband.
      Cork?
      Is that better than tobacco?

2053   I want a cigar for my husband.
      Fairly strong?
      Yes, please. The ashes kept breaking off the last one.

2054   I always know a good cigar when I see it.
      Yeh?
      Yeah . . . if there's not too much mud on the band.

RELATED SUBJECTS
Male (the) 912-924
Female (the) 925-938

DRINKING

2055   So you were upta Montreal, last week, eh?
      Yeah — that's what I hear.

2056   They are hard drinkers. In fact, they had their water cut off
      on Monday and didn't discover it until the following Saturday.

2057   Man: (Staggering out of dive at 4 A.M.) Good Lord, what is
      that strange odor around here?
      Doorman: That, sir, is fresh air.

2058   How did you get arrested?
      Well, my friend told me when I got home late to take off
      my clothes and shoes and sneak up the stairs quietly.
      Well, how could you get arrested doing that?
      When I got upstairs I found it was the elevated station.

2059   Officer: So you're sober, eh? Let me see you walk that chalk
      line.

(Drunk manages to walk line straight)
Officer: Well, I guess you are sober.
Drunk: That's right, officer. Now, let me see you walk the chalk
line.

2060   Stop drinking — there are about forty empty bottles around here
now. I don't want any more.
Thash funny, I can't 'member bringin' home any empty bottles.

2061   It takesh me an hour or sho to get to shleep when I go home
drunk.
Thash funny. I alwaysh fall ashleep ash soon ash I hit the bed.
Sho do I. My trouble ish in hitting the bed.

2062   She: So! — Drunk again!
He: Yeah — and thish time I had a speshial reason for gettin'
drunk.
She: Yeah? And what was the special reason?
He: Whash the difference — as long as it sherved the purpose?

2063   He's a glass blower.
You mean, he makes these fancy little glass ornaments?
Naw —he blows the glass to remove the foam.

2064   I had a bad cough. I went to a party where they had some
draught beer and I sat in the draft too long.

2065   Your uncle is always drunk. I'd think he'd get run over crossing
the streets.
He'll never get run over. He always carries a box marked
DYNAMITE and no one ever hits him.

2066   You know liquor makes a lot of people loosen up.
Sure, and a lot of loose spenders are going to get tight, too.

2067   You put in whisky to make it strong; water to make it weak;
lemon to make it sour and sugar to make it sweet. It makes
me cockeyed to think of it.

2068   My father's selling gasoline.
Your father wouldn't work even if somebody gave him a job.
What makes you think he's selling gasoline?
Well, the police station telephoned today and said: Better come
down and bail your papa out, because he has a tank full.

2069   Have a cocktail — have a Custer's Last Stand?
What is that?
One more and you'll fall.

2070   He was so drunk, he spent all night throwing pennies in the
sewer and looking up at the clock on the City Hall to see how
much he weighed.

2071   Drunk: Has Mike been here?
       Man: Oh, yes, he was here about an hour ago.
       Drunk: Was I with him?

2072   Did you ever drink all you wanted?
       No, I can't hold a bottle long enough.

2073   Blessed are the pure in spirits for there is nothing worse than a
       mixed drink.

2074   Was the party last night a good one?
       It was great — while I lasted.

2075   Does it hurt to mix your drinks?
       Not if you don't drink them.

2076   I've never been so drunk before.
       Yeah?
       That is, before midnight.

2077   So you went out last night and raised the roof. I suppose you
       finally got drunk?
       No — not finally. You have to get drunk first to get the way I
       was finally.

2078   He likes to take a drink because it makes him see double and
       feel single.

2079   I was driving with Bob the other day and I looked at the speed-
       ometer — he was going eighty miles an hour. Suddenly he
       turned to me and said: Hey, who's driving?

2080   Did you have a good time at the party?
       I had a fine time — so they tell me.
       How did you find yourself in the morning?
       I just looked under the table and there I was.

2081   You drink too much.
       I don't drink.
       Why, I saw you drinking Scotch the other night.
       Oh, I didn't mean to drink it. I was gargling with it and it
       slipped.

2082   Why is that you're much more affectionate after a few drinks?
       All I can get to drink is rubbing alcohol.

2083   What's the matter with you?
       I'm a little stiff from bowling.
       You're a little stiff most of the time.

2084   Let me pour you another drink. I've heard you like good liquor.
       Sure, but pour me another one, anyway.

2085   Drinking makes you look beautiful.
       I haven't been drinking.
       I know, but I have.

2086   What's the matter with your clothes?
       I live with my sister, you know — and she's very careless. She
          left this dress lay on the floor all night.
       What's the matter? Couldn't she pick it up?
       I don't think so. I was in it.

2087   What was that noise?
       The mate heaved the anchor.
       My word! What was he drinking?

2088   Did you go out last night?
       No, I knew what I was doing all the time.

2089   I had a wonderful time at your party last night.
       Why, I had no party last night.
       That so? Well, believe me, I was at somebody's party.

2090   I have no sympathy for a man who gets drunk every night.
       A man who gets drunk every night doesn't need sympathy.

2091   Taxi, sir?
       Drunk: Thanksh, I wash wunnerin' wat it wash!

2092   He was so drunk he looked in the cuckoo clock for eggs.

2093   I was glad to see you in church Sunday, Pat.
       My God — was that where I was?

2094   What'll you have to drink?
       Week-end whisky.
       Week-end whisky? What's that?
       Drink it and the week ends right there.

2095   Scotch or Rye?
       Don't tell me — let me guess.

2096   I can't understand you Americans — you mix a drink and say:
          Here's to you. Then you drink it yourself.

2097   Will you stop drinking for me?
       Who said I was drinking for you?

2098   Is he a hard drinker?
       No, it's the easiest thing he does.

2099   You're drunk.
       Well, if I'm not I've been cheated out of twenty bucks.

2100   I've been drunk for three days—yesterday—today and tomorrow.

2101   We've been everywhere and we've seen everything.
Have you ever had delirum tremens?
No.
Then, you've never been anywhere and you haven't seen anything.

2102   Why don't you drink wine? It makes blood.
I'm not blood thirsty.

2103   I saw you coming out of a saloon last night, late.
Well, I had to come out sometime.

2104   He drank so much whisky that when the mosquitoes bit him they
died of alcoholic poisoning.

2105   I believe in justice.
What do you mean?
I believe in getting justice drunk as you can.

2106   (Officer arresting speeder) Let me see your license.
Drunk: I haven't got a license; I can't read and I'm color blind.
I'm going to give you a heavy fine unless you have a good excuse.
I have a good excuse.
What is it?
I'm intoxicated.

2107   Jack: Fred just gave me twenty bucks!
Jim: From Fred? I always thought he was pretty tight.
Jack: He was.

2108   Where is this town Bond?
What town?
Bond — the place where all whisky is bottled.

2109   (Woman looking underneath table) Oh, I'm sorry, I was looking for a lady's husband!
I'm one, lady — *crawl under!*

2110   How was that liquor I gave you last night?
Just right. If it had been any better you wouldn't have given it
to me. And if it had been any worse it would have killed me!

2111   Butler: Did the master smack his lips after drinking that fine old
whisky I served him last night?
Maid: No, sir. He smacked mine.

2112   He's learning to hiccup.
Why?
He wants to be a successful drunkard like his father.

2113   What did you mean when you said you got an optical cocktail
yesterday?
I almost went blind after drinking it.

2114 Why, dad, you drink coffee like anybody else, don't you?
      Of course — why not?
      Mom told me you drank like a fish.

2115 Have you got rheumatism?
      No, why?
      Mon said you got stiff in every joint.

2116 He was so drunk that when he came out of the hotel and saw a
      man with gold braid and medals on his chest, he said: Will
      you call me a cab?
      So the man was insulted and he said: How dare you insult me—
      I'm no doorman — I'm an admiral in the Navy.
      So the drunk said: All right—call me a boat, I'm in a hurry.

2117 Life is just six of one and a half dozen of the other.
      That's what I said the other night when I had those seven drinks
      straight. I was sick of one and half dozing from the others.

2118 This is the first day of January — I'll give you one day to stop
      drinking.
      All right — I'll take the Fourth of July.

2119 You didn't tell me he was a hard drinker.
      He isn't — he takes it easy.

2120 You had better stick to drink mixing. As a rancher you're a fail-
      ure. And the last drink you mixed for me was terrible. It was
      the worst mixture I ever tasted. It wasn't fit for a hog.
      Yes, but that was the first mixture I ever mixed for a hog.

2121 Why do you drink liquor?
      What would you suggest I do with it?

2122 We had a party and had a big bowl of punch, but the cats came
      in and drank up the punch.
      They did?
      Yeah — sort of a punch in the puss.

2123 I saw a drunken man lean out of his car window and ask a cop: Is
      this the way to go to a football game?
      The cop looked at the drunk and said: It sure is — if I wasn't a
      cop I'd go the same way.

2124 Take back that glass of beer and bring me a whole stein.
      Mooooo! Mooooo! Mooooo!

2125 Whash yer looking for?
      We're looking for a drowned man.
      Whash yer want one for?

2126   Ginger ale, please.
Pale?
No, just a glass.

2127   (Knock on door)
Are you Mrs. Schmitz?
Yes, I am.
Are you sure you're Mrs. Schmitz?
Surely, I'm sure I'm Mrs. Schmitz!
Well, come down and pick out Mr. Schmitz. The rest of us
    want to go home.

2128   I'll take a Doctor Jekyll and Mr. Hyde cocktail.
A Doctor Jekyll and Mr. Hyde cocktail?
Yeah, one drink and you're another man.

2129   The doctor gave me a powder to cure my husband of drinking.
    I have to put it in his coffee.
Has it cured him?
Yes, of drinking coffee.

2130   Did you ever taste moonshine whisky?
Certainly not! Anybody who can't swallow fast enough to keep
    from tastin' it has no business tryin' to drink it.

2131   Now, Macpherson, why don't you fight against your longing for
    drink? When you're tempted, think of your wife at home.
When the thirst is upon me, I am absolutely devoid of fear.

2132   If you don't give up gin it will shorten your life.
Do you think so?
I'm sure of it. If you stop drinking it will prolong your days.
I guess that's right. I went twenty-four hours without a drink
    six months ago, and I never spent such a long day in my life.

2133   Have you a cocktail shaker at home?
No, she's at finishing school.

2134   What do they mean by "nip and tuck"?
One nip and they tuck you away for the night.

2135   My old gent can mix the smoothest cocktails you ever saw.
Who wants to look at them?

2136   The stuff I had here yesterday tasted like kerosene.
Well, you wanted to get lit, didn't you?

2137   Have a drink?
No, thanksh, jush had one.
Have another.
Jush had another.

Well, start in wherever you stopped.
Can't. Haven't stopped yet.

2138   How do you know he's a college man?
He doesn't stop drinking long enough to get a hangover.

2139   He dropped a bottle of liquor on the floor and it spilled all over.
That's too bad. I bet he feels terrible about that.
He'll be all right as soon as they get all the splinters out of his
tongue.

2140   Drunk: What time is it?
Drunker: Tuesday.
Drunk: Then I've missed my train.

RELATED SUBJECTS
Boast 2285-2304
Not Myself 2485-2487
Hospitality 3564-3660
Restaurant 4738-4883

BARTENDER

2141   So your uncle lifts faces—he's a plastic surgeon?
But he doesn't lift *faces*.
You told me he did.
I told you he lifts *mugs* in a bar.

2142   I come from a family of tenders.
Cattle tenders?
No — bartenders.

RELATED SUBJECTS
Restaurant 4738-4883

BOUNCER

2143   I want to apply for the job of bouncer.
What makes you think you can bounce?
I was a rubber in a Turkish bath.

2144   How would you like to go to work? We need a bouncer.

What is that?

All you have to do is get rid of people we don't need around here.

All right. I'll take it. When do I start?

Right now. Your first job is bouncing yourself right out of the window.

RELATED SUBJECTS
Conduct 1802-1862
Restaurant 4738-4883

ACTION

FIGHT

2145   My father and a man named McSniff have been fighting for twenty years, but they've finally stopped.

Why, did they bury the hatchet?

No, they buried McSniff.

2146   When I hit a man he remembers it.

When I hit a man he is through remembering.

2147   My wife and I had an argument and she went home to her folks in Maine.

Bangor?

I didn't even touch her.

2148   Did you strike that man in an excess of irritability?

No, sir, I struck him in the stomach.

2149   Did you ever win an argument with your wife?

Yes, just once — just once.

And when was that?

I can't remember just *when* it was, but I got a distinct recollection that her mouth was full of hairpins at the time!

2150   Go to it! You ain't half licked yet.

Well, come on, you can have the other half. I ain't greedy.

2151   You're a funny guy. I call you a skunk, a rotter, a bum and a crook — and you stand there and smile!

Sure. I used to be a baseball umpire.

2152   Well, Peter, so you and your wife have been fighting again? Liquor, I suppose?

No, she licked me this time.

2153   Really, Bill, your argument with your wife last night was most amusing.

Wasn't it though? And when she threw the ax at me I thought I'd split.

2154   If you laugh at me again, I'll knock your block off.

Haw, haw, you wouldn't even know what club to use.

2155 She threw a bowl of alphabet soup at him and hot words passed
      between them.

2156 We like a man that comes right out and says what he thinks,
      providing he agrees with us.

2157 He claims his wife was untractable, your Honor, so he beat her
      into subjection with a golf club.
      How many strokes?

2158 Your Honor, he hit me in the nose, he hit me in the eye, he
      punched me in the head, he . . .
      Don't pay any attention to her, Judge, she's punch drunk.

2159 I'm sore at my wife. She threw a suit of my clothes out of the
      window.
      Well, that won't hurt you.
      No? I was in the suit.

2160 Hey, you, why don't you fight it out?
      My wife won't let me.
      How could she know you'd been fighting?
      She'd see the doctor coming out of your house.

2161 As soon as my wife and I start to quarrel, my wife becomes
      historical.
      You mean, hysterical?
      No, she rakes up the past.

2162 Well, where I come from that's a fight.
      Why don't you fight?
      I ain't home.

2163 What was you running up the street for this morning?
      I was running to stop a fight.
      Who was fighting?
      Me and another fellow.

2164 He knocked you down — and then I punched him in the nose.
      We fought over you like two dogs over a bone and you didn't
      even get up — you just laid there.
      Did you ever see two dogs fighting over a bone?
      Uh huh!
      Did you see the bone get up and do anything?

2165 One more word out of you and I'll fight.
      Scram!
      That's not the word.

2166 (Wife throws dishes at husband — then picks up salt shaker)
      Man: Don't throw the salt shaker, darling, that means a quarrel.

2167   Nothing but the law makes me keep my hands off you.
       Nothing but the law makes you keep your hands off a lot of
       things.

2168   I wouldn't take advantage of you because I come from fighting
       stock.
       Don't let that stop you. My father and mother fight all the time,
       too.

2169   I have a notion to beat you to a jelly.
       What flavor?

2170   Where did you get the black eye?
       Oh, I was talking when I should have been listening.

2171   How did you get that black eye?
       Oh, I went to a cabaret last night and I was struck by the beauty
       of the place.

2172   What's that noise overhead?
       Mother is dragging father's pants across the floor.
       Pants shouldn't make that much noise.
       I know, but father is still in them.

2173   Why are you learning to be a fighter?
       I believe in preparedness.
       Preparedness? What's fighting got to do with that?
       I'm going around with a married woman and I'm getting in
       shape to go ten rounds with her husband.

2174   My brother got into a fight the other day in a restaurant and the
       bouncer punched him in the eye and kicked him out the door.
       Did your brother get hurt?
       Yeah, he's got a black eye.
       Which proves that the hand is quicker than the eye.
       It also proves that the foot is quicker than the seat of the pants.

2175   That man quarreled with his wife and she told him to go to blazes.
       What happened then?
       Oh, he joined the fire department.

2176   I can see that you won't be convinced, and I'm not going to
       stand here any longer and waste my good breath on you.
       Don't fool yourself. Your breath isn't so good.

2177   I'm going home to mother and I never want to see you again.
       Too late — your mother went home to grandmother last night.

2178   Never hit a man when he's down — he may get up.

2179   The devil must have inspired you to bite that man's ear off and
       stamp his head in.
       Biting his ear off was my own idea.

2180 Why did you hit your wife with a chair?
Because I couldn't lift the piano.

2181 So you broke a cane over his head, did you?
It was an accident.
How could it be an accident. You did it deliberately.
I had no intention of breaking the cane.

2182 I feel like punching him in the nose again.
Again?
Yeah, I felt like that once before.

2183 Fighting is all right, provided you do it intelligently.
Yes, but you can't always find a smaller man.

2184 There are two sides to every question — her side and the **wrong** side.

2185 My wife is so temperamental, the least thing I do starts a fight.
You're lucky — mine starts her own fights.

2186 Judge: Do you mean to say that such a physical wreck as he is gave you that black eye?
Joe: Yer Honor, he wasn't a physical wreck till he gave me the black eye.

2187 What was the terrible row upstairs last night between young Peck and his wife?
Oh, Peck's a long-suffering chap, but he finally lost control when his wife kept flicking cigarette ashes all over the floor he had just swept.

2188 I'd like to dot your eyes.

2189 What do you mean — kicking me on the calf?
I couldn't reach any higher.

2190 What were you and your wife fighting about?
She was trying to drive a nail in the wall with the hair brush and I said: You can't drive that nail with that brush.
Is that all you said?
Well, I added — why don't you use your head?

2191 Pardon me, but would you mind having your wife stop banging her head on the wall?
Why?
My wife is tired of drinking cement with her coffee.

2192 If I were you, Percy, I should tell him just what I think of him.
How can I? The cad has no telephone.

2193   Here, young man, you shouldn't hit that boy when he's down.
G'way! What do you think I got him down for?

2194   Look here, I'll give you just five minutes to take that back.
Is that so? And suppose I don't take it back in five minutes?
Then I'll extend the time.

2195   Come quick, Mr. Policeman! There's a man been fightin' my
father for half an hour.
Why didn't you tell me before?
'Cause father was gettin' the best of it until a minute ago.

2196   They're taking him away in the ambulance for beatin' his wife.

2197   Well, I'm glad I was able to bring you two enemies together and
effect peace between you. Now shake hands.
Mrs. Brady: Well, Mrs. Tyler, I wish you all you wishes me.
Mrs. Tyler: And now, I'm askin' you, Mrs. Brady, who's saying
nasty things now?

2198   Then in order to settle the fight he took his wife apart and tried
to reason with her.
Suppose he had been unable to re-assemble her?

2199   You admit tearing a handful of hair from your husband's head?
Yes — I wanted some to put in a locket.

2200   Ever pick a quarrel with your wife?
No, I leave it to her. She picks much better ones.

2201   And then my wife hit me on the head with an oak leaf.
Well, that couldn't have hurt you, surely.
Oh, couldn't it? It was the oak leaf from the center of the dining
room table.

2202   Oh, she's very dignified. Every time she throws a cup at her husband she always takes the spoon out.

2203   Before he left her he settled all the furniture on her. In fact, he
settled so much furniture on her she couldn't get up.

2204   When they were married he took her out to the little house he
had built for her and said: Just a little world for you and
me — and they've been fighting for the world's championship
ever since.

2205   I am very careful; whenever I quarrel with my wife, I send the
children for a walk.
They look healthy.

2206   You're a henpecked little shrimp!
I'll bet you wouldn't dare say that in the presence of my wife.

2207   You say you never clash with your wife?
       Never. She goes her way and I go hers.

2208   She's been throwing things at me ever since we was married.
       Then why have you not complained before?
       This is the first time she's hit me.

2209   This officer states that he found you two fighting in the middle
           of the street.
       The officer has misled you. When he arrived we were trying to
           separate each other.

2210   When two bodies come together, is heat generated?
       No, sir. I hit a guy yesterday and he knocked me cold.

2211   Married couples have fewer arguments in winter than summer,
       because a lot of husbands wear earmuffs in the winter.

2212   My girl and I are on the outs.
       Only a lover's quarrel.
       No, this is serious. We got into a political discussion.

2213   If you were my husband, I'd give you poison.
       If I were your husband, I'd take it.

RELATED SUBJECTS
Conduct 1802-1862
Temper 2276-2284
Courage 2320-2339
Revenge 2488-2489
Apology 2519-2520
Prizefight 4495-4499

TOUGH PERSON

2214   Smith is a man who takes his hat off to nobody.
       How does he get his hair cut?

2215   What makes him so tough?
       He was raised on marble cake, rock candy and brick ice cream.

2216 I saw you with the toughest man in town yesterday — you were both eating hamburgers. What have you in common with that terrible man?
Indigestion.

2217 Believe me, men shiver in front of my father.
I didn't know he was so tough.
He isn't — he heats towels in the Turkish bath.

2218 My brother's got a job and he sure tells them where to get off.
He does? Where is he working?
He's a conductor on the street car.

2219 Jones says his wife jumps whenever he speaks.
Yes, she does — all over him.

2220 He's so tough — the only way I could get him to go to bed was to play strip poker with him.

RELATED SUBJECTS
Swearing 1498-1500
Courage 2320-2339

SLEEP

2221 What time does the sandman come to your house?
After my old man goes to work.

2222 Did you give her a night cap?
Yeah — and she drank it down in one gulp.

2223 What time do you go to sleep?
I used to sleep between 8 and 10 — but two of my brothers left home, so now I sleep between 6 and 8.

2224 When I went to college I lived in a dormitory.
A what?
A dormitory! You know what a dormitory is. What did you sleep in?
My underwear.

2225 How late do you usually sleep on Sunday morning?
It all depends.
Depends on what?
The length of the sermon.

2226 Oh, she was asleep in the arms of Morpheus?
Well, I don't know — I didn't look in her room.

2227 Can you imagine anybody sleeping with his shoes on?
No, who did that?
My horse.

2228   Well, what was the matter? Didn't the alarm clock go off?
        Oh, yes, sir, it went off all right, but the trouble was that it
        went off while I was asleep.

2229   He was so henpecked he cackled in his sleep.

2230   I can stay awake any length of time by simply forcing myself
        to it.
        I see — the triumph of mind over mattress.

2231   What time do you get up in the summer?
        As soon as the first ray of the sun comes in my window.
        Isn't that rather early?
        No. My room faces West.

2232   Hired Hand: I never sleep late. I always rise with the lark.
        Farmer: Well, you can't work that old gag on me. We ain't got
        any larks here, and if you waited for a lark to wake you, you'd
        sleep till doomsday. Here's an alarm clock set for five, and
        you get up when it rings.

2233   I haven't been able to sleep a wink since my wife ran away.
        Why don't you try counting sheep?
        I'm too busy counting my lucky stars.

2234   Doctor, my husband talks in his sleep.
        Oh, that's not serious. I can give you a prescription that will cure
        him of that.
        Don't you dare! That's the only time he ever talks to me!

2235   Is it your custom to sleep between sheets, summer and winter?
        No. I sleep between my roommate and the window.

2236   Our baby keeps us up all night. We can't get him off to sleep.
        What do you suggest?
        If your baby can't sleep at nights, just move him over to the
        edge of the bed and I'm sure he'll drop off.

2237   My brother stands in front of a mirror with his eyes closed.
        What for?
        Oh, he just wants to see what he looks like when he is asleep.

2238   Let's sleep in the gutter.
        Why?
        Plenty of room with running water.

2239   If I got eight hours of sleep a night I would die of sleeping
        sickness.

2240   Hey, wake up!
        What's the matter?
        Just wanted to tell you you had two more hours to sleep.

2241 Wake up! Wake up!
      What's the matter? What happened?
      I forgot to give you your sleeping powder.

                    RELATED SUBJECTS
                    Ambition 1874-1893
                    Boat 4174-4200
                    Airplane 4208-4217
                    Train 4218-4242

INSOMNIA

2242 I also have insomnia.
      Well, she'll have to register too.
      Who?
      Your wife, Insomnia.

2243 I'm sure tired. Didn't get much sleep last night. Had insomnia
      all night.
      Why didn't you try counting sheep?
      I did. I counted 10,000 sheep. I put them in the cattle car and
      shipped them to market and after I had figured out how much
      money I lost on the deal, it was time to get up.

2244 (Counting out loud) One hundred five, one hundred six, one
      hundred . . .
      What are you doing?
      Counting sheep.
      Do you have to count out loud?
      Yes — I lose track when I count in my head.

2245 What do you take as a remedy for your insomnia?
      A glass of wine at regular intervals.
      Does that make you sleep?
      No, but it makes me content to stay awake.

2246 My wife has insomnia very badly, Doctor. She very often remains
      awake until 2 o'clock in the morning. What shall I do for her?
      Go home earlier.

                    RELATED SUBJECTS
                    Worry 2348-2355

SOMNAMBULIST

2247 Hotel Clerk: (To guest parading through lobby in pajamas)
      Here, what are you doing?
      Guest: (Awakened) Beg pardon! I'm a somnambulist.
      Hotel Clerk: Well, you can't walk around here like that, no
      matter what your religion is.

2248 I think I should tell you something — I'm a somnambulist. You
      know what a somnambulist is?

Sure — it goes (makes a noise like siren) and takes people to the hospital.

2249   I walk in my sleep.
       Oh, you're a policeman.

2250   I can cure you of walking in your sleep and it will cost you only ten cents.
       How?
       Buy a box of tacks.

2251   Will you marry me?
       I must tell you I'm a somnambulist.
       That's all right — you can go to your church and I'll go to mine.

2252   Do you ever walk in your sleep at night?
       No, I've never been asleep at night.

2253   If you walk in your sleep don't forget to take carfare with you when you go to bed.

2254   He has three automobiles, four airplanes and three motorcycles — yet he still walks in his sleep.

RELATED SUBJECTS
Hitch Hiking 4038-4041

SNORE

2255   Boy, did you snore last night.
       I wasn't snoring. I don't snore.
       Don't fool yourself — you sounded like a buzz saw.
       I wasn't snoring — I was dreaming about a dog and that was the dog growling.

2256   Give me a sentence using the word "miniature."
       The miniature asleep you begin to snore.

2257   (Loud snoring on train)
       Man: Sounds like I'm in the cattle car.
       (Snoring with a nose whistle — popular song)
       Man: Boy — that's a hot snore.

2258   I didn't get a wink of sleep last night.
       You snored so loud, you woke up the engine.
       How could an engine hear?
       Haven't you ever heard of engineers (engine ears)?

2259   You snored, wheezed and whistled.
       I wish you had awakened me.
       Why?
       Because I can't sleep when I snore.

2260 I went to church with my aunt last Sunday. And she surely did embarrass me. She snored so loud it woke me up.
How did the preacher like that?
He didn't like it. He said: You'd better wake your auntie up.
And I said: You wake her up yourself. You put her to sleep.

RELATED SUBJECTS
Sleep 2221-2241

TALK IN SLEEP

2261 I know a couple who talk in their sleep. He plays golf, and she loves to go to auction sales. The other night the golfer yelled: "FORE!" And the wife yelled: "FOUR TWENTY-FIVE!"

2262 The preacher mumbled a few words in his throat and they were married. A few months later the husband mumbled a few words in his sleep and they were divorced.

2263 Wake up — you're talking in your sleep.
My goodness, do you begrudge me those few words?

2264 My wife tells me I talk in my sleep, doctor. What should I do?
Nothing that you shouldn't.

RELATED SUBJECTS
Secret 1565-1575
Marriage 2882-3051

DREAM

2265 I ate lobster last evening for dinner and all night I dreamed.
Bad dreams?
Yeah—I dreamed I paid the check.

2266 Last night I dreamed I died and went to Heaven. When I got there they told me I couldn't come in unless I was mounted. So I came back and got you. When I got back to Heaven, St. Peter said: Just hitch your donkey outside and come in.

2267 I dreamed last night of Clark Gable. He held me in his arms and then he hugged me and kissed me.
Then what happened?
It was time to get up—but I'm going to bed early this evening.

2268 I dream of you all day.
What do you do nights?
Oh, nights — I go out.

2269 I dreamed about the funniest thing last night. Wasn't it a funny dream?

How do I know what your dream was about?
You ought to know. You were in it.

2270　A girl gave me a piece of her wedding cake. I put it under my
　　　　pillow and I dreamed of my future wife.
　　　　I did that once, and I dreamed of a Notre Dame football team.

2271　A man kicked his wife out of a four poster bed and do you know
　　　　what his alibi was?
　　　　No. What?
　　　　He said he was dreaming he was back in college playing football
　　　　and his team needed the extra point.

2272　He dreamed last night he was eating shredded wheat and when
　　　　he woke up this morning, half the mattress was gone.

2273　I dreamed I was dancing with you last night.
　　　　Did you?
　　　　And when I woke up I found it was a policeman hitting me on
　　　　the bottom of my shoes with his club.

2274　My wife had a dream last night and thought she was married to
　　　　a millionaire.
　　　　You're lucky! My wife thinks that in the daytime.

2275　What's it a sign of if a married man dreams he's a bachelor?
　　　　It's a sign he's going to be disappointed when he wakes up.

RELATED SUBJECTS
Sleep 2221-2241

AFFECTIONS

TEMPER

2276　It's the same thing, night in and night out. No matter what I say.
　　　　Compose yourself. Don't fly off the handle.
　　　　Who's got flies on the handle?
　　　　Get hold of yourself. Get a grip!
　　　　Get a suitcase yourself.

2277　Is your wife hard to get along with? Has she a quick temper?
　　　　She has an even temper — the most even temper I ever knew in
　　　　my life — she's always mad.

2278　She's a nice little girl — even disposition — always mad.

2279　My girl's very dove-like.
　　　　Soft and cooing?
　　　　No, pigeontoed.

2280   My first wife and I separated because she had such a temper.
       Well, how is your last wife?
       Even.
       Even what?
       Even worse than the first one.

2281   From what I hear, your wife is a bit of an angel.
       Oh, rather. She's always going up in the air and harping on
          something or other.

2282   I've been nursing a grouch all day.
       I didn't know your wife was sick.

2283   Did you get up with a grouch today?
       No, she got up ahead of me.

2284   You must not grow angry and say naughty things. You should
          always give a soft answer.
       Mush!

RELATED SUBJECTS
Swearing 1498-1500
Conduct 1802-1862
Fight 2145-2213
Revenge 2488-2489
Marriage 2882-3051

BOAST

2285   Chugwater makes very sure of himself before he does any bragging.
       Oh, yes, he's a safe blower.

2286   I take a cold shower every morning.
       Why brag about it?
       Gosh, that's why I take it.

2287   There was a chicken-stealing case before the court. The culprit
          pleaded guilty, and was sentenced. But the curious judge still
          questioned the guilty man about the case—how he had
          managed to take those chickens right from under the window
          of the owner's house, and with a savage dog loose in the yard.
          But the thief was not minded to explain:
       It wouldn't do any good to try to explain it, Judge. If you were to
          try it, you wouldn't get chickens, just a hide full of shot. If you
          want to try any rascality, you'd better stick to the bench,
          where you are accustomed to being.

2288   My dad is a great man — he's a trustee at a University!
       Shucks! My dad is a trusty at the State Penitentiary.

2289   My father is worth $5,000 in Missouri.
       How could he be worth $5,000 in Missouri?
       That's what the Sheriff offered for his return.

2290   I have a white hen that lays brown eggs.
       What's so wonderful about that?
       Can you do it?

2291   When it comes to men, I knock 'em dead.
       That's nothing. I get 'em dead and bring 'em back to life again.

2292   I'm a millionaire, I could buy you and sell you!
       Well, I'm a billionaire, I could buy you and keep you. I don't
          have to sell you.

2293   Remember Joe, the man who boasted that some day he would
          tell his wife where she could get off?
       Yes.
       He's in the hospital.
       What for?
       She heard him boasting.

2294   I never go out with the same man twice.
       If I were you, I wouldn't boast about it.

2295   Young man, do you know how I made my money?
       Sure, but I won't tell your daughter and let it ruin our happiness.

2296   I was a beauty in my day.
       Just another day wasted away!

2297   Well, this conversation isn't a line — it's a gift.
       Well, give it back.

2298   Hear that fellow blowing about his business?
       Yeah. Trade winds!

2299   Do you know that it's hell to be born rich, for then one is de-
          prived of the privilege of bragging about his humble start.

2300   One of my pet canaries ate a lot of frankfurters. He felt so happy
          he started to chirp. My cat heard him chirp and ate 'em up.
       Your cat ate the frankfurters?
       No, he ate the canary.
       What has that got to do with me?
       You should keep your mouth shut when you're full of bologna.

2301   I'll let you know my father is a wealthy man. He owns a
          newspaper.
       That's not so much. A newspaper is only 25 cents.

2302 (Drunk boasting) I've got a million dollars, a yacht, a country
house, a town house, six automobiles — a chauffeur, a butler,
a maid, a cook, etc., etc. Whatta you got?
I've gotta go.

2303 Once while I was having a meal in the jungle a lion came so
close to me that I could feel his breath on the back of my neck.
What did I do?
Turned up your collar?

2304 He boasts he runs things in his house.
He does — the lawn mower, washing machine, vacuum sweeper,
baby carriage and the errands.

RELATED SUBJECTS
Exaggeration 1507-1517
Lying 1540-1564
Pride 2361

EGOTISM

2305 You're not a bad looking sort of fellow.
You'd say so even if you didn't think so.
Well, we're square then. You'd think so even if I didn't say so.

2306 Isn't it peculiar that famous writer's name is Brown, too? Is he
related to you?
Well — not exactly, but indirectly he is — you see, he is famous,
too.

2307 (The inebriated young actor lurched into the lobby of a large
hotel far from Hollywood. He looked into a mirror and smiled
with pleasure.)
Actor: Look! They've got a picture of me here, too!

2308 Judge: Who do you think is the best movie actor?
Actor: Myself.
Judge: Don't you think that is a bit egotistical?
Actor: Perhaps, your Honor, but you must remember that I'm
under oath.

2309 My only sin is vanity. I look into my mirror every morning and
think how beautiful I am.
That's not a sin — that's a mistake.

2310   Is he conceited?
       Conceited? Why, every time he hears a clap of thunder he runs
       to the window and takes a bow.

2311   Your head is so big they'd have to pin your ears back to get you
       through the Grand Canyon.

2312   I know I'm not good looking, but what's my opinion against
       thousands of others?

2313   Is it a sin to be pleased when a man says I'm pretty?
       Sure, it's a sin, but it's a terrible responsibility for the man.

2314   An egotist is one who, reading a book and not understanding
       something in it, decides it is a misprint.

2315   Dearest, I always think of you — always.
       You do think of the most wonderful things.

2316   You have such confidence in yourself, it's a pleasure to insult you.
       Now do you want to know what I think of YOU?
       No, you may be right.

2317   Of course, I'm only one person.
       You ought to count yourself up more often — you ain't so many.

2318   What do you do when you see an unusually beautiful girl?
       Oh, I look for awhile, then I get tired and put my mirror down.

2319   I hope you don't think I'm conceited?
       Oh, no. But I'm just wondering how you can keep from giving
       three cheers whenever you look at yourself in the glass.

                         RELATED SUBJECTS
                         Success 1945-1966
                         Snob 2357-2360

COURAGE

2320   Don't be afraid — just look the lion in the eye!
       I can't — I'm cross-eyed.

2321   Mr. Doakes — the lion tamer — will now engage in a hand to
       hand combat with a ferocious beast. He will enter the cage
       without arms.
       Yeah — and come out without legs.

2322   Once when I was in the Foreign Legion, the Captain said: I
       want someone to step out of this line to go on a dangerous

mission. He stepped forward and picked me.
Did you really step out of line?
No, the rest of the army stepped back.

2323   I come from a family of strong men — my brother was so strong he walked right up to Muhammad Ali and hit him right on the nose.
I'd like to meet your brother — I'd like to shake hands with him.
Don't be silly. You don't think we're going to dig him up just to shake hands with YOU.

2324   The next time you are walking in a tough neighborhood, remember that people often whistle to keep up their courage.
And remember also that a police whistle is as good as any.

2325   My mother heard a noise in the bedroom last night. She jumped out of bed and there were a man's feet sticking out from under the bed.
A burglar's?
My father's. He'd heard the burglar, too.

2326   Did Jack remain cool when that burglar came in?
Yes, he was positively shivering.

2327   All you have to do is look the lion in the eye and show him you're not afraid.
Yeah, but the lion would know I was just being deceitful.

2328   My uncle has twelve medals — he won them during the war.
He must have been a great sharp-shooter.
No — a great crap-shooter.

2329   Last week when that bear got out you ran away and left me, and once you told me you would face death for me.
Yes, I would — but that bear wasn't dead.

2330   The man I marry must be a hero.
Oh, you're not so bad as all that.

2331   A man down the street just insulted me.
I'll go knock his block off. What did he look like?
A great big brute with a scar on his cheek.
Oh, well — forget it — he was probably joking.

2332   This is a very dangerous mission—do you suppose we'll ever return alive?
Well, I don't know about you—but if they start shooting and the first shot don't get me—the rest will fall short.

2333   Man may have more courage than woman, but he doesn't get half the chance to show his backbone.

2334 And I rushed right straight at the big brute and knocked him
      down.
      You, Billy? A big fellow? I don't believe it.
      What's wrong with you? I told you I was driving the sedan.

2335 One night when you were away I heard a burglar. You should
      have seen me going downstairs three steps at a time.
      Where was the burglar — on the roof?

2336 My uncle died with his boots on.
      What did he do that for?
      Well — er — maybe he couldn't get them off.

2337 Colonel: Did you keep your heads during the last attack?
      Private Jones: Yes, sir.
      Colonel: And you, Smith?
      Private Smith: Yes, Jones and me talked some.
      Colonel: Oh? Then it looked to me like a *running* conversation.

2338 I've told thousands of women where to get off.
      You must be a lady killer.
      No, I run an elevator in a department store.

2339 A real man is always willing to face the music.
      Yes—even the well-known march from Lohengrin.

RELATED SUBJECTS
Fight 2145-2213

FEAR

2340 I wonder what makes him so high strung?
      He inherits that from his grandfather. He was a horse thief.

2341 Wait a minute — somebody's knocking at the door.
      That's not the door — that's my knees.

2342 You're afraid of lightning! The last time there was lightning you
      ran and hid. Why did you run down into that dark cellar and
      hide?
      You don't have to tell me about lightning—I protect myself!
      If lightning's going to hit you, it's going to hit you, no matter
      where you go.
      If it's going to hit me, let it look for me.

2343 And then there was the timid collegian who preferred blondes,
      because he was afraid of the dark.

2344 For a long time I had the feeling someone was following me.
      But you don't feel that way any more?
      I still feel that way — but I found out what it was. It was just
          my underwear creeping up on me.

2345 Hear those castanets — oh boy!
      Those aren't castanets — that's my teeth chattering.

2346 He won't hurt you — he's harmless. He was raised on milk.
      So was I, but I'm eating meat now.

2347 Papa, when you see a cow ain't you afraid?
      Of course not, son.
      When you see a great big worm, ain't you afraid?
      No, of course not.
      When you see a horrid, big, black bumblebee, ain't you afraid?
      No, certainly not.
      Ain't you afraid when it thunders and lightnings?
      No — you silly child.
      Papa, ain't you afraid of nothing in this world 'ceptin' mama?

RELATED SUBJECTS
Cemetery 173-176
Ghost 177-183
Fight 2145-2213

WORRY

2348 Well, if your wife has left you, come on and drown your sorrow
          in drink.
      I'm afraid I couldn't do that.
      What's the matter? No liquor?
      No — no sorrow.

2349 Dearest, something is troubling you, and I want you to tell me
          what it is; your worries are not your worries now, they are
          our worries.
      Oh, very well. We've just had a letter from a girl in New York
          and she's suing us for breach-of-promise.

2350 Cheer up, old man. Why don't you drown your sorrow?
      She's bigger than I am and besides it would be murder.

2351 I'll give you $100 to do my worrying for me.
      Great! Where's the hundred?
      That's your first worry.

2352   I never take trouble home with me from the office.
I don't have to either; mine's usually there at home waiting for me.

2353   I shall love to share all your troubles.
But, darling, I have none.
No, but I mean when we're married.

2354   You look sad lately.
Yeah, it always makes me sad to see someone else sad.
Who has been looking sad?
My mother-in-law — for a long time she worried about going to the poor house.
But now she doesn't have to worry any more?
No — she's in the poor house now.

2355   Why don't you drown your troubles?
I would, but I can't get her to go in swimming with me.

RELATED SUBJECTS
Curiosity 1323-1324
Advice 1978-1989
Sympathy 2445-2448
Marriage 2882-3051

WISH

2356   You are always wishing for what you haven't got.
Well, what else can one wish for?

SNOB

2357   Don't you know her? Why, she lives in the same square with you.
Yes, but she's not in the same circle.

2358   She certainly is a snob. Her nose is turned up so high she nearly drowned.
How?
It rained into it.

2359   So your girl broke your engagement?
Yeah. You know she lived at 125th Street and I lived at 47th St.
What's that got to do with your engagement?
Her mother told her she should never marry any one beneath her station.

2360   Gee, I'd like to meet that swell-looking girl over there. Who is she, anyway?
Oh, she belongs to the Nodding Club.
What's that?
Nodding doing.

RELATED SUBJECTS
Nobility 1134-1135

PRIDE

2361   Why doesn't your horse hold her head up?
It's her pride. I haven't paid for her yet.

OPTIMIST

2362   An optimist is anybody who don't care what happens as long as it happens to somebody else.

2363   An optimist is a man who goes into a restaurant without a dime and figures on paying for the meal with the pearl he hopes to find in the oyster.

2364   An optimist is one who puts fifteen cents on a letter and marks it "rush."

HUMOR

2365   A gag is something you push down the people's throats whether they like it or not.

2366   I thought it was funny the other day when that fellow fed you all those green apples.
Yeah, I had to hold my sides.

2367   Excuse me — is this a general store?
Yes.
I would like to speak to the general.
Is that supposed to be a funny remark?
Yeah — it made *me* laugh.
Looking at you would make anybody laugh.

2368   Who said women haven't a keen sense of humor? The more you humor them the better they like it.

2369   A funny thing happened to my mother in Paris.
I thought you said you were born in Ohio.

2370   What are you laughing at?
       Nothing, sir. I'm just practicing so I can be ready when you say
          something funny.

2371   He had proposed — she had refused.
       She: You are just a joke to me.
       He: Well, can't you take a joke?

2372   I got a good joke on Johnson. Last week ven I vos at lodge
          Johnson kissed my ole voman an' giff her fifty cents — an' I
          kiss her annie time for notting.

2373   What would the world be without its little joke?
       You wouldn't be alive.

2374   You are a little Dove; may I hold your Palmolive?
       Not on your Lifebuoy; your head's solid Ivory.
       This is where I get the Colgate . . .
       I Woodbury that joke if I were you.

2375   That was one of my mother's jokes.
       Really? I suppose you were one of your father's jokes?

2376   I heard a new one the other day. I wonder if I told it to you?
       Is it funny?
       Yes.
       Then you haven't.

2377   You know my uncle nas a good joke on the police department.
       What is it?
       They locked him up for robbing a house and he didn't do it.

2378   Nudist Colony jokes: Without any toppers.

2379   That chiropractor joke was pretty good.
       Yeah — it has a new twist.

2380   You know the other night at the theatre a man fell out of the
          balcony and everybody laughed but me.
       Why didn't you laugh?
       I was the man.

RELATED SUBJECTS
Fat People 348-370
Scotchman 1102-1133
Writer 1612-1642
Theatre 4506-4512
Actor 4514-4585
Radio 4598-4610

PESSIMIST

2381 Daddy, what is a pessimist?
A man who wears a belt as well as suspenders, my son.

2382 What is a pessimist?
A man who won't milk a cow because he is afraid the milk's already sour.

RELATED SUBJECTS
Worry 2348-2355

POPULARITY

2383 What makes you so popular?
It's my line.
What is your line?
The line of least resistance.

2384 You know my brother doesn't believe in signs any more.
No? Why not?
Well, he spent six months trying to get rid of halitosis, and found out he was unpopular anyway.

2385 You certainly have a lot of girls.
If I should die tonight, at least thirty girls would go back in circulation again tomorrow.

2386 She is very popular. Last night she went out with a party of seventy-five. He was her granddaddy.

2387 What's the cause of Janet's unpopularity?
She won a popularity contest.

2388 Have you ever speculated on why you are so popular in your neighborhood?
No, except that I told my neighbors that I always played the saxophone when I got lonely.

2389 I had a quiet little evening alone with a book last night.
I'm afraid that's going to happen to me some night, too.

RELATED SUBJECTS
Friend 1037-1056
Enemy 1057-1058
Society 1136-1144
Hospitality 3564-3660

LIKE

2390 My girl's father doesn't like me.
He doesn't — on what grounds does he object to you?
On any grounds within ten miles of the house.

2391 And you say there are three reasons why you didn't like Archie?
Yes. I simply can't stand him — I simply can't stand him — I simply can't stand him!

2392 Yes, he's the kind of a guy who, when you first meet him, you don't like him. But when you get to know him, you hate him.

2393 I hate you.
What?
I said: I hate you! Hate — hate — hate!
Three hates make twenty-four.

2394 There are several people in this world I hate and you're all of them.

2395 You know, at first people don't care so much about me, but I grow on people.
I'll say you do, you little wart.

2396 Bobby, why are you so unkind to nurse? Don't you like her?
No, I hate her. I'd like to pinch her cheeks like daddy does.

> RELATED SUBJECTS
> Friend 1037-1056
> Enemy 1057-1058
> Popularity 2383-2389
> Love 2595-2640
> Marriage 2882-3051

FRESH PEOPLE

2997 A man I've never seen before, asked me for a kiss.
A fresh guy, eh?
Yeah.
Did you slap his face?
As soon as he got through.

2398 I saw that stranger kissing you.
Yeah — he kissed me a lot of times.
Where is that guy? I'll teach him a thing or two.
I don't think you could.

2399 That fresh taxi cab driver offered me a quarter for a kiss.
What are you looking in your pocketbook for?
Gee! I thought I'd lost the quarter.

2400 How about a little ride, cutie?
Are you going north?
Yes, I am.
Give my regards to the Eskimos.

2401 Oh, officer! There's a man following me and I think he must be drunk.
(Officer gives the woman the once-over) Yes, he must be!

2402 Listen, cutie, would you like to make a bet? I'll bet I can kiss you without even touching you.

I'll take you up.
Get ready. This is going to be a cinch.
(He kisses her several times)
You touched me when you kissed me.
All right — here's your nickel.

2403   Fresh Guy: Where do you live, cutie?
        Girl: I live at 210 West First Street—now, don't you dare
           follow me.

2404   Who was that guy that kissed you today on the street?
        I don't know, but he evidently knew me pretty well.

2405   Officer, this man is annoying me.
        But this man isn't even looking at you.
        I know it — that's what's annoying me.

2406   (Couple out driving in automobile—car stalls)
        He: Outa gas, by golly.
        Girl: Oh, yeah? (Pulls out flask)
        He: Ah ha! What's in the flask?
        Girl: Gasoline.

2407   (Man slips up to woman sitting on park bench and kisses her)
        How dare you!
        Pardon me, I thought you were my sister.
        You dumb ox, I AM your sister.

2408   What's a chiropractor?
        A guy who gets paid for what I get slapped for.

        RELATED SUBJECTS
        Golddigger 1029-1036
        Love Making 2641-2719
        Flirtation 2779-2784
        Lady Killer 2792-2793

NUTS-TO-YOU—NUTS

2409   You have some doughnuts there. Why not give me a few?
        Well—I'll give you half—dough to me and nuts to you.

2410   I saw your girl and she crochets beautifully.
        She doesn't crochet; she knits.
        I say she crochets.
        I say she knits.
        All right — crochets to me and knits to you.

2411   Some Hoochie Koochie dancers!
        You mean Nautch dancers.
        I say, Hoochie Koochie!
        I say, Nautch.
        All right — Hoochie Koochie to me and Nautch to you!

2412   He: (Bringing box of candy to girl) You know — sweets to the sweet.
She: Yeah—I figure that way, too. Help yourself to the nuts.

2413   There's something wrong with my automobile—my motor rattles something awful.
You mean, the motor knocks.
I said, it rattles.
I say, knocks.
All right — rattles to me — knocks to you!

2414   The only reason I come home at all is that the mosquitoes were biting me.
They weren't mosquitoes — they were gnats.
What are you talking about? They were mosquitoes.
They were gnats.
All right—mosquitoes to me, but gnats to you!

2415   That boat did 25 miles an hour.
Twenty-five miles? You mean knots.
Well, miles to me — knots to you.

2416   This girl is nuts.
That's my daughter. What do you mean she's nuts?
Nuts-so-bad.

2417   Name me three kinds of nuts.
That's easy! Peanuts, walnuts and forget-me-nuts.

GRATITUDE

2418   All that I am I owe to my mother.
Why don't you send her thirty cents and square the account?

2419   I must say that I owe everything I have to my wife.
Hey, you're not forgetting my bill, are you?

RELATED SUBJECTS
Friend 1037-1056
Kindness 2449-2465

COMPLIMENT

2420   I think she's as pretty as she can be.
Most girls are.

2421   You are very clever, if I may say so.
You may say so, but not in front of these people.
You are very clever, but not in front of these people.

2422   I hear a big blonde busted you in the eye at the masquerade party last night.
Yes. I told her how well she looked in a bustle.

What's wrong with that?
She wasn't wearing one.

2423 They were priceless.
What do you mean — they were priceless?
I don't want them at any price.

2424 You look sweet enough to eat.
I do eat. Where shall we go?

2425 You look like a clean cut young man.
Yes, ma'am, I just finished shaving.

2426 Little girl, you remind me of the ocean.
Why? Because I'm deep, restless and romantic?
No, because you make me sick.
Well, you're no tonic to *me!*

2427 You look like a million bucks.
Yes, and I'm just as hard to make.

2428 I've heard so much about you.
You'll have an awful time proving it.

2429 Your hat is becoming . . .
Oh, thank you.
. . . becoming a little worn out.

2430 You're one in a million, kid.
So are your chances.

2431 You're beautiful when I'm in the mood.
Do you really think I'm beautiful?
When I'm in the mood, anybody is beautiful.

2432 You know, you've changed since I saw you last.
And how? For better or worse?
My dear, you could only change for the better.

2433 I've heard a lot about you.
That's not strange — I've done a lot.

2434 Why, hello there, Janet.
I wonder how you remembered me?
I wouldn't forget a face like yours.

2435 That wasn't half bad.
It was ALL bad.

2436 Does your husband ever pay you compliments?
Well, sometimes he says: You're a fine one!

2437 He spoke very highly of us. He said we were perfect nonentities.

2438   That girl certainly looks good from a distance but she can't get far enough away.

2439   (Driving along country road)
        He: You look lovelier to me every minute. Do you know what that's a sign of?
        She: Sure. You're about to run out of gas.

RELATED SUBJECTS
Description of People 263-303
Conduct 1802-1862
Beauty 4725-4735

TOAST

2440   Make a toast to the Hay Fever Club.
        Here's looking at-choooo!

2441   I propose a little toast.
        You'll have to do better than that — I'm hungry.

2442   I feel just like a loaf of bread. Wherever I go — they toast me.

RELATED SUBJECTS
Hospitality 3564-3660
Speech 5111-5123

CONGRATULATION

2443   I want to congratulate you. This is one of the happiest days of your life.
        But I'm not getting married until tomorrow.
        That's why I say today is one of your happiest days.

2444   I'm glad to hear you're married.
        I don't know why you should be glad — I never did you any harm.

RELATED SUBJECTS
Compliment 2420-2439

SYMPATHY

2445   I wouldn't cry like that, my little man.
        Cry as you damn please; this is my way.

2446   Never think of him without a choking sensation.
        That's too bad.
        Yeah. Everytime I think of him I want to choke him.

2447 She's awful mean to me. Why, when I had my finger cut she cried over it — just so she could get salt in the wound.

2448 (Woman crying)
Bystander: I wouldn't cry like that!
Woman: And if I were you I wouldn't cry like this, either.

RELATED SUBJECTS
Friend 1037-1056
Marriage 2882-3051

KINDNESS

2449 Oh, no — I'm sure he's a kind man. I just heard him say he put his shirt on a horse that was scratched.

2450 George is the most generous man in the world — he gives me everything credit can buy.

2451 Oh, I always do a good deed every day.
That's fine — what good deed have you done today?
Why, there was only castor oil enough for one of us this morning, so I let my little brother have it.

2452 She's so tender-hearted she won't even whip cream. She can't even stand to beat a rug, and tears come to her eyes when she has to skin little onions.
I suppose she's kind to insects?
She never loses an opportunity to pat a mosquito on the back.

2453 My uncle's the meanest man in the world — he fed his cat peanuts so the cat would be too thirsty to drink anything but water.

2454 What is the matter? You have tears in your eyes.
My mother drowned one of my little kittens.
And that made you cry?
Sure. She promised me I could drown it.

2455 You know, I think everyone should divide their worldly goods with the other fellow.
That's a good idea. If you had $2,000 — would you give me one-half?
Sure.
And if you had two automobiles, would you give me one?
Sure.
And if you had two shirts, would you give me one?
No.
Why?
Because I've got two shirts.

2456   I tell you lady, I'm hungry. I'm broke — and I'm starving. I
haven't tasted food for three days.
Don't worry about it — it still tastes the same.

2457   I want to get some ice cream — will you lend me a dime?
I'm giving you this dime because it makes me happy to do it.
Why don't you give me a quarter and really enjoy yourself?

2458   Will you please send someone to chloroform three cats which are
outside my door? I'm afraid they'll freeze to death.

2459   Here's a nickel. Run out and buy yourself a steak.
But a steak will cost more than a nickel.
That's all right. I'll trust you for the rest.

2460   She's very kindhearted. The horse kicked her through the barn
door and she cried all night because she thought the horse was
mad at her.

2461   I got big-hearted this morning and gave a bum five dollars.
What did your husband say about it?
Thanks!

2462   Yes, I feel an intense longing to do something for others.
Just who do you mean by others?
Well, I suppose almost anybody outside of my immediate family.

2463   My father's so kindhearted he picks stray dogs up on the streets
and brings them home and feeds them.
I didn't know you called your relatives dogs.

2464   What are you fellows weeping about?
The elephant's dead.
Did you love the big animal so dearly?
No, ma'am — love 'im nothing — the boss just told us we've
got to dig his grave.

2465   If I saw a man beating a donkey and stopped him from doing
so, what virtue would I be showing?
Brotherly love.

RELATED SUBJECTS
Friend 1037-1056
Conduct 1802-1862
Gratitude 2418-2419
Beggar 5518-5537

CHIVALRY

2466   I noticed you got up and gave that lady your seat in the train the other day.
Since childhood I have respected a woman with a strap in her hand.

2467   After all, Sir Walter Raleigh established chivalry when he let Queen Elizabeth step on his coat.
I was just thinking . . .
Thinking what?
What if it had been Queen Elizabeth and Mahatma Gandhi?

2468   If he stands uncovered while talking to a lady it is not chivalry.
It's either that he is collegiate or he is proud of his hair.

2469   He can't bear to see the ladies stand in the street cars. So he closes his eyes.

2470   My sweetie took me down to the picture show last night and we had to ride on a crowded street car. Gee! Was he mad!
Because you had to ride on the crowded street car?
Well, that's part of the reason, but the thing that made him the sorest was that there was only one seat when we got on and I had to stand up all the way downtown.

2471   What do you do when in doubt about kissing a girl?
Give her the benefit of the doubt.

2472   Chivalry is the notion that the girl you married is better than the ones you go out with.

2473   When we was school kids I was crazy about her. I used to pick her up and carry her across the mud puddles.
I suppose you'd do the same now?
No. I couldn't. She weighs two hundred and forty pounds.

2474   I saw a fellow strike a girl today.
You didn't let him get away with it, did you?
I went up to him and said: Only a coward would hit a woman — why don't you hit a man?
Then what happened?
That's all I remember.

RELATED SUBJECTS
Male (the) 912-924
Conduct 1802-1862
Apology 2519-2520

PATRIOTISM

2475 My uncle just got back from Europe. The minute he stepped on American soil, he fell right down and kissed the ground.
In a burst of patriotism?
No, on a banana peel.

2476 Three cheers for the red, white and blue!
Thas not enough — only makesh just one cheer for each color.

2477 What's that waving up there on the pole?
The flag, dear.
The flag?
Yes, the flag. Your flag and my flag . . .
Then, let's go up and get it.

2478 He was a Scotch anarchist, but he got killed.
How?
He lit a bomb and hated to let go of it.

> RELATED SUBJECTS
> Gun 4454-4461
> Navy 5131
> Army 5134-5147
> War 5148-5152

BASHFULNESS

2479 I won a prize in a recent contest for bashfulness.
What was the prize?
I don't know — I was too bashful to go up and get it.

2480 She's so modest she pulls down the shade to change her mind.

2481 He is so modest he carries extra fuses around with him just in case his girl's lights go out.

2482 She's so modest she blindfolds herself while taking a bath.

2483 He's one of those modest fellows — if he was sitting in the parlor with his girl and the lights went out — he'd go down to the cellar to fix them.

2484 Has the canary had its bath yet?
Yes, ma'am — it's all right for you to come in now.

> RELATED SUBJECTS
> Conduct 1802-1862
> Girl 2588-2594

NOT MYSELF

2485 He told her he wasn't himself tonight, so she beat him up because she doesn't allow strangers in the house.

2486   This isn't your room.
       That's all right, I'm not myself tonight.

2487   What's your name?
       Don't know what my name is.
       You don't know what your name is?
       No.
       Why not?
       I'm not myself tonight.

RELATED SUBJECTS
Conduct 1802-1862
Drinking 2055-2140

REVENGE

2488   My friend had injured me, and I itched for revenge. Two months
       later my friend was found in his office, a shrieking madman
       thrashing about in an enormous wastebasket . . . I had simply
       put his name on every mailing list in the country.

2489   Tell me about this girl you went with.
       We had an argument. I said it was only a flirtation and I was
       through. She said she was going to get revenge.
       And did she get revenge?
       I'll say she did — she married me.

RELATED SUBJECTS
Enemy 1057-1058
Conduct 1802-1862
Fight 2145-2213

HONESTY

2490   There are millions of ways to make money, but only one honest
       way.
       How is that?
       I don't know.

2491   You shouldn't lie — look at George Washington.
       I'll look at him — where is he?
       He was a model man and he was honest.
       No, you're wrong. He wasn't — to this day whenever it's his
       birthday, the banks all close.

2492   Come with me and we'll sit beneath that pine tree.
       Not me!
       Why — can it be you can't trust me?
       Well — I trust you — and I trust myself — but I can't trust
       the two of us together.

2493   Never trust a girl who says she loves you more than anybody
       else in the world. It proves that she has been experimenting.

2494   Did you vote for the honor system?
Bet I did — four times!

2495   What are you doing nowadays?
Trying to earn an honest living.
Well, you certainly won't have much competition.

2496   Here, hold my horse a minute, will you?
Sir, I'm a member of Congress.
That's all right. I'll trust you.

2497   Joe is certainly an awful flirt. I wouldn't trust him too far.
Huh! I wouldn't trust him too near!

2498   Trust me for a pair of shoes, will you?
I wouldn't even trust my brother.
I know him, too, and I wouldn't trust him myself.

2499   He doesn't trust her any more.
How is that?
One morning he sneaked in the kitchen of her home, and kissed
her on the neck. Without turning around, she said: All right,
just leave a quart of milk and a pint of cream.

RELATED SUBJECTS
Conduct 1802-1862
Politician 5099-5110
Election 5124-5130
Thief 5178-5214
Policeman 5225-5228

DISHONESTY

2500   He's so crooked I always count my fingers after shaking hands
with him.

2501   Before he did everybody he had time to do — now all he has to
do is time.

2502   You're so crooked you have to screw your sox on.

RELATED SUBJECTS   Conduct 1802-1862
Description of People 263-303 Election 5124-5130
Thief 5178-5214

RIGHT

2503   See that girl over there?
Yeah.
She's fresh from the country and it's up to us to show her the
difference between right and wrong.
Okay, Pal. You teach her what's right.

2504   How do you get along with your relatives?
I never speak to them.
Is that right?
No, it isn't right, but I don't speak to them.

2505 He: May I kiss you?
      She: Would it be right?
      He: I'll try my best.

2506 The dancing teacher showed me something new today.
      Is that right?
      No, but it's lots of fun.

2507 Last night I did some n-e-k-k-i-n-g.
      N-e-k-k-i-n-g? That isn't right!
      I know it — but it's lots of fun.

> RELATED SUBJECTS
> Lying 1540-1564
> Conduct 1802-1862
> Honesty 2490-2499
> Unfaithfulness 3057-3088

INSULT

2508 What do you call frozen water?
      Iced water.
      What do you call frozen ink?
      Iced ink.
      You're telling me.

2509 The butcher insulted me today.
      What happened?
      I asked him for 10 cents worth of dog meat, and he said: Shall I
      wrap it up or will you eat it here?

2510 When he insulted me, I told him I never wanted to see his face
      again.
      What did he say to that?
      Nothing. He just got up and turned out the light.

2511 Will you do me a favor?
      Gladly.
      Step in front of a steam roller sometime so I can use you for a
      bookmark.

2512 The maid just gave notice. It seems you insulted her this morning
      over the telephone.
      Oh, I thought it was you on the wire.

2513 Mrs. Brown must be offended at something. She hasn't been over
      for several days.
      Be sure to find out what it is when she does come over, and
      we'll try it on her again.

2514 I wanted to call my dog "Shakespeare" but my mother wouldn't
      let me — said it would be an insult to the man. Then I

wanted to name him after you, but my mother wouldn't let me.
Good for your mother!
She said that would be an insult to the dog.

2515   You're a sap.
What?
You're a sap — sap — sap! You know what comes out of trees.
Monkeys like you.

2516   You remind me of the ocean.
Why? Because I'm so uncontrollable and restless?
No, because you're all wet.

2517   One of your guests insulted me!
Only one?

2518   Now, just a minute, Mr. Camembert . . .
Camembert? That's a cheese.
You're telling me?

RELATED SUBJECTS
Insanity 1399-1417
Conduct 1802-1862
Fight 2145-2213
Apology 2519-2520

APOLOGY

2519   (After making insulting remarks)
If I said anything I'm sorry for, I'm glad of it.

2520   I say, dear, you nearly hit me. Be careful where you aim your
gun. You just missed me.
Gee, I'm awfully sorry.

RELATED SUBJECTS
Conduct 1802-1862
Fight 2145-2213
Fresh People 2397-2408

PUNISHMENT

2521   Who are you?
I'm guilty.
Were you arrested?
No. But I want to be punished. In a moment of weakness, when
no one was looking, I expectorated on the sidewalk and I want
to be chastised properly.
If it will make you feel better — two dollars fine.

2522   Do you think it's right to punish folks for things they haven't
done?
Why, of course not, Willie.
Well, I didn't do my homework.

2523 Son, I'm spanking you because I love you.
Dad, I'd like to be big enough to return your love.

2524 This makes the fifth time I've punished you this week. What
have you to say?
I'm glad it's Friday, sir.

RELATED SUBJECTS
Conduct 1802-1862
Fight 2145-2213
Fines-Sentences 5276-5282

CHURCH

2525 Preacher Simmons says things are getting better because he's
getting much better buttons in the collection.

2526 Where have you been, little girl?
To Sunday School.
What have you in your hand?
Oh, just an ad about Heaven.

2527 What is your religion?
Militia, sir.
Oh, no, I said "religion."
Oh, religion, sir. I beg your pardon, I'm a plumber.

2528 I was sorry for your wife in church this morning when she had
a terrific attack of coughing and everyone turned to look at her.
You need not worry about that. She was wearing a new spring
hat.

2529 Confessor: I have stolen a fat goose from a poultry yard!
Priest: That is very wrong.
Confessor: Would you like to accept it, father?
Priest: Certainly not — return it to the man whom you stole
it from.
Confessor: But I have offered it to him and he won't have it.
Priest: In that case you may keep it yourself.
Confessor: Thank you, Father.
(The Priest arrived home to find one of his own geese had been
stolen).

2530 You know your guardian angel is always with you.
Does he eat with me?
Yes.
Does he sleep with me?
Yes.
Well, I'll bet he's the fellow that kicked me out of bed last night.

2531   What is the difference between a preacher and a politician?
        What?
        A preacher makes up his bed and lies in it — a politician makes
        up his bunk and lies out of it.

2532   You know that church on Tenth Street? It accommodates ten
           thousand souls.
        How many heels?

RELATED SUBJECTS
Right 2503-2507
Prayer 2550-2554

BIBLE

2533   Say, dad, our lesson in Sunday School told about the evil spirits
           entering the swine.
        Yes, my son. What do you wish to know?
        Was that the way they got the first deviled ham?

RELATED SUBJECTS
Prayer 2550-2554

ADAM AND EVE

2534   I was told that radio started in the Garden of Eden. Do you be-
           lieve that?
        Well, whoever told you that radio started in the Garden of Eden
           was probably referring to the time they took a rib out of Adam
           and used it to make the first loudspeaker.

2535   The reason I want to be Adam is, if I pulled a joke, I know no one
           could say: I heard that one before.

2536   (Father explaining beginning of world to son)
        In the beginning of the world, Adam was born.
        Was he born in the morning?
        No, a little before Eve. A rib was taken from his side while he
           slept, and that was Eve.
        Didn't he need the rib?
        It was a spare rib.
        (Boy starts to cry) I've got a pain in my side. Oh, daddy, I think
           I'm going to have a wife.

2537   Is it true Adam discovered love in a garden?
        If he did it must have been a beer garden for he saw snakes.

2538   Why did you strike your little sister?
Well, we were playing Adam and Eve, and instead of tempting me with the apple, she ate it herself.

RELATED SUBJECTS
Male (the) 912-924
Females (the) 925-938

NOAH'S ARK

2539   (Noah's Ark as three camels come on board)
Noah: Hey, one of you will have to stay ashore.
1st: Not me. I'm the camel so many people swallow while straining at a gnat.
2nd: I'm the camel whose back is broken by the last straw.
3rd: And I'm the camel which shall pass through the eye of a needle sooner than a rich man shall enter the Kingdom of Heaven.
So Noah, deciding posterity would be lost for illustrations without them, let them all come aboard.

2540   What was the difference between Noah's Ark and Joan of Arc?
Noah's Ark was made of wood and Joan of Arc was maid of Orleans.

2541   Why did Noah take two of each kind of animal in the ark?
Because he didn't believe that story about the stork.

2542   Did you know all the animals came on the ark in pairs?
All except worms and they came in apples.

RELATED SUBJECTS   Pets 3667-3740
Church 2525-2549   Animals (wild) 4640-4668

PROVERBS

2543   Remember — bread cast on•the water always returns.
Bread cast on the water may return, but the dough this country cast across the ocean didn't.

2544   Late to bed, early to rise, makes a fan radio-wise.

2545   Let him among us to run the fastest throw the first stone.

2546   You spoiled my article by a misprint.
I'm sorry. What did we get wrong?
A proverb I used. You printed "a word to the wife is sufficient."

RELATED SUBJECTS
Church 2525-2549
School 4885-4894
Speech 5111-5123

QUOTATIONS

2547   You want to remember this: Crime doesn't pay.
No, it doesn't pay, but the hours are optional.

2548   Give me a quotation from the Bible.
Judas went out and hanged himself.
And another one?
Go thou and do likewise.

2549   Cleanliness is next to godliness.
Maybe in the Bible it's next to godliness, but in Chicago it's next to impossible.

> RELATED SUBJECTS
> Bible 2533
> Speech 5111-5123

PRAYER

2550   The middle-aged, childless farmer and his wife resorted to prayer that their loneliness might be relieved. After a time they were receiving congratulations on the birth of triplets.
Friend: Prayers are always answered.
Farmer: Yes, but I never prayed for no bumper crop like that.

2551   In India the Mohammedans pray in the street.
That's nothing. Pedestrians do that here.

2552   "Oh Lord," prayed Sally, "I'm not asking for a thing for myself, but please send mother a son-in-law."

2553   Little Clarence, climbing a tree, began to fall swiftly toward the ground: Oh, Lord, save me! Save me! . . . (pause) . . . Never mind, Lord, my pants caught on a branch.

2554   Do you say your prayers every night?
No, some nights I don't want anything.

> RELATED SUBJECTS   Superstition 1422-1431
> Spiritualism 1276-1277   Church 2525-2549
>   Luck 5588

HEAVEN

2555   Don't you believe in the hereafter? — I want a kiss.
What's the hereafter got to do with the kiss?
That's what I'm hereafter.

2556   Tell me those three words that will send me right up to Heaven!
Go shoot yourself.

2557   There will be weeping, wailing and gnashing of teeth among the wicked who pass on to the next world.
What about those who haven't any teeth?
Teeth will be provided.

2558   St. Peter: How did you get here?
Man: Flu.

2559   Do you believe in the hereafter?
Sure I do.
Then, hereafter please don't bother me.

2560   Saton: Hey, you act as if you owned this dump.
New arrival: I do. My wife gave it to me.

2561   St. Peter: And here is your golden harp.
Arrival: How much is the first payment?

2562   Sergeant: Hey, there, you, John! Come back here! Suppose you do get killed, what of it? Heaven is your home.
John: Yes, sir, Sarge, I know that. But right now, I'm not homesick.

2563   Do you believe that a missionary goes to Heaven and a cannibal that eats people goes to the other place?
Of course, I believe it. A missionary always goes to Heaven.
But answer this question: What happens when the missionary is inside the cannibal?

2564   Yesterday I saw a man knocked right up in the air, and he lay stretched out under the telegraph wires unconscious, and when he woke up he found the wires all around his wrists. He said: Thank goodness, I've led a clean life. They've given me a harp.

2565   Don't you know that matches are made in Heaven?
They aren't either. They're made in Sweden.

RELATED SUBJECTS
Death 124-145
Church 2525-2549

MORMON

2566   (Preacher marrying Mormon to his wives)
Preacher: John Smith, do you take these women to be your lawful wedded wives?
Man: I do.

Preacher: And do you girls take John Smith to be your lawful
wedded husband?
Women: (Faint) We do.
Preacher: Pardon me, but you girls in the back will have to speak
louder if you want to get in on this.

2567   You're the fellow who was so worried about the Salt Lake City
earthquake.
Will, I'm not worried any more because I just found out there
wasn't any earthquake in Utah.
No earthquake? There must have been some reason for the earth
to vibrate the way it did.
Yeah — Mae West walked over Brigham Young's grave.

RELATED SUBJECTS
Church 2525-2549

II.–INSTITUTIONS

MATRIMONY

COURTSHIP

OLD MAID

2568 Why do old maids wear cotton gloves?
I don't know — why?
'Cause they haven't any kids.

2569 You know my old maid aunt lets the dust accumulate under the
bed because she heard that man is made out of dust.

2570 I have a mad, crazy, insane desire to crush you in my arms.
You aren't insane, baby, you're talking sense.

2571 What is the difference between a young girl and an old maid?
A young girl goes out with a Johnny and an old maid stays home
with the Willies.

2572 Miss Priss, the office spinster, is taking lessons now in "How to
become a contortionist" so she can sit on her own lap.

2573 She's an old maid — and she's got sixteen children.
An old maid and she's got sixteen children?
Yeah, she teaches the kindergarten.

2574 Husbands are such a worry.
Oh? I didn't know you had one?
I don't—that's what worries me!

2575 1st Old Maid: There's some one in the room; hand me the mirror.
2nd Old Maid: So that you can look under the bed?
1st Old Maid: No. So I can powder my nose.

2576 Is this the janitor speaking?
Yes, Miss Sourpuss, what do you want?
I just found two strange men in my apartment and I want you
to throw one of them out.

2577 An old maid rang the fire alarm and twenty firemen responded.
When they arrived she said: There's no fire, so nineteen of you
can go back.

2578 Old Maid: (Calling fire department) A man is trying to get
into my room.
You don't want the Fire Department — what you want is the
Police Department.
Old Maid: I don't want the Police — I want the Fire Department — a man is trying to get into my room — and we're on
the second floor and he needs a ladder.

2579   So the waiter said to me: How would you like your rice? So I
        says wistfully — thrown at me, big boy!

2580   Have you ever been kissed by a big, strong, handsome man?
        No, could you fix it up for me some night?

2581   You say, Tillie, you were engaged to a promising young lawyer?
        Yes, but he didn't keep his promise.

2582   Imagine my embarrassment when, according to my usual habit,
        I looked under the bed before retiring — I had forgotten that
        I was in an upper berth.

                    RELATED SUBJECTS
                    Age 45-107
                    Description of People 263-303
                    Love 2595-2640
                    Mouse 3902-3907

BACHELOR

2583   A bachelor is a man who thinks before he acts, and then doesn't
        act.

2584   He has always been very lucky in love.
        You mean, he always gets his woman?
        No — he's still a bachelor.

2585   Did your uncle ever marry?
        Well, he was two-thirds married one time. He was there and
        the preacher was there, but the bride never showed up.

2586   What excuse have you for not being married?
        I was born that way.

2587   Hasn't Harvey ever married?
        No, and I don't think he intends to, because he's studying for
        a bachelor's degree.

                    RELATED SUBJECTS
                    Marriage 2882-3051

GIRL

2588   Do you ever expect to find the perfect girl?
        No, but it's lots of fun hunting.

2589   What is the difference between a girl and a horse?
        I don't know.
        I'll bet you have some swell dates.

2590   Pete: I'm going to get married as soon as I find my opposite.
        Hal: Fine. Then I'll introduce you tonight to a girl who's good-
            looking, intelligent, and cultured.

2591   I gave you a girl.
        You gave me a girl you didn't want.
        Boy! The girl I don't want don't live.

2592   Have you ever met the only girl you could be happy with?
        Yeah, lots of times.

2593   I want a girl that cooks, sews, keeps house and doesn't smoke
            or pet.
        Why don't you go down to the graveyard and dig up one?

2594   Was that a new girl I saw you with last night?
        No, just the old one painted over.

                            RELATED SUBJECTS
                            Male (the) 912-924
                            Female (the) 925-938
                            Flirtation 2779-2784
                            Dates 2785-2791

LOVE

2595   Haven't you ever met a girl you cared for?
        Only recently, it was love at first sight.
        Why don't you marry her?
        I took a second look.

2596   Real love is that something — that certain something that makes
            a girl marry her boss and work for him for the rest of her
            life without salary.

2597   I traded my sweetheart to an Indian for a sack of peanuts. Now
            I wish I had him back.
        So, you found out you really loved him?
        No, I'm hungry for peanuts.

2598   Love — the delusion that one woman differs from another.

2599   I'm getting so I can't sleep for love of you. Let's get married.
        Why?
        So I can sleep.

2600   Darling, will you love me when I'm old and feeble?
        Of course, I do.

2601   I wonder if my girl loves me.
        Of course; why should she make you an exception?

2602   Love beats its tattoo on every lover's pocketbook.

2603   You don't love me any more. I'm going back to mother.
        Don't bother. I'll go back to my wife.

2604   I don't like you any more. Take your ring back; I love Joe.
       Where is Joe?
       You're not going to tell him, are you?
       No, I'm going to try to sell him the ring.

2605   Ah, you Arabians! You are such intense lovers.
       Of course, we do everything in tents.

2606   Then there is the fellow who wears his girl's picture in his watch
       case because he thinks he will learn to love her in time.

2607   I can't learn to love you.
       But I've saved ten thousand dollars.
       Give me one more lesson.

2608   You don't even know what love is.
       I surely do. Love is the tenth word in a telegram.

2609   Mrs. Pecksniff must think a lot of her husband. She kisses him
       every time he comes home.
       Yes, but she kisses him to see if he's been drinking.

2610   Then we're engaged?
       Of course.
       Am I the first girl you ever loved?
       No, dear, but I'm harder to suit now than I used to be.

2611   Do you love me?
       Yes, dear.
       Would you die for me?
       No — mine is an undying love.

2612   Was it a case of love at first sight?
       No, it was a case of whiskey first — then love came natural.

2613   (Reading book on love)
       What does it say on the first page?
       It says when you meet a girl you like you take her hand in
            yours . . .
       Then what?
       Then you squeeze it . . .
       Yes . . .
       Then you put your arm around her waist . . .
       Yes, yes — go on . .
       You're getting ahead of the book. Then you take her for a stroll.
       Then what does the book say?
       The next page is torn out.

2614   Are I in love with her?
       What English! You should say: I am in love with her, we are in
            love with her, they are in love with her.
       Gee, what a girl I picked!

2615 When a woman loves a man he can make her do anything she
      wants to do.

2616 Do you think you could learn to love me?
      Yes, but if I were a man I'd hate to think I was an acquired
      taste.

2617 Don't turn out the lights, John. Don't you know that love is
      blind?
      Yeah, but your old man's not in love.

2618 If all the world loves a lover, a lover's lover ought to get jealous.

2619 Darling, I've lost all my money. I haven't a cent in the world.
      That won't make any difference, dear. I'll love you just as much
      — even if I never see you again.

2620 Tell me that you love me.
      Sure, but don't ask me to write it.

2621 I luf my goil more effry day. She ees so capable, so efficient. She
      ees on the thoid tub at the laundry now, and as soon as she
      gets on de foist tub, I'm goin' to marry her.

2622 Do you realize what happens to nine out of every ten men that
      fall in love?
      No. What?
      They get married.

2623 Could you love two girls at once?
      Yes, immediately.

2624 It's a very simple question after all. The only thing she must
      decide is whether she loves him or not.
      Yeah, but what's puzzling her is whether she can do any better.

2625 It's mostly you I care for, I care for your money only up to a
      certain point.
      The decimal point?

2626 Do you believe in love at first sight?
      Well, I think it saves a lot of time.

2627 But how can I be sure that you love me?
      Well, I can scarcely sleep at night thinking of you.
      That doesn't prove anything. Papa can hardly sleep thinking of you.

2628 Do you love me still?
      I might if you'd stay still long enough.

2629 I can't marry you as I don't love you, but I will be a sister
      to you.
      Fine. How much do you think our father is likely to leave us?

2630   And you'll love me always when we are married?
       Of course, Henry! I've begun to dread getting a divorce already.

2631   I'd like a pencil.
       Hard or soft?
       Soft. It's for writing a love letter.

2632   I wonder if my husband will love me when my hair is grey.
       Why not? He's loved you through three shades already.

2633   Love — the delusion that one woman differs from another.

2634   And will you love me as much as this when we are married?
       How can you doubt me? You know I've always liked married
       women best.

2635   Would you love me just the same if my father had lost all his
          money, Ole?
       He hasn't lost it, has he?
       No.
       Of course, I would, you silly girl.

2636   Oh, darling, I love you so. Please say you'll be mine. I'm not
          rich like Percival Brown. I haven't a car, or a fine house, or a
          well-stocked cellar, like Percival Brown, but, darling, I love
          you, and I cannot live without you!
       And I love you, too, darling; but where is this man Brown?

2637   Captain Randall proposes in this letter. I wonder if he really
          loves me — he's only known me a week.
       Oh, then, perhaps he does.

2638   We met one day and married the next.
       Oh, love at first sight?
       Yeah, but I wished I'd taken another look.

2639   What's your idea of love?
       Taking a girl out and fattening her up for somebody else.

2640   Do you really love me?
       What do you think I'm doing — shadow boxing?

RELATED SUBJECTS
Courtship 2568-2881
Marriage 2882-3051

LOVE MAKING

2641 My uncle is going with a woman 85 years old. She's very rich.
It's what you call a football romance. He's waiting for her to
kick off.
How does a romance like that ever start?
I think they were thrown together in a rumble seat.

2642 Where did he meet her?
They met in a revolving door and he's been going around with
her ever since.

2643 Why won't you sit on my lap, dear?
Because you're bowlegged and I'm afraid I'll fall through.

2644 Why are you wearing a fireman's hat and a bathing suit?
I promised my girl I'd go through fire and water for her.

2645 My uncle got married. It was a garden romance.
A garden romance? How beautiful!
Yeah. He has always been a dead beat and she was an old tomato.

2646 He objected to my clothes, my friends and my singing. Then he
married another girl, so I made up my mind to have nothing
more to do with him.

2647 Can you support her in the way she's been accustomed to?
No, perhaps I cannot support her in the manner to which she has
been accustomed to, but I can support her in the way to which
her mother was accustomed when she was first married.

2648 I don't get much of a kick out of petting girls.
I never heard one complain either.

2649 I would go to the end of the world for you!
Yes, but would you stay there?

2650 Darling, I'm groping for words to express my love for you.
Well, do you think I have part of the dictionary tattooed on me?

2651 He was wonderful. Divine. He said things to me no man has
ever said.
What was that?
He asked me to marry him.

2652 Why, darling, your kisses are hotter than hot.
Yeah, but your nephew says they're hotter than hotter than hot.

2653 I would love to go out with Bing Crosby again.
Again?
Yes, once before I felt I'd like to.

2654 I bought her a fine dinner, took her to a show, then to a night
club. Then do you know what she said?

No.
Oh, then you've had her out, too.

2655   I've got a hotel heart — always room for one more.

2656   You know I used to go around with her until I found out she
        spent $5,000 a year on dresses.
        So you broke up over that?
        Yeah. Now I'm going with her dressmaker.

2657   I was bursting with love — she said I could kiss her every time a
        star fell. So I kissed her, and I kissed her and I kissed her and
        now she's mad at me.
        Why did she get mad?
        Because she found out the neighborhood was full of lightning bugs
        last night.

2658   What would you do if you had had five dates with a man and he
        had never attempted to kiss you?
        I'd lie about it.

2659   I love you — I adore you. I have always wanted you. Will you
        kiss me?
        What for?

2660   You say she only partially returned your affection?
        Yes, she returned all the love letters but kept the ring.

2661   If that boy never necks you, why do you go around with him?
        Oh, he's such a relief after a hard day at the office.

2662   He's been taking her out to dinner every night.
        Yes, and I hear she's all fed up on him.

2663   A love affair may be said to have progressed beyond the prelimi-
        nary stages when a man stops fighting for his girl and begins
        fighting with her.

2664   A courtship begins when a man whispers sweet nothings, and
        ends when he says nothing sweet.

2665   She sat on my lap for at least two hours.
        Quite a lapse of time, eh?

2666   I'm fifty-eight years old and never been kissed. Did I miss any-
        thing?
        It's too late to find out now.

2667   Now, you hardly speak to me any more — and you used to call me
        your heart's delight.
        Yes — delight that failed.

2668   I've known a lot of girls, too.
What happened to them?
I started paying attention to them and now I'm paying alimonv

2669   Why does a boy have to hold a girl's hand?
Self-defense, you sap!

2670   Do you believe in necking?
Why, of course not.
Neither do I, you liar!

2671   The way to a man's heart may be through his stomach, but who
the heck wants to go through his stomach?

2672   Margie, I love you! I love you, Margie!
In the first place, you don't love me; and in the second place, my
name isn't Margie.

2673   Why did your sister throw that farmer over for the Duke?
She said love in a cottage was all right, but she preferred passion
in a palace.

2674   Hello, Ruth, do you still love me?
Ruth? My name is Helen.
I'm so sorry — I keep thinking this is Wednesday.

2675   Somebody loves me, too.
Who loves you?
Don't you know that beautiful girl who moved into the corner
house last week? I sang a serenade under her window last night,
and she threw me a beautiful red, red rose.
In a moment of mad love?
No, in a three pound pot.

2676   Are you going to take your girl to the movies?
We don't have to go to the movies.
Why not?
Her mother and father are going.

2677   He bought a new shirt, and on a slip pinned to the inside found
the name and address of a girl with the words: Please write and
send a photograph.
"Ah," he said, "here is romance."
He wrote to the girl and sent a picture of himself. In due
course an answer came, and with a heart aflutter, he opened it.
It was only a note reading: I was just curious to see what kind
of looking fellow would wear such a funny shirt.

2678   If you see a pretty girl, you stop! She turns around and you LOOK!
And after you're married, HOW you listen!

2679   I kept all her letters for years, but yesterday I burned them up.
       Why — after keeping them for years?
       I just found out she always wet them on her Pekinese's nose.

2680   Do you think you could be happy with a girl like me?
       Perhaps, if she isn't too much like you.

2681   What kind of a husband do you think I should look for?
       Better leave the husbands alone and look for a single man.

2682   Ah, look at the cow and the calf rubbing noses in the pasture. That
       sight makes me want to do the same.
       Well, go ahead — it's your cow.

2683   Is Madge still looking for her ideal man?
       Good Heavens, no! She's far too busy looking for a husband.

2684   Listen, daughter, I don't want to be narrowminded about how late
       your boy friend stays. I don't care if he stays till morning, but
       I wish you would tell him to stop taking the morning paper
       when he leaves.

2685   Am I good enough for you, dearest?
       No, you're not; but you're too good for any other girl.

2686   I notice that your policeman friend calls frequently. Do you think
       he means business?
       I think he does. He's already beginning to complain about my
       cooking.

2687   No, Tom, I can never be yours. Sorry, but that's that.
       All right — what about my presents?
       I'll return them, of course.
       Yes, I know you will, but who's going to return all those cigars I
       gave your father and the pennies I gave your little brother?

2688   Darling, I could die for your sake.
       You are always saying that, but you never do it.

2689   I'd go through everything with you.
       Let's begin with your bank book.

2690   So you and your boy friend were reading. Well, just how could
       you do that with the lights out?
       Why, mother, we were lip reading.

2691   It was a beef stew romance.
       What is that?
       She was always beefing and he was always stewed.

2692   I don't stand for necking.
       You don't.
       No, standing makes me tired.

2693 I'm in love with a beautiful girl, but she's poor. And there's a homely girl with plenty of money in love with me. Would you marry the rich girl or the poor girl?
I'd marry the rich girl and be good to the poor.

2694 Since I met my new girl I can't eat, I can't sleep, I can't drink.
Why not?
I'm broke.

2695 Doesn't that young man know how to say goodnight?
I'll say he does!

2696 Myra, did I see that young man stroking your hair on the porch last night?
It's a mere habit with him, Mother. He used to stroke on the varsity eight.

2697 How come you go steady with Eloise?
She's different from other girls.
How so?
She's the only girl who will go with me.

2698 You must be pretty strong.
Strong? What makes you think so?
My daddy said you can wrap any man in town around your little finger.

2699 Mother, I advertised under a different name that I would like to make the acquaintance of a refined gentleman with an eye to romance.
Gladys, how awful! Did you get any answers?
Only one — from father.

2700 She hooked him on the pier last night.
Oh? Well, I think she should have thrown him back.

2701 He: Oh, my dear, how can I leave you?
She: By train, plane or taxi.

2702 You never show contempt for any man, do you?
No, I'm saving my hisses for the man I marry.

2703 Gladys, do you love me?
Yes.
Would you be willing to live on my income?
Yes, if you'll get another for yourself.

2704 I'll never forget you — never.
I'll tell you something that will make you forget me.
What is it?
Tomorrow is my birthday.

2705 I'd love to have a little home of my own.
Wouldn't that be great! Then we could get married.

2706 Why do you want your letters returned? Are you afraid that I'll
take them to court?
No, but I paid to have those letters written by an expert, and I
may use them again some day.

2707 Daughter, is that young man serious in his intentions?
Guess he must be, dad. He asked me how much I make, what
kind of meals we have, and how you and mother are to live with.

2708 How dare you say my father is a wretch!
Well, I told him I could not live without you and he said he would
be willing to pay the funeral expenses.

2709 You deceiver, I hate you!
But yesterday you said you loved every hair on my head.
But not every hair on your shoulder.

2710 But surely, you didn't tell him straight out that you loved him?
Goodness, no. He had to squeeze it out of me.

2711 Daughter: I wish you would make some allowances for Jimmy's
little shortcomings.
Father: I'm not complaining about his shortcomings; it's his long
stayings.

2712 I called on my girl one night and her mother jerked me into the
hall and said: Young man, what are your intentions regarding
my daughter?
Just then my girl called down from upstairs: Mama, that ain't
the one.

2713 Well, and how are you getting on with your courtship of the
banker's daughter?
Not so bad. I'm getting some encouragement now.
Really, is she beginning to smile sweetly on you, or something?
Not exactly, but last night she told me she had said no for the
last time.

2714 Boy, some doll! She ain't got a friend, has she?
Yep.
Oh, heck! Who?
Me.

2715 So Helen gave her boy friend the sack?
Yes, but she kept the presents which came in it.

2716 Stop it — you'll squeeze the life out of me!
Impossible! You haven't any life in you.

2717   Do you love me with all your heart and soul?
Uh-huh.
Do you think I'm the most beautiful girl in the world?
Uh-huh.
Do you think my lips are like rose petals?
Uh-huh.
Oh, you say the most beautiful things!

2718   I went to see my girl last night.
Did you stay late?
Well, I guess I did, but I kept turning the clock back and finally my girl's father yelled down from upstairs and said: That clock has struck twelve three times now — would you mind letting it practice on one for a while?

2719   You can't blame young folks for making love in a taxi. After all, that kind of thing has been going on ever since the days of Adam and Eve.
That taxi I had the other day must have been the one Adam and Eve rode in.

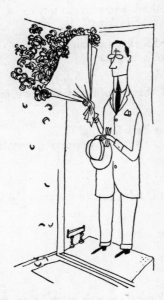

RELATED SUBJECTS
Fight 2145-2213
Courtship 2568-2881
Married Life 2882-3131
Boast 2291
Egotism 2315
Courage 2330
Worry 2353
Nuts-to-You 2412
Compliment 2426
Right 2507
Insult 2516
Prayer 2552
Heaven 2556; 2565
Old Maid 2570; 2580
Girl 2588; 2592; 2593
Love 2605; 2611; 2612
Love Making 2655
Kiss 2728
Marriage 2913
Unfaithfulness 3062
Birds 3677
Proprietor (Restaurant) 4748
Seasons-of-Year 5584

KISS

2720   Where did you get that black eye?
For kissing the bride after the ceremony.
Isn't that the usual custom?
But this was three years after the ceremony.

2721   I got a good one on you, Mike.
What do you mean?
I went by your house last night, and you forgot to pull your shades down. And I saw your wife kissing you. Had a good laugh on that.
Ha, ha, but the joke's on you, Joe!
How's that?
I wasn't home last night.

2722   Please give me a kiss.
My lips are chapped.
Well, one more chap won't hurt them.

2723   I went to a party last night, and what food! We had mushrooms.
Did you sit in one?
Did I sit in one? What do you think a mushroom is?
A mushroom is a place where couples kiss.

2724   All my life I've been saving my kisses for a man like you!
Get ready to lose the savings of a lifetime.

2725   What kind of a kiss was it?
It was wonderful — the kind that would cost you two dollars in a taxi.

2726   Why did you kiss that girl in the dark last night?
Since seeing her in the daylight, I've been wondering myself.

2727   I want to give you a kiss.
What?
I said, I want to give you a kiss. Don't you know what a kiss is?
It's wonderful.

2728   What would you take to give me a kiss?
Would you really like to know?
Yes.
Chloroform.

2729   What's the difference between kissing your sister and your sweetheart?
About twenty-five seconds.

2730   I just received a letter from my sweetheart and she put a couple of X's at the bottom of the letter. I sure am blue about it.

Why be blue about that? She's just sending you a couple of kisses. Don't you know what the X's are for?

Sure — they mean she's double-crossing me.

2731   The only men I kiss are my brothers.
What lodge do you belong to?

2732   So your last boy friend went with you a year before asking for a kiss?
Yes, up to then he'd just been taking them.

2733   A kiss is a peculiar proposition. Of no use to one, yet absolute bliss for two. The small boy gets it for nothing, the young man has to ask for it, and the old man has to buy it. The baby's right, the lover's privilege and the hypocrite's mask. To a young girl — faith; to a married woman — hope; and to an old maid — charity.

2734   So you never let a man kiss you goodnight?
No, by the time he leaves me it's always morning.

2735   My wife asked me for a check for $50 for a new dress and I gave her a check for kisses — 1,000 kisses. Well, what are you laughing at?
I cashed it.

2736   Come on, give me a kiss.
No, I've got scruples.
That's all right — I've had them twice.

2737   I'm going to kiss you tonight or I'll die in the attempt, I told my girl.
Well, did you?
You didn't see my name in the obituary column, did you?

2738   She said to me: Stop! My lips are for another.
What did you say to that?
I said: Well, if you hold still, you'll get another.

2739   I'm a kissing fool — he exclaimed.
And I'm kissing a fool — she replied.

2740   I'm going to kiss you like you've never been kissed before!
Oh, yes, I have.

2741   Do you think we can make a kiss last an hour?
An hour? Say, that one I just gave you is going to last you all evening.

2742   I told you to stop kissing me!
I did — several times.

2743   Mother: You let that man kiss you in the parlor!
       Daughter: But, mother, you must be considerate; the hall is so
       cold.

2744   What are your views on kissing?
       I haven't any — my girl's hair always gets in my eyes.

2745   How did your girl do selling kisses at the charity bazaar?
       She did all right. I let her sell six or seven and then I told her I
       had better take her home.
       Why?
       Charity begins at home.

2746   Mistress: Hilda, I saw the milkman kiss you this morning. In the
       future I'll take the milk in.
       Maid: Val, it ain't no use, by yimminy, 'cause he promise to kiss
       no one but me!

2747   How did you ever learn to kiss like that?
       Well, I used to be a vacuum cleaner salesman.

2748   If I give you one kiss, will you be good?
       If you give me one kiss, you'll know I'm good.

2749   I'd give five dollars for just one kiss from a sweet little girl
       like you.
       Oh, how terrible!
       Oh, beg pardon, I didn't mean to offend you.
       No, I was just thinking of the big fortune I gave away last night
       for nothing.

2750   I'm telling you for the last time you can't kiss me!
       Oh, I knew you would weaken.

2751   He who kisses and runs away will live to kiss another girl.

2752   Every time I kiss my wife I put a quarter in her bank. I opened
       the bank the other day, and I found three five-dollar bills
       there. I don't know how to account for it.
       You don't think *I'm* as stingy as you are, do you?

2753   Oh, isn't he sweet. Little boy, if you give me a kiss, I'll give you
       a bright new penny.
       Little boy: I get twice as much as that at home for just taking
       castor oil.

2754   My girl is selling kisses at the charity bazaar.
       How much does she charge?
       That depends.
       Depends on what?
       Well, she charges one dollar if you kiss her; two dollars if she
       kisses you, and for three dollars you just hang on.

2755 Do you believe kissing is unhealthy?
I couldn't say — I've never . . .
You've never been kissed?
I've never been sick.

2756 I was quite upset when Jack kissed me.
Oh, I say — you've been kissed before.
Yes, but never in a canoe.

2757 I understand your kisses speak the language of love.
Yes.
Well, let's talk things over.

2758 Guess who it is. If you don't guess who it is in three guesses, I'll
kiss you.
Santa Claus — Jack Frost — Mother Goose?

2759 Why does my sweetheart always close her eyes when I kiss her?
Look in the mirror, and you'll find out.

2760 How is it that you can kiss so divinely?
Oh, I used to blow the bugle in the Boy Scouts.

2761 They say kisses are the language of love.
Well, why don't you say something?

2762 George, dear, why do you shut your eyes so tight when you kiss
me?
I'm trying to make myself believe you're Raquel Welch.

2763 The doctors still insist that kissing is dangerous.
Thank heaven, all men aren't cowards.

2764 My wife won't speak to me just because I awakened her with some
kisses this morning.
Gracious, what kind of kisses were they?
Some kisses I was giving the maid.

2765 When you kissed him it brought out the beast in him?
Yes — the jackass.

2766 I just kissed him like a brother.
Yeah, a fraternity brother.

2767 Some kiss hot.
Some kiss cold,
Some don't kiss
Until they're told.
Some kiss fast,
Some kiss slow,
Those that don't kiss,
I don't know.

2768   Do you know you are the first man to kiss me?
Then you must have taken a correspondence course, for you certainly don't act like a beginner.

2769   I haven't been kissed for ages.
Yeah, the middle ages.

2770   I kissed her under the mistletoe.
I wouldn't kiss her under anaesthetic.

2771   Come, Freddy, and kiss your Aunt Martha.
Why, ma — I ain't done nuthin'!

2772   There's only one man I ever care to have caress me — isn't that the way you feel?
Yeah — only one — at a time.

2773   What's the best way to make you stop kissing me?
Let me get tired.

2774   Many a girl who saves her kisses for a rainy day finds that the man who calls for them is all wet.

RELATED SUBJECTS
Flirtation 2779-2784
Marriage 2882-3051
Unfaithfulness 3057-3088

JEALOUSY

2775   Is Jim's wife jealous?
Is she jealous? Why whenever Jim comes home with a hair on his coat he has to show her the horse.

2776   He is so jealous. I bought him some underwear. Now he is going around looking for a fellow with the initials B.V.D.

2777   Did you shoot him because of jealousy?
No, because of publicity.

RELATED SUBJECTS
Suspicion 1418-1421
Conduct 1802-1862
Love 2595-2640
Marriage 2882-3051
Divorce 3089-3105

FLIRTATION

2778　When you go to a restaurant, why do you always flirt with the
　　　　waitress?
　　　　I'm playing for big steaks.

2779　My girl is such a flirt that when she passes a field of waving corn,
　　　　she waves back at it.

2780　I see you have an eye for beauty.
　　　　Yes, but you ain't my type.

2781　Did you see that young lady smile at me?
　　　　That's nothing — the first time I saw you, I laughed right out loud.

2782　My, but Mary is a flirt.
　　　　How so?
　　　　She even thinks the ocean is waving at her.

2783　I hear the new cook's quite a gal.
　　　　Yeah. If she can't make the milkman she starts mashing potatoes.

2784　I wonder what's wrong with that tall blonde guy over there. Just
　　　　a minute ago he was getting awful friendly, and then all of a
　　　　sudden' he turned pale, walked away, and won't even look at
　　　　me any more.
　　　　Maybe he saw me come in. He's my husband.

> RELATED SUBJECTS
> Girl 2588-2594
> Love Making 2641-2719
> Party 3575-3579
> Automobile 4042-4146
> Boat 4174-4200
> Airplane 4208-4217
> Train 4218-4242

MATRIMONIAL AGENCY

SEE:
Description of People 302
Love Making 2699

DATES

2785　What are you doing with that feed bag?
　　　　Haven't we got a date with a couple of chorus girls?
　　　　Yeah, but what's the idea of the feed bag?
　　　　Didn't you tell me they eat like horses?

2786　Went on a double date last night with Eddie.
　　　　How can you go on a double date with a single man?

2787 Don't rush me! I'll make a date with you when I'm good and
      ready.
      Well, I can't wait until you're good, but I will wait until you
      are ready.

2788 Give me a date sometime, will you?
      Sorry, but I can't go out with a baby.
      Pardon me. I didn't know about it.

2789 I was out with Dick last night.
      Both of you? It must have been potent liquor.

2790 Where do blind dates come from?
      They are girls disappointed in love who have cried their eyes out.

2791 Says Flapper Fannie: Coffee isn't the only thing that's fresh
      when dated.

RELATED SUBJECTS
Drinking 2055-2140
Love Making 2641-2719
Dancing 3584-3603
Lateness 5388-5392
Hour (the) 5567-5575

LADY KILLER

2792 I'm a lady killer.
      Yeah, they take one look at you and drop dead.

2793 They say he's a regular lady killer.
      I'll say he is. He starves them to death.

RELATED SUBJECTS
Fresh people 2397-2408
Love Making 2641-2719

PROPOSAL

2794 I've been asked to get married lots of times.
      Who asked you?
      Mother and father.

2795 Where in the world are you going with that candy bag?
      I've got a 14 carat diamond ring in it and I'm goin' to propose to
      my girl.
      Do you think she'll accept you?
      Sure — it's in the bag.

2796 What would you say if I asked you to be my wife?
      Nothing — I can't talk and laugh at the same time.

2797 I want you for my wife!
      What does your wife want me for?

2798 Without you everything is dark and dreary — the clouds gather
and the wind beats the rain — then comes the warm sun — you
are like a rainbow.
Is this a proposal or a weather report?

2799 You know I'm in love.
I didn't know that.
Yes, but I don't know how to propose to her.
All you have to do is look into her eyes and say: I love you, Ann.
But how can I say that when her name is Sarah?

2800 Don't worry about Jane refusing your proposal. You'll soon forget
her and be happy again.
Oh, no, I won't. I bought too many things for her on time payments.

2801 Oh, he's proposed to every girl he knows.
That so?
Yeah, he's been turned down so often he looks like a bed spread.

2802 You know, I would like to have you for my wife.
What would your wife ever want me for?

2803 Refuse me, will you?
Why?
So I'll be driven to drink.

2804 I asked her for her hand.
What happened?
I got it — on the ear.

2805 I'll support you in the style you are accustomed to.
Then I won't marry you.

2806 Dearest, I love you and want you for my wife.
Heavens! I didn't know you had a wife.

2807 A local Romeo had a very bad experience. He tried to break off
his engagement by telling the girl he was a smuggler. Now she
wants a bigger diamond.

2808 You must marry me — I love you, there can be no other . . .
But John, I don't love you — you must find some other woman
— some beautiful woman . . .
But I don't want a beautiful woman — I want you.

2809 I have had my good eye on you for years. I'm rich. Marry me and
you'll have anything your heart desires.
Anything?
Yes!
How about a new jack knife?

2810   Timid man proposing over phone: Miss Simkins?
       Woman: Yes, Miss Simkins speaking.
       Man: Well, er — will you marry me, Miss Simkins?
       Woman: Yes! Who's speaking?

2811   Did you ever do any public speaking?
       Well, I proposed to a girl in the country over a party line.

2812   I know what's passing through your mind. I know, too, why you
          are calling here night after night, appropriating my time to your-
          self and keeping other nice young men away. You want to marry
          me, don't you?
       Why — I — Yes, I suppose so.
       I thought so. Very well, I will.

2813   Darling, will you be my wife?
       Will you always let me do just what I like?
       Certainly.
       Can mother live with us?
       Of course, dear.
       Will you give up the club and always give me money when I ask
          for it?
       Willingly, my pet.
       I'm sorry, I could never marry such a boob.

2814   You! You want to marry me.
       Yes.
       But, my dear boy, you've only known me three days.
       Oh, much longer than that, really! I've been two years in the bank
          where your father has his account.

2815   What's worrying you, David?
       I was just wonderin' if Dad would see to the milkin' while we're
          on our honeymoon, supposin' you said "yes" if I asked you.

2816   What made you quarrel with Merlin?
       Well, he proposed to me again last night.
       Where was the harm in that?
       My dear, I had accepted him the night before.

2817   My boy friend proposed to me twice and I'm sure sore.
       Why should that make you sore?
       Well, my mother married my father, my aunt married my uncle
          and I'll be darned if I'm going to marry a stranger.

2818   You haven't said a word for twenty minutes.
       Well, I didn't have anything to say.
       Don't you ever say anything when you have nothing to say?
       No.
       Well, then, will you be my wife?

2819 Did Joe propose?
Yeah, but I turned him down on account of the book I was reading.
What could your reading a book have to do with your refusing him?
Well, my sister's husband proposed to her while she was reading *The Three Musketeers* and she had triplets.
I don't see the connection.
When Joe proposed, I was reading *The Birth of a Nation*.

2820 I have something I have to ask you — er — er — something — er — very close to my heart — and er — er . . .
I think I can guess what it is!
Ah, you have divined. You know — you — er —
Yes, you want to ask me where I put your hat when you came in.

> RELATED SUBJECTS
> Love Making 2641-2719
> Kiss 2720-2774
> Breach of Promise 3055-3056
> Gift 3943-3962

ASKING FOR DAUGHTER'S HAND

2821 Your daughter promised to marry me.
What do you expect, hanging around our house very night?

2822 I want to marry your daughter.
How much money do you make?
One thousand a month.
Well, her allowance is six hundred a month — and that'll make . . .
No, I've already figured that in.

2823 When I asked my girl's father if I could marry her, he acted just like a lamb.
Like a lamb?
Yeah. When I asked him if I could marry his daughter, he said "Bah!" Just like a lamb.

2824 Did you take father apart and speak to him?
Not exactly, but he almost fell to pieces when I spoke to him.

2825 May I marry your daughter?
What is your vocation?
I'm an actor.
Then get out before the foot lights.

2826 I've come to ask you for your daughter's hand.
All right — take the one that's always in my pocket.

2827   Father: So you want to marry my daughter? You know that she
has a perfectly good home?
Suitor: Exactly, sir, and I think it would be rather cruel to take
her away from it, don't you?

2828   I'd die for your daughter.
Don't do that — she knows enough dead ones already.

2829   Sir, er — that is — I would like to — er, that is, I mean, I have
been going with your daughter for five years . . .
Well, waddya want — a pension?

2830   I would like to marry your daughter.
Well, sir, you can leave your name and address, and if nothing
better turns up, we can notify you.

2831   I wish to marry your daughter, sir.
Do you drink, young man?
Thanks a lot, but let's settle this other thing first.

2832   Oh, good! You've asked father for my hand!
No, my dear. I've been in a motor smash up.

2833   I — er — suppose you are aware that I've been making advances
to your daughter?
Yes, put it there, son. And now what about her poor old father?

2834   She gave me her lips — she gave me her heart. Now I want her
hand.
What are you doing — piece work?

2835   And you think you will be able to give my daughter all she wants?
Yes — she says she only wants me.

2836   I wish to marry your daughter.
Can you support a family?
Yes.
But there are eight of us!

2837   In asking for your daughter's hand, I would remind you that I
am the possessor of an old and honored name.
Ah! And will you be good enough to inform me at what bank it
will be honored, and for how much?

2838   (The all-important question had been put up to the girl's father)
Father (Turning to young suitor with rage): You impudent,
young puppy! Do you mean to tell me that you want to marry
Ella? Do you think for a moment that you could give her what
she's been used to?
Er — yes, I think so. I've got a bad temper myself.

2839 Did you ask father for my hand?
Yes.
What did he say?
Well, he asked me how I was fixed and I told him I had $3,000 in the bank.
And what did he say to that?
He borrowed it.

2840 I have only $25,000 a year, sir, but I think I can support your daughter on that.
Support her, my dear boy? You can support her entire family on it.

2841 You want to marry my daughter? What are your means?
I expect shortly to come into a fortune of between one thousand and four hundred thousand dollars.
Why are you so uncertain about the amount?
It's a ticket I have in a Sweepstake.

2842 How do you know you love my daughter enough to marry her?
Why — er — why, I'd marry her, even if she lost her job.

2843 Didn't you ask father for my hand?
I haven't the courage to tell your father of my debts.
What cowards you men are! Father hasn't the courage to tell you of his debts.

2844 Well, dearest, what did your father say when he found I wanted to marry you?
At first, he demurred because he didn't want to lose me, but I explained that he could have me, and that he would have you to boot.
That sounds all right, except for the to boot part.

2845 Sir, I want your daughter for my wife.
And I, sir, am not willing to trade.

2846 Was father violent when you asked for my hand?
Was he violent? I thought he would shake my arm off.

2847 What is your reason for wishing to marry my daughter?
I've no reason, sir. I'm in love.

RELATED SUBJECTS
Marriage 2882-3051
Family 3209-3217

ENGAGEMENT

2848 If that's the kind of a fellow you are, I'm going to break our engagement this minute. My feelings toward you are changed. I don't want anything more to do with you.

Give me back my ring then.
My feelings toward you have changed, but I feel just the same about the ring.

2849   Do you believe in long engagements?
Yes — the longer the better.

2850   You know, you've been engaged to her a long time, why don't you marry her?
I've been thinking about it — but where would I spend my evenings if I did?

2851   If we become engaged, will you give me a ring?
Certainly. What's your number?

2852   Howdy, Tom, old man. Congratulations upon your engagement to Jean. I guess you're a pretty lucky man. She certainly has a pile of cash. But then again she's pretty fussy, I hear, and she'll probably make you cut out drinking and smoking.
Oh, well — I suppose so. But if we hadn't become engaged I would have had to cut out eating.

2853   (Phone rings)
There goes that phone. I broke my engagement off this afternoon and she's returning the ring.

2854   Well, since you don't want to marry me after all, perhaps you'll return my ring.
If you must know, your jeweler has called for it already.

2855   Are you engaged to marry Bob?
Yes, I've promised to marry him as soon as he has made his fortune.
That isn't an engagement — that's an option.

2856   So Ethel returned your engagement ring?
Yes, she mailed it to me and she had the nerve to paste a label on the outside of the package: GLASS — handle with care.

2857   So you broke your engagement to Evelyn. Why was that?
Well, I was only doing to the engagement what it did to me.

2858   I hear you're engaged. Who's the lucky woman?
Her mother.

RELATED SUBJECTS
Courtship 2568-2881

ELOPEMENT

2859   Come — flee with me.

I can't flee with you. I'm wearing my father's pants. It would be terrible to see the headlines in tomorrow's papers: FLEES IN FATHER'S PANTS.

2860   (Eloping bride receives wire from parent) — Do *not* come home and all will be forgiven.

2861   Darling, have you made all arrangements for our elopement?

Yes, my love. We take a plane to South America, get married in Rio, announce our marriage from New York, ask for forgiveness in Cherbourg, and wire from Paris for the return fare home.

2862   Lover (Eloping with loved one) (To taxi driver): How much is the fare?

Driver: That's all right, sir. The lady's father settled all that.

RELATED SUBJECTS
Courtship 2568-2881

WEDDING

2863   It's a dollar and sense wedding.

What do you mean?

He hasn't a dollar and she hasn't any sense.

2864   A wedding is a funeral where you smell your own flowers.

2865   They had an up to date wedding.

Up to date?

Yeah. With their marriage license they got a ticket to Reno with a one day stop over in Niagara Falls for their honeymoon.

2866   A friend of mine was engaged to a movie star and on his wedding day his car stalled and so he sent her a wire saying: Delayed for a few hours, don't marry anyone until I get there.

2867   What are you doing with that rice?

I bought it by mistake.

Most people go shopping on purpose.

Yes —·but this was funny. I saw a man coming down the street with a shotgun, so I followed him.

So what?

I thought there was going to be a wedding.

So you stopped and got the rice?

Yes, but it was a joke on me. It turned out to be just a bank robbery.

2868   Usher: (at wedding) Are you a friend of the groom?
Lady: Indeed no, I'm the bride's mother.

2869   The groom didn't get his pants back in time for the wedding so he sued the tailor for promise of breeches.

2870   On which side of the church should the parents of the bride and bridegroom be seated?
On opposite sides and as far apart as possible. A church is no place to start anything.

2871   Don't you know what a bridegroom is?
Sure, it's a thing they have at weddings.

2872   What would you do if you married a rich woman?
Absolutely nothing.

2873   You know when I was married I couldn't find the ring. Boy! I got an awful fright.
Yeah — and you still got her.

2874   A shoe hit me the day I got married.
I bet your wife's dad had a hand in it.
G'wan, I bet he had a foot in it.

2875   I went to a wooden wedding.
What's that?
The gal next door married a blockhead.

2876   Do you like big weddings or little ones?
Well, without big weddings you can't have little ones.

2877   We're going to give the bride a shower.
Count on me — I'll bring the soap.

2878   Do you take this man to be your wedded husband, for better or for worse?
Just as he is, Parson. Just as he is. If he gets any better I know the good Lord will take him, and if he gets any worse, why, I'll tend to him myself.

RELATED SUBJECTS
Toast 2440-2442
Congratulations 2443-2444
Home 3197-3205
Gift 3943-3962

HONEYMOON

2879   And the honeymoon is over when the bridegroom can taste his
        wife's kisses in his coffee.

2880   I think you should make up with your wife and go on a second
        honeymoon.
        I can't.
        Why can't you?
        I ain't taken a first one yet.

2881   How long do you want to be away on your honeymoon?
        Well — sir — er — how long would you say?
        How do I know? I haven't seen the bride.

> RELATED SUBJECTS
> Love 2595-2640
> Elopement 2859-2862
> Marriage 2882-3051
> Travel 3971-4246

MARRIAGE

2882   Will you hold my money, please?
        What's the idea? Are you trying to be funny?
        I've just got married.
        And you want me to keep your money?
        Yeah. You don't think I should keep my money in the house with
        a strange lady around?

2883   Everything in marriage should be on a 50-50 basis. You should
        give your wife a $50 dress and spend 50c for a shirt.

2884   There's my friend, Joe. He's a Napoleon of Finance.
        Why?
        He had his salary raised three months ago and his wife hasn't found
        out about it.

2885   Tell me how long has your brother been married?
        He has been married the best part of a year.
        When was the wedding?
        Ten days ago.

2886   Lately my wife has the habit of not going to bed until three o'clock
        in the morning.
        Does she go out to night clubs or parties?
        Neither. She sits up waiting for me.

2887   My wife and I have a joint checking account.
        Isn't that hard to keep straight?
        No. I put in the money and she takes it out.

2888   When we get married, we're going to have a good cook in our
        house.
        I didn't know your girl could cook.
        She can't. Her mother is coming to live with us.

2889   My father's home was broken up by a twister.
        A twister? Do you mean a tornado?
        No — a Hula Hula dancer.

2890   Does your wife pick your clothes?
        No — just the pockets.

2891   It was thirty years ago today when I lost my wife — the only wife
        I've ever had.
        That's too bad. I didn't know about that. It must be hard to lose
        your wife like that.
        Hard? It's darn near impossible.

2892   My wife and I don't have a home.
        Why don't you live with your folks?
        We can't, because they're still living with *their* folks.

2893   Why do you cringe like that when you hear an automobile horn.
        Are you afraid of being hit?
        No. Last week a man ran off with my wife in an automobile and
        now when I hear a horn honking, I'm afraid he is bringing
        her back.

2894   Before we were married every time you'd see me you'd always
        catch me in your arms.
        Yeah — and since we're married, I catch you in my pockets.

2895   Were you ever married?
        Yeah, but my wife ran away.
        How did it happen?
        She ran away when I was taking a bath.
        I'll bet she waited years for the opportunity.

2896   I let my wife do all the cooking and mending and washing.
        She must be a hard working wife?
        You said it.
        Don't you ever help her with her work?
        Sure. On Monday I wash dishes — Wednesday night I clean the
        furniture with her and tonight I'm going to mop up the floor
        with her.

2897   My wife and I have a partnership. She takes care of and decides
        on all the small things, and I take care of and decide on all the
        big things.
        How are you doing?
        So far no big things have come up.

2898 Officer: How many times have you kissed that girl?
      Man: I don't know with that thing in my eyes. Anyway, she's
      my wife.
      Officer: Oh, I didn't know she was your wife.
      Man: Neither did I until you put the flashlight in my eyes.

2899 She's a very nice wife. Every time her husband returns home late
      at night, the minute he gets in the house he gets his pipe, slippers
      and pajamas and if anything else is handy she lets him have
      that too.

2900 How can you live without your wife?
      Much cheaper.

2901 Does your wife select your clothes?
      No, but she picks the pockets.

2902 He told me his wife left him ten days ago and hasn't come back.
      What did you tell him?
      I told him to wait a few days before celebrating.

2903 Remember that your wife still enjoys candy and flowers. Let her
      know that you remember by speaking of them occasionally.

2904 My husband and I agree on one point; he doesn't think anything's
      too good for me, and neither do I.

2905 My wife is threatening to leave me.
      That's tough. Can't you get her to promise?

2906 Now that we are married, perhaps I might venture to point out a
      few of your little defects.
      Don't bother, dear. I'm quite aware of them. It was those little
      defects that prevented me from getting a much better man than
      you are.

2907 A tornado blew my house away with my wife in it.
      Say, that's terrible.
      Oh, it's all right — my wife has been wanting to take a trip for
      a long time, anyhow.

2908 My wife kisses me only when she needs money.
      Don't you think *that's* often enough?

2909 Aren't your relations pleasant?
      Mine are, but his are terrible.

2910 I think men should wear something to show they're married. Wo-
      men wear rings to show they're married.
      Men wear something to show they're married. They wear last
      year's clothes.

2911 Wife: (to returning husband) So you finally came back. I guess
home is the best place after all.
Husband: It's the only place open.

2912 I accused my wife of taking a quarter out of my pocket. She said
she didn't know I had a quarter, and in the second place she
never put her hands in my pockets in her life, and in the third
place, she says the pocket where I had the quarter had a hole
in it.

2913 I bet you can't remember the day when you were married.
Yeah—I do remember that day. It was the day my favorite mule
died.

2914 How are your uncle and his wife getting along?
For two years now he hasn't been out one night.
Well, that's what I call love.
You may call it love, but the doctor calls it rheumatism.

2915 What is he so angry at you for?
I haven't the slightest idea. We met on the street and we were
talking just as friendly as could be, when all of a sudden he
flared up and tried to lick me.
And what were you talking about?
Oh, just ordinary small talk. I remember he said: I always kiss
my wife three or four times every day.
And what did you say?
I said: I know at least a dozen men who do the same — and then
he had a fit.

2916 Do you know who the greatest dictator in the world is?
Know her — say, I married her!

2917 We've been married ten years today.
Wonderful — shall I kill a chicken and celebrate?
Why punish a poor chicken for something that happened ten
years ago?

2918 You'll never get another wife like me.
Who says I would ever want one like you?

2919 Wife: Before we were married you told me you were well off.
Husband: But I never knew how well off.

2920 You loved me more when we were only engaged.
Well, to tell the truth, my dear, I never cared for married women.

2921 Don't divorce your wife. Give her an automobile. The shock will
kill her, and you can use the machine for the funeral.

2922 We read of a woman who didn't kiss her husband for ten years.
He must have been dead or else she had money in her own name.

2923   How do you get along at home so well?
       My wife is Secretary of the Treasury, her mother is Secretary of
           War, the cook is Secretary of Interior . . .
       And you're the president?
       No, I'm the public that pays the taxes.

2924   His wife ran away from home — so he ran away, too.
       Why did he run away?
       He was afraid she might change her mind and come back.

2925   How do I know you're a chauffeur?
       I got a license to show for it.
       Let me see it! Why, this is a dog license.
       Yeah — my wife leads me a dog's life.

2926   What's the difference between a single man and a married man?
       What?
       A single man has no buttons on his shirt, and a married man has
           no shirt.

2927   I'm going home to my mother.
       For goodness sakes — don't do that, because then it will be her
           turn to visit us.

2928   Some wives leave their husbands and take everything; others take
           everything, but don't leave.

2929   I lost my wife at sea. My wife fell overboard and I threw her a tire.
       Well, the tire should have held her up.
       I know, but I forgot to take the rim out.

2930   And then there's the Hollywood hostess who sends out elaborate
           invitations for "Bearer and One Wife."

2931   Tell me, Tom, did you marry that girl, or do you still darn your
           own socks and do your cooking?
       Yes.
       Yes, what?
       I married the girl and I still darn my own socks and do my own
           cooking.

2932   Before marriage he said nothing would be good enough for her and
           after marriage he still seemed to think it was.

2933   Father gave us the house and furniture.
       Did he also give you your car?
       I should say not! George wouldn't accept such a thing. All that
           father pays for is the rent and the housekeeping expenses.

2934   You swore you'd always treat me like a queen!
       Well, hang it — I'm not Henry the Eighth.

2935   Is she considerate of her husband?
       Very. She's joined the Nudist Cult for a while, to give him a chance
       to pay her dress bills.

2936   I've decided to leave my husband.
       How come? Have you started to economize?

2937   I'm sorry I ever became your wife.
       Oh, you were no young bird when I married you.
       No, but considering what I got I was an early bird.

2938   Husband: You have kept my nose to the grindstone for forty years.
       Wife: I've done more than that. I've made you turn the grind-
          stone.

2939   Husband: Let's have some fun this evening.
       Wife: Okay, and please leave the light on in the hallway if you
          get home before I do.

2940   Were you excited when you first asked your husband for money?
       Oh, no, I was calm — and collected.

2941   Is your wife dependent upon you?
       She sure is. If I didn't go out and get the washings for her to do
          she'd starve plum to death.

2942   Old Man: What were you thinking about?
       Old Woman: I was just thinking how long we had lived together
          and that it couldn't go on forever like this and the time will soon
          come when one of us will have to go.
       Old Man: Yes, but it's no use to worry about that now.
       Old Woman: No, but I was just thinking that when it does hap-
          pen, I would like to go to California to live.

2943   They started fighting at the altar. When he said: I do, she
       said: Oh, no, you don't.

2944   Are you satisfied with married life?
       Yeah, I'm satisfied — I've had all I want of it.

2945   Well, I can tell you're a married man all right. No holes in
       your stockings now.
       No. One of the first things my wife taught me was how to
       darn 'em.

2946   I say, why is Jones pacing up and down outside his house like
       that?
       He's awfully worried about his wife, poor chap.
       Why — what has she got?
       The car.

2947   You didn't have a rag on your back when I married you.
       Anyway, I've plenty of them now.

2948   So your married life was very happy? What was the trouble —
          December wedded to May?
       Lan' sake no! It was Labor Day wedded to de Day of Rest.

2949   Does your husband expect you to obey him?
       Oh, dear, no. You see he's been married before.

2950   Why did you tell Mrs. Tuff her husband was dead when he
          had only lost all his money?
       I thought I'd better break it to her gently.

2951   Let's get our wives together tonight and have a big evening.
       Okay. But where shall we leave them?

2952   You're home early from the court, Mrs. Murphy.
       They shoved me out for clapping when me husband got three
          months.

2953   Why did you tell Joe you married me because I'm such a won-
          derful cook? I can't boil a potato.
       But I had to give some excuse.

2954   I heard your wife came to you on her knees yesterday.
       Yeah — she did. She dared me to come out from under the bed.

2955   Your wife has beauty, brains and charm. What more could
          you ask?
       I couldn't — she does all the asking.

2956   I want to see the head of the house.
       You'll have to wait a minute — they're just deciding it.

2957   I have a clever wife.
       Mine finds out, too.

2958   How long have you been married?
       Long enough to learn that there are some things you can't say
          with flowers.

2959   They should be happy because they played golf together during
          their courtship.
       But did they play bridge? That's the supreme test.

2960   I'm thinking of marrying and feathering my nest.
       So you're marrying a fan dancer?

2961   Listen! I can marry anyone I please.
       Why don't you then?
       I don't please anybody.

2962   How would you like to marry a fan dancer?
        I'd rather be one of her fans.

2963   Are there any more at home like you?
        Yes, there are six of us.
        Then your dad has six mouths to feed?
        No — twelve.
        How do you figure twelve?
        We're all married.

2964   I can see from your remarks that matrimony is a serious word.
        It's worse than that — it's a sentence!

2965   I'm a very happy man. I was the best man at my girl's wedding.
        Your girl got married and you're happy?
        Yeah, I'm happy I was only the best man.

2966   I hear your daughter has married a side-show freak.
        Yes — the living skeleton, thinnest man on earth. I don't see
          how she could do it.
        Well, you know how crazy women are about anything that's
          reduced.

2967   Do you believe in marriage?
        Only as the last resort.

2968   What is the future tense of marry?
        Divorce.

2969   She's been married so often that the wedding bells sound just
          like an alarm clock to her.

2970   Are you married?
        No, sir, I make my own living.

2971   You should get married; you know marriage is an institution.
        I'm not ready for an institution yet.

2972   Why don't you marry her?
        Okay — I'll do it for a lark.
        All right — I'll give you the bird.

2973   I don't want to marry him — he couldn't keep me in hand-
          kerchiefs.
        But you're not going to have a cold all your life.

2974   I can't marry her. I don't know everything about her.
        What difference does that make? In Africa a man doesn't know
          his wife until after he marries her.
        What do you mean — in Africa?

2975 What is your ambition? You certainly must have some ambition in life.
I want to be married and have a lot of husbands.
A lot of husbands! You know the penalty of having a lot of husbands, don't you? Suppose you married twice, what is that?
Bigamy.
And if you are married only once?
Monotony.

2976 Marriage: The foreclosure of a mortgage on a man's future happiness.

2977 Why is it that when a fellow spends time and money showing a girl a good time, she thinks he is putting himself under so much obligation to her that she ought to marry him.

2978 You seem to like his attentions. Why don't you marry him?
Because I like his attentions.

2979 When I marry, I'm going to cook, sew and darn my husband's socks, lay out his pipe and slippers, and read to him evenings. What more could a husband ask for than that?
Nothing — unless he wants beauty and romance.

2980 Who did she marry?
She married Bill when she was engaged to Joe so she could have a place to entertain Sam.

2981 She's going to marry her former husband. Just think of marrying your ex-husband.
X-husband? I didn't know she kept her husbands alphabetically.

2982 He did me out of $50,000.
How was that?
He wouldn't let me marry his daughter.

2983 Love is blind — and marriage is an eye opener.

2984 Before you marry her, there's something you should get off your chest.
What?
That tattooed heart on your chest with Mabel's name on it.

2985 I'm never going to marry.
That's what they all say — but they're still building school houses.

2986 I think she married me for my money.
Well, she earned it.

2987 Don't you believe in monogamy?
I like oak better.

2988   I have a cousin who was a dude. He got married and now he
       is sub-dued.

2989   Marriage is like a prizefight — the preliminaries are generally
       better than the main event.

2990   An elderly gentleman was asked by one of his sons to go with
       him to a boxing exhibition.
       Son: Now, dad, you'll see more excitement for your two dol-
       lars than you've ever seen in your life before.
       Father: I've got my doubts about that. Two dollars is all that
       my marriage license cost me.

2991   There's something wrong with present day marriage.
       How is that?
       The best man doesn't get the bride.

2992   I don't see how we can marry, dear. I'm not making expenses.
       That's all right. Just marry me and I'll make expenses.

2993   Modern marriage is like a cafeteria. A man grabs what he
       wants and pays for it later.

2994   What do you think of trial marriages?
       I must be frank — all marriages are trial marriages.

2995   She married him for better or for worse. It was better for her
       and worse for him.

2996   An American film actress was applying for a passport.
       Examiner: Unmarried?
       Actress: Occasionally.

2997   Poor old Tomkins has two wives to support now.
       Good heavens! You don't mean to say he's a bigamist.
       Oh, no. Nothing like that. But his son got married last week.

2998   It was a radio marriage.
       A national hook-up, eh?

2999   Before marriage a man yearns for a woman. After marriage
       the "y" is silent.

3000   I suppose you've had lots of chances to get married.
       Yes, but I'm not taking chances.

3001   Which do you prefer — trial, companionate or fight-to-the-
       finish marriage?

3002   Marriage is like a card game. They start with a pair; he shows
       a diamond; she shows a flush and they end up with a full
       house.

3003   Eight girls married two brothers.
       Eight girls married two brothers? Impossible! Who were they?
       The Marx Brothers and the Mills Brothers.

3004   I don't want to marry Pete.
       You've got to marry him tomorrow.
       Why?
       I rented out your room today.

3005   He wanted to marry me.
       What's wrong with marrying a ship builder?
       Who wants a lot of little tug boats running around the house?

3006   I took her for better or worse — but she's so much worse than
           I took her for.

3007   Maud has made some swell marriages, but divorced all her
           husbands.
       Yes, she moves in the best triangles, so to speak.

3008   You said if I'd marry you, you'd be humbly grateful.
       Well, what of it?
       You're not — you're grumbly hateful.

3009   (Widow marrying again)
       Mom, I want to ask you something.
       What is it, dear?
       Do you get this daddy cheaper because he is second hand?

3010   Would you marry a man for his money?
       Not exactly. But I'd want my husband to have a lovely disposi-
           tion, and if he didn't have money he'd very likely be worried
           and ill-natured.

3011   What did her father settle on them when they married?
       The rest of the family.

3012   Remember the fellow who said marriage is a state fit for a king
           may have been an anarchist.

3013   Married life isn't much different from single blessedness. She
           used to wait up half the night for her boy friend to go; now
           she waits up for him to come home.

3014   Offsher, you'd better lock me up. Just hit my wife over the head
           with a club.
       Did you kill her?
       Don't think so. Thash why I want to be locked up.

3015   I did not marry beauty, my boy — I did not marry wealth or
           position — I married for sympathy.
       Well, you have mine.

3016   I'm not against marriage — only up against it.

3017   What do you call it when a woman gets married three
       times — bigotry?
       You ignoramus. When a gal gets married two times, that is
       bigotry; when she tries it three times, that is trigonometry.

3018   Does m-i-r-a-g-e spell marriage?
       Yes, my child.

3019   If your mother married again, you'd have a step-father.
       Wouldn't be any different.
       No different?
       No — we drag the one we've got off the steps every night.

3020   One of the greatest lotteries in the world is licensed by law
       and sponsored by clergymen — marriage.

3021   I wonder why so many marriages are failures.
       It must be because so many inexperienced people go into it.

3022   Could I see the man who was arrested for robbing our house
       last night?
       Why do you want to see him?
       I want to ask him how he got in the house without awakening
       my wife.

3023   My wife doesn't understand me, does yours?
       I don't know, I've never heard her even mention your name.

3024   My husband is just the opposite of me — whilst I sing he
       grumbles and growls.
       Then why not leave off singing?

3025   Who is really the boss in your house?
       Well, of course, Maggie assumes command of the child, the
       servants, the dog, the cat, and the canary. But I can say
       pretty much what I please to the goldfish.

3026   Remember, dear, you took your husband for better or for worse.
       But I didn't take him for good, did I?

3027   Then you believe that your husband's death was due to a broken
       heart?
       Yes, if he hadn't broken my heart, I wouldn't have shot him.

3028   Ain't you the mugg who once escaped from prison for a few
       days just to make your wife awfully happy?
       Yeah, she turned me in and got a reward.

3029   Which is the more important, a man's wife or his trousers?
       Well, there are lots of places a man can go without his wife.

3030 What's your husband's average income?
Oh, around midnight.

3031 Do you sometimes have doubts about your husband's love being
genuine?
Yes, I don't think he really loves half the other women he says
he does.

3032 It seems to me that I shall have to report that your husband
died from unknown causes.
Yes, I don't know yet why I poisoned him.

3033 We were happily married, and a year later a little stranger
arrived.
A baby — how nice.
No, my wife's uncle — he's a midget.

3034 I married an adagio dancer — we've been married three weeks
and I've never kissed her yet.
What's the matter — don't you love her?
Sure, I love her, but I can't catch her.

3035 I've had bad luck with both my wives.
How come?
The first one ran off with another man.
And the second?
Didn't.

3036 Last night I held my wife so tight I cracked one of her ribs.
I'll bet she was furious.
That's why I held her tight.

3037 It says that the man was shot by his wife at close range.
Then there must have been powder marks on his body.
Yes, that's why she shot him.

3038 I thought your sister and her husband were inseparable.
Yeah, it takes about six people to drag them apart.

3039 That's an accomplished girl Ben is going to marry. She can
swim, ride, dance, drive a car, and pilot a plane. A real all-
around girl.
They should get along fine. You know Ben is a good cook.

3040 D'ya know, Mrs. Harris, I sometimes wonder if me husband's
grown tired of me.
What ever makes you say that, Mrs. Jiggs?
Well, he ain't been home for seven years.

3041 How long have you been married?
This time — or altogether?

3042   We hadn't been married a week when he hit me with a piece
       of sponge cake.
       Disorderly conduct. Five dollars and cost.
       And I'd made the cake with my own hands.
       Assault with a deadly weapon — one year.

3043   You are called as a witness of the quarrel between your friend
       and his wife. Were you present at the beginning of the
       trouble?
       Certainly! I was a witness at their wedding.

3044   Is it true that your husband ate his dinner in silence after your
       quarrel?
       No — we had soup.

3045   Why does every man call a woman "his better half"?
       If your wife asks you for money, you better have some.

3046   Is it true a man lays down the law to his wife?
       It is. But how she repeals it!

3047   They tell me you married your wife because her aunt left her
       a fortune.
       Well, that ain't so. I'd have married her no matter who left it
       to her.

3048   I was just talkin' to Cap Winter. He's a retired sea captain,
       you know. His wife just ran away with another man. Cap
       Winter took her for a mate, and she turned out to be a skipper.

3049   Mr. Peck, your wife has been arrested and is being held incom-
       municado. But the police chief is easy and a little money . . .
       Fine! Fine! And tell him that there's ten dollars for him for
       every day he can keep her that way.

3050   Do you know your wife is telling around that you can't keep
       her in clothes?
       That's nothing. I bought her a home and I can't keep her in
       that either.

3051   What do you do when your wife begins crying?
       As my wife is a head taller than I am and she cries copiously, my
       first move is to stand from under and get an umbrella.

BIGAMY

3052 Do you know what bigamy is?
Two mothers-in-law.

3053   They sold him two cars; they sold him a duplex; two phones in his house; a suit with two pairs of pants; and now I hear they got him for bigamy.

3054   Paw, does bigamy mean that a man has one wife too many?
Not necessarily, my son. A man can have one wife too many and still not be a bigamist.

RELATED SUBJECTS
Marriage 2882-3051
Attorney 5235-5244

BREACH OF PROMISE

3055   Why so sad, dearie?
That big sap I'm suing for breach of promise wants to marry me now.

3056   Judge: It isn't often a man sues his wife for breach of promise. On what ground do you base your claim?
Husband: She promised to divorce me, and never did.

RELATED SUBJECTS
Proposal 2794-2820
Marriage 2882-3051
Attorney 5235-5244

UNFAITHFULNESS

3057   How did you get that black eye?
Well, you know that beautiful blonde whose husband is in China?
Yes. What about it?
Well, he isn't in China.

3058   You're just like that guy Noah Webster — he corrected everybody — claimed they said the wrong word. One day Mrs. Webster went back in the garden and found Noah kissing the maid. She said: I'm surprised!
And what did he say?
He said: No, dear, you are astonished — I am surprised.

3059   Listen, I was sitting in a theatre with my wife when an old girl friend of mine came to where we were sitting and said "hello."
That's nothing. I was sitting in a theatre with my girl and my wife came in and said "hello."

3060   My husband's car is the latest car out, you know.
Yes, so all the neighbors say — and every night, too, at that, my dear.

3061   Can you let me have six-fifty? I'm having dinner with a very charming woman in the dining room and I'm stuck for the money.

Okay. I'll go with you. How did this happen?
She flirted with me on the porch and swept me off my feet.
That's a woman for you. Where is she?
That's the lady over there.
That's the lady?
Yeah — will you pay the bill?
What? You take my wife to dinner and I should pay the bill?

3062 A man never gets into trouble chasing women — it's after they're caught that the trouble begins.

3063 When I came home today our house was full of smoke and I asked my wife who had been there. She said: Why, Mary, you know — my girl friend — dropped in to leave her regards.
Well, Mary left her pipe on the piano.

3064 Tell me — have you been true to your wife all your life?
I haven't lived all my life yet.
Don't evade the issue. Tell me the truth. Have you ever kissed another man's wife?
Yes. I'll confess I've kissed the wife of another man.
Who was she?
My grandmother.

3065 Long hair makes a man look intelligent.
I saw a wife once pick one off her husband's coat and he looked foolish.

3066 When is the Fuller Brush man gonna play pool with pa?
Well, Willie, that's a foolish question.
Well, didn't you tell him this afternoon that you'd give him his cue when you saw pa coming?

3067 A sweet young thing upon parting from a young man at the railroad station was observed to go into tears. The manner in which she expressed her grief stirred up the sympathy of a passenger.
Passenger: My dear young lady, are you crying because you have to leave your husband?
Girl: N-n-n-n-no. I'm crying because I'm going back to him.

3068 This suit was a surprise from my wife. I came home one night and found it right on the back of a chair.

3069 I just got a letter from a man saying if I didn't stay away from his wife he was going to shoot me.
Well, I suppose you're going to take heed of the warning.
I can't — he didn't sign his name.

3070 Wife: Who's that woman over there staring at us?
Husband: Shhh — not so loud! I'll have a time explaining to her tomorrow who you are.

3071   I suppose you kiss them and run away.
       He who kisses and runs away, never has to hop out of some
       other guy's window.

3072   Papa, why don't you go away so I can see mama dump that
       salesman off the fire escape?
       Why, Willie, what on earth are you talking about?
       Well, I heard her tell him that she'd tip him off just as soon
       as you leave.

3073   Man returning home in the wee small hours of the night finds
       a burglar jimmying his front door.
       Man: Wait a minute, old man. Let's strike a bargain. I'll open
       the door if you'll go in first.

3074   Little boy, I need a dozen eggs from the store. Do you suppose
       you could go for me?
       No, but I heard my pa say he could.

3075   So, you wanted to steal my girl away without any warning?
       Oh, no — what warning did you want to give me about her?

3076   You're not my type.
       Well, I'm glad there's one type of man you don't go for.

3077   I went by your house about three this morning, and I saw a
       light burning. Who was up?
       I was sitting up waiting for my mother to get home from her date.
       Don't be silly — you didn't have to sit up for your mother.
       Well, somebody had to let grandma in anyway.

3078   My brother received a letter today and it said: I understand you
       have been running around with my wife. Please call at my
       office and we'll discuss this matter.
       Pretty serious. What did your brother do?
       He answered it promptly — he said: Received your circular
       letter, and will be tickled to death to attend the meeting.

3079   When you called up my wife and told her I would be detained
       at the office, and would not be home until very late, what did
       she say?
       She said — Can I depend on that?

3080   (Woman calls up ex-husband who has just arrived in town)
       Woman: Hello darling. How are you? Why don't you come
       out and see me?
       Man: But, my dear, you forget I'm a much married man now.
       Woman: Well, that didn't seem to bother you when you were
       married to me.

3081   Does your husband go out much at night?
       I don't know; I'll have to ask him the next time I see him.

3082   Listen, man, if I ever hear of you going out with my girl again,
          I'll shoot you.
       Well, if I do, I'll deserve it.

3083   Night before last you didn't come until yesterday; last night
          you came home today; if you don't come home tomorrow, I'm
          through with you.

3084   Girlie, why are you always looking in the mirror?
       Your wife told me to watch myself when you were around.

3085   You look more gorgeous every day. What do you say we make
          a date for Saturday night?
       I can't make it Saturday — I'm getting married Saturday. How
          about Sunday?

3086   Hear about Johnson being in the hospital?
       In the hospital? Why, I saw him last night dancing with a dizzy
          blonde.
       That's why he's in the hospital. His wife saw him, too.

3087   What do you mean by coming home at this hour?
       I didn't mean to come home at this hour — but the darn place
          was raided!

3088   So you've been going around with a married woman?
       Yeah. I was over there last night and her husband came home
          unexpected.
       What happened?
       Well, I told him I was the plumber.
       That was pretty fast thinking.
       Not so fast — you see — he's a plumber himself.

RELATED SUBJECTS
Conduct 1802-1862
Love Making 2641-2719
Jealousy 2775-2777
Marriage 2882-3051

DIVORCE

3089   Why do you want a divorce?
       Every time I sit in my husband's lap, he starts dictating letters.

3090   What's this divorce evil they're always talking about?
       Alimony.

3091   What are your grounds for divorcing this man?
       I had to wash his back every Saturday night.
       Do you consider that a sufficient reason for divorce?
       No, but his back was clean last Saturday night.

3092   She wanted to know what it was that parted me and my last
          husband and I told her the truth.
       What?
       The police!

3093   Woman charges her husband with reckless driving. His care-
          lessness consisted of driving with another woman.

3094   Now that Mrs. Hodge is divorced I suppose she's after a man
          again.
       Yes, she's got back her maiden aim.

3095   He spent twenty years of his life in the penitentiary for arson,
          but his wife divorced him because he wouldn't start the fire
          in the kitchen stove.

3096   I want something to quiet my nerves, Lawyer Jones.
       But I'm not a doctor — I'm a lawyer.
       Yes, I know. I want a divorce.

3097   Can't afford a divorce — so she shot her husband.

3098   I want to know if I have grounds for a divorce.
       Are you married?
       Yes.
       Then, of course, you have.

3099   I'd like to know if I can get a divorce.
       What has your husband done?
       Is it necessary to tell that?
       Well, we must, of course, make some charge against him. State
          what he's done.
       Well, as a matter of fact, he hasn't done anything. I haven't
          got a husband, but I'm engaged to a man and I just wanted to
          see how easy I could get a divorce in case of need.

3100   About all that is needed for a divorce these days is a wedding.

       You only have to mumble a few words in church to get married.
          And a few in your sleep to get divorced.

3101   I've had enough. Next week I'm divorcing that faithless husband of mine!
Ah, so you're part of a triangle?
Triangle — nothing! I'm part of an octangle!

3102   Are the divorce laws in your state as liberal as I've heard?
Liberal! I should say so. They are so liberal that nobody ever heard of a woman crying at a wedding out there.

3103   I want to get a divorce from my husband.
What are your charges?
My charges? I thought I had to pay you.

3104   I'm divorcing you, John. I need a Spanish type for the new apartment.

3105   Why do you want a divorce, my man?
My wife has not spoken to me in three months.
Some men do not deserve good wives.

RELATED SUBJECTS
Marriage 2882-3051
Mother-in-Law 3116-3131
Attorney 5235-5244
Judge 5245-5250
Trial 5251-5275

ALIMONY

3106   I understand you've got your divorce, Sally. Did you get any alimony from your husband?
No, but he done give me a first-class reference.

3107   When the Judge ruled Jones had to pay alimony, how did he feel about it?
Chagrined.
And how did his wife feel about it?
She grinned.

3108   The word alimony is merely a contraction of "all his money."

3109   Just been down to the jail to see my friend Joe.
What's he in for?
For not paying alimony, and he's the guy that said marriage wouldn't get him anywhere.

3110   What is alimony?
A man's cash surrender value.

RELATED SUBJECTS   Attorney 5235-5244
Marriage 2882-3051   Trial 5251-5275
                          Money 5457-5479

WIFE

3111   And the kind of wife I'm looking for is one who can sew. The kind you can give a handful of buttons to and say: Here — sew some shirts on these.

3112   Will you please tell me what a wife really is? Some of my friends say their wife is an angel and others say theirs is a she-devil.
Well, a wife is a woman who will stick by you in all the trouble you wouldn't have gotten into if you hadn't married her in the first place.

RELATED SUBJECTS
Age 45-107
Description of People 263-303
Names of People 939-1017
Talk 1432-1481
Fight 2145-2213
Marriage 2882-3051
Divorce 3089-3105
Family 3209-3217
Mother 3262-3266
Beauty 4725-4735

HUSBAND

3113   Your husband has a new suit.
No, he hasn't.
Well, something's different.
It's a new husband.

3114   It says here that a woman in Omaha has just cremated her third husband.
Heigho! Isn't that just the way? Some of us can't get one and other women have husbands to burn.

3115   Is that fellow you're looking at one of your former husbands?
No — I think he's one of my children.

RELATED SUBJECTS
Description of People 263-303
Names of People 939-1017
Ambition 1874-1893
Economy 1997-2030
Marriage 2882-3051
Unfaithfulness 3057-3088
Family 3209-3217
Father 3267-3270
Children 3326-3333

MOTHER-IN-LAW

3116 Will you donate something to the Old Ladies' Home?
With pleasure. Help yourself to my mother-in-law.

3117 Yesterday while we were out hunting you almost shot my mother-in-law.
Sorry, here's my gun. Take a shot at mine.

3118 When is your mother coming?
Wednesday of next week. Why?
I just wanted to find out when I was going.

3119 My wife threatened to go back to her mother. I said: Is that a threat or a promise?
What's the difference?
If she goes back to her mother, that's a promise. But if she says she's going to bring her mother home — that's a threat.

3120 Where did you get that medal?
I saved a life.
How?
I shot at my mother-in-law and missed her.

3121 Mother-in-law: Just look at you! Why don't you pull yourself together! Just look at you! Why don't you go out and get a haircut! You look like a woman!
Son-in-law: So do you.

3122 My mother-in-law was kidnapped last week. The kidnappers said if we didn't send $24,000 quick we would have to take my mother-in-law back.

3123 Why did you break off your engagement, Jack?
Well, we were looking over a flat when her mother remarked that it was rather small for three.

3124 Turkey — you know what turkey is?
Uh huh.
You know what you had for Thanksgiving dinner?
Oh, my mother-in-law, but we call her an old buzzard.

3125 To my mother-in-law: When I'm hanging socks this Christmas, let me hang one on your jaw. You'll find a mistletoe on my shoe strings, just for you, mother-in-law.

3126 George, what do you think? Mother wants to be cremated.
Right! Where is she? Tell her to put her things on.

3127 Why did you bite your husband's mother?
'Twas his fault, your honor, he was always throwin' her in my teeth.

3128 Wife: Mother says she nearly died laughing over those stories you told her.
Husband: Where is she? I'll tell her some funnier ones.

3129 And when you sassed your mother's mother your dad took you out into the woodshed, did he?
Yeah. He didn't want my mother to see him slip me a quarter.

3130 I don't like my mother-in-law.
Listen, don't you realize that you wouldn't have your wife if it hadn't been for your mother-in-law?
Yes, that's why I don't like her.

3131 Do you mean to tell me you've been married for five years and your mother-in-law has only been to visit you once?
Yeah. She came the day after we were married and never left.

RELATED SUBJECTS
Description of People 263-303
Shapes (Physical) 341-347
Marriage 2882-3051
Family 3209-3217
Back-Seat-Driver 4128-4135

HOUSE (CONSTRUCTION)

3132 Why do you have your front door leading right into your dining room?
So my wife's relatives won't have to waste any time.

3133 Why did you have a winding stairway put in your house?
To give me something to do — I wind it up every night and unwind it in the morning.

3134 I wish I could have a den in my house.
That's easy. Tell your wife that if you can have a den you won't growl all over the kitchen, dining room and the front porch.

3135 Say, I lived in a house four years before I found out it didn't have a roof.
How did you find out the house didn't have a roof?
I happened to be at home once and it rained.

3136 What kind of house did you build?
A regular California bungalow. It's made out of tar paper, chicken wire and slats.
Some of these California bungalows are not to be sneezed at.
You don't dare sneeze at 'em.

3137 My paper hanger put paper on over the old paper.
Why didn't he take the old paper off?
If he took the old paper off, the house would collapse.

3138 Your roof must be leaking. Does the roof always leak?
      No — only when it rains.

3139 Why did your uncle move after living eighteen years in his home?
      He decided to move when he didn't find a bathroom.
      Oh — after eighteen years he didn't find a bathroom?

3140 We have a special knob for agents.
      What kind is it?
      When you say: Come in — the door knob comes off in the agent's
        hands.

3141 I tried to find your house yesterday but I couldn't find it. Didn't
        you say it was near the water?
      Yeah.
      Well, I didn't find any water.
      You didn't look in the basement.

3142 Marie! Marie! Y'hooo!
      Yes — what is it?
      Let's see the mail order catalog. I've just got some money and
        now we can order those steps up to the third floor.

3143 Charming place this old mansion — seen the old wing?
      Oh yes, I had it for lunch.

3144 Nice building. What style of architecture is it?
      I'm not quite sure — but I think it's Reminiscence.

3145 We're building the ceilings in our house of rubber.
      What's the idea?
      So when mama gets mad and hits the ceiling all she'll do is bounce
        around.

3146 Now there is a house without a flaw!
      My gosh, what do you walk on?

3147 Have you any suggestions for the study, Mr. Quickrich?
      Only that it must be brown. Great thinkers, I understand, are
        generally found in a brown study.

3148 It ain't sanitary to have the house built over the hog pen that way.
      Well, I dunno. We ain't lost a hog in fifteen years.

3149 I noticed that at the banquet you were eating soup when every-
        body was finished eating.
      Well, it was raining and there was a hole in the ceiling.
      What's that got to do with it?
      Well, my soup plate was right under the hole and I had to keep
        eating to keep from being drowned.

3150   The door key that you have had for twenty-five years does not fit?
       When did you discover it?
       After the death of my wife.

3151   It was one of those Hollywood apartments. You know, one of
       those apartments where if you are in the living room and want
       to go to the kitchen or the bathroom you just stand where
       you are.

                                         RELATED SUBJECTS
                                         Insurance 208-216
                                         Home 3197-3205
                                         Family 3209-3217
                                         Flies 3790-3800
                                         Finance 5457-5537

LEASE

3152   That's a very quiet apartment house you live in, isn't it?
       I'll say. When I rented the apartment the landlord asked if I had
       children and I said no. Then he asked, "Any dogs?" And I
       said no. Then he wanted to know if I had a canary or other
       pets and I said, "No, but I've got a fountain pen that scratches
       a little."

3153   What were you doing to cause all that racket last night?
       We were playing a game — every one jumps around and hollers
       and sings — and the one who makes the most noise wins.
       What is the name of the game?
       Breaking the lease.

3154   How much are they asking for your apartment rent now?
       About twice a day.

3155   Your singing is very instrumental.
       You wouldn't call singing instrumental?
       Yes, I would. It's instrumental in breaking our lease.

3156   I'm going to raise your rent.
       I'm glad of that, because I can't raise it.

3157   I want you to pay your rent.
       Let me tell you this — in a few years time people will look up at
       this miserable studio and say: "Doakes, the famous artist, used
       to work there."
       If you don't pay your rent by tonight, they'll be able to say it
       tomorrow.

3158   Is this the bird store?
       Yes.
       Well, send me 30,000 cockroaches at once.
       What in heaven's name do you want with 30,000 cockroaches?

Well, I'm moving tomorrow and my lease says I must leave the premises here in exactly the same condition in which I found them.

3159   I'm awfully sorry I can't pay you this month.
That's what you said last month.
You see — I keep my word.

3160   I'm sorry if our hammering disturbed you. We were hanging a picture.
Oh, that's all right. I just came over to ask if it was all right if we hung a picture on the other end of the nail.

3161   I'm afraid this apartment is too small. I might want to grow a beard.

3162   If you don't pay your rent, I want your room.
You wouldn't like it here.

RELATED SUBJECTS
Home 3197-3205
Family 3209-3217
Attorney 5235-5244

FURNITURE

3163   What's that thing over the bed?
That's a canopy — you know what a canopy is?
Yes. What's the matter? Does the roof leak?

3164   After being away from home for two months, the husband returned and said: What do you call that new piece of furniture in the corner?
She: Hi-boy.
He: How'ya, kid?

3165   I want to get an easy chair for my husband.
Morris?
No — Horace.

3166   Isn't this antique furniture gorgeous? I wonder where Mrs. Betts got that huge old chest?
Well, they tell me her old lady was the same way.

3167   Give me an example of period furniture.
Well, I should say an electric chair — because it ends a sentence.

3168   I don't like that chair.
It's a Louis the 14th.
Well, it's too small. I want a Louis the 16th.

3169   I'm going to buy a book.
A book?

Yes, my husband bought me the most adorable reading lamp yesterday.

3170 Woman: I am redecorating my living room, and I would like to see what you have in armchairs.
Clerk: This is our latest style. How do you like it?
Woman: Like it? Why it doesn't have any arms!
Clerk: Of course not. It's our Venus de Milo model.

RELATED SUBJECTS
Home 3197-3205
Department Store 5418-5429

INSTALLMENT PLAN

3171 I wouldn't buy a car. It's too complicated.
What's complicated about buying a car?
Well, all I know is my uncle is still paying part payments on the car he sold in part payment of the car he has now.

3172 Pay for it on the installment plan — as you drive.
All right, but remember, I'm a very slow driver.

3173 I paid the plumber the last installment today.
Thank goodness! I can at last take a bath with a clean conscience.

3174 Mrs. Higgins had just paid the last installment on the perambulator.
Shopkeeper: Thank you, ma'am. How is the baby getting on now?
Mrs. Higgins: Oh, he's quite all right. He's getting married next week.

3175 Why do you always buy your clothes on the installment plan?
They try to give me stuff that will last until the installments are paid.

3176 You should be ashamed to be late.
Yes, but it's not my fault I'm not on time.
On time? What does "on time" mean to you?
A few bucks down and the rest on easy payments.

3177 What do you know about the installment plan?
All I know is that if it wasn't for the installment plan, a lot of animals could wear their own furs this winter.

3178 He bought a suit from me on time and then his watch stopped.

3179 One more payment and the furniture is ours.
Good! Then we can throw it out and get some new stuff.

3180   Late again — have you ever done anything on time?
       Yeah — I bought a car.

RELATED SUBJECTS
Budget 3315-3316
Clothing 3391-3502
Automobile 4042-4146
Stores 5393-5402
Department Stores 5418-5429
Money 5457-5479

MORTGAGE

3181   There are so many mortgages on her car she has to drive it in
       second gear.

3182   I just mortgaged the home.
       Why did you do that?
       Oh, it's only temporary.
       What do you mean — only temporary?
       Until they foreclose.

3183   This paper says one quarter of the United States is covered with
       forests.
       And I suppose the other three quarters is covered with mortgages.

RELATED SUBJECTS
Attorney 5235-5244
Businessman 5309-5321
Finance 5457-5537

FIRE

3184   What are those buckets for on the shelf in the backroom?
       Can't you read? It says on them "For Fire Only."
       Then why do they put water in them?

3185   I say, conductor, will you please get me a glass of water?
       That's the tenth glass of water I've gotten you in the last five
       minutes. I never heard of anyone drinking so much.
       I'm not drinking it. My berth is on fire. I'm trying to put it out.

3186   Every time I come over to see you that cat is sitting in exactly the
       same place.
       Yeah, he's a hole cat.
       A hole cat?
       Yeah, my brother burned a hole in the carpet and he's trained the
       cat to sleep over the hole.

3187   Suppose you were driving your automobile and a fire engine came
       along. What would you do?
       Follow the engine. I'm crazy about fires.

3188   Do you know, you'd make a wonderful fireman.
       How's that?
       You never take your eyes off the hose.

3189   Yes, always spread newspaper in front of the fireplace so if any
       sparks come out they won't get on the rug.

3190   You know what an emergency call is?
       Sure I do. A private house burned down to the ground last night.
       I rang the doorbell, but no one answered the door, so we went
       back to the firehouse.

3191   There was a fire in the dressing room of the star backstage. The
       firemen were there six hours.
       Six hours to put out a fire in a dressing room?
       Oh no — it only took them one hour to put out the fire, but it
       took five hours to put out the firemen.

3192   I was working until yesterday. I worked at a place where they
       sell fire extinguishers and all kinds of things to put out fires.
       Why aren't you working there now?
       The place burned down last night.

3193   I'm so glad my uncle's house burned down. It was the first time
       it was warm this winter.

3194   Is this the fire station?
       Yes.
       Well, I have just had a new rock garden built and I've put in
       some new plants . . .
       Where's the fire?
       Some of these new plants are very expensive, and . . .
       Look here — you want the flower shop.
       No, I don't. I was coming to that in a minute. My neighbor's house
       is on fire, and I don't want your firemen to run all over my
       garden when you come here.

3195   Mama, when the fire goes out where does it go?
       My dear boy, I don't know. You might just as well ask me where
       your father goes when he goes out.

3196   Why does the whistle blow for a fire?
       It doesn't blow for the fire, it blows for water. They've got the
       fire.

3197　Where do you live?
　　　I live with my sister.
　　　Where does your sister live?
　　　She lives with me.
　　　Where do you both live?
　　　We both live together.
　　　Oh, you moved, huh?
　　　That's where we live now.

3198　I lived in one house ten years.
　　　You did?
　　　Yeah, I'd have been there yet if the Governor hadn't pardoned me.

3199　I'm going home.
　　　Why?
　　　I live there.

3200　Where do you live?
　　　Nowhere. Where do you live?
　　　I live in the next block from you.

3201　Why didn't they stay in their new home?
　　　The house was too damp — there was too much due on it.

3202　We're going into the home of Pete Smith, the great comic.
　　　Oh — we're going slumming.

3203　Close that door — where were you raised — in a barn?
　　　(Man cries)
　　　Oh, well, I'm sorry I yelled at you like that.
　　　I'm not crying because you yelled at me — I'm crying because I
　　　was raised in a barn and every time I see a jackass it makes me
　　　feel homesick.

3204　After all, isn't a home what we make it?
　　　No — it's the neighbors who make it noisy, our friends who mess
　　　it up and the landlord who makes it expensive.

3205　Did you say you lived in Duluth all your life?
　　　Yep — it's getting so it's just like home to me.

RELATED SUBJECTS
Insurance 208-216
Installment Plan 3171-3180
House 3132-3151
Family 3209-3217
Neighbors 3661-3666
Radio 4598-4610
Cooking 4798-4824
Food 4825-4878
Table Manners 4881-4883

HOMESICKNESS

3206   I'm homesick.
Isn't that your home?
Yes, but I'm sick of it.

3207   I don't feel very well today.
Homesick?
No, I'm here sick.

3208   Honest, weren't you ever homesick?
Not me, I never stay there long enough.

RELATED SUBJECTS
Travel 3971-4246

FAMILY

3209   My uncle has a large family. The other day while he was out walking a policeman stopped him and said: You're under arrest. My uncle said: Why? I ain't done nothing. And the policeman said: What's the big crowd following you for?

3210   I've got another mouth to feed.
Good Lord — you don't mean to tell me that you . . .
Heck, no, I've got a tapeworm.

3211   Is Mary your oldest sister?
Yep.
And who comes after her?
You and two other guys.

3212   Why were you late this morning?
On account of my alarm clock. Everybody in the house got up except me.
How was that?
There are eight of us and the alarm clock was only set for seven.

3213   My father was a bank robber; my sister is a shoplifter; my oldest brother was hung; and I have a brother in Harvard Medical College.
Do you mean to tell me out of a family of that kind, you have a brother who is a student in the Harvard Medical College?
I didn't say my brother is a student of the Harvard Medical College. He's just there — they have him in a little bottle of alcohol.

3214   I passed your house this morning and I saw all your family wash in the yard.
Don't be silly! My family wash in the bathroom.

3215   Your uncle sure has a large family, hasn't he?
I don't know exactly, but it's quite big. I know a sack of flour lasts awfully quick. .

3216 Have you any brothers or sisters?
No, my parents were orphans.

3217 The average American family consists of 4.1 persons, we read,
and you have one guess as to who constitutes the .1 person.

RELATED SUBJECTS
Description of People 263-303
Names of People 939-1017
House 3132-3151
Home 3197-3205
Heredity 3248-3252
Salary 3271-3280
Clothing 3391-3502
Food 4825-4878

ANCESTRY

3218 Here take this pill — it will take you back to your childhood.
Back to the early Boones.
I didn't know he came from the Boones.
Sure — his grandfather was named "babboon."

3219 Why won't you marry me?
I couldn't think of it. I have royal blood in my veins. My father
was offered a crown three times, but he refused it.
What's the matter? Was he holding out for a porcelain filling?

3220 How many people came over on the Mayflower?
One hundred and twenty.
You're crazy — I know three million people that took that trip.

3221 I'm proud of my forebears.
What are you — an animal trainer?

3222 Daddy, is it true I came from a tribe of monkeys?
I don't know — I never saw your mother's folks.

3223 Let me tell you we have a wonderful family tree.
The tree is all right, but the crop is a failure.

3224 A king touched my grandfather on the head with a sword and
made him a duke.
That's nothing. Once an Indian hit my uncle over the head with
a tomahawk and made him an angel.

3225 Were any of your ancestors on the stage or screen?
My cousin was the principal character at a public function once,
but the platform fell.
Did he fall to the floor?
No — the rope stopped him.

3226   My whole family follow the sea. My brother is an officer on a ship.
       Really? What is his capacity?
       About four or five quarts.

3227   I can trace my ancestors back to the Stone Age. You know, that
          was the age when if a man saw something he wanted he just up
          and took it.
       I understand your relatives still have that habit.

3228   I suppose he is one of the first families?
       Yes, one of the first as you turn left off San Fernando Boulevard
          and First.

3229   How far back do you trace your ancestors?
       Well, I had an old uncle who was traced way out to San Fran-
          cisco before they got him.

3230   He spent a thousand dollars to have his family tree looked up,
          and found out he was a sap.

3231   My father was Sir Andrews, Knight of the Garter, Golden Fleece,
          Pearly Teeth . . .
       Shake hands. My father was a duke, my grandfather was a duke,
          my great grandfather was a duke . . .
       Oh, you're looking for an argument.
       I'll match my ancestry with yours any time.
       All right, put up your dukes.

3232   We all spring from animals.
       Yeah — but you didn't spring far enough.

3233   I think we are descended from either birds or monkeys. What
          do you think?
       There are no feathers on *you*.

3234   My family goes way back. My ancestors fought William the
          Conqueror and the Spanish Armada and Napoleon's armies.
       Yeah, your family never got along with anybody.

3235   I understand you have been having your family tree looked up.
       Yes and it cost me five thousand dollars.
       Quite expensive, wasn't it?
       Yes, but it cost only two thousand to have it looked up. The other
          three thousand was what I paid to have it hushed up.

3236   I've got Spanish blood in me.
       By your mother?
       No, by transfusion.

3237   Oh, you mustn't blame me for my ancestors.
       I don't. I blame them for you.

3238   Poor Frank married Miss Nobody and just to think his ancestors
          came across on the Mayflower.

Yep, but don't forget to remember her folks came across with a couple hundred thousand dollars.

3239 (To man picking up scraps of paper with jabbing stick)
Don't you find that work very tiring?
Not so very, Mum. You see, I was born to it — my father used to harpoon whales.

3240 Dad, what are ancestors?
Well, my boy, I'm one of your ancestors. Your grandfather is another.
Then, why do people brag about them?

3241 My ancestors spring from a long line of peers.
Well, I had an uncle that jumped off the dock.

3242 My uncle died awfully young, but he left a lot of money behind him.
I know — they shot him crawling out of a bank window and he had to leave the money behind.

3243 (Loud yipping and yelling)
What's the idea making all that noise?
It's the Indian in me.
On what side are you Indian?
On the inside. I just swallowed a buffalo nickel.

3244 Has anyone told you about my forebears?
Goodness, no! Is it catching?

3245 I understand your wife came from a fine old family?
Came is hardly the word — she brought it with her.

3246 He's a blue blood. His blood's so blue, he's been despondent for years.

3247 This makes the second of my husband's family in the Peerage.
Have you any relation in the House of Lords?
No, but I've got two maiden aunts in the Kingdom of Heaven.

RELATED SUBJECTS
Resemblance 304-317
Nationalities 1059-1101
Success 1945-1966

HEREDITY

3248　Do you believe in heredity?
Absolutely — that's how I got all my money.

3249　What is heredity?
Something a father believes in until his son begins acting like a darn fool.

3250　Collecting must be in your blood.
Yeah, my father was a collector.
What did he collect?
Garbage.

3251　She loves to dance — dancing is in her blood.
She must have poor circulation — it hasn't got down to her feet yet.

3252　He takes after his father.
In what way?
He's good for nothing.

RELATED SUBJECTS
Description of People 263-303
Resemblance 304-317
Marriage 2882-3051
Family 3209-3217
Children 3326-3333

RELATIVES

3253　When he has money, a distant relative can be very distant.

3254　Who is that man over there? He annoys me.
He's my cousin — once removed.
Well, remove him again.

3255　All you need is a sponge.
But I haven't got a sponge.
That's all right — I'll lend you some of my relatives.

3256　Have you any close relatives?
Yes — all of them.

3257　Mother, let me go to the zoo to see the monkeys.
Why, Tommy, what an idea. Imagine wanting to go to see the monkeys when your Aunt Betsy is here.

3258　He's her second cousin — the first one didn't turn out so well.

3259　My brother got married last month.
Well, maybe a year from now you'll be an uncle.
No — I don't think so — I'll be out of town.

3260 See that man out there? He's my grandfather.
On your mother's or father's side?
Oh, he sticks up for both of them.

3261 Say — h'ja like to see our jail?
Full of my husband's relatives.

RELATED SUBJECTS
Mother-in-law 3116-3131
Home 3197-3205
Family 3209-3217
Ancestry 3218-3247
Loan 5503-5513

MOTHER

3262 I saw your mother for the first tme in three weeks. She has aged
a lot. Do you know what those wrinkles on your mother's brow
mean?
Yeah — she hasn't been to a beauty parlor for the last two days.

3263 A woman waved to a clergyman.
Daughter: Who's that?
Mother: That's the man who married me.
Daughter: Oh, really, Then who's that man back home?

3264 A modern mother is one that can hold safety pins and a cigarette
in her mouth at the same time.

3265 Little boy, is your mother engaged?
I think she's married.

3266 I've got a little riddle I want to ask you. When skies are blue,
who is always ready to comfort you?
I don't know.
Your mother. Who is it when skies are gray will chase Joe's
blues away?
I don't know.
Why, it's Joe's mother. What is it that has a long neck and long
legs and sticks its head in the sand when it is frightened?
I know that one.
What is it?
Your mother.

RELATED SUBJECTS
Description of People 263-303
Names of People 939-1017

Ambition 1888   Advice 1978-1989
Gratitude 2418   Marriage 2882-3051
                             Family 3209-3217
                             Children 3326-3333

FATHER

3267   Does your family live here on the desert?
        My father is a rich merchant in Africa. He makes suitcases.
        Oh — a bag-dad!

3268   "I'm a father!" cried the young man as he burst into the office.
        "So's your old man," replied the boss.

3269   My father was a sailor. He deserted my mother the day before
            I was born.
        Maybe he knew what was coming.

3270   Daughter of First Film Star: How do you like your new father?
        Daughter of Second Film Star: Oh, he's very nice.
        Daughter of First Film Star: Yes, isn't he? We had him last year.

RELATED SUBJECTS
Description of People 263-303
Names of People 939-1017
Marriage 2882-3051
House 3132-3151
Home 3197-3205
Family 3209-3217
Children 3326-3333
Automobile 4042-4146

SALARY

3271   Remember to remind me to reduce your salary so when I fire you
            you'll only be out half as much.

3272   When I went to work for you, didn't you say something about
            my getting a raise?
        I did say that if you did your work well.
        I knew there was a catch in it somewhere.

3273   I understand his salary goes to five figures . . .
        Yeah — a wife and four children.

3274   Does he make any money?
        He gets $50 a week and his wife gets $50 a week.
        That makes $100 a week . . .
        No, it's the same fifty. He earns it and she gets it afterwards.

3275   You want me to give you a raise in salary, eh? Well, give me at
            least two good reasons.
        Twins!

3276   How do you spend your income?
About thirty percent for shelter, thirty percent for clothing, forty percent for food and twenty percent for amusement.
But that adds up to one hundred and twenty percent.
That's right.

3277   Er — er — um —aw — my wife and I are finding it terribly difficult to live together on my salary, sir.
Well, what do you want me to do? Arrange a divorce for you?

3278   Does your husband get what he earns?
Yes, that's why we are always so hard up.

3279   I understand Lamb commands a good salary.
No, he only earns it. Mrs. Lamb commands it.

3280   You shouldn't divorce your husband. He's the kind that brings home the bacon.
Yes, but the man who owns the bacon has found out about it.

RELATED SUBJECTS
Work 1894-1944
Income Tax 3317-3323
Businessman 5309-5321
Occupations 5362-5380

BILLS

3281   I noticed a man sitting around your studio. Is he posing for you?
No — that's the furniture man — he's laying for me.
Why don't you pay him?
He told me he was going to keep the rest of the collectors away from here until he gets his.

3282   My wife used to buy in three or four stores and her bills were terrific. Now her bills are much smaller.
How does she do it?
She buys from thirty or forty stores.

3283   Are you going to pay me what you owe?
Yes — I'll pay. Here's a dollar down.
What about the rest of it?
I'll give you a dollar every day I work.
That's fine. What do you do?
I decorate Christmas trees.

3284   It's true that an apple a day keeps the doctor away, but you have to use tomatoes on bill collectors.

3285   I didn't have any money, so I asked him for some.
       Did he give it to you?
       All he had was a thirty dollar bill.
       There is no such thing as a thirty dollar bill.
       No? You should see our grocery bill sometimes.

3286   I ought to punch you in the eye. You owe me five bucks.
       We'll fight — that will make it a war debt and you'll never
         collect that.

3287   You have to pay me what you owe me.
       I admit I owe you the money—but what were the terms?
       You were to pay me in two months.
       Yeah, but you didn't say which two months, and I'm taking
         September of 1982 and April of 1996.

3288   Do you have trouble meeting your obligations?
       No — I never have any trouble meeting 'em — what troubles me
         is ducking them.

3289   The man can't deliver your groceries until you pay your bill.
       Tell him to cancel the order, I'll be dead by then.

3290   Didn't I see you coming out of a doctor's office today?
       Yeah — he ordered me to go to a warmer climate.
       What did you go to see him about?
       About collecting a bill.

3291   What! You want me to pay thirty-five dollars for my room in
         this hotel? Say, that is outrageous.
       But this is on the American plan; your meals are included in
         that price.
       But I didn't eat a meal here.
       They were right there for you — that's your fault.
       Then you owe me thirty-five dollars.
       What for, may I ask?
       For kissing my wife.
       But I didn't kiss your wife, I tell you.
       Well, that's not my fault; she was right there for you.

3292   There's something bigger than money.
       Yes — bills.

3293   Can you pay your bill now?
       No — see me Thursday.
       Thursday I'll be out of town.
       So will I.

3294   My good man, how is it you have not called on me for my account?
       Oh, I never ask a gentleman for money.

Indeed! How, then, do you get on if he doesn't pay?
Why, after a certain time I conclude he is not a gentleman and
   then I ask him.

3295   Sir, your creditors await you without.
Without what?
Without the door.
Well, give 'em that, too.

3296   Where is that twenty dollars you borrowed from me?
I'm broke, and you can't get blood out of a turnip.
(Whereupon the man hit him on the nose and it bled and he found
   out he wasn't a turnip.)

3297   Sir, how about this little bill?
What about the little bill?
This is pay-what-you-owe-week.
I'm observing extension-of-credit-week.

3298   I haven't paid a cent for repairs on my machine all the ten months
   I have had it.
So the man who did the repairs told me.

3299   I want you to help me hold down the bills.
That's easy! The last place I worked at, I didn't have no trouble
   keeping down the bills.
That's fine. How did you do it?
I just used paper weights.

3300   I'm sorry, old man, but I haven't a cent. And you know you can't
   get blood out of a stone.
Yeah? But what makes you think you're a stone?

3301   Judge: Haven't I seen you before?
Speeder: Maybe — so many men owe me money I can't remember
   their faces.

3302   But my dear daughter, your husband owes me a lot of money.
I don't think he should expect me to lend him more.
Well, father, he has to get it somewhere and he has a certain
   sentiment about keeping his creditors in the family.

3303   Husband: What became of that unpaid bill Dunn and Company
   sent us?
Wife: Oh, that? I sent it back marked insufficient funds.

3304   You should be in Congress — you bring so many bills in the
   house.

3305   Look here, you've been owing me this bill for a year. I'll meet you
   half way. I'm ready to forget half what you owe me.
Fine! I'll meet you. I'll forget the other half.

3306   What is your occupation?
It isn't an occupation, it's a pursuit. I'm a bill collector.

3307   Here's my new dress, dear. I bought it for a song.
All right, send in the collector and I'll sing to him.

3308   How are you?
Oh, I'm about even.
Even?
Yes, I figure I owe about as many people as I don't owe.

RELATED SUBJECTS
Marriage 2882-3051
Family 3209-3217
Budget 3315-3316
Clothing 3391-3502
Money 5457-5479

WOLF-AT-DOOR

3309   You know I'm having a struggle to keep the wolf away from
the door.
That's not so bad. We haven't got a door to keep the wolf away
from.

3310   Why are you looking so sad?
For three long years the wolf has been howling at our door.
Now I suppose you haven't any door for the wolf to howl at?
No — yesterday we let him in.

3311   What is an opportunist?
One who meets the wolf at the door, and appears next day in a
fur coat.

3312   Girl: The way prices keep going up, I don't know how I'm going
to make ends meet!
Guy: I know how to keep the wolves from *your* door.
Girl: How can I do that?
Guy: Stop wearing such tight sweaters.

3313   If the wolf doesn't go away from my door, I'll lock him in the
ice box and let him starve to death.

3314   The wolf at our door is getting fat. I measured him today, and
he is one yard wide across the back.
I get it. All wolf and a yard wide.

RELATED SUBJECTS
Finance 5457-5537

BUDGET

3315   I bought some sheets, pillow cases and blankets today. Shall I
       put them down in my budget as cover charges or overhead?

3316   Are you saving any money since you started your budget system?
       Sure. By the time we have balanced it up every evening, it's too
       late to go anywhere.

RELATED SUBJECTS
Economy 1997-2030
Installment Plan 3171-3180
Family 3209-3217
Salary 3271-3280

INCOME TAX

3317   Have you a wild man?
       Yes, he is good and wild today. He just sent in his income tax.

3318   Our whole family is going over to live with Uncle Felix until
         April 15th.
       Why until April 15th?
       So Uncle Felix will have more dependents to put in his income
         tax statement.

3319   They ought to have special schools to tell you how to fill out forms.
       There is one person the Government won't have to tell how to
         fill out her form.
       Who's that?
       Mae West.

3320   That reminds me. Interest can be deducted.
       Swell! I have a terrific interest in Charlie McCarthy.

3321   My husband left me on April 15th without any explanation.
         Why do you think he did that?
       He probably left you on that date because he figured he couldn't
         support the government and a wife on one salary.

3322   What is untold wealth?
       That which does not appear on income tax reports.

3323   Advice on how to make out your income tax:
       List as your dependents: Your wife — car — three goldfish and
         two children.
       Now, multiply your grandfather's age by six and seven-eights,
         subtract his telephone number. Next, add the size of his hat
         and subtract the number of his car.
       Then, deduct one thousand dollars for keeping your wife a blonde

for the whole year, then divide the remainder by the number of lodges you belong to, multiply by the number of electric lights in the house, and divide by the size of your collar.

Now, then you have the gross income, which, after dividing by your chest measurement, and subtracting your blood pressure, gives you the net amount owed to the Government.

> RELATED SUBJECTS
> Father 3267-3270
> Salary 3271-3280
> Attorney 5235-5244
> Businessman 5309-5321
> Money 5457-5479
> Wealth 5480-5486

TAXES

3324   They're now talking about personal tax: size and weight. So much a pound. Every man will be worth his weight in gold, and Uncle Sam will live off the fat of the land. The tax on the Greenbay Packers would cover the national deficit. And between Orson Welles and Jackie Gleason, we could float the Navy.

3325   I'm going to be a Nudist — you can't tax them.
The government will get them, too.
No, it won't. You can't pin anything on a Nudist.
> RELATED SUBJECTS
> Money 5457-5479

CHILDREN

3326   How do you know how many children you have?
When the house gets full, we lock the doors and go to sleep. Once a man threw a brick through the window and children ran out of the house for three days.

3327   How many children have you?
I don't know — but every time they get in the yard, it looks like recess.

3328   Which would you rather have? Ten thousand dollars or ten children?
Ten children. When a man has ten thousand dollars he always wants more.

3329   We have a nice big family. There are (counting) 1 — 2 — 3 — 4 — 5 — 6 — Six of us.
Six altogether?
No — one at a time.

3330   So you have nine children. Quite a family. I suppose before long you'll be having another child.
Oh, no.

What makes you so positive?
Because every tenth child born is a Chinese.

3331 Some friends of ours sent their little boy to stay with us because in their town they had had several large landslides. After we had the boy a week we sent him back and told them to send us the landslides.

3332 He has two sons. One is a politician and the other isn't much good either.

3333 Mary, why do you yell and scream so? Play quietly like Tommy. See, he doesn't make a sound.
Of course he doesn't. That is our game. He's papa coming home late, and I am you.

RELATED SUBJECTS
Description of People 263-303
Names of People 939-1017
Family 3209-3217
Baby 3359-3389
Games 3604-3613
School 4885-4894

KID BROTHER - SISTER

3334 Small Brother: Ha! Ha! I just saw you kiss sis.
Suitor: Here. Keep still. Put this quarter in your pocket.
Small Brother: Here's ten cents change. One price to all, that's the way I do business.

3335 Suitor: (To little brother) Here, take this quarter and go to see a show.
Kid: No, I'll give you fifty cents to let me stay and watch.

3336 Little boy, are you sure you can cut your meat?
Oh, yes, ma'am — we often have it as tough as this at home.
RELATED SUBJECTS
Love Making 2641-2719
Family 3209-3217
School 4885-4894

BATH

3337 Where do you bathe?
I bathe in the spring.
I didn't say when — I said where?

3338   Today my little girl asks me: Why do I have to wash my face
       all the time? I told her because it was dirty.
       What did she say?
       She said: Why can't I powder over the dirt like mama does?

3339   An American tourist, traveling through England: Driver, can
       you tell me when we get to Bath?
       Driver: When you're dirty, mum.

3340   When I went home last night I found a horse in the bathtub.
       What did you do?
       Oh, I just pulled the plug out.

3341   I'm going home — I expect a phone call.
       Who from?
       I don't know.
       Then how do you know the phone will ring?
       I'm going to take a bath.
       That's right — the phone generally rings when I take a bath.
       Yeah, but sometimes I have to take two or three baths to make
       it ring.

3342   What was the idea of sending the porter for water all night? He
       must have brought you three quarts of water. What did you do
       with all that water?
       Well, I learned my lesson. I'll never try to take a bath in an upper
       berth again.

3343   Do you want to hear an odd noise?
       Sure.
       Well, let the water run in the bathtub. That will be strange
       to you.

3344   How long does it take you to dress in the morning?
       'Bout half an hour.
       Only takes me ten minutes.
       Well, I wash.

3345   Hotel Guest: There's a man taking a bath in my room!
       Desk Clerk: Sh! Please be quiet, or everybody else will want one!

3346   The best time to take a bath is just before retiring.
       No wonder these boys retire at a ripe old age.

3347   If all the bath mats were placed end to end, a person could walk
       to New York from San Francisco in his bare feet.

3348   Bellhop: I just saved a life.
       Clerk: Give me the particulars.

Bellhop: Well, the lady in 301 fainted in her bath and I dragged her out.

3349   Did you use the thermometer like I told you when you bathed the baby?
No, ma'am; I can tell without that. If it's too hot, the baby turns red, and if it's too cold, he'll turn blue.

3350   A new teacher had a very dirty pupil in her class. At first she didn't know what to do, but finally she sent the boy home with a note to his mother, saying that he was not clean and that he should bathe more often. The next morning the boy came back to school, and pinned to his dirty shirt was the following note: Tommy isn't a rose. Don't smell him—teach him!

RELATED SUBJECTS
Description of People 263-303
Family 3209-3217

CLEANLINESS

3351   Have you taken every precaution to prevent spread of contagion in your family?
Absolutely, doctor, we've even bought a sanitary cup and we all drink from it.

3352   The cat is a wonderful animal — just as clean as a whistle.
Oh, cats aren't so clean.
Don't argue with me — cats are very clean. Take a look at the little pussy cat in the corner. Its always washing its face.
I don't know about that. Cats don't wash their faces — they wash their feet and wipe them on their faces.

3353   See here, waiter, this knife isn't clean.
Why, it must be. The last thing I cut with it was a bar of soap.

3354   You certainly do keep your car nice and clean.
It's an even deal — my car keeps me clean, too.

3355   Your face is clean, but how'd you get your hands so dirty?
Washin' my face.

3356   After I wash my face I always look in the glass to see whether it is clean.
I don't have to. I look at the towel.

3357 Tramp: No, ma'am, I ain't dirty from choice. I'm bound by
       honor. I wrote a testimonial for a particular soap once and
       promised to use no other.
       Woman: Well, why don't you use that?
       Tramp: Because, ma'am, the firm that made the soap went
       bankrupt during the depression.

3358 Your wife must be very clean — because everything I have tasted
       so far tastes of soap.

RELATED SUBJECTS
Description of People 263-303

BABY

3359 My aunt is coming over with her baby — it's just three weeks old.
       What's its name?
       I don't know. I can't understand a word it says.

3360 What caused all the bumps on your baby's head?
       Well, the doctor told me he was a bouncing baby boy, but I can't
       make him bounce.

3361 We're expecting a baby boy at our house.
       You mean, you're expecting a baby at your house . . . boy or girl.
       No — a boy.
       Why are you so positive it's going to be a boy?
       Last year mother was sick in bed and she got a baby girl. Now,
       dad is sick in bed.

3362 Has your baby called you daddy yet?
       No, my wife isn't going to tell him who I am until he gets a little
       stronger.

3363 I'm the father of a bouncing baby.
       A bouncing baby? Boy or girl?
       I don't know — it hasn't stopped bouncing yet.

3364 I get blamed for everything that goes on around here. Even as a
       baby, they were always pinning things on me.

3365 The India Rubber man and his wife have a bouncing baby boy.
       What does it look like?
       Like they caught it on the first bounce.

3366   We got a new baby at our house.
Did you turn in the old one?

3367   I love babies. Especially those born about twenty years ago.

3368   By the way — how's your younger brother?
That's a long story. Didn't you know he got married?
No — tell us all about it.
My father was very fond of George, and the day he got married
he promised to give him a thousand dollars to apply on the
mortgage on their little home for each baby they had — The
first year his wife presented him with a baby girl. Father gave
him the thousand dollars toward the mortgage. The second
year his wife had twins and the old man kicked in with two
thousand dollars more; the third year they had triplets and
father gave him three thousand dollars more toward the mortgage; and then the next year my brother died.
Your brother died?
Yeah — he killed himself trying to pay off the mortgage.

3369   Every time his wife presents him with a baby, he brings home an
accessory — something to put on the baby buggy. When the first
baby was born, he brought home a new top; when the second
one came along, a new set of bumpers for the buggy; the next
time she gave him twins and he bought a pair of wind wings and
tires for the buggy. Now, he's got me very, very worried. He's
got another baby and he doesn't know what to get for the baby
buggy.
That's easy.
What do you mean?
I think he ought to get a stop light.

3370   We've got a new baby at our house.
Where did you get him?
We got it from Doctor Brown.
We take from him, too.

3371   We have a new baby at home.
Has the baby come to stay?
I think so — he's taken all his things off.

3372   Daughter: Oops! Mom, I just dropped the baby's blanket out
the window!
Mother: You shouldn't have done that—he'll catch cold.
Daughter: No, he won't. He was in it.

3373   Well, Joe, how do you like your new little sister?
Oh, she's all right, I guess; but there are lots of things we needed
worse.

3374   We have a new baby at our house. It weighs seven pounds. How much was it a pound?

3375   What's the matter, little boy?
We got a new baby at our house and I get the blame for everything.

3376   So God has sent you two more little brothers, Dolly?
Yes, and He knows where the money's coming from; I heard Daddy say so.

3377   Say, Mom, was baby sent down from Heaven?
Yes, son.
I guess they like to have things quiet up there, huh?

3378   My brother's wife just had a baby.
Boy or girl?
He didn't say — and now I don't know whether I'm an aunt or an uncle.

3379   Your wife just had a baby.
Boy or girl?
What?
Boy or girl — am I a father or a mother?

RELATED SUBJECTS
Birth 11-34
Stork 35-44
Names of People 939-1017

TRIPLETS

3380   Didn't I tell you about Mrs. Smith? She had triplets and two weeks later she had twins.
That's impossible. How did it happen?
Well, one of the triplets got lost.

3381   A friend of mine is very excited. He just became the father of triplets. He can hardly believe his own census.

3382   Nurse: Mr. Politician, you are the father of triplets.
Man: What?
Nurse: You're the father of triplets. TRIPLETS!
Man: I'll demand a re-count.

3383   They offered the father of triplets a job in the movies.
Acting?
No, in the production department.

RELATED SUBJECTS
Stork 35-44

TWINS

3384   Just got a telegram from my wife: Just had twins — more by mail.

3385   When did you live in New York?
When I was twins.
When you were twins? You were twins?
Yeah, my mother has a picture of me when I was two.

3386   How old are you?
I don't know.
Ask your mother.
How would she know?
Well, how old is your brother?
He's three years younger than I am and we're twins.
How could you be twins if he is three years younger?
I'll prove it to you. What's in a hat box?
A hat.
What's in a bookcase?
Books.
Okay — my brother and I sleep in twin beds, so we're twins.

3387   You and your sister are twins, are you not?
We were in childhood. Now, however, she's five years younger
than I am.

3388   Well, Dick, my boy, my congratulations! I hear you're engaged
to one of the pretty Robbins twins.
Yeah.
But how on earth do you manage to tell them apart?
Oh, I don't try.

3389   I guess your brother was pleased when he found himself the
father of twin boys.
Was he! He went around grinning from heir to heir.

RELATED SUBJECTS
Birth 11-34
Stork 35-44

ORPHAN

3390   Ever since I was two years old I was left an orphan.
Is that so? Did it live?

RELATED SUBJECTS
Children 3326-3333

CLOTHING

3391 How do you like the fit?
      Fit? It's a convulsion.

3392 Is he wealthy?
      When I first met him, he didn't have a stitch of clothes on his
         back.
      Where did you meet him — in a bathtub?

3393 Girls worry too much about their clothes, but this is only much
         ado about nothing, so to speak.

3394 When did bustles go out of style?
      When revolving doors were invented. They just couldn't take it.

3395 My pants aren't as baggy as yours.
      They would be if you weren't knock-kneed.

3396 You certainly look cute in that gown.
      Oh, this? I wear it to teas.
      To tease whom?

3397 The latest fashion fad in Paris is to wear wigs to match the gown.
         From all indications, bald heads will soon be quite the rage.

3398 What can I do for you?
      I want a hat.
      Fedora?
      No — for me.

3399 After tomorrow, I'm not going to wear these pants any longer.
      Why?
      Because they're long enough.

3400 A woman may put on a golf suit and not play golf — she may
         put on a bathing suit and never go near the water — but when
         she puts on a wedding gown, she means business.

3401 Mary was quite décolleté at the dance last night, wasn't she?
      Why, I didn't know that she ever touched a thing.

3402 Miss Trumpet is a very particular dresser. When she goes out
         walking, she wears walking clothes; when she rides she wears
         riding clothes; when she goes out in the evening, she wears
         evening clothes . . .
      I'm going to give a birthday party and invite Miss Trumpet.

3403 The girls look lovely in those new gowns.
      That girl over there looks as if she was poured into her dress.
      She looks as if she overflowed.

3404 That dress is too tight for you. It's skin tight.
It's tighter than my skin.
How could anything be tighter than your skin?
I can sit down in my skin, but I'll be darned if I can sit down in this dress.

3405 Can you tell whether a girl is wearing stockings?
Sure. If their legs have seams, they're wearing stockings.

3406 That's a good looking hat you have.
Yes, I bought this hat two years ago. I had it cleaned twice, exchanged it in a restaurant once, and it still looks as good as new.

3407 Are you a college man?
No, I'm wearing these clothes to pay an election bet.

3408 I never wear an overcoat or a hat when it rains.
Gone collegiate?
No. I don't go out when it rains.

3409 I'd like to see something cheap in a straw hat.
Try this one on. The mirror is on your left.

3410 I have a suit for every day in the year.
You have a suit for every day in the year?
Yeah — the one I'm wearing.

3411 There will be very little change in men's clothing this season; especially very little change in their pockets.

3412 It was the year 600 B.C. — before clothing.

3413 It fits you like a glove.
It fits me like a glove?
Yeah — a boxing glove.

3414 Where did you get that lovely dress?
Everything I make I put on my back.
You must have been out of work a long time.

3415 Why is it his hat always looks so nice, and his coat looks so well, but his pants! They're just about the shabbiest I've ever seen.
You can't get pants in a restaurant.

3416 Do you know you can't clean a suit with two pairs of pants?
Why can't you clean a suit with two pairs of pants?
Because you have to use cleaning fluid.

3417 Bob: I want to apologize for my appearance this evening. This was rather unexpected and I didn't have an opportunity to dress. You know I always like to dress for the occasion — sometimes

I change my clothes four or five times a day — if the occasion demands.

Pete: Bragging, huh? Well, that's nothing — I've got a brother who changes his clothes four or five times an hour if the occasion demands.

Bob: How old is he?

Pete: Six months.

3418 (Wearing a suit made of the map of the United States)
Why, you have Wyoming on one arm, Oregon on your chest — Kansas on your back . . .
That's nothing — when I sit down, I have Virginia on my lap.

3419 Do you wear suspenders?
No. Why should I wear suspenders?
To support your pants.
Why should I support my pants? They never did anything for me.

3420 You ask me — if I put my hand in my pants pocket and found some money, what would I think?
Okay — if you put your hand in your pants pocket and found some money, what would you think?
I'd think I had somebody else's pants on.

3421 Does she dress like a lady?
I don't know — I never saw her dress.

3422 Why does your uncle wear such a large collar?
He found it, but it'll fit him in time.
How?
He's raising a goitre.

3423 She looks like she was poured into that dress and forgot to say when.

3424 Why do you carry that cane?
Because it can't walk.

3425 Will you give me the address of your tailor?
Yes, if you won't give him mine.

3426 Are you going to the party?
Is it formal — or do we wear our own clothes?

3427 Why did you buy that hat?
Because I couldn't get it for nothing.

3428 He wears clothes well.
No better than I do — I wore one suit for six years.

3429 How do you like my new suit?
It would look just as well on a nail.

3430 (Girl wears low neck dress)
She's showing her heart's in the right place.

3431 She wore one of those baseball dresses.
What's that?
A baseball dress? It had a diamond back, a grandstand view in front, and it showed a lot of beautiful curves.

3432 I want some winter underwear.
How long?
How long? I don't want to rent 'em — I want to buy 'em.

3433 Have you heard Janet rave about the silk stockings she bought in Paris?
I asked her how much they cost and she said: You can't touch them for any amount of money.

3434 What's the idea, Pete, wearing your socks wrong side out?
There's a hole in the other side.

3435 Bill's lost his coat again.
How's that?
Can't find mine.

3436 I wonder why this suit of mine has only three pockets in it.
No doubt the manufacturer knew that anyone who buys a cheap suit like that wouldn't have much to put in the pockets.

3437 Pants are made for men and not for women. Women are made for men and not for pants. When a man pants for a woman and a woman pants for a man, that makes a pair of pants. Pants are like molasses, they are thinner in hot weather and thicker in cold weather. There has been much discussion as to whether pants is singular or plural; but it seems to us when men wear pants it's plural, and when they don't it's singular. If you want to make the pants last make the coat first.

3438 I'd like to buy that hat in the window.
That's not necessary. They sell it to you over the counter.

3439 Where is your brother?
I took his pants down to get pressed.
Then he had to stay home and wait for them?
Oh, no, he went along for the ride.

3440 Why do you think Jim is a little off?
Because he wears wooden clothes?
What — wears wooden clothes?
Yeah — just this morning I heard him say he was goin' to buy a lumber jacket.

3441 Eloise is always in fashion.
      I hope to strangle! She's so up to date she gets spring fever in
          October.

3442 Where ja get the soup and fish?
      Holy smoke, I t'ought I wiped dem spots off.

3443 Salesman: Now that, sir, is the most becoming hat you've tried on
          so far.
      Customer: I agree with you entirely — it's my own.

3444 I am a physical culture teacher and I want to buy a pair of
          bloomers to wear around my gymnasium.
      Well, how big is your gymnasium?

3445 What could be worse than coming here with your underwear on?
      Coming here without any underwear on.

3446 My wife will overlook every stain on my clothes but one.
      And what's that?
      Lipstick on the collar.

3447 This is my traveling suit.
      Traveling suit?
      Yeah, it traveled from my father down to me.

3448 I just bought a new suit with two pairs of pants.
      Well, how do you like it?
      Fine, only it's too hot wearing two pairs.

3449 I want you to make me the outfit for my trial.
      Let me see — you'll want a direct testimony suit, a cross-examina-
          tion gown and something dainty and clinging to faint in.

3450 What a lovely fur coat you have, Mrs. Astor. But I can't help
          thinking of the poor animal that had to suffer in order that
          you might have that coat.
      How *dare* you call my husband an animal!

3451 Those are pretty stockings you have on.
      Those are my baseball stockings.
      I suppose you call them that because they are your white sox?
      No, I call them my baseball stockings because they have three runs.

3452 Did you see a pair of my socks around here?
      Well, we'll never find them on this black carpet.

3453 How about a sombrero — a ten gallon hat?
      That's a barrel. How much is it?
      Ten dollars.
      My goodness! A dollar a gallon. Haven't you got a half pint?

3454   What's the idea coming in here wearing that long beard?
       I've got to wear that.
       Why?
       My girl makes my ties.

3455   She wears a low cut gown, doesn't she?
       Yes, her coming out dress.
       She was coming out so far the other night, I wanted to push her
          back.

3456   His clothes are made to order.
       I know, but not to his order.

3457   Look at those stockings you have on — all full of holes. What
          kind of stockings are those?
       Those are my golf stockings — 18 holes.
       Why do you run around with your stockings full of holes like
          that?
       I don't give a darn.

3458   Do you like these long dresses the women are wearing these days?
       It don't worry me. I got a good memory.

3459   By the way, I know where you can buy some wool sox cheap.
       Where?
       From my brother. He was in an automobile accident and now his
          bones are beginning to knit.

3460   Jack, you sure are a scream in those clothes.
       Well, you don't exactly remind me of silence, yourself.

3461   What use would you have for a trunk?
       I'd put my clothes in it.
       What? And go around naked!

3462   What will men wear this spring?
       The clothes they bought in 1930.

3463   My wife is always pleased with the latest wrinkle.
       So is mine — provided it isn't on her own face.

3464   Pardon me, young lady, but in the matter of dress, don't you
          think you could show a little more discretion?
       My gosh, some of you guys ain't never satisfied.

3465   Now, you asked me to come here to help you pick out material
          for your clothes. You don't like my choice . . . so please your-
          self. I suppose you are the one who will wear the clothes.
       Well, I didn't suppose you'd wear the coat and vest.

3466   Don't you think George dresses nattily?
       Natalie who?

3467 Say, what's the idea of wearing my raincoat?
You wouldn't want your new suit to get wet, would you?

3468 Why do you wear such looking clothes?
Well, I don't make money enough to dress differently.
Don't you know, personal appearance is a great factor in getting
more money?
And more money is a great factor in getting a better personal
appearance.

3469 How many shirts do you wear a week?
You mean, how many weeks does he wear his shirts?

3470 His coat and vest always look so nice but his trousers look terrible.
Yeah, his trousers seem to be the seat of all his trouble.

3471 Why do you always wear those funny looking clothes and that hat?
Well, one time I didn't wear them and they threw me in jail.

3472 How do you like my new dress?
Fine — but you didn't take the hanger out.
Hanger! That's my shoulder blades.

3473 Men who criticize the modern apparel of women should be forced
to spend one hour looking through the old family album.

3474 Look at that outfit. What are you dressed up for?
About $45.00

3475 I'm going to buy a shirt for my brother. What size shirt do you
wear?
Fifteen — but what has that to do with it?
Oh, you're always wearing his shirt.

3476 Have you noticed her hat? Looks as if it had been stepped on.
Well, she had it in the ring, but now she's out of politics.

3477 You call that a hat? My dear, I shall never stop laughing.
Oh, yes, you will. The bill will probably arrive tomorrow.

3478 Do you know what became of my evening gown? I can't find
it anywhere.
I just saw a moth fly out of your clothes closet.

3479 Ever buy anything at a rummage sale?
Yes, I bought back my Sunday pants the last time our church
gave one.

3480 Why don't you put on your slicker?
I can't. I got a book in one hand and it won't go through the sleeve.

3481 Look at that sign.
Whazzit shay?

Shays ladies ready to wear clothes.
Well, ish damn' near time, ain't it?

3482 Why did he wear a business suit when he called on you last night?
He meant business — I owe him money.

3483 My dad is too old fashioned. He thinks everyone should wear
red woolen underwear.
Well, why not?
People are too restless the way it is.

3484 What is the idea of standing there with a straw hat on your head,
an umbrella in your hand, a fur coat on your arm, and wearing
a bathing suit?
No matter what the weather — I'll be prepared.

3485 This suit has a rubber collar for falling dandruff.
Why the rubber collar?
So the dandruff can jump back in its place.

3486 Why did you cut the sleeve out of your overcoat?
So I could put it on without taking my books out of my hand.

3487 Hole-proof hose don't wear well.
I think they do.
I mean, they don't seem to stand up.
Maybe you don't wear them long enough.

3488 There's an old clothes man at the door.
Tell him I've got all I need.

3489 What's the matter with your suit? It's getting threadbare!
Threadbare? Why, the last time I took it into town to get it
cleaned, they sent it back on a spool.

3490 How many shirts do you get out of a yard?
Well, that depends on what yard I get into.

3491 According to a certain ladies' fashion magazine, girls will be
wearing their legs longer this summer.

3492 I lost all my trunks.
You did!
Yeah, and in London I nearly froze to death.
How come?
Did you ever try running around London without your trunks?

3493 He called it his bridge clothes — it was his weakest suit.

3494 He wore a celluloid collar and he got so excited his collar caught
on fire.

3495   Wife: (After trying on numerous dresses) Dear, wouldn't you
        like to see me in something flowing?
        Husband: Yes, go jump in the river.

3496   Do you believe that tight clothes stop circulation?
        Certainly not. The tighter a woman's clothing the more she's in
        circulation.

3497   Did you ever wear two-pants suits?
        No, they're too hot.

3498   Starch — starch — starch. What's in your shirt?
        My brother — he borrowed it.

3499   Are you good at grammar?
        Now that was my best study.
        Is trousers singular or plural?
        I know that one — singular at the top and plural at the bottom.

3500   My uncle joined a Nudist Colony.
        Why, I saw him just yesterday and he was wearing a blue serge
        suit — the night it was three below zero.
        You saw him the other night in a blue serge suit when it was
        three below zero? That wasn't a blue serge suit — he was
        freezing.

3501   Have you a hunting suit?
        Yes, this one I'm wearing.
        That's not a hunting suit.
        My brother is hunting for it.

3502   The neck of her dress is so low, you can't tell if the dress is
        slipping or if she is coming up.

RELATED SUBJECTS
Shape (Physical) 341-347
Installment Plan 3171-3180
Bills 3281-3308
Laundry 3556-3563
Raccoon Coat 5097
Stores 5393-5402
Department Store 5418-5429
Shoe Store 5454-5456

Installment Plan 3175
Bills 3307
Bath 3344
Furs 3510
Worm 4414

SOCKS

3503   Mother: Go and change your socks. You've got on one blue sock and one yellow one.
Son: Well, if you don't like them, then why did you buy that other pair that's in my drawer?

3504   These are my church socks. They're my holy pair.

FURS

3505   I think it's cat fur. You better watch out or some dog will chase you up a tree.

3506   She had just received a beautiful skunk coat as a gift from her husband.
She: I can't see how such a nice coat comes from such a foul smelling beast.
He: I don't ask for thanks, dear. But I do demand respect.

3507   Many an alley cat can look at an ermine coat and say: There goes papa.

3508   I heard two rabbits talking. One rabbit said to the other: Well, goodbye. Winter is here — and you'll soon be an ermine and I'll be a seal.

3509   How would you like to raise rabbits for ladies' fur coats? They don't live long. You know, here today and gone tomorrow.
You mean — hare today and mink tomorrow.

3510   I wish when you come out with me you would dress a little better. That fur coat looks terrible.
This is my insomnia coat.
What do you mean insomnia coat?
It hasn't had a nap for three years.

3511   Is that a mink fur?
If it is some rabbit has been living under an assumed name.

3512   That fur coat is so cheap the moths hired doubles to eat it up.

3513   Joe, what animal is most noted for its fur?
The skunk—the more fur you get away from him, the better it is for you.

3514   You know my new boss gave me a lovely fur coat.
To keep you warm?
No, to keep me quiet.

3515   Honey, I'll be needing a new fur soon.
What? Say, I bought that fur not quite two seasons ago.
Yes, dear, I know, but you must remember that the fox wore it.

> RELATED SUBJECTS
> Female (the) 925-938
> Marriage 2882-3051
> Hunting 4423-4453
> Animals (Wild) 4640-4668
> Raccoon Coat 5097

MOTH

3516   Moths held a party at our house. It was a swell party.
What are you talking about?
Haven't you ever heard of moth balls?

3517   How did Santa Claus treat you?
He brought me this lovely woolen sweater.
That isn't wool. It's plainly marked "cotton."
Yes, I know — that's to fool the moths.

3518   The moths are eating up our living room furniture.
I'll speak to them about it.

3519   What's a myth?
A myth's a female moth.

3520   You know I've been experimenting with moths and asbestos —
I've finally succeeded in crossing them.
Why?
So the moths can play around the flame without getting burned.

3521   I was out with the insects listening to 'em talking.
What are you talking about?
Didn't you ever hear of moths chewing the rag?

3522   A moth leads an awful life.
How come?
He spends the summer in a fur coat, and the winter in a bathing
suit.

3523   What did the moths live on before Adam and Eve wore clothes?
I don't know — I give up.
That's what the moths did.

3524   I'm crossing moths with glow worms. So the moths can find their
way around in dark closets.

RELATED SUBJECTS
Clothing 3391-3502
Raccoon Coat 5097

SERVANTS

3525   What became of your valet?
     I fired him for removing a spot from my dress suit.
     That was part of his duty.
     Yes, but this was a five spot.

3526   Do you want the porter to call you?
     No, thanks. I awaken every morning at seven.
     Then, would you mind calling the porter?

3527   Be careful not to drop those china dishes, Norah.
     Don't worry, mum. If they did fall they're too light to hurt my
       feet.

3528   Jane, you were a long time coming up here. Didn't you hear me
       calling?
     No, ma'am — not until you called the third time.

3529   Tell me, my dear, how do you manage to get the maid up so
       early in the morning?
     It was rather clever of me. I introduced her to the milkman.

3530   You are discharged for allowing my husband to kiss you. What
       sort of reference do you expect from me after that?
     Well, you might at least say that I tried to please everyone.

3531   And you have had the same servant for two years?
     Yes. She says she doesn't believe in changing after she has gone
       to the trouble of teaching a family her ways.

3532   Just look at this table. Why, I can write my name in the dust.
     It must be wonderful — I wish I was educated.

3533   So your brother lost his job as butler.
     Yeah — they told him to call the names of all the guests as they
       arrived at the party.
     Well, couldn't he do that?
     Yeah, but some of the names he called them can't be repeated.

3534   (Loud crash)
     Mistress: Whatever is the matter, Huldah?
     Huldah: I'm sorry, ma'am. I wiped the legs off the piano.

3535   Did you sweep the room, Bridget?
     Faith an' I did, Mum. If yez don't believe me, look under the bed.

3536   John, I wish you would go out in the kitchen and give Bridget a
       good talking to before you go to business.

How's that? I thought you were very satisfied with her.
So I am, dear, but she's beating some carpets for me this morning, and she does it better when she's angry.

3537 Oh, Janet, how did you come to break that ornament?
I'm sure I'm verra sorry, mum; I was just accidentally dustin' it.

3538 I'm a woman of few words. If I beckon with my finger, that means come.
Suits me, mum. I'm a woman of few words myself. If I shake me head that means I ain't comin'.

3539 You know, ma'am, how you've been trying to match that Japanese vase in the living room?
Yes.
Well, ma'am, you needn't try any more. I've broken it.

RELATED SUBJECTS
Family 3209-3217
Salary 3271-3280
Trades People 3547-3563
Cooking 4798-4824

SHOPPING

3540 How much do you want for that horse over there?
Two hundred dollars, and I'm a one-price-man.
I'm a one-price-man, too. I'll give you five dollars.
Sold.

3541 You see, darling, this hat only costs twenty dollars. Good buy!
Yeah — goodbye twenty dollars.

3542 It cost her two dollars taxi fare to go to a sale, where she won a glass vase worth ten cents on a free coupon.

3543 How much is your hamburger steak?
$2.25 a pound.
But at the corner store it is only $2.10
Why don't you buy it there?
Because they haven't any.
Oh, I see. When I don't have it, I sell it for $2.00 a pound.

3544   My uncle bought a swell car and he only paid fifty-five dollars for it.
Fifty-five dollars? I can't get over it!
Neither can he. He's always under it.

3545   Salesman: (Demonstrating car) Now, I will throw in the clutch.
Farmer: I'll take her then; I knew if I held off long enough you'd give me something for nothing.

3546   Do you like tobogganing?
It always pays to bargain a little — you get a reduced rate.

> RELATED SUBJECTS
> Spendthrift 1990-2030
> Economy 1990-1996
> Stores 5393-5402
> Salesman 5403-5416
> Profit 5417
> Department Store 5418-5429

PHOTOGRAPHER

3547   Have you heard from Al lately?
Didn't you know? He died last summer.
Did he? Why, what happened?
He was photographing on the beach and died of overexposure.

3548   Photographer (to pretty model): Let's go into the darkroom and see what develops.

3549   What did the photographer tell Snow White?
I don't know—what?
"Don't worry, miss. Someday your prints will come."

3550   I didn't mind posing nude in front of the camera.
You didn't mind? But what if they publish the photos?
Oh, don't worry. There wasn't any film in the camera.

3551   Photographer: Your face ought to be on a magazine cover.
Model: Oh? Which? *Vogue? Harper's Bazaar? Glamour?*
Photographer: No, *Popular Mechanics.*

> RELATED SUBJECTS
> Marriage 2882-3051
> Cooking 4798-4824

MILKMAN

3552   Mrs. Jones is sure sore at her milkman.
Why, did he leave her sour milk?
No, he left the wrong husband on her doorstep.

> RELATED SUBJECTS
> Flirtation 2779-2784
> Cow 3810-3838
> Bills 3281-3308

GARBAGE MAN

3553 Am I too late for the garbage?
      Oh, no, madam — climb right in.

3554 He used to be a street cleaner.
      He was?
      Yeah, he never had to buy cigars.
      SEE ALSO
      Ancestry 3239
      Heredity 3250

PLUMBER

3555 Who put that statue under the sink?
      That's no statue — that's the plumber.

                              RELATED SUBJECTS
                              Bath 3337-3350

LAUNDRY

3556 I have five handkerchiefs here but no shirt. Where's my shirt?
      I notice one of the handkerchiefs has a sleeve. Why don't you
         send the handkerchiefs back? Maybe they would send you a
         shirt.

3557 I have a new job now.
      What are you doing?
      I'm working down at the Eagle Laundry.
      Eagle Laundry?
      Uh-huh.
      I didn't know they washed eagles.

3558 I can get your brother a job at the Model Laundry.
      I don't think he could do it — he's never had any experience at
         washing models.

3559 How did the laundry finish your shirts, sir?
      There is not a cuff in the carload. They came back with their
         sides splitting.

3560 You look grand. By the way, who does your laundry?
      Nobody. I tear the buttons off myself.

3561 Why do you charge two cents extra for each of my cuffs?
      Because you make pencil notes on them.
      Why should that make such a difference?
      The girls waste so much time trying to make them out.

3562 The hand laundry is the place where your mother takes you when
         you get your hands so dirty she can't get them clean.

3563 A new laundry exhibition is soon to be held in London. It will
         probably be declared open by the tearing of a shirt by the guest
         of honor.

Related Subjects
Wife 3111-3112
Family 3209-3217
Clothing 3391-3502

HOSPITALITY

3564 Guess I'll be going now. Don't trouble to see me to the door.
It's no trouble, it's a pleasure.

3565 Are you sure your wife knows you're bringing me home for
dinner?
Certainly. Didn't I argue about it this afternoon for hours?

3566 I live in Paris — if you ever come across the ocean, drop in.

3567 I passed your house yesterday.
Thanks. We appreciate it.

3568 Really, old chap, I haven't the nerve to impose upon your hospitality longer. Could I ask you for a bottle of nerve tonic?

3569 Good gracious! How could you think of bringing that Mr. Higgins home to dinner when you know I'm spring cleaning?
Hush, my dear! He's the only man I know who can help move the
sideboard.

3570 Do you remember that couple we met on the steamer we took such
a violent fancy to — I mean, the couple we invited to visit us?
Yes.
Well, they thought we meant it when we asked them — they're
coming next week.

3571 This is a rare treat.
I know I don't treat often, but why rub it in?

3572 How do they treat you here?
Not very often.

3573 I'm certainly glad to be back.
(Silence)
I'm certainly glad to be back. I've been away three weeks. It seems
like ages.
Oh, hello! Have you been gone?

3574 Are you glad to be home?
Yeah — and did you notice the signs all over the studio?
No — what did they say?
"Welcome home, Joe." But they sure spelled "home" funny.
They spelled "home" — H-A-M.

PARTY

3575   It ought to be quite a party.
Do you think they'll bob for apples?
Bob for apples? They'll clutch for cocktails.

3576   Did you ever have a party soda?
Party soda? What's that?
Well, last night we had a party so da landlady true us out.

3577   Are you going to the big ball tomorrow night?
No, I'll be out of town tomorrow night.
I didn't get invited either.

3578   So Joe was the life of the party?
Yeah. He was the only one who could talk louder than the radio.

3579   We're going to that masquerade party tonight.
So are we. How are we supposed to dress?
To match the color of your boy friend's hair.
Gee, I can't go.
Why not?
My boy friend is bald.

CLUBS

3580   Did you go to your lodge meeting last night?
No, we had to postpone it.
How is that?
The Grand All-Powerful Invincible Most Supreme Uncon-
querable Potentate was beaten up by his wife.

Drinking 2055-2140
Hospitality 3564-3660
Restaurant 4738-4883

INVITATION

3581   Hello, darling, would you like to have dinner with me tonight?
Oh, I'd be delighted, dear!
Okay. Tell your mother I'll be over at six o'clock and please not
to have hash.

3582   You have three invitations. One from the Van Astors — one
from the De Puysters — and one from the Traffic Court.

3583   I'm sorry that I forgot to invite you to my picnic tomorrow. Won't
you come?
No, you're too late. I've already prayed for a violent thunder storm
tomorrow.

RELATED SUBJECTS
Hospitality 3564-3660

DANCING

3584   You should see the way I kick the back of my head.
That explains everything.

3585   So your girl's a dancer?
Yeah — she's a toe dancer — she dances all over my toes.

3586   Let's dance Scotcher.
How's that?
Closer.

3587   This floor is so slippery that one can hardly keep on your feet.
Oh, did you really mean it? I thought it was accidental.

3588   Hula Hula dancers have an easy time of it.
Why?
All they have to do is stand around and twiddle their tums.

3589   Can I have this dance?
Sure, if you can find some one to dance with.

3590   No wonder you can't dance — you're bustle bound.

3591   I am the most graceful dancer in this state.
You may be in *this* state, but you're not when you're sober.

3592   Ah, I believe this is my dance.
Quite so. Keep it, won't you?

3593   I could dance like this all night.
Yeah, but would they allow it?

3594   I learned to dance in one evening.
       I thought so!

3595   They are a couple of hula hula dancers. There's a hungry horse approaching — so they'll be doing a fan dance before long.

3596   What is that new dance you're doing?
       That isn't a new dance — I'm losing my garter.

3597   The dance floor is slippery.
       Don't be silly — that ain't the floor, I just had my shoes shined.

3598   I hope you'll dance with me tonight.
       Oh, certainly! I hope you don't think I came down here merely for pleasure.

3599   It is a funny thing, but every time I dance with you the dances seem very short.
       They are. My fiancé is leader of the orchestra.

3600   He's a great dancer. He one steps in the morning, two steps in the afternoon and side steps his wife in the evening.

3601   I'll bet you never saw any dancing like this back in the twenties eh, uncle?
       Once — then the place was raided.

3602   Do you care for dancing, Peggy?
       No.
       Why not?
       It's merely hugging set to music.
       Well, what is there about it that you don't like?
       The music.

3603   What are you doing in the South Seas?
       I'm a hula hula dancer.
       Okay, let's pull straws for her, buddy.

RELATED SUBJECTS
Legs 433-439
Music 1747-1752
Orchestra 1753-1758
Flirtation 2779-2784
Party 3575-3579
Chorus Girl 4563-4565

GAMES

3604   Let's play the auto show game.
       What's that?
       I'll kick you where I ought to, but it won't show.

3605   We'll play the garage game — you break down and I'll give you a
       tow — maybe five toes where it would do you the most good.

3606   Is football your favorite game?
       No — I prefer wild duck.

3607   Say, that boy of ours in college must be gettin' on purty handy
           with carpenter tools.
       What's he been doin'?
       He sez he just made the basketball team.

3608   Let's play house.
       Okay — you be the door and I'll slam you.

3609   We had a big party and all the folks at the party played a game
           I invented. It's called "Christmas Tree."
       I never heard of the game. What is it like?
       Every one stands in the corner and tries to get lit up.

3610   I'm sore — we've missed half the game.
       But the score board says nothing to nothing — so you can see
           we didn't miss a thing.

3611   Are you the game warden?
       Yes, ma'am.
       Well, I'm so thankful I have the right person at last! Would you
           mind suggesting some games suitable for a children's party?

3612   Did you enjoy the winter sports?
       One tried to get smart with me and I slapped his face.

3613   My father says fencing is a great art.
       I'll say it is! My father built half the fences in this town.

>   RELATED SUBJECTS
>   Hospitality 3564-3660
>   Baseball 4350-4351
>   Football 4352-4379
>   Gambling 4500-4505

BRIDGE

3614   Papa and mama never play bridge together.
       Why not — do they fight?
       Well, not exactly — but papa is bowlegged and when mama kicks
           him under the table, she always misses his shin.

3615   Well, I can't imagine what you bid no trump on when I had three
           aces and four kings.
       Well, if you want to know, I bid it on one jack with two queens
           and three cocktails.

3616   I held a perfect hand last night.
Shook hands with yourself, I suppose.

3617   By the way — you saw our bridge game last night. How would
you have played that last hand of mine?
Under an assumed name.

3618   Is she a good partner in bridge?
She was awful. You couldn't tell by the expression on her face
how she would play.
Poker face?
No, but I wanted to.

3619   What's a kibitzer?
Well, a kibitzer can't do anything himself, but tells you everything
you should play. The greatest pleasure a kibitzer can have is
for you to lose money. He is so happy his tears run down your
face.

3620   I beat him in bridge. I played bridge and won sixteen rubbers and
twenty-one coats.

3621   Hello! City Bridge Department?
Yes. What can we do for you?
How many points do you get for a little slam?

3622   He went home with a couple of bridge lamps. His wife gave them
to him after he trumped her ace.

3623   Shall we have a friendly game of cards?
No, let's play bridge.

3624   Did you ever play football?
No, sir, but at dear old Oxford we played Rugby.
How is that played?
Well, sir, it consists of a lot of shin kicking.
Well, in this country we call that bridge.

3625   What would you do if you held the Queen alone?
That depends.
Depends? On what?
On when the king is expected.

RELATED SUBJECTS
Gossip 1518-1537
Smoking 2031-2054
Drinking 2055-2140
Hospitality 3564-3660

PRIZES

3626 I took my chow dogs to the Dog Show and won first prize.
You won first prize with those dogs of yours?
Well, I'd been eating blueberry pie, and as the Judges passed by,
I yawned and they pinned the first prize ribbon on me.

3627 I took first prize at a bridge game the other night.
Why cry about that?
They caught me and I had to take it back.

3628 I heard your uncle won a swimming match last week.
Oh, yes — he has been swimming for twenty years.
I'll bet he's tired out by now.

3629 (Mrs. Boopeep, the old scrub woman, won $1,000,000)
Mrs. Boopeep, what are you going to do now that you have all
this money?
I've been scrubbing floors all my life. I've often wondered what
I would do if I had money, and now I'm going to do it.

3630 I won $50,000.
Fifty thousand dollars? Clear?
No, I had to pay two dollars for the ticket.

> RELATED SUBJECTS
> Games 3604-3613
> Gift 3943-3962

RIDDLES

3631 What's the difference between a gold filling, an expensive wedding
and a maple syrup bucket?
A gold filling is an inlay, an expensive wedding is an outlay. But
why did you mention the maple syrup bucket?
To catch you, you sap!

3632 Who are the children of an automobile?
I give up.
The automobile skids.

3633 When is a goat nearly?
I don't know.
When it's all butt.

3634 Listen, I'll come out with a sweater on and carrying a shoe. You
guess what I represent.
Well, the sweater is New Jersey — but what is the shoe for?
I knew you'd put your foot in it.

3635   Why is trying to put your arms around a fat lady like breaking in
         on a party?
       Because you'll never know who you will meet.

3636   Why is a newspaper like a woman?
       Because every man should have one of his own and not run after
         his neighbor's.

3637   What has three heads, five eyes and sings?
       I don't know.
       A trio.
       But you said five eyes.
       Well, can I help it if one of them only has one eye?

3638   What animal has eyes, but can't see; legs, but can't walk; but
         can jump as high as the Empire State Building?
         (No answer.)
       The answer is a wooden horse.
       But how does it jump as high as the Empire State Building?
       The Empire State Building can't jump.

3639   What's the difference between Jack Dempsey, Max Schmeling
         and a piece of bologna?
       Don't know — what is the difference?
       Jack Dempsey and Max Schmeling have done great feats.
       That's right, but where do you get the bologna?
       At the butcher's.

3640   Do you know the difference between taxis and trolleys?
       No.
       Good — then we'll take a trolley.

3641   Do you know how to get down from an elephant?
       No.
       You don't get down from an elephant; you get down from a duck.

3642   If a jackass is tied to a fence and there's a bale of hay ten feet
         away — how does he get the bale of hay?
       I don't know — I give up.
       That's what the jackass did.

3643   What's the difference between a man that makes $100.00 a
         week, a nudist and a bale of hay?
       I don't know—what is the difference?
       A man that makes $100.00 a week makes a bare living; and a
         nudist is living bare.
       Yeah, but what's the bale of hay for?
       You're a jackass—you should know.

3644   What is twice as cold in the winter time than an icebox at the
         North Pole?

I don't know, what?
Two nudists on a motorcycle.

3645   What has twenty-four feet, green eyes and a pink body with pur-
        ple stripes around it?
        I don't know — what?
        I don't know, either, but you better pick it off your neck.

3646   Why is a raven like a writing desk?
        Because they both stand on their legs and ought to be made to
        shut up?
        Because each can produce a few notes that are very flat?
        Because Poe wrote on both?
        Frankly, I haven't the slightest idea what the answer is!

3647   What's the difference between a jeweler and a jailer?
        I don't know. What is the difference?
        One sells watches and one watches cells.

3648   Now I'll do something and you guess what I'm doing.
        All right.
        What am I doing?
        Nothing.
        Yes, I am.
        What are you doing?
        I'm going upstairs.
        But you're not moving.
        I know — I'm on an elevator.

3649   What is the difference between the so-called old-fashioned woman
        and the so-called modern woman?
        The old-fashioned woman used to darn her husband's socks while
        the modern woman socks her husband.

3650   What does a dog do on three legs, a man standing up, and a
        woman sitting down? Answer: Shake hands.

3651   Why is a zoo like a sideshow?
        I don't know — but you'd do all right in both places.

3652   Well, what is it that is shaped like a finger, the same color as a
        finger and the same size as a finger?
        I don't know — what is it?
        A thumb.

3653   What has four legs and flies?
        I don't know.
        Your dinner table.

3654   You're good at conundrums, try this one. Take away my first
        letter, take away my second letter, take away all my letters,

and I'm still the same. What am I ?
That's easy. You're a mailcarrier.

3655   What is black and white and red all over?
Oh, that's easy. A newspaper.
No, it's not.
Then what is it?
A sun-burned zebra.

3656   Why is a woman wearing rolled stockings like a special delivery
boy on a bicycle?
I give up. Why?
Ah, gimme time. I haven't figured out the answer yet.

3657   What is it that has four legs, eats oats, has a tail and sees equally
well from both ends.
I don't know — what?
A blind horse.

3658   Why are hogs like trees?
I don't know — why?
Because they root for a living.

3659   What do you call those little white things in your head that bite?
I know the name but I don't like to speak of such things.
I fooled you that time. All I meant was your teeth. They're white
and they bite, don't they?

3660   What's the difference between a sewing machine and a kiss?
I don't know — what is the difference?
One sews seams nice and the other seems so nice.

RELATED SUBJECTS
Games 3604-3613

NEIGHBORS

3661   Can I have one of those calendars you're giving away to your
customers?
But your mother doesn't trade with us, sonny.
I know she doesn't — but she borrows from Mrs. Rains, and Mrs.
Rains trades with you.

3662   My uncle's very generous — he's always borrowing things from
his neighbors, and the other night just to let them feel that he

would be glad to return the favors, he said: If you'll let me fry
my eggs in your butter, I'll let you boil your ham in my cabbage.

3663 Hello, Mr. Brown.
      I guess he's sore at you. He didn't return your greeting.
      Oh, he's my neighbor — he never returns anything.

3664 (Woman calling to husband to come to dinner)
      Woman: Come in and get your roast duck, apple pie and cham-
         pagne.
      Man: Are you trying to kid me?
      Woman: No, the neighbors.

3665 What are the products of the West Indies?
      I don't know.
      Come, come. Where do we get sugar from?
      We borrow it from our next door neighbor.

3666 Does your neighbor return what he borrows?
      Yes, he returns our snow shovel in the spring and borrows our
         lawn mower.

PETS

BIRDS

3667 Did you ever shoot an American Hawk?
      A what?
      An American Hawk — hawk! Hawk! HAWK!
      Did you swallow a fish bone?

3668 What's the state bird of Texas?
      Lady.
      Lady?
      Sure. Lady Bird—she's the best-known bird in the whole state of
         Texas.

3669 You mean ostriches — they're the largest living birds.
      Even when they're dead.

3670 Some people can't tell a bird from a beast. Yesterday I heard a
         conversation — two girls were talking — one said: Who was
         that bird I saw you with yesterday? And the other girl an-
         swered — That was no bird — he's a beast.

3671 That's $3 altogether — $2.50 for the cage. I'm practically giving
         you the bird.
      I think I'll take it.

3672 The first time my city cousin saw our peacock she said: Look at
         the rooster in full bloom.

3673   Oh, look at the eagles.
    Those aren't eagles — they're seagulls.
    Well, eagles, seagulls — seagulls, eagles, what's the difference as
       long as you're healthy?

3674   When I was out hunting — I shot at a bird but missed him. He
       must have been a jail bird.
    Why?
    He flew into Sing Sing prison.

3675   Why does the African woofle bird fly backwards?
    Dunno.
    It doesn't give a damn where it's going — it wants to know where
       it's been.

3676   The woods were full of wild animals.
    What wild animals?
    Pigeons.
    Pigeons aren't wild animals.
    But I'm wild about them.

3677   One night last summer my girl and I were on the back porch and
       the birds were singing . . .
    Wait a minute — the birds don't sing at night.
    These were a couple of jail birds.

3678   Can any boy tell me what a canary can do that I can't?
    Please, teacher, can you take a bath in a saucer?

3679   That certainly is a large canary!
    That's not a canary — that's my parrot. He has yellow jaundice.

3680   I spent ten dollars on a canary yesterday.
    That's nothing. I spent fifty on a lark.

3681   Tommy, the canary has disappeared.
    That's funny. It was there just now when I tried to clean it with
       the vacuum cleaner.

RELATED SUBJECTS
Home 3197-3205

GOLD FISH

3682   If I ate a gold fish would I swim like one?
    That's silly, it would kill you.
    Well — it didn't.

3683   Did you give the gold fish some fresh water this morning?
    Huh?

I said, Did you give the gold fish fresh water this morning?
No. They haven't finished the water they got yesterday.

HOMING PIGEON

3684   (Cooing noise)
What's that man cooing for?
He isn't cooing. The Finance Company took his house last month,
and he has to carry his homing pigeons in his pocket.

PARROT

3685   That's a parrot.
Does he talk?
No. He's an underworld parrot. He won't talk.

3686   I have crossed a walnut and a chestnut and have created a new nut.
That's nothing. My uncle in Scotland crossed an overcoat with
a parrot. When anyone attempts to take the overcoat, the pocket
opens up and says: "Hoot, mon! McGregor, some one is makin'
away with your coat."

3687   I crossed my hens with parrots to save time.
Why did you do that?
I used to waste a lot of time hunting for eggs. Now the hen comes
up to me and says: I just laid an egg — go get it.

3688   Is it possible that you are teaching the parrot to use slang?
No, mama, I was just telling him what not to say.

SEE ALSO
Canary 3679

CAT

3689   You remember the $5 check you gave me to drown your cat?
Yes, I remember.
Well, the check came back.
So did the cat.

3690   I was down to the Cat's Whiskers.
What do you mean — the Cat's Whiskers?
You know — that new joint.
Never been there. Where is the Cat's Whiskers?
Four feet from its tail.

3691   Your brother isn't here. Dynamite Dan is on the rampage again
and your brother went out to get a posse to capture him.
How silly — why didn't he come to me? I could get him a posse.
You can?
Yeah, my cat has ten of the cutest little posses you ever saw.

3692   Our cat is rather distinguished. He's sort of a swordsman.
What do you mean swordsman?
Well, he is the best fencer in the neighborhood.

3693   Our cat swallowed a ball of yarn and when she had kittens they
all had sweaters on them.

3694   Your cat was making an awful noise last night.
Yes, ever since she ate the canary she thinks she can sing.

3695   Why are you trying to feed the cat bird seed? I told you to feed
the canary.
Well, that's where the canary is.

RELATED SUBJECTS
Birds 3667-3677
Mouse 3902-3907

DOG

3696   Do you have any bloodhounds?
Yes. Come here, Pete.
But he doesn't look like a bloodhound to me.
Bleed for the lady, Pete.

3697   Why is that dachshund so close to the ground?
He was born under the stove.

3698   They're photographer puppies. They're always snapping people.

3699   Papa's buying a dog to help him hitch hike.
What kind of a dog could help him hitch hike?
He's buying a pointer.

3700   (Dog barks)
Don't be afraid — a barking dog never bites.
You mean, he never barks while he's biting.

3701   We've lost our St. Bernard dog — and it's all mother's fault.
You mean your mother got lost and you sent the dog out to find
her and the dog hasn't come back?
No, the dog got lost and we tied a bottle of whisky around mother's
neck and sent her out to look for the dog and neither one of
them have come back.

3702   See my new dog. Notice how soundly he sleeps.
       Naturally.
       Why naturally?
       He's a police dog.
       He doesn't look like a police dog to me.
       Naturally.
       Why naturally?
       Because he's in plain clothes.

3703   I think your dog is cute, but what puzzles me is he's so covered
          with hair you can't tell which end is which.

3704   Is your dog trained?
       Yeah. When I say: Sit up, or won't you? he either sits up or he
          doesn't.

3705   What's the idea of the chain on Fido?
       Well, isn't he a watch dog?

3706   I had to get rid of my dachshund.
       Why?
       It took him so long to get in and out of the door, he let all the
          flies in.

3707   What kind of a dog was he?
       He was an entymologist.
       Why, an entymologist is a collector of rare insects.
       He collected them.

3708   I don't want a Scottie or a Police Dog. I want a dachshund.
       Why do you want a dachshund?
       So the kids can pat him — all at the same time.

3709   I have to stop on the way home and get a muzzle for my dog.
       Why? Is he vicious? Does he bite?
       Yesterday he took a bite out of my apple.
       Well, that's nothing. You could always get another apple.
       Yeah — but that was my Adam's apple.

3710   Well, well, what a cute pup. Is he a bird dog?
       Sure. Here, Fido, give the lady the bird.

3711   I paid a hundred dollars for that dog — part Collie and part
          bull.
       Which part is bull?
       The part about the hundred dollars.

3712   I make a lot of money off my dachshunds.
       How?
       I rent them out as stove pipe cleaners.

3713   What happened to your dog?
       I told my uncle to take him out for some air and he took him down
          to the nearest filling station.

3714   I've got a St. Bernard dog. He is so proud — he walks with his
          head 'way up in the air — boy, is he proud!
       What about?
       He is serving real brandy again.

3715   (Little girl walking her dog.)
       Girl: Here Broker, here Broker!
       Man: Oh, is your dog on the stock market?
       Girl: No, he does his trading on the curb.

3716   This is my new dog.
       A chow?
       Gesundheit!

3717   Say, what's the matter with that dog of yours? Every time I come
          near the water cooler, he growls.
       Oh, he won't bother you.
       Then what is he growling about?
       He's probably a little sore because you're drinking out of his cup.

3718   This dog will eat off your hand.
       That's what I'm afraid of.

3719   I see you have a dog.
       Yeah — he used to be a hunting dog — a pointer. But my mother
          spoiled him.
       How?
       She taught him it wasn't polite to point.

3720   Did you see the mountain peaks?
       What kind of dogs are those?

3721   What do you call that low, thin German dog?
       Frankfurter.

3722   He must be a police dog — he's always hanging around the cook.

3723   Rufe Johnson's pet hound disappeared. Rufe put the following ad
          in the paper: Lost or run away — one liver-colored bird dog
          called Jim. Will show signs of hydrofobby in about three days.
       The dog came home the following day.

3724   What kind of a dog is that?
       He's a sitter-pointer. He sits in the kitchen all day and points at
          the ice box.
       He looks like a wirehaired terrier. Does he scent the bird?
       He doesn't scent them. He hears them. He's wired for sound.

3725 My dachshund died.
   Too, bad! What happened?
   He met his end going around a tree.

3726 I shot my dog.
   Was he mad?
   Well, it didn't seem to exactly please him.

3727 Is he a good watch dog?
   Rather. If you hear a suspicious noise at night you have only to
    wake him and he begins to bark.

3728 I say, Smith, didn't you say your dog's bark was worse than his
    bite?
   Yes.
   Then for goodness sake, don't let him bark. He just bit me.

3729 Is that a bull dog?
   Oh, my, no — it's a female.

3730 I know a dog worth seven thousand dollars.
   How could a dog save so much?

3731 What kind of a dog is it?
   Well, his father was an airedale, but his mother was a female, so I
    don't just know what he is.

3732 I bought him for a lap dog but they lied to me.
   What makes you think so?
   Because the first time I sat on his lap he bit me.

3733 My dog swallowed a tape worm and died by inches.
   That's nothing, my dog crawled in on my bed and died by the foot.
   I had another dog that went out of the house and died by the yard.

3734 Doc, I've just been bitten by a dog.
   Well, was he a rabid dog?
   No, he was just a plain old bird dog.

3735 What have you done to Fido? He's all corners.
   I asked the maid to wash him, and she starched him as well.

3736 I see you have a new dog.
   Yeah, and he's very accommodatin'.
   Accommodating?
   Yeah. He loves children, don't chase de chickens — why, he even
    carries his tail curled up so dat de fleas can loop de loop.

3737 I wonder why a dog hangs his tongue out of his mouth.
   To balance his tail, you simp.

3738 What are you doing with that dog in the bird cage?
   Well, it's like this. It's a bird dog.

What do you mean, bird dog?
Well, the bird is in the cat.
Where's the cat?
In the dog.

3739   Say, boy, your dog bit me on the ankle.
Well, that's as high as he could reach. You wouldn't expect a little
pup like that to bite you on the neck, would you?

3740   He lost his job. For twenty years he was a dog catcher.
What happened?
The dogs started catching him.

RELATED SUBJECTS
Dog Racing 4481-4482
Fleas 3778-3789

FARMING

FARMER

3741   How's your uncle doing with his farm?
Not so good. There ain't so much money in milk and eggs any
more. So he sits up all night trying to think of something else
for the hens and cows to do.

3742   It's pretty hard on the farm. You go to sleep with the chickens,
get up with the roosters, work like a horse, eat like a pig, and
we treat you like a dog.

3743   On our ranch we have 'hundreds and hundreds of cattle.
That's a lot of cows.
And thousands and thousands of bulls.
That's a lot of bull.

3744   When I left the ranch, I was a three-letter man.
Did they have a football team?
No, I sat on the branding iron.

3745   How's your father getting along with his farm?
Not so good. Things are so bad, he can't pay the hired man his
wages. So the hired man works until he has enough money coming to buy the farm and then my father works for the hired
man until the hired man owes him enough money and then my
father takes the farm back.

3746 What became of the hired hand you got from the city?
He used to be a chauffeur, and he crawled under a mule to see why it didn't go.

3747 What is the hardest thing to learn about farming?
Getting up at 5 A.M.

3748 You look like a real rancher. What are you doing with a boxing glove on?
I'm practicing cow punching.

3749 What's that I smell?
That's fertilizer.
For the land's sake!
Yes, ma'am.

3750 What does your son do?
He's a bootblack in the city.
Oh, I see, you make hay while the son shines.

3751 Say there, Abner, be that new hand of yours intelligent?
Wal, mebbe so, mebbe so, Si, but he must be awful humorous, 'cause you see, when I asked him to call the cows, he up and queried what their names might be.

3752 She was a country girl.
From what country?
Bulgaria.

3753 I've been spending a holiday at a watering place.
Why, Harry told me you were on a farm.
Yes, a dairy farm.

3754 Tourist: Pardon, sir, but what do you do with all that corn?
Farmer: Well, we eat what we can and what we can't we can.
Tourist: Oh, I see.
Tourist's wife: What did he say, dear?
Tourist: He said, they ate what they could, and what they couldn't they could.

3755 What's the name of this ranch?
This is the Bar "B" — over yonder is Bar "Q".
I get it — Bar — B — Q (barbeque).

3756 Where's the dog ranch?
Dog ranch?
Yeah, the K-9!

3757 So he is a gentleman farmer, now?
Gentleman farmer's right. Believe me, he even has his scarecrows changed into evening dress at dusk.

3758   Where's the other windmill gone to?
        We only had wind enough for one, so we took the other one down.

3759   On the farm we get up at three in the morning to harvest the oats.
        Are they wild oats?
        No.
        Then why do you have to sneak up on them in the middle of the night?

3760   Have you a monkey-wrench here?
        Naw. My brother bane got a cattle rench over there; my cousin got a sheep rench down there; but it's too cold for a monkey rench here.

RELATED SUBJECTS
House 3132-3151
Installment Plan 3171-3180
Home 3197-3205
Family 3209-3217
Animals (Domesticated) 3806-3866

GARDEN

3761   You've ordered flower seeds that take two years to bloom.
        Mind your business. This is last year's catalogue.

3762   Please tell me why they always have such beautiful illustrations in seed catalogues.
        The beautiful floral pictures are to show people what the seeds they planted would look like if they had ever come up.

3763   Why are you turning those cucumber seeds inside out before you plant them?
        So when they grow they will have dimples instead of warts.

3764   You know they raise the largest vegetables in the world in New York. I heard the Police Captain say yesterday he found two policemen asleep on one beat.

3765   I can get you a job digging potatoes.
        Why don't you get the man that planted them? He knows where he hid them.

3766   (Man jumping up and down in garden)
        What are you raising?
        Mashed potatoes.

3767   What are you planting?
        Cucumbers, tomatoes, celery, onions and lettuce.

Yeah, but why plant them all together?
I'm raising combination salad.

RELATED SUBJECTS
Birds 3667-3677
Chicken 3872-3901

FLOWERS

3768 Papa got an invitation to be a judge at the flower show.
What does he know about flowers?
He can't tell one flower from another. Everybody says papa
doesn't smell so good.

3769 What's that you got in your buttonhole?
Why, that's a chrysanthemum.
It looks like a rose to me.
Nope, you're wrong, it's a chrysanthemum.
Spell it.
K-r-i-s . . . by golly, that is a rose!

3770 Now, this plant belongs to the Begonia family.
Ah, yes, and you're looking after it for them while they're away
on a holiday?

3771 My new boy friend is studying all about flowers.
Oh, he's a botanist.
A what?
A botanist — you know — a naturalist.
No — he never goes out without his clothes.

RELATED SUBJECTS
Love Making 2641-2719
Home 3197-3205
Gift 3943-3962

INSECTS

3772 This is an ideal spot for a picnic.
It must be. Fifty million insects can't be wrong.

3773 Aren't ants funny little things? They work and work, and never
play.
Oh, I don't know about that. Every time I go on a picnic they
are there.

RELATED SUBJECTS
Worm 4414-4418

CATERPILLAR

3774 Do you know what fish worms are?
No, what are fish worms?
Nudist Colony caterpillars.

3775 What's the trouble?
Has gooseberries got legs?
No.
I must have swallowed a caterpillar.
A caterpillar is harmless.
Do you know what a caterpillar is?
What is it?
A fish worm with a raccoon coat.

CENTIPEDE

3776 And my poor centipede — he came home last night and he was
afraid of waking his wife. He wanted to sneak upstairs and
the poor guy spent all night taking off his shoes.

3777 Oh, I say, what's worse than a giraffe with a sore throat?
A centipede with chilblains.

FLEAS

3778 I used to have a Flea Circus — I overslept one day and the fleas
didn't get anything to eat.
Were they mad at you?
Mad? They hopped all over me.

3779 You know that trained flea of mine? He's all tired out.
What's the matter with him?
I don't know — he was on a tramp for about three days.

3780 You know I discovered a new kind of flea powder.
Does it kill the fleas?
No, it makes the fleas itch.

3781 What are you looking so sad about?
I just got thinking of fleas — fleas always know that their children
will go to the dogs.

3782 I've got a new kind of flea in my circus. A sailor flea.
Where'd you find him?
In a permanent wave.

3783 I've discovered a new way to get rid of fleas.
How?
I take my dog up in an airplane, do a few stunts and the fleas get
scared and jump off.

3784   What is your favorite sport — I asked my trained flea.
        What did he say?
        Following the hounds.

3785   I've got a new idea for a flea circus.
        Well, keep it under your hat.

3786   Mention a difference between an elephant and a flea?
        Well, an elephant can have fleas, but a flea can't have elephants.

3787   How do you get rid of fleas?
        That's easy. Take a bath in sand and a rub-down in alcohol. The fleas get drunk and kill each other throwing rocks.

3788   I took in the show last night.
        What did they have?
        Educated fleas.
        How were they?
        Fine. I took the leading lady home.

3789   I had a flea circus once and I had to give it up when the leading lady ran off with a poodle.

RELATED SUBJECTS
Dog 3696-3740
Animals (Domesticated) 3806-3866
Animals (Wild) 4640-4668

FLIES

3790   What was the most pathetic sight you ever saw?
        A horse fly sitting on an automobile boring into a radiator cap.

3791   My, the flies are thick around here!
        Ah — I see you like your flies thin.

3792   What was all that hammering this morning? What in the world were you doing?
        Just taking off the screens from the windows to let the flies out.

3793   My brother has a new job catching flies.
        You mean he catches and kills the flies?
        No — he doesn't kill them. He just catches the flies and puts them in my uncle's new fly catching machine.

3794   I certainly don't like all these flies.
        You just pick out the ones you like and I'll kill all the rest.

3795   He is a blacksmith in a candy store.
        What does he do?
        He shoos flies.

3796   Aha, my dear, there are a tremendous number of casualties, I see
         by the paper.
         What paper?
         The fly paper.

3797   Here's your fly paper. Anything else today?
         Yes, I want about six raisins.
         Do you mean six pounds?
         No, about six — just enough for decoys.

3798   Don't you ever shoo the flies here?
         No, we just let them run around barefooted.

3799   What is your uncle doing now?
         Selling fly paper.
         Fly paper in winter? What's the idea?
         He figured there would be no competition.

3800   Professor: The progeny of a single fly may number many millions.
         Co-Ed: Gee, what must the progeny of a married fly be?

                         RELATED SUBJECTS
                         House 3132-3151
                         Food 4825-4878

MOSQUITOES

3801   Every time I crawled in bed, I was eaten up with mosquitoes.
         Cinnamon bears kill mosquitoes.
         Who wants to get in bed with Cinnamon bears?

3802   You show me one good feature in favor of Nudists.
         They must be right. They have millions of followers . . .
         Who?
         Mosquitoes.

3803   The Nudist Colony is going to be a lot more popular next summer.
         With whom?
         The mosquitoes.

3804   How do you find the mosquitoes?
         You don't have to — they'll find you.

3805   If you miss your mosquitoes this summer the reason will probably
         be that they have gone to join a Nudist Colony.

                         RELATED SUBJECTS
                         Farmer 3741-3760
                         Vacation 3965-3970
                         Fishing 4380-4413
                         Hunting 4423-4453

ANIMALS

3806 I'm going to open a pet shop. When next you find me, I'll be among my little dumb animals.
Wear a hat so we'll know you.

3807 I'm working on a National Animal Week.
How are you going about it?
The way I figured it — every dog will have its day, the cats will have the nights and Sundays will be for the road hogs.

3808 He has a couple of new pets — Calls them his flannel trousers.
Why?
Because they're a pair of white ducks.

3809 My duck always holds one foot off the ground.
Why does she hold one foot off the ground?
If she held both feet off the ground she would fall over on the ground.

RELATED SUBJECTS
Home 3197-3205
Pets 3667-3740
Farmer 3741-3760

COWS

3810 Been experimenting with a cow. I've been using a toothbrush on the cow's teeth — now she's giving dental cream.

3811 My uncle can't decide whether to get a new cow or a bicycle for his farm.
He'd certainly look silly riding around on a cow.
Yeah, but he would look a lot sillier milking a bicycle.

3812 Why does your uncle keep his cows in the house?
Well, he has to keep them contented, doesn't he?

3813 How's your father coming with his dairy farm?
Grand. He makes all the cows sleep on their backs.
What's the idea?
So the cream will be on top in the morning.

3814 Did you ever live in a farm? And listen to the cow bells?
Don't be silly. Cows haven't bells — they have horns.

3815 Name five things for me that contain milk.
That's easy. Ice cream, butter, cheese and two cows.

3816 I'm going to sue the railroad company on account of my cows.
What happened — did a train run over your cows?
No. The trains run so slowly the people lean out the windows and milk my cows.

3817   What makes this milk so blue?
       Because it comes from discontented cows.

3818   How much milk does that cow give?
       I don't know exactly, but she's a darn good-natured critter, and
       she'll give all she can.

3819   He knows all about the farm, I suppose. Does he know how long
       cows should be milked?
       The same as short ones.

3820   Is this milk fresh?
       Fresh? Three hours ago it was grass.

3821   I have to drink a quart of milk every day.
       Why?
       To keep it from getting sour.

3822   Say, what kind of a cow gives evaporated milk?
       A dry cow.

3823   We milk our cow ten and twelve times a day.
       That's preposterous. Does she give milk each time?
       No, but she tries hard.

3824   The best way to prevent milk from going sour is to keep it in
       the cow.

3825   How much milk does your cow give?
       She gives me five gallons.
       How much milk do you sell?
       I sell ten gallons. I'm a milkman of the first water.

3826   How does it come that there is never any cream on top of your
       milk?
       Well, you see, we fill our bottles so full that there's no room left
       for the cream.

3827   My brother has a job dairying in the tropics.
       Is it as hard work as over here?
       No, but he has to sit on a higher stool to milk the cocoanuts.

3828   We play music when we milk our cows.
       And the way this tastes you must have played Old Man River.

3829   Somebody stole my cow, but it won't do them any good.
       What do you mean, it won't do them any good?
       I took all the milk out of her yesterday.

3830   I bought a new cow today.
       Does she give milk?
       No, she doesn't give it — you gotta kinda take it away from her.

3831   What marvelous milk you get on the ranch.
       Not me. I get mine from the milkman

3832   During the war — my brother stayed home — worked on the
       farm instead. One day while he was milking a cow, a soldier
       came along and said: You slacker! Why aren't you at the front?
       What did your brother say?
       He said: Because there isn't any milk at that end.

3833   What is cowhide chiefly used for?
       To keep the cow together.

3834   I've been sliding my cows down a rough plank — trying to raise
       my own planked steak.

3835   Hey, this milk is colored.
       Sure. This is the blue grass country.

3836   That cowboy broke his neck at the rodeo.
       How did he break his neck?
       They gave him a bum steer.

3837   Don't bring me any more of that horrid milk. It is positively blue.
       It ain't our fault, lady. It's these long, dull evenings as makes the
       cows depressed.

3838   He forgot to turn off the electric milker and when he got home,
       his cow was turned inside out.

                              RELATED SUBJECTS
                              Milkman 3552
                              Food 4825-4878

GOAT

3839   On what side of a goat is the most hair?
       On the outside.
       Not my goat. He just ate a hair mattress.

3840   My children is going to miss that old gentleman.
       They liked him, did they?
       There is no man they didn't like better than they liked him. Only
       Christmas he bought them a goat and a wagon, and he'd drive
       all nine of them around the yard at once.
       You mean to say the goat could pull nine of them around the
       yard at once? He must have been a powerful, strong goat.
       He is pretty strong, but we're getting used to that.

RELATED SUBJECTS
Animals (Domesticated) 3806-3866

HOG

3841   I've got a pet pig — I call him Waterman.
Is that his real name?
No, that's his pen name.

3842   My brother's gone into the pig business. He's raising fancy
hogs.
What's he planning on — showing them at fairs?
No. He feeds them one day and starves them the next.
Why does he do that?
That's the way people like bacon — a strip of fat and then a strip
of lean.

3843   Do you know anything about pigs?
My father raised a big hog once.
You're telling me?

3844   What is a hog's favorite food?
Corn. Any hog knows that.
Well, you ought to know.

RELATED SUBJECTS
Butcher Shop 5449-5453

HORSE

3845   We call our horse "Baseball."
Why call him "Baseball"?
Because he's covered with horse-hide.

3846   I just saw a man making a horse.
That isn't possible.
Well, I just saw him tacking on the feet.

3847   That's an awfully skinny looking horse you have there.
Yes. You see it's this way — every morning I toss up to see
whether he gets his hay or I get my beer, and that unlucky horse
has lost six mornings straight.

3848   Are you a pretty good judge of horse flesh?
No, I've never eaten any.

3849   Do you care for horses?
No, I wait on tables.

3850   Would you look a gift horse in the mouth?
That's silly! I ain't goin' to buy no horse.

3851 Hey, Clem, I want my money back! That horse you sold me is blind!
Well, I told you he's a fine horse, but he didn't look good!

3852 One thing about a horse, you don't have to fill him up with alcohol to keep him from freezing.

3853 What's your uncle doing now?
Oh, he's hanging around town — they caught him stealing horses.

3854 So your uncle was a horse thief?
No, not really. You see he had a great sense of humor and he was always talking about his wild oats, and sometimes the horses would hear him and follow him home.

RELATED SUBJECTS
Horse Racing 4462-4480
Horseback Riding 4483-4494

JACKASS

3855 I got assets. Do you know what assets mean?
Sure. Assets is little donkeys.

3856 Have you a red colored jackass in your house?
No — why?
Then it must have been you I saw.

3857 Bill, I see your mule has "U.S." branded on his hindquarters. Was he an army mule before you got him?
No, that "U.S." doesn't stand for Uncle Sam—that stands for "unsafe."

3858 Mr. Missouri, why does the State of Missouri stand at the head of mule-raising in this country?
Because the other end is too dangerous, sir.

3859 If you stand alongside of a jackass what fruit would you look like?
If I stood alongside of a jackass what fruit would I look like?
Well, I don't know. What would I look like?
A beautiful pair.

3860 I heard a mule kicked you yesterday.
Yes, he did.
Where did he kick you?
Well, if my head was in New York and my feet in California, he'd have kicked me in Omaha.

RELATED SUBJECTS
Description of People 263-303

RABBIT
3861 I'll put my rabbit in the other room.
You don't mean to say you have a rabbit in the house?
I can't let him out.
Why?
This is an ingrown hair.

3862 Mammals are classified thus: man and lower animals. Of course, man does the classifying.

RELATED SUBJECTS
Hunting 4423-4453
Magician 4566-4567

SCARECROW

RELATED SUBJECTS
Garden 3761-3767
Beauty 4725-4735

SHEEP
3863 He owned a lot of sheep and he wanted to take them over a river that was all ice, but the woman who owned the river said: "No." So he promised to marry her and that's how he pulled the wool over her ice.

3864 The wife was working out a crossword puzzle, when suddenly she turned to her husband and asked: What is a female sheep? Ewe, he replied without looking up from his paper — and then the battle raged.

3865 I own more sheep than any other man.
Really?
Yeah, in the United States I'm the head sheepman.
That's right — you're a mutton head.

3866 Get off my ranch! You're fired!
How come?
I caught you sound asleep in the barn.
Don't blame me!
Why not?
If you counted as many sheep as I did, you'd go to sleep, too.

CROSS-BREEDING

3867 He succeeded in crossing a kangaroo with a raccoon — now he is raising fur coats with pockets.

3868 I once crossed a bridge with an automobile.
Amazing! And what was the result?
I got to the other side.

3869 And I crossed a dachshund with a zebra.
What did that give you?
Striped sausages.

3870 I've been trying to cross a turkey with a centipede so everybody can have a drumstick.

3871 I've been trying to cross a turkey with an octopus.
Why?
So there'll be enough legs to go around.

       Related Subjects
       Inventor 1784-1801
       Animals (Wild) 4640-4668

CHICKEN

3872 I can't eat this chicken.
Why not?
It's an incubator chicken.
What makes you think it's an incubator chicken?
No chicken with a mother could be this tough.

3873 What were all your chickens doing out in front of your house?
They heard some men were going to lay a sidewalk and they wanted to see how it was done.

3874 How is your uncle doing with his chicken ranch?
Swell, he's found a new way to make his chickens lay. He puts a mirror alongside the hens, then the hen lays an egg, and when she looks in the mirror she thinks it's another hen laying the egg and she gets jealous and lays another egg.

3875 Yeah, this is a spring chicken all right. I just bit into one of the springs.

3876 Here's your dinner.
You may lay the table.
Yes, sir.

Say, what's wrong with these eggs?
Don't blame me — I only laid the table.

3877   Are you sure these eggs are not fertile?
Certainly. They've all been tried and failed to hatch.

3878   Those eggs just came from the country.
What country?

3879   What hens lay longest?
Dead ones.

3880   Rooster looks over football: Opposition, eh? I'll have to look to
my laurels.

3881   I had an egg for breakfast this morning.
That so?
Yes, and it was a bird.

3882   Be sure to bring my egg soft-boiled this time.
Waiter: Yesterday I barely dipped it in hot water and still it was
overdone. I know it'll be all right this morning, 'cause I just
carried it through a hot kitchen.

3883   That's rather a small egg, isn't it?
Give it a chance. It was only laid yesterday.

3884   Do you raise chickens on your ranch?
I'm getting lots of chickens and more eggs all the time.
Is it true that hens will lay more eggs if you put cod liver oil in
their food?
Yes, but they won't like you any more.

3885   Is it correct to say: A hen is sitting—or a hen is setting.?
The question don't interest me at all. What I wants to know when
I hear a hen cackle is whether she is laying or lying.

3886   It's a funny thing about chickens.
What's funny?
You know a chicken is the only animal you can eat before it's born.

3887   How did you make your neighbor keep his hens in his own yard?
One night I hid half a dozen eggs under a bush in my garden and
next day I let him see me gather them. I wasn't bothered after
that.

3888   How is that incubator doing that you bought?
I suppose it's all right, but I'm a little worried about it. It hasn't
laid a single egg yet.

3889   Are you sure these eggs are not fertile?
Not exactly — but we gave them every chance to prove they were.

3890 Our hen kicked a porcelain egg out of her nest. She said they weren't going to make a brick layer out of her.

3891 What are you doing to those chickens?
Dressing them.
You mean, you have to undress and dress them every day?

3892 These are the best eggs we've had for years.
Well, bring me some you haven't had so long.

3893 So you like country life. Are your hens good layers?
Toppin'! They haven't laid a bad egg yet.

3894 Are these eggs fresh?
Fresh! Why, the hens haven't missed 'em yet.

3895 Is your car a roadster?
Roadster?
Yeah — don't you know what a roadster is?
Sure — a roadster is a chicken's husband.

3896 He's in jail again — and it's all on account of a misunderstanding.
How was that?
Well, I left him on my chicken ranch and told him to raise chicks.
He thought I told him to raise checks.

3897 I was buying some chickens.
Pullet?
No, I carried them home.

3898 A football landed in the chicken yard. The rooster called all the chickens together and said: I'm not grumbling, you understand, but I just want you all to see for yourselves what is being done in other poultry yards.

3899 Old Hen: Let me give you a piece of good advice.
Young Hen: What is it?
Old Hen: An egg a day keeps the ax away.

3900 Why so blue, Tom?
I lost my chickens.
Don't worry; chickens go home to roost.
That's the trouble — they went.

3901 Talking of hens, reminds me of an old hen my dad once had. She would hatch out anything from a tennis ball to a lemon. Why, one day she sat on a piece of ice and hatched out two quarts of hot water.
That doesn't come up to a club-footed hen my mother once had. They had been feeding her by mistake on sawdust instead of oatmeal. Well, she laid twelve eggs and sat on them, and when

they hatched eleven of the chickens had wooden legs and the twelfth was a woodpecker.

RELATED SUBJECTS
Farmer 3741-3760
Garden 3761-3767
Worms 4414-4418

MOUSE

3902   I heard your brother bought himself a fruit store.
Yeah — and they caught a rat 100 years old.
How did they know that the rat was 100 years old?
He had a date in his mouth.

3903   Don't you think we ought to get some rat biscuits?
Say, if those rats don't like what they can get to eat around here, let them starve.

3904   I wanna quarter's worth o' rat poisoning.
Do you wanna take it with you?
No, I'll send the rats in after it.

3905   One mouse to another: Sure, go ahead and swipe the cheese — it'll be a snap.

3906   I want twenty-five cents worth of rat paste.
Do you want it on white bread or rye?

3907   I'm sure I heard a mouse squeak.
Well, do you want me to get up and oil it?

RELATED SUBJECTS
Female (the) 925-938
Cat 3689-3695

HOLIDAYS

THANKSGIVING

3908   So you had a nice Thanksgiving?
Yeah.
Well, I wanted to come over to your house for dinner, but I couldn't make it. What did you have to be thankful for?
I was thankful you couldn't come over for dinner.

3909   I like turkey all right, but that turkey skeleton is going to last for weeks.
You shouldn't say skeleton — it's a carcass.
It may be a carcass when you get through with it, but when I get through with it, it's a skeleton — the inside is out and the outside is off.

3910 I suppose you got the best part of the turkey.
      You bet. But I was fourteen yours old before I knew a turkey
      had anything else but a neck.

3911 First turkey on way to market: This is the first time I have been
      to the city.
      Second Gobbler: You'll be all right, if you don't lose your head.

3912 Turkey: (As he is about to be eaten) It serves me right. If I
      hadn't lost my head, I wouldn't be in this fix.

3913 What have you been eating?
      Some giraffes left from New Year's.
      I thought you had turkey.
      We did. It might just as well be giraffe — I just had a neck.

3914 The poor turkey, he's hit in the neck, loses his head, they break
      his legs, knock the stuffing out of him, cut him to the heart
      and pick on him for weeks.

3915 James the First introduced the turkey to this country. And this
      must be the beggar he introduced.

3916 The poor turkey was so thin, my uncle said it should be a little
      more Mae Westish.

3917 So you had Thanksgiving dinner at your house? Did you like the
      turkey?
      Well, that turkey couldn't have gone any faster if it had been
      streamlined.

3918 A lot of nice fat turkeys would strut less if they could see into
      the future.

In many cases, Thanksgiving would be much more heartily
enjoyed if it came before Election Day.

RELATED SUBJECTS
Drinking 2055-2140
Hospitality 3564-3660
Cooking 4798-4824
Food 4825-4878
Table Manners 4881-4883

EASTER

3919 By the way, where did you get that nice Easter tie?
      What makes you think it's an Easter tie?
      It's got egg on it.

3920 I'm going to buy a peacock.
      Why?
      So I can have colored Easter Eggs without coloring them. The
      peacock will lay colored eggs.

CHRISTMAS

3921 It must be heck to live in Miami. They never have Christmas there
How come?
Haven't you seen that sign: "It's Always June in Miami"?

3922 Have you ordered your Christmas tree, sir?
Yes, and I'm going to have my broker decorate my tree.
Why your broker?
It's the only thing he hasn't trimmed.

3923 What does it mean — "Yuletide Greetings"?
Lend me $5 — you'll tide me over for a few days.

3924 Did you hang your stocking up last year?
Yeah.
What did you get in it?
A hole in the heel.

3925 There's one thing about Santa Claus that's been puzzling me.
What is it?
Whether he sleeps with his beard inside the covers or outside.

3926 At Christmas time, every girl wants her past forgotten and her
present remembered.

3927 What did you get in your stocking for Christmas?
Nothing but a runner.
Well, what did you expect — a pole vaulter?

3928 They wanted to give me some Red Cross Seals for Christmas but
I told them I didn't want them — I didn't even know how to
feed them.

3929 Is Santa Claus a myth or a moth?
Well, moth grows on trees so Santa Claus can't be a moth, because if you think Santa Claus grows on trees you're screwy.

3930 I'm going to find out whether there is a Santa Claus.
How?
Christmas eve I'm going to put fish hooks in my chimney.

3931 I gave him a sock on the nose.
A sock on the nose?
Yeah — he wouldn't know it was Christmas without a sock on
the nose.

3932   I'm not going to hang up my stocking this year.
        Why not?
        Last year I hung up my stocking and it walked away with the
          mantel.

3933   My wife hung my socks up and boy did I have a headache.
        How could hanging up your socks give you a headache?
        She forgot to take me out of them.

3934   We're having a rubber Christmas this year. I'm going to let my
          wife and family go in and look at the tree and stretch their
          imagination.

3935   Last year we had an electric Christmas.
        What do you mean?
        Well, my little brother got an electric train, my sister got an
          electric iron, my mama got an electric washing machine and
          papa got the electric chair.

3936   Mother, where did all these pretty toys come from?
        Why, dear, Santa brought them.
        Did he bring everything? Did he bring the electric train — the
          baseball glove — the ice skates . . .?
        Yes, my love, he brought everything.
        Well, mother, may I ask who buys all the things in the stores?

3937   I think I'll wait till Christmas and hang up my stockings.
        By that time you won't need to — they'll stand alone.

3938   Are you sure this is Christmas morning?
        If it ain't, I washed my socks for nothin'.

3939   Where are you going?
        To the zoo.
        And what for?
        My mother told me to buy some Christmas seals.

3940   We were walking along the snowspread streets on Christmas Eve,
          and we noted to our companion the holly wreaths in the win-
          dows, the vari-colored lights on the trees, and the mistletoe
          over the threshold of our friend, Jones.
        Jones certainly does this Christmas spirit thing up brown. Look
          and observe that none of the sanctioned touches are lacking at
          his establishment. And see — there they are carrying in the
          yule log.
        Say — that ain't no yule log — that's Jones.

3941   Well, Bobby, did you see Santa Claus this time?
        No, Auntie. It was too dark to see him, but I heard what he said
          when he knocked his toe against the bedpost.

3942 Why do they call Santa a myth?
I don't know. I've always thought it was baby talk for mither.

RELATED SUBJECTS
Drinking 2055-2140
Bills 3281-3308
Children 3326-3333
Party 3575-3579

GIFT

3943 I want to buy my girl a present. What do you think she would like?
Does she like you?
Oh, yes, I'm positive she likes me.
If she likes you, she'll like anything.

3944 See these stockings. I just paid five dollars for them. They're a gift for my girl. Think she'll like them?
Why, there's a run in each stocking.
Yeah — I did that — I wanted to get a run for my money.

3945 Your boy friend sure has a lot of automobiles — he has a Cadillac and a Dodge and a Buick that I know of. Did he give you the Buick.
No, all he ever gave me was the dodge.

3946 (One burglar's wife to another)
What did your old man give you for your birthday?
Not a thing. The cops caught him just as he was bringing it home.

3947 Remember — last Christmas I bought my girl some perfume and my brother a shotgun? I sent my girl a note with her present saying I hoped she would try it on herself sometime. She got the note all right, but I made a mistake and sent her the shotgun.

3948 Why not buy him a couple of book ends?
Oh, he won't have time to read them.

3949 I came in here to get something for my wife.
What are you asking for her?

3950 Here's a present for you.
Oh, I think it's wonderful — it's just what I needed — isn't it grand!
Well, I'm glad you like it.
Yeah — but tell me — what is it?

3951 I want to buy a present for my wife.
Can I interest you in something in silk stockings?
Well, let's see about the present first.

3952 Weren't you kinda nervous when he gave you all those beautiful
         gifts?
      No — I just kept calm and collected.

3953 What are you going to give your children for Christmas?
      Well, if my husband doesn't stop staying out until three in the
         morning — I'll give them a new papa.

3954 What are you going to give me for Christmas?
      Close your eyes and tell me what you see.
      Nothing.
      That's what you're going to get for Christmas.

3955 Are you interested in book ends?
      Yeah, that's the part I read first.

3956 What are you going to give me for Christmas?
      Take the number four.
      Yeah.
      Subtract 2.
      Yeah.
      What've you got?
      Two.
      Now subtract two.
      Yeah.
      What have you got?
      Nothing.
      That's what I'm going to give you for Christmas.

3957 That mouth organ you gave me for my birthday is easily the best
         present I've had.
      I'm glad you like it.
      Yes — mother gives me a quarter a week not to play it.

3958 What shall we get dad for Christmas?
      I hear he's buying us a car — let's get him a chauffeur's outfit.

3959 How did you like those Chinese backscratchers I gave you?
      Is that what they are? My wife's been making me eat salad with
         them.

3960 I gave him a bridge for his violin.
      What's the idea?
      To help him get his music across.

3961 Wouldn't you be surprised if I gave you a check for your birth-
         day, dear?
      I certainly would.
      Well, here it is, already made out, ready for you to sign.

3962   According to one of our tragediennes, the ability to weep at a
        moment's notice is a great gift. More important, it generally
        results in one.

                        RELATED SUBJECTS
                        Birthday 108-120
                        Engagement 2848-2858
                        Wedding 2863-2878
                        Flowers 3768-3771
                        Salesman 5403-5416
                        Department Store 5418-5429

NEW YEAR

3963   I'll bet you didn't keep your New Year's resolution about necking
            when you went out with that saxophone player last night.
        Sure I did — I kept it to myself.

3964   I'm making a resolution that you won't drink, smoke or stay out
            late nights with other girls.
        Oh, you're making that resolution?
        Yeah, and it's not going to be broken either.

                        RELATED SUBJECTS
                        Drinking 2055-2140
                        Hospitality 3564-3660

VACATION

3965   What's the idea going around in your shorts?
        I want everybody to see my tan. It cost me a fortune.
        How long did it take to get your tan?
        Five days. Sort of a Woolworth vacation — five and tan.

3966   I went to a hotel for a change and rest.
        Did you get it?
        The bellboy got the change and the hotel got the rest.

3967   Did you enjoy your weekend trip?
        The trip going was terrible.
        Have a flat tire?
        Yeah — but I made her walk home.

3968   On our vacation in Italy, I'm going to see Florence.
        But won't your wife get jealous?

3969   You really ought to come to Shrimpton with me next summer. I
            had a wonderful time there this year. I won a beauty com-
            petition.
        No, I think I'd rather go to a more crowded place.

3970 Don't you ever take a vacation?
I can't get away.
Why? Can't the firm do without you?
Quite easily. That's what I don't want them to find out.

RELATED SUBJECTS
Mosquitoes 3801-3805
Travel 3971-4246
Beach 4280-4304
Fishing 4380-4413
Hunting 4423-4453
California 5564-5566

TRAVEL

DIRECTIONS (How to Locate)

3971 It's a lovely house up North where we're living in the South.
You can't live in the North and South at the same time. If you are facing east, what would be on your left hand?
My fingers.

3972 Never ask a girl how to get to her house — she is liable to tell you all the taxi drivers know the way.

3973 Orator: In this great and glorious country of ours there is no North, no South, no East, no West . . .
She: No wonder we don't know where we're at.

3974 Can you tell me where the Grand Hotel is?
What's the matter — lost?
No — the hotel's lost.

3975 Where do you live?
Why?
I always like to know how far I can go with a girl.

3976 Your sister seems to be a sensible woman. Where can I get hold of her?
I don't know — she's awful ticklish.

3977 Are you sure we're traveling in the right direction?
Oh yes — didn't we find the River Nile in the right part?
Yeah — you hit the Nile right on the head.

3978 How do you get to Doakesville from here?
Well, I believe I would go back about a mile and take the first right hand road. No, I believe I would take the left hand road. Come to think of it, stranger, if I were trying to get to Doakesville I wouldn't start from here at all.

3979   Don't you know your way around this town?
        No, if I knew my way around it, you don't suppose I'd have gotten
        mixed up in it, do you?

3980   I told you to take the Fourteenth Street car. Didn't you take it?
        I waited and waited for the fourteenth street car, but after the
        tenth went by, I fell asleep.

3981   Which road shall I take?
        Oh, it doesn't make any difference.
        It doesn't make any difference?
        No, whichever you take you'll be sorry you didn't take the other
        one.

                        RELATED SUBJECTS
                        Foreign Cities 3990-3999
                        Famous Places 4000-4015
                        Cities 5558-5562

DISTANCE

3982   We're ten miles from land.
        What direction?
        Straight down.

3983   How far is it to the next town?
        Oh, about ten miles — you can walk it easy in two hours, if you
        run.

3984   Is it true that scientists claim a straight line is the shortest distance
        between two points?
        Yes, a straight line is the shortest distance between two points, but
        Mae West got there quicker with curves.

3985   It's ten miles to town as the flow cries.
        No, ten miles as the cry flows!
        Both wrong. Ten miles as the fly crows.

3986   Why, you said it was only a hop, skip and a jump here. It's at
        least two miles from the station.
        Sure, at the station you hop in a cab, skip a couple of miles, and
        jump out here.

                        RELATED SUBJECTS
                        Automobile 4042-4146
                        Boat 4174-4200
                        Airplane 4208-4217
                        Train 4218-4242

SCENERY

3987   I've got a new job.
      What doing?
      Boring knot-holes in billboards so people can see the scenery.

3988   Have you seen any of the sights around the city?
      Seen any? I was out with one last night.

3989   Tourist: What beautiful scenery! Lived here all your life?
      Farmer: Not yet.

RELATED SUBJECTS
Vacation 3965-3970
Famous Places 4000-4015

FOREIGN CITIES—COUNTRIES—RIVERS

3990   Do you know what those crooks will do to you if they catch you?
      No, what?
      They hang you by the nails.
      Not me.
      Why not?
      I bite my nails.

3991   In America we drink our coffee out of cups — in China they drink
      their tea out of doors.

3992   I went to Switzerland on a vacation last summer.
      So did I. While over in Switzerland, how did you like the Swiss
      Alps?
      They are the nicest people I ever met.

3993   What do you call all the little rivers that run into the Nile?
      The Juveniles!

3994   Cry on the Nile: Egypt me.

3995   I have been painting as an amateur for several years now, and
      those landscapes were done on the Riviera.
      That's Nice?
      Why, thank you!

3996   (Touring through Europe)
      Where are we now?
      Half way between Paris and Marseilles, sir.
      Don't bother me with niggling details. What country are we in?

3997   An American tourist in France, realizing he had a two hour wait
      for his train, went exploring. Finding himself lost, he ad-
      dressed a passerby in the best French he could remember from
      college, mispronouncing it greatly. He voiced his request for
      information as follows:
      Pardonnez-moi. J'ai quitté ma train et maintenant je ne sais pas
      où le trouver encore. Est-ce que vous pouvez me montrer le
      route à la train?

Let's look for it together, said the stranger. I don't speak French either.

3998   How do they figure the population of a Swiss village?
Oh, I guess they count the number of echoes and divide by the number of mountains.

3999   Didn't you ever hear of Naples?
Sure, n'aple a day keeps the doctor away.

RELATED SUBJECTS
Automobile 4042-4146
Boat 4174-4200
Airplane 4208-4217
Train 4218-4242
Foreign Languages 4996-5002
Geography 5003-5014
History 5015-5026
Cities 5558-5562

FAMOUS PLACES

4000   I had a grand time seeing the sights of New York.
Is that so?
But something has been puzzling me all day.
What is that?
What famous General is buried in Grant's tomb?

4001   And this was where the great Colonel fell.
No wonder! I almost tripped over it myself.

4002   I know why they call this the Great White Way. It's the place where Brown and White and Yellow play together, and are in the pink of condition, turn green with envy and purple with rage when they don't get anywhere singing the blues — That's the Great White Way.

4003   Have any big men ever been born in Hollywood?
No — only little babies.

4004   Lincoln's Gettysburg address: 725 Court Street.

4005   See that house? That's where Uncle Tom lived.
Uncle Tom from Uncle Tom's Cabin?
Yes.
I never even heard of him.

4006   We saw that famous volcano.
What?
Volcano — you know, one of those things that belches and spits fire.
Oh sure — landsakes, I married one.

4007   Washington sure must have had a great memory.
       Why do you think he had a great memory?
       Well, they built a big monument to it.

> Train 4218-4242
> Geography 5003-5014
> History 5015-5026
> Famous People 5029-5042

GRAND CANYON

4008   My uncle fell into a ditch in Arizona and they never found him.
       Fell into a ditch and never came out? That's ridiculous!
       You mean you've never heard of the Grand Canyon?

NORTH POLE

4009   First Eskimo: How far is it to Iglooton?
       Second Eskimo: Six months by dog sled.
       First Eskimo: All night ride, eh?

RUINS

4010   Just think, some of those ruins are five thousand years old.
       Say, I'm not that dumb.
       Don't you believe they are five thousand years old?
       How could they be — it's only 1980?

4011   These mummies are thousands of years old.
       Yeah? Where are the poppies?

4012   I found a wonderful myth in the old baths of Rome.
       I hoped you begged her pardon and left.

4013   Listen to this. This article states that in some of the old Roman
       prisons that have been unearthed they found the petrified re-
       mains of the prisoners.
       Gracious! Those must be what they call hardened criminals, I
       expect.

4014   Do you like romantic old ruins?
       If they'd only stop asking to marry me.

4015   I heard they just found Columbus' bones.
       I never knew he was a gambling man.

CANNIBAL

4016   A man was captured by man-eating cannibals. They formed a
       rescue party. The man's son said: I hope we reach my father
       before he's scratched off the menu.

4017   Yeah, but if these cannibals catch you, they'll eat you.
       I don't care. Let them kill me — let them throw me in the pot
       and cook me — but they'll be sorry.
       Why?
       Because I'm not what I'm cooked up to be.

4018   Cannibal: We've just captured an actor.
       Chief: Hurray! I was hoping for a good ham sandwich.

4019   Wasn't it the polite cannibal king who remarked to the recently
       captured missionary: We would like very much to have you
       for dinner tomorrow?

4020   Look — we're surrounded by cannibals.
       I hope they don't find out I'm an actor.
       Why?
       You know how everybody loves boiled ham.

4021   You know, all these natives are carniverous . . .
       I don't care about their politics. I just hope they are vegetarians.

4022   What would a cannibal be who ate his mother's sister?
       I'll bite — what?
       An aunt-eater, of course.

4023   Why did Miss America break off her engagement to the cannibal
       chief?
       He told her she looked good enough to eat.

4024   The missionary was captured and eaten by cannibals — gave the
       cannibals their first taste of religion.

4025   The cannibal king of the Mambas assures Britain that he has given
       up the habit of eating small boys. Youth, it appears, will no
       longer be served.

4026   Why do cannibals always eat missionaries?
       Because missionaries don't get on the right side of the cannibals.
       They always get in the inside instead of the right side.

4027   Good heavens! Cannibals!
       Now, now, don't get in a stew.

4028   Why is that cannibal always looking at us?
       You see, he's the food inspector of the tribe.

RELATED SUBJECTS
Directions (How to Locate)
3971-3981

MODES OF TRAVEL

PEDESTRIAN

4029   Do you realize that eighty percent of the pedestrians here in
          Chicago don't realize that if they would raise their hands while
          they're crossing a safety zone all automobiles would have to
          stop?
       Do you mean to say that eighty percent of the pedestrians here in
          Chicago don't realize that if they would raise their hands while
          they're crossing a safety zone all automobiles would have
          to stop? Well, what about the twenty percent that do know it?
       They're in the Receiving Hospital.

4030   It's getting so nowadays that a pedestrian can't go through traffic.
       All you have to do is just be calm and collected.
       Yeah? My uncle went through the traffic yesterday — he was
          calm — and he is still being collected.

4031   We're out in the country.
       I can't see anything. How can you tell we're out in the country?
       Because we're not hitting as many people.

4032   Where's the driver that hit him? Get him!
       Wait, Mr. Policeman, wait. I was trying to cross the street and
          the driver stopped and motioned me to go across. The shock
          was too much, I fell down.

4033   I read where a kangaroo was run over by an automobile today.
       What about it?
       It's most discouraging. You know how a kangaroo can leap.
       Yes, I know.
       Well, what chance has a pedestrian got?

4034   Autoist: I tell you, Judge, there are too many people on the streets
          for safety.
       Judge: Why not buy an airplane? Then the pedestrians won't
          bother you. Thirty days!

4035   What is a pedestrian, daddy?
       It's a person with a wife, daughter, two sons, and a car.

4036   Say, look out, how you drive! You knocked down a pedestrian.
       Say, it's a slow day — sometimes I get two or three a day.

4037   The way some pedestrians walk you'd think they owned the
       streets.
       Yeah, and the way some motorists drive you'd think they owned
       their cars.

                              RELATED SUBJECTS
                              Accident 615-709
                              Directions (How to Locate)
                              3971-3981
                              Automobile 4042-4146
                              Policeman 5225-5228

HITCH-HIKING

4038   Why do you go around twiddling your thumbs?
       I'm a hitch-hiker and I'm training for the spring.

4039   (Two hitch-hikers trying to get a ride)
       One: Why don't you try hailing a few cars?
       Other: I'm saving my thumb for the ride back.

4040   Things are picking up. Hitch-hikers at intersections this season
       are thumbing in only two or three directions instead of four.

4041   I hear your boy friend had a finger in a big transportation deal.
       Yes, he thumbed a ride across the country.

                              RELATED SUBJECTS
                              Directions (How to Locate)
                              3971-3981
                              Foreign Cities 3990-3999

AUTOMOBILES (In General)

4042   Mama, what becomes of an automobile when it gets too old to run
       any more?
       Why, somebody sells it to your father for a used car — as good
       as new.

4043   So your husband refused to buy you an auto of your own?
       He didn't exactly refuse. He said he thought I ought to become
       more familiar with machinery in general and so he bought me a
       washing machine to start on.

4044   You looked at my car like it was the first car you've ever seen.
       Well, your car looks like the first car I ever saw.

4045   Do you think the automobile has contributed anything toward
       your prosperity?

I know it has. Last year I built a new hospital for the town and this year they have given me a contract to build an addition to it.

4046   You sold me this car two weeks ago?
Yes, sir.
Tell me again all you said about it then. I'm getting discouraged.

4047   Statisticians claim the automobile has actually cut down the deaths from old age in this country.
How's that? Prevents over-exertion, I suppose?
No, not that so much, but fewer people escape to reach old age.

4048   So your father is crazy over his car.
Whenever I see him, he's crazy *under* it.

4049   I'm going to buy a car.
Why do you want to buy a car?
I just found a parking space.

4050   I have a good idea how to keep the front bumpers from getting bumped up in front.
How?
Put them on the rear of the car.

4051   I hear your new car goes like a top.
Yes, I have just been for a spin.

4052   Sir, your car is at the door.
Yes, I hear it knocking.

4053   I call my car "Snake."
Why?
Because it always rattles before it strikes.

4054   I call my new car "Straight Rye."
Why?
Because I use a motorcycle cop for a chaser.

4055   That son of mine is the dumbest boy I ever saw.
How come?
I sent him to put water in the car, and when I went out I found a bucket of water in the back seat.

4056   Well, your car sure does run smoothly.
Wait a minute — I haven't started the engine yet.

4057   Is your car in good condition?
Sure — everything makes a noise except the horn.

4058   What'll it cost to have my car repaired?
What's the matter with it?

I haven't any idea whatever.
Sixty-four dollars and fifty cents.

4059 Automobile roads today are like mirrors.
I'm glad. Maybe the women drivers will keep their eyes on the
road now.

4060 My car has an indifferent horn.
What kind of a horn is that?
Oh, it just don't give a toot.

4061 I read in today's paper that scientists have discovered an animal
that can twist itself into all kinds of shapes. What do you think
about that?
At last they have found something that can get in and out of
some of those new foreign sportscars.

4062 What would your wife say if you bought a new car?
Look out for that traffic light. Be careful now! Don't hit that
truck! Why don't you watch where you're going? Will you
never learn? And a lot more like that.

4063 The abundance of autos in America suggests to some that the
national flower should be changed from the golden-rod to the
car-nation.

4064 What caused the fight?
He said he'd like.to get one of those police sirens for his car.
What caused the fight — why did she hit him?
Well, his wife heard us talking, and when he said he'd like one of
those police sirens for his car she hit him with a plate and said
if she ever caught him two-timing her, she'd fix him.

4065 Transportation itself is wonderful, when you think of the way it
has progressed. First came the bicycle, then came the horse,
then came the trains and then came the automobiles — and
what comes after the automobiles?
Motor cops, as a rule.

4066 Didn't you guarantee when you sold me this car that you would
replace anything that broke?
Yes, sir. What is it?
Well, I want a new garage door.

4067 You'd never think this car was a second-hand one, would you?
No, it looks as if you had made it yourself.

4068 An automobile engineer claims the car of the future will have a
wheelbase of 150 inches. However, the width will remain
about that of a prostrate pedestrian.

4069   Your car has a good pick-up.
I'll say — the first day I was out I picked up two sailors, a barber and an ice cream man.

4070   Cop: (Looking at man in gutter) Drunk?
Man: Certainly not! I'm just holding this parking space for a friend.

4071   My brother's in jail for not buying a license for his dog.
But he hasn't a dog.
I know, but his car growls so much, the neighbors complained of our dog.

4072   My uncle just had his car overhauled and it cost him $50.
Fifty dollars for overhauling a car?
Yes, he was driving on the highway and a policeman overhauled him.

RELATED SUBJECTS
Accidents 615-709
Installment Plan 3171-3180
Pedestrian 4029-4037
Policeman 5225-5228

MODELS (Automobile)

4073   Mechanic: (Repairing old, broken-down car) Mister, you've got a good horn here. Why don't you jack it up and run a car under it?

4074   Well, I think I will just have to trade in my new Thunderbird. I just can't afford those big cars anymore.
Well, you know what they say about the automobile.
No, what?
It's an invention that made people go fast and money faster.

4075   The automobile has increased the mortality rate, created appalling traffic problems, contributed to juvenile delinquency, showed half of America how to live beyond its income, and relieved us of the horsefly.

4076   Someone stole my Toyota last night. It makes me so mad. If I were a magistrate, I would make sure that all car thieves were driven out of town!
Really? Well, I think they should be made to walk!

4077　You don't know what fractures are? Fractures are breaks.
　　　　Oh — I got four-wheel fractures on my car.

4078　What kind of a motor horn would you like? Do you want a good, loud blast?
　　　　No, I want something that just sneers.

4079　The latest models from Detroit are supposed to save you half the fuel.
　　　　Oh, really? Well, then I'll take two, so I can save *all* the fuel.

4080　I just had an argument with a man in the parking station. He made me pay a parking charge and then made me leave a $10 bill with him.
　　　　How come?
　　　　To make sure I would come back and take it away.
　　　　Well, you know it isn't a Rolls Royce.
　　　　No, it isn't a Rolls Royce, but I've got it so that now it backfires with an English accent.

4081　You know, the manufacturers say it takes three thousand bolts and nuts to hold an automobile together.
　　　　Well, it only takes one nut to scatter it all over the country!

4082　Did you stop in Detroit on the way out here?
　　　　Yeah — that's the place they make automobiles.
　　　　Oh, yes — they make other things, too.
　　　　I know — I've ridden in them.

4083　A prehistoric skeleton found with its legs wrapped around its neck would seem to indicate that the sports car was older than we had supposed.

4084　Daughter: What happens to a car when it gets too old?
　　　　Mother: Someone sells it to your father.

4085　Help! My Jaguar just hit a deer and turned turtle!
　　　　You don't need a mechanic — you need a veterinarian.

4086　Too bad about Dave.
　　　　I thought his business was booming. What happened?
　　　　I see he's gone on welfare.
　　　　How do you know?
　　　　He just drove by in a new car.

4087　A trade note claims that the automotive industry gives employment to millions of people in the United States. And that's exclusive of policemen and morticians.

4088　Yes, sir, of all our cars, this is the one we feel confident and justified in pushing.
　　　　That's no good to me. I want one to ride in.

4089   Is your car an eight or a twelve?
       Both. Eight cylinders — twelve payments.

RELATED SUBJECTS
Insurance 208-216
Installment Plan 3171-3180
Family 3209-3217

TOOLS

4090   You hammer nails like lightning.
       I'm fast, you mean?
       No, you never strike twice in the same place.

4091   Have you a wrench? Have you anything heavy?
       Here's a sponge.
       A sponge isn't heavy.
       It is if you dip it in hard water.

DRIVING (Automobile)

4092   I was driving a car down the street and turned into a big tree.
       What's the idea running into a tree?
       Well, how else was I to stop the car?

4093   How fast will your car go?
       Oh, about three hundred billboards per hour.

4094   What does it mean when a woman is holding out her hand?
       It means she's turning left, turning right, backing up, waving at
          somebody or going to stop.

4095   Present-day drivers are too finicky. The old hansom cabmen
          never complained of back-seat drivers.

4096   Three men were repairing telephone poles. A woman passed by
          in her car and when she saw the men climbing the telephone
          poles, she said: Look at those darn fools — you'd think I had
          never driven a car before.

4097   You drive too fast. Don't you know where the brake is?
       The what?
       The brake. There are two brakes on every car — the foot brake
          and the hand brake. The hand brake is put on in case of emer-
          gency.
       Oh sure — like a kimono.

4098   How is your sister getting along with her driving lessons?
       Fine. The road is beginning to turn now when she does.

4099   Your tail light is out.
I disconnected it. I thought — what's the use of driving with a light in back when you have one in front of you?

4100   Is he a good driver?
Well, when the road turns the same time he does, it's just a coincidence.

4101   What's the idea — don't you know this is a one way street?
Well, I'm only going one way.

4102   Jones is so old-fashioned.
Why so?
He always goes back after hitting anyone.

4103   Do you run a car?
Nope. Let the engine do that.

4104   Cop: (To man driving past a Stop sign) Hey there, can't you read?
Motorist: Sure, I can read, but I can't stop.

4105   How do you like driving a car?
There is one thing I don't like about driving. I don't like steering the brakes.

4106   I stalled my car at a traffic light and couldn't get it started.
That's bad.
It was terrible. The lights went from green to yellow and back from yellow to red and then to green again. But I couldn't move the car. A cop came over and said: What's the matter? Haven't we got any colors you like?

4107   What happened to your speedometer?
I sold it — I didn't need it any more.
How can you get along without a speedometer?
Easy — at twenty miles, the fenders rattle — at thirty miles, the doors rattle — and at forty miles, I rattle.

4108   I wouldn't advise people to drive to Florida right now.
Why not?
They would have to take the Freeway — all the detours are being repaired.

4109   I see you were arrested for driving eighty miles an hour on the wrong side of the street, in the middle of the night, without any lights. What have you to say?
It was necessary, your Honor. The car was stolen.

4110   Cop: (To lady stalled in auto) Use your noodle, lady, use your noodle!

Lady: My goodness! Where is it? I've pushed and pulled everything in the car.

4111 Hey! You're blocking up traffic. Can't you go any faster?
Yes, but I don't want to leave the car.

4112 How did your father know we used his car yesterday?
Well, you know that fat guy we ran into?
Yes.
That was father.

4113 I say, Briggs, don't you ever take your wife out with you in
the car?
No. I can't contend with both of 'em together.

4114 But, lady, you put out your hand.
Sorry. I didn't mean anything by it. I was just admiring my new
ring.

4115 What happened, George?
Puncture.
You should have watched out for it. The guidebook warned us
there was a fork in the road about this point.

4116 Speed? Say, that car can't be stopped on the hills.
Mine was that way, too, before I had the brakes fixed.

4117 Now, lady, this is the gear shift; down there is the brake; yonder
is the accelerator, and over here is the clutch.
Let's take one thing at a time — teach me to drive first.

4118 How's your brake?
You should worry. It's my car.

4119 What is the best thing to do when the brakes of one's car give way?
Hit something cheap.

4120 Don't you know that you should always give half of the road to a
woman driver?
I always do, when I find out which half of the road she wants.

4121 At times my wife seems to be trying to be an angel.
You mean when she wants something from you?
No, when she drives a car.

4122 Let me see your driving license.
Well, as a matter of fact, officer, I don't happen to have it on me,
but if it will save you any bother I can assure you it's very much
like any other old driving license.

4123 Tell me, George, quick! Which is the right side of the road to
keep on when you're running down a hill backward like this?

4124 Isn't it dangerous to drive a car with one hand?
Yeah, many a guy has run into a church that way.

4125 Having any serious trouble with your new automobile?
Not a bit. So far I haven't hit a single man without being able to get away before he got my number.

4126 The candidate for a chauffeur's job was being examined by the car owner. He got along all right until the questioner asked whether he had traveled much in other states. The applicant said he had.
All right, let's see you fold this road map.

4127 What are your favorite colors?
Stop and Go!

> RELATED SUBJECTS
> Insurance 208-216
> Accident 615-709
> Directions (How to Locate) 3971-3981
> Pedestrians 4029-4037

BACK-SEAT-DRIVERS

4128 I got rid of that rear noise in my car.
How did you do it?
I made her sit up front with me.

4129 My wife doesn't like these new cars. The ones that look the same at both ends. She's a back-seat-driver and she doesn't know which end to get in.

4130 Are you a back-seat-driver?
Indeed, I'm not. I sit right here where I can grab the wheel if he doesn't do what I tell him.

4131 Has your wife learned to drive the car yet?
Yes, in an advisory capacity.

4132 All this talk about back-seat-drivers is bunk. I've driven a car for ten years and I've never had a word from behind.
What sort of car do you drive?
A hearse.

4133 Now remember, Herbert, the brake is on the left, or is it the right, but don't . . .
For heaven's sake stop chattering. Your job is to smile at the policeman.

4134 My father said he didn't like women that drive from the back seat.
What did your mother say to that?
She said back-seat-drivers were no worse than men who cook from the dining room table.

4135 A man was driving an auto with his wife in the back seat and stalled his car on a railroad track with the train coming. His wife hollered: Go on! Go on! And the husband said: You've been driving all day from the back seat. I've got my end across, see what you can do with your end.

RELATED SUBJECTS
Marriage 2882-3051
Mother-in-law 3116-3131

SPEEDING (Automobile)

4136 Miss, you were doing sixty miles an hour!
Oh, isn't that splendid! I only learned to drive yesterday.

4137 What's the idea going seventy-five miles an hour in a twenty-five mile zone?
I wasn't going seventy-five miles an hour — I wasn't going sixty, I wasn't going fifty. I wasn't even going forty — I wasn't . . .
Look out! In a minute you'll be backing into something.

4138 Why did you have the policeman put eighty miles an hour on the ticket when he arrested you for driving sixty miles an hour?
I want to get a better price for the car when I sell it.

4139 Driving a car eighty miles an hour is a criminal offense.
I can't help it. I do everything fast.

4140 Do you know that you are going fifty miles an hour?
Impossible, I have only been out of the garage twenty minutes.

4141 Officer: (Arresting girl for speeding) Say, didn't you see me wave at you?
Girl: Yeah, and I thought you were awfully fresh.

4142 Yesterday, I got pinched for speeding. The judge said: I'll fine you today, but if it happens tomorrow I'll have you thrown in the cooler.
I get it. Fine today — cooler tomorrow.

4143   How does the motorcycle policeman know when people are going too fast?
         If they go too fast for him to catch them, he gives them a ticket.

4144   Don't you know you can get into trouble speeding? You're liable to get forty dollars or thirty days in jail.
         Well, I'll take the forty dollars.

4145   Well, what is your alibi for speeding fifty miles an hour?
         I had just heard, your Honor, that the ladies of my wife's church were giving a rummage sale and I was hurrying home to save my other pair of pants.

4146   Why are you racing through town at this rate?
         My brakes are out of order and I wanted to get home before there was an accident.

RELATED SUBJECTS
Accident 615-709
Pedestrian 4029-4037
Airplane 4208-4217
Policeman 5225-5228

GAS STATION

4147   Attendant: Ten gallons enough, sir?
         Customer: Yes.
         Attendant: Check your oil, sir?
         Customer: No, it's okay.
         Attendant: Got enough water in your radiator?
         Customer: Yes, filled up.
         Attendant: Anything else, sir?
         Customer: Yes, would you please stick out your tongue so I can seal this letter?

4148   I'm in a hurry. Give me a gallon of gas.
         What are you doing — weaning your car?

4149   Fill her up, sir?
         No, no, thanks. Just give me a glass of water.
         Glass of water?
         Yeah, for an Alka Seltzer. I already got gassed in Mexico.

4150   Do you know what petrol is?
         Sure, I rode in one.
         Rode in one what?
         A police petrol.

4151   How much gas do we have?
         It points to one-half, but whether the thing means half full or half empty, I don't know.

4152   When you get your car fixed in a garage, what do they charge for
        the oil in the car?
        What do you mean?
        How much do they charge for the oil the mechanics always leave
        on the upholstery?

4153   Check your oil?
        No, I'll take it with me.

4154   I can't believe the high cost of gasoline!
        Well, what did the station attendant say to you?
        "Stick 'em up!"

4155   How much gasoline does the tank in your car hold?
        I don't know. I've only had it ten years and I never had enough
        money to pay for getting it filled clear up.

4156   What kind of oil do you use in your new car?
        What?
        What kind of oil do you use?
        Oh, I usually start off by telling them how lonesome I am, and
        then . . .

RELATED SUBJECTS
Accident 615-709
Automobile 4042-4146
Stores 5393-5402
Salesman 5403-5416

TAXI

4157   Drunk to Taxi Driver: Home, James.
        Taxi Driver: What d'ya mean — "Home James?" This is a
        public taxi.
        Drunk: Oh, very well, home, Jesse James.

4158   I've got a taxi cab now.
        How're you doing?
        Not so good. I hardly make enough to pay for the damage I do
        to the other cars.

4159   You say you've never driven a car while sober?
        Yeah, that's a fact.
        You say you purposely ran down ten people last year?
        That's right.
        And you are willing to drive only in the middle of the street and
        just miss hitting the fenders of other cars when passing them?
        You got it straight, mister.
        Fine! You're just the man to drive one of our company's taxi cabs.

4160   My uncle got into a taxi cab and fell asleep. When he woke up
        in the taxi cab and the meter registered six dollars and twenty

cents he found he only had forty-five cents in his pocket.
So what did he do?
He made the driver back up to forty-five cents.

4161   I came in a taxi. The fare was $3.10 but the driver didn't have
the change for a five, so I had to ride around until the fare was
five dollars.

4162   How does he like his new girl friend?
He likes the girl, but he claims she is too expensive.
Why is that?
Every time she sees a taxi cab she gets paralyzed from the hips
down.

4163   Look at those colors! The yellow of the butterfly — the passionate
purple of a tropical night — the crimson of . . .
What is it, a rainbow?
Naw — a gypsy cab.

4164   How do we get to your home from here?
Oh, any taxi driver knows the way!
That's all right — I'll ask a conductor.

4165   Taxi! Taxi!
Were you calling me?
Yes.
Well, I'm already engaged.
Oh, are you? Well I hope you'll be awfully happy.

4166   Man: Well, cabbie, how much?
Cabman: Well, can you beat that? I had the meter going back-
wards and I owe you a dollar and a half.
Man: Thanks! Hey, where's my tip?

4167   I saw a car today and suddenly the fenders became wings and the
darn thing flew over my head like a canary.
A canary?
Yes, it was a yellow cab.

4168   Go over to Riverside Drive and pick up a lady.
Not *me*.
Why?
Because if I can pick her up, she's no lady.

4169   A statesman was being driven rapidly by his chauffeur, when the
car struck and killed a dog. The chauffeur stopped, and the
statesman got out to address the owner placatingly. But she
turned on him wrathfully, and told him just what she thought.
At last, the statesman said:
Madam, I shall be glad to replace your dog.
The woman hissed: Sir, you flatter yourself!

4170   I hate taxi cabs.
        Why?
        If I ride backwards I get sick and if I ride frontwards, I feel worse
            because I can see the meter.

4171   Call me a taxi!
        Okay — you're a taxi.

4172   He was riding in a taxi and the cab driver kept sticking his hand
            out the window, so he said: Keep both your hands on the wheel
            — I'll tell you when it starts raining.

4173   I can't pay this taxi cab bill.
        Then I'll take you to the police station.
        I'll pay it — but first take me to the poorhouse and leave me.

                              RELATED SUBJECTS
                              Directions (How to Locate)
                                  3971-3981
                              Distance 3982-3986
                              Driving 4092-4127

        BOAT
4174   Can you tell me where the Captain is?
        The Captain's forward.
        That's all right — this is a pleasure trip.

4175   Shall I bring your lunch on deck, sir?
        Just throw it overboard and save time.

4176   To win a yacht race you have to be about three sheets in the wind.

4177   They put the trunks down the hatchway.
        Huh?
        I said, they put the trunks down the hatchway. Don't you know
            what a hatchway is?
        Sure — that's where baby chickens are born.

4178   All hands on deck, the ship's leaking.
        Aw, put a pan under it and come to bed.

4179   Are you nautical?
        What did you say?
        I said, are you nautical?
        Well, I have my moments.

4180   I even went in one of those glass bottom boats.
        I never did get a chance to see one. What is the idea of those glass
            bottom boats?

So the fish can see how big the man is they got away from.

4181   He used such nautical terms.
       Yes, sailors do talk dirty.

4182   I understand the food on some ocean going liners is terrible.
       Yeah, even the seagulls are complaining.

4183   Why do they refer to ships and boats as "she"?
       Because they make their best showing in the wind.

4184   Close that porthole.
       Do you feel a draft?
       No, but my steak has blown out of my hand four times.

4185   How do you tell the starboard from the port?
       Did you look for labels on the bottles?

4186   So your uncle took a boat trip. How's he feeling?
       Fine. The ocean gave him a new lease on life. But he gave the
          ocean just as much as it gave him.

4187   Where did you put your clothes?
       In that little closet with the glass door.
       You boob — that's the porthole.

4188   I'll find out just how much you know about a boat. What would
          you do if a sudden storm sprang up on the starboard?
       Throw out an anchor.
       What would you do if another storm sprang up aft?
       Throw out another anchor.
       And if another terrific storm sprang up forward, what would
          you do?
       Throw out another anchor.
       Hold on. Where are you getting all your anchors from?
       From the same place you're getting your storms.

4189   Can't something be done for that ship in distress?
       It's all right, mum. We sent a line to the crew to come ashore.
       Good gracious! Must they have a formal invitation?

4190   I love canoeing and you paddle so well. Where did you learn?
       At Gamma Sigma Pi initiations.

4191   Go up forward and box the compass.
       Which hand shall I use — my right or my left?

4192   I would like to get some information about a sea berth.
       You'll have to see the ship's surgeon, second door to your left.

4193   My uncle was wrecked on a desert island with twenty-five girls
          and when they found him he was nearly dead.

From exposure?

No — from pulling down the distress signals the girls put up.

4194   If the boat foundered, whom would you save first, the children or me?

Me.

4195   Three men fell overboard. The captain yelled to me: When they come up grab them by the hair and pull them into the boat.

Two of them came up and I grabbed them by the hair and pulled them in the boat. Then the third man came up but he was baldheaded.

What did you do?

I pushed him under and told him to come up like he should.

4196   There's a tramp steamer signalling us.

What do they want?

They want a dime for a cup of coffee.

4197   Tell me, Billy, why they use knots instead of miles on the ocean?

Because they've got to have the ocean tide.

4198   Can you tell me at what time I'm most likely to see this sea serpent they tell about?

Yes, right after the cocktail hour.

4199   Where is Jimmy this afternoon?

If he knows as much about canoes as he thinks he does, he is out canoeing, but if he doesn't know any more about it than I think he does, he's swimming.

4200   I never could see why they always call a boat "she."

Then I guess you never tried to steer one, did you?

RELATED SUBJECTS
Sleep 2221-2241
Fresh People 2397-2408
Flirtation 2779-2784
Dancing 3584-3603
Games 3604-3613
Vacation 3965-3970
Distance 3982-3986
Tip 4274-4276
Restaurant 4738-4883
Telegram 5550-5557
Weather Bureau 5589-5596

SEASICKNESS

4201   We were out at sea — the boat was rolling and rocking something awful. One sailor got pretty sick, and he was leaning over the

rail. The captain comes along and says: You can't be sick here.
The sailor regarded the Captain a minute and said: Watch.

4202   There is something in my throat that goes up and down.
       You must have swallowed an elevator.

4203   What will I do if I get seasick?
       Don't worry — you'll *do* it.

4204   Many a tourist has wondered what to do about seasickness and
       then given up.

4205   A wife to her seasick husband: Do you want me to have the
       steward send up some dinner?
       No, but I wish you would have him take it on deck and throw it
       over the rail for me.

4206   Sweetheart, you aren't sick, are you?
       No, but I'd hate to yawn.

4207   My husband is particularly liable to seasickness, Captain.
       I've heard of the complaint before, ma'am.
       Could you tell me what to do in case of an attack?
       Tain't necessary, ma'am. Instinct will tell him.

       SEE ALSO   RELATED SUBJECTS
       Scotchman 1132   Sickness 741-801
       Boat 4175; 4182   Airplane 4208-4217
                                Train 4218-4242

AIRPLANE

4208   How would you like to ride in an airplane?
       I wouldn't like it. It's de terra-firma for me, and de firmer de
       groun' de lesser de terror.

4209   Where is your plane?
       Over there — the tri-motor plane.
       What do you mean tri-motor plane?
       If one motor goes bad, we'll try the other.

4210   So you have a plane with a kitchen in it. How did you like cooking
       in the air?
       It was swell for making flapjacks.
       For making flapjacks? Why?
       Oh, we just put the flapjacks on and then looped the loop.

4211   It was wonderful of you to drop ten thousand feet in a parachute.
       Do tell me your sensation.
       Oh — er — er, it was just a kind of sinking sensation.

4212   Why did he go in the air service?
       He was no earthly good.

4213   No one has ever complained of a parachute not opening.

4214   Young lady parachutist: (to traveling companion — making a jump) This is frightfully slow. Isn't there some way of speeding these things up?

4215   Flying is one of those things in which most of us would rather start at the bottom — and stay there.

4216   Only the wife of an aviator is glad to see her husband down and out.

With birds being hit by planes, it won't be long until birds will be considered the pedestrians of the air.

4217   It must be wonderful to be a parachute jumper. I suppose you've had some terrible experiences.
Yes, miss, terrible. Why, once I came down where there was a sign "Keep off the grass."

RELATED SUBJECTS
Sleep 2221-2241
Fresh People 2397-2408
Flirtation 2779-2784
Distance 3982-3986
Scenery 3987-3989
Seasickness 4201-4207
Tip 4274-4276

TRAIN
4218   The train was so crowded I had to sleep in an upper berth. It was so small I stuck my feet out the window and in the morning I found two mail bags on them.

4219   I manufactured this train.
Who said so?
I said so.
Don't make me laugh.
Okay — I'll prove it. What times does this train leave?
Six o'clock.
If I got here at six five?
You would have missed it.
At six ten?
You'd still miss it.
But I got here on time. So I made it. If I made it, I manufactured it.

4220   Who shined my shoes last night?
I did.

One is brown and one is black.
What a coincidence.
What do you mean — a coincidence?
A man got off at Buffalo complained of the same thing.

4221   I had a terrible time falling asleep. There was a terrific noise over
        my head.
        I know what that was. That was a couple of midgets in the upper
        berth rehearsing a tap dance.

4222   I want to catch a late train to New York.
        Take No. 9 — that's usually as late as any.

4223   Do you want to go by Buffalo?
        No, I want to go by train.

4224   You can't use this ticket — it says: "New York fo Chicago," not
        "Chicago to New York."
        That's all right — I'll ride backwards.

4225   Be careful when you cross the railroad tracks.
        Yeah — I always slow down at railroad crossings. You can never
        tell what those crazy railroad men are going to do.

4226   Did you miss that train, sir?
        No! I didn't like the looks of it, so I chased it out of the station.

4227   So you missed your train?
        Yes!
        By how much did you miss it?
        I missed it by just a minute.
        So don't get so excited. The way you're carrying on, it's like you
        missed it by an hour.

4228   Last night he gave up his drawing room on the train to an elderly
        woman. He wired his wife: Home soon. Just gave berth to an
        old lady.

4229   Upper or lower?
        I'll take the lower.
        Sorry, but they're all taken.

4230   Do you want an upper or lower berth?
        Well, what's the difference?
        An upper is lower and a lower is higher.
        That's clear — what other differences are there?
        In the morning if you have an upper you have to get down and
        if you have a lower you have to get up.

4231   Did you meet your son at the station?
        No, I knew him for years.

4232 I was riding on the train, and the conductor threw my suitcase out the window because I didn't pay my fare and my little brother brought back the suitcase.
How could your little brother bring it back?
He was inside of it.

4233 That boy looks over seven years old. I'll have to have a full ticket for him.
He was just seven last week.
He looks pretty old to me.
You are just seven, aren't you, Junior?
Junior starts crying.
Did the conductor offend my little boy?
Junior (Husky voice) No, my pipe burned a hole in my pocket.

4234 Conductor: Sorry, Madam, but we have learned that the station where you intend to get off has been burned to the ground.
Lady: That's all right. They'll probably have it rebuilt by the time this train gets there!

4235 I was just reading about a fellow who has been employed in this country for seven years and can't speak a word of English.
Impossible! What is his employment?
He's a train announcer at the Union Station.

4236 We came in on a radio train.
A radio train?
Yeah, it stopped every five minutes for a station announcement.

4237 How much to carry baggage?
Twenty-five cents the first parcel, then fifteen cents each for each additional parcel.
I will carry the first parcel and you take the other.

4238 What has happened, conductor?
Nothing much — we ran over a cow.
Was it on the track?
No, we chased it into a barn.

4239 Give me a sentence with the word diadem in it.
People who drive onto railroad crossings without looking diadem sight quicker than those who stop, look and listen.

4240 You know that sign downtown that says: This will take you to 42nd Street. The one near the subway?
Yes.
Well, I sat on the sign for two hours and it never moved an inch.

4241 Porter: (on train) Do you want to sleep with your feet to the engine?
Man: No, I don't think they're long enough.

4242 Conductor, we are like sardines here. Can't you prevent our being crushed?

Certainly, sir. Number off the passengers and then make the even numbers breathe in while the odd numbers breathe out.

RELATED SUBJECTS
Accidents 615-709
Sleep 2221-2241
Fresh People 2397-2408
Flirtation 2779-2784
Distance 3982-3986
Scenery 3987-3989
Boat 4174-4200
Airplane 4208-4217
Tip 4274-4276
Food 4825-4878

TICKET

4243 Here's our train. Where are the tickets?
I haven't got them.
Where are they?
In your suit.
(Looks) No, they aren't. They aren't in my coat.
They're in the vest.
I can't find them.
Not that suit — they're in your brown suit.
Where's the brown suit?
In your trunk.

4244 This ticket costs you fifty dollars and allows you a three-day hangover in St. Louis.
And how much if I don't get drunk?

4245 Are you sure the tickets are all right?
Sure, they are. Didn't I put them in the safe just before we started?

4246 Ticket Seller: You'll have to change twice before you get to New York.
Lady: Goodness me! And I've only brought the clothes I be standing up in!

RELATED SUBJECTS
Age 45-107
Admission 4513
Money 5457-5479

HOTEL

HOTEL ACCOMMODATIONS

4247 You want to know our weekly rates? Well, I don't know any one who has ever stayed here a week.

4248 Bellhop: Is there anything else I can do, sir?
Guest: If there was anything else you could do, then you wouldn't have to be a bellhop.

4249 How about a room with a bath?
I'll take the room, but I never take baths.
I noticed . . . We've got one room with a shower.
I'd rather have a bed — I can't sleep standing up.

4250 (Conversation over phone)
Hello.
Say, I want you . . .
Can I do something for you?
Yes. I want you to come here and . . .
I'll be happy to . . .
I want you to remove something from my room . . .
With pleasure. Is it a piece of furniture you don't like?
No — it's a burglar.
Are you sure?
Positive.
Well, in that case I'll send up the house detective.

4251 Do you have hot and cold water in this hotel?
Yes, hot in the summer and cold in the winter.

4252 What was the name of the hotel we stopped at in Detroit?
Wait, I'll look through my towels.

4253 Is this room quiet?
It's never made a sound.

4254 The sign in hotels — Stop, have you left anything? — should be changed to: Stop, have you anything left?

4255 How much is the room?
Fifty dollars a week.
Couldn't you make it a little cheaper?
Well, being as it's you — I'll make it ten dollars a day.

4256 I left a call for seven o'clock. Why didn't you call me?
Well, you didn't come home until seven-thirty.

4257 You see you have to be careful in that hotel — when you turn on the hot water faucet cold water comes out. And when you turn

on the cold water faucet hot water comes out. But it doesn't make any difference.
Why not?
There's no hot water.

4258   What a small room you have — why don't you get a suite?
The doctor told me to stay away from sweets.

4259   I want a room.
Tub or shower?
It makes no difference — I just want to wash my hands.

4260   What do you charge for your rooms?
Twenty dollars and up.
Yes, but I'm a student.
That being the case, the price is twenty dollars down.

4261   There's no door to my room.
Well then, you won't have to worry about losing the key.

4262   I shall have to ask you to pay in advance. Your luggage is too — er — emotional.
Emotional?
Yes, easily moved.

4263   Where's the stationery, please?
Are you a guest of this hotel?
Certainly not — I'm paying sixty dollars a day.

4264   M'friend, I wanna room on the shecond floor.
But you're Mr. Brown, aren't you? We have you registered as occupying room six twenty.
Thash perfectly correct, ol' boy, but I jush fell out of it.

4265   I suppose one dresses for dinner here in your hotel?
Well, suit yourself, sir. But I might add that we charge extra for meals served in bed.

4266   I'd like a room.
Single?
What difference does it make whether I'm single or married, I still want a room.

4267   How about your supper tonight? Shall we bring it up to your room?
If it's going to come up, I'll bring it up myself.

4268   Do you want a single bed or double?
Single — I'm not expecting company.

4269 The hotel clerk was growing impatient because the traveler took
      a long time to read the names on the register.
      Just sign on that line, please.
      Young man, I'm too old a hand to sign anythin' without readin' it.

4270 What have you overlooking the front of the hotel?
      The house detective.

4271 What have you in the way of a suite?
      Oh, I haven't any time for girls.

4272 Lady: Can you give me a room and bath?
      Hotel Clerk: I can give you a room, madam, but you'll have to
      take your own bath.

4273 First Drunk: This hotel's bar is so good, that after one more
      drink, I think I'd buy it!
      Second: Wait! Give me one more, and I'll sell it to you!

RELATED SUBJECTS
Sleep 2221-2241
Waiter 4749-4795
Food 4825-4878

TIP

4274 Do you ever give them any tips?
      Sure. I just gave the bellhop a tip — not to bet on horses and not
      to drink.

4275 What is the difference between valor and discretion?
      Well, to travel on an ocean liner without tipping would be valor.
      I see.
      And to come back on a different boat would be discretion.

4276 So your wife came back from the mountains?
      Yeah, just got back.
      Didn't she stay longer than usual?
      Yes. Couldn't afford to leave there while there were so many
      servants to tip. She had to stay until most of them were gone.

RELATED SUBJECTS
Spendthrift 1990-1996
Economy 1997-2030
Waiter 4749-4795
Money 5457-5479

DETECTIVE

4277 He's a great detective — he's always got his ear to the ground. In fact, he's always in the gutter.

4278 We should be careful who we show our badges to. Yeah, they might take them away from us.

4279 Did he ever solve a great mystery? Yeah — boarding house hash.

RELATED SUBJECTS
Gun 4454-4461
Officers 5132-5133
Criminals 5178-5224
Policeman 5225-5228
Arrest 5229-5230

BEACH

BATHING BEAUTY

4280 How do you like bathing beauties? I don't know — Never bathed any.

BATHING SUIT

4281 (Woman wearing a loud looking bathing suit) Man: If a seagull saw you, he'd go into a tailspin.

4282 Susie was my rival at the beaches all last year. Which of you outstripped the other?

4283 What color bathing suit was she wearing? I couldn't tell. She had her back turned.

RELATED SUBJECTS
Body 338-340
Shape (Physical) 341-347
Fat People 401-404
Flirtation 2779-2784

SUNBURN

4284 How do you keep from getting sunburned? I have a secret — not one chance in a thousand to get sunburned. What is it? I wear an overcoat.

4285 Maybe we should stay indoors and we wouldn't get sunburned. My little sister got sunburned in school. How on earth could your sister get sunburned in school? She came in late and the teacher tanned her hide.

4286 Why don't you get your girl a sunlamp? A sunlamp?

Yeah, I bought my girl one.

She bakes herself with it?

Sure. Yesterday she baked herself six hours and now she's the toast of the town.

4287 Where were you sunburned?

On the beach. It's my own fault. I put on so much oil and butter, I could have sautéed a steak.

4288 I'm having a great time on the beach — I lie on the beach all afternoon — and I lie on the beach all morning — and my maid serves cool drinks. What do you do all day?

I lie, too.

> RELATED SUBJECTS
> Vacation 3965-3970
> Nudist 4305-4318

SWIMMING

4289 How far can you swim?

I don't know.

Could you swim from one end of the boardwalk to the other?

Don't be silly. No one could swim from one end of the boardwalk to the other.

Why not?

There's no water up there.

4290 I'll never forget that wonderful dive you made into the river.

And all I wonder is, who pushed me in?

4291 Do you know all my family were great swimmers?

Yes, I know that. I heard your brother was killed in a dive on the west side.

4292 I went diving in my new swimming pool today, but it will be more fun tomorrow.

Why will it be more fun tomorrow?

Because tomorrow I'm going to put water in it.

4293 Can you swim?

Only at times, ma'am.

Only at times? How strange. And when do these moments of ability come to you?

In the water, ma'am.

4294 I can't swim.

Why?

I ain't in the water.

4295   Never go into the water after a hearty meal, for you'll never find it there.

4296   My sister's been taking swimming lessons and she got a lot of splinters in her hand.
How did she get splinters in her hand swimming?
Crawling on the floor. You see she is taking them by correspondence and she hasn't come to the water part yet.

4297   I've eaten beef all my life, and now I'm as strong as an ox.
That's funny. I've eaten fish all my life and I can't swim a stroke.

> RELATED SUBJECTS
> Shape (Physical) 341-347
> Exercise 382-400
> Nudist 4305-4318

LIFE GUARD

4298   Did you save my little boy from drowning?
Yes.
Well, where's his cap?

4299   What are you doing to my daughter?
She nearly drowned and we're giving her artificial respiration.
The heck you will. There's going to be nothing artificial about it. You give her the genuine. I can afford it.

4300   It must have taken a lot of courage to rescue me as you did.
Yeah. I had to knock down three other guys who wanted to do it.

4301   Just look at you.
I'm a Life Guard. See the sign on my suit? Voluntary Life Saving Corps — that's me!
How did you get to be a Voluntary Life Saver?
I was drafted.

4302   I'm glad to have been of some assistance. Can't we meet again somewhere?
Yes. Save my life tomorrow about the same time.

4303   Help! Help! I'm going down for the third time.
Don't worry, old man. If you don't find it this time, I'll help you.

4304   Marge ought not to go in alone. She was nearly drowned yesterday and Jack had to use artificial respiration.
You mean, Marge had to use artificial drowning.

NUDIST CAMP

NUDIST

4305 How are things at your Nudist Colony?
Well, pretty good. I opened up a little store out there. I'm selling underthings to the Nudists.
What kind of underthings could you sell to Nudists?
Cushions.

4306 So you're not a Nudist any more.
No, I didn't mind it so much when a fellow hung his hat on me, but when a fellow scratched a match on me, that was too much.

4307 My friend the aviator joined the Nudist Colony and when he went back to his firm they fired him. I can't understand why they did it.
That's easy. You can never be an aviator after becoming a Nudist. You can never take off again.

4308 Who is that old fellow over there?
He's a new member.
Was he just initiated into a fraternity?
No, he just backed into a hot stove.

4306 So you're not a Nudist any more.
I lost my hat in a restaurant, suit, coat and shirt in a laundry, and those are the bare facts.

4310 I can't blame him for being a Nudist.
Why?
He was born that way.

4311 My uncle is champion golfer out at the Nudist Colony.
What makes you think he's champion golfer out there?
Because yesterday he went around the whole course in nothing.

4312 I've got a job at the Nudist Colony.
What doing?
Keeping all tattoo artists out of the colony.
Why?
They don't want any skin games going on there.

4313   And then there was the conscientious Nudist who drove into the Nudist Colony and stripped his gears.

4314   Did you go to a Nudist Colony?
       Yeah — and it reminded me of my first trip in an airplane.
       Why?
       I'll never forget the first take-off.

4315   What happened to your husband?
       He has a new job. He is out at the Nudist Colony. He's teaching horseback riding. He's teaching the nudists how to ride bareback.

4316   Simile: As careful as a Nudist crossing a barbed wire fence.

4317   I've just invented a way for Nudists to carry cigarettes, matches and toothbrushes.
       How do they do it?
       With adhesive tape. Just tape a loop each for the brush, the cigarette pack and the matches.

4318   Simile: As broke as a pickpocket in a nudist colony.

RELATED SUBJECTS
Shape (Physical) 341-347
Description of People 263-303
Mosquitoes 3801-3805
Vacation 3965-3970
Swimming 4289-4297

SPORTS

ATHLETE

4319   Where are all the angry farmers you told me about?
       What angry farmers?
       Didn't you tell me to come over and see the cross-countrymen?

4320   Did you have many athletes in your college?
       Oh no — we wouldn't have any athletes around our college.
       Why not?
       Well, haven't you heard about their feet?

4321   Did you ever notice during the Gay Nineties there were very few girl athletes in those days? I wonder why.
       Because they were all bustle-bound.

4322   You say you have done other racing?
       Sure, I got this medal for racing.

What kind of racing?
Raising a family.

4323   What race did you run in?
The human race. Ha-ha — I got you then.
What are you laughing at? You weren't in it.

RELATED SUBJECTS
Stupidity 1337-1381
Sports 4319-4505
School 4885-4894

GOLF

4324   A man was cured of deafness when a golfball struck him on the
head. He was cured of hanging around golf courses, too.

4325   Last Sunday while I was playing golf a man hit me with a golf
ball. I said: That will cost you five dollars.
The man said: Well, I yelled "Fore"!
And I said: I'll take four instead.

4326   What can I do to prevent me from topping all my drives?
Turn the ball upside down.

4327   I like to play golf.
What's your favorite shot?
Scotch, with a little soda.

4328   When you were playing golf, did you ever shoot a birdie?
No, but I once shot at a duck.

4329   You made a pretty drive this afternoon.
Which one do you mean?
The one where you hit the ball.

4330   Well, caddie, I guess I'm about the worst golfer in the world.
Oh, no, sir, there are a lot worse than you, but they don't play.

4331   So the judge fined you fifty dollars for hitting your wife with a
club?
Oh, it wasn't so much for hitting her as it was for using the
wrong club.

4332   There are two times to address a golf ball, before and after
swinging.

4333   So you're a golfer! What's your favorite course?
Soup.

4334   Did you go around the golf course in eighty-one?
What?
I said, I heard you went around the golf course in eighty-one.
Gosh no, I wasn't born in eighty-one.

4335   Do you think it's a sin for me to play golf on Sunday?
       The way you play golf — it's a crime to play any day.

4336   Does he play much golf a day?
       Oh, thirty-six holes roughly speaking.
       And how much without cursing?

4337   Murphy got rich quick, didn't he?
       He got rich so quick that he can't swing a golf club without
       spitting on his hands.

4338   Say, caddy, why do you keep looking at your watch?
       It isn't a watch, sir, it's a compass.

4339   There's a new dictionary of golfing terms just out.
       Well, if it's complete it will be banned.

4340   Your trouble is that you don't address the ball properly.
       Well, I was polite to the darn thing as long as possible.

4341   Hi, caddie! How many strokes did Major Pepper have to take
       to get out of that bunker?
       Seventeen ordinary ones, sir, and one apoplectic.

4342   How's your daughter's golf?
       She says she is going around in less and less every week.
       I don't doubt that, but I asked you about her golf.

4343   Golfer: Pardon, but would you mind if I played through? I've
       just heard that my wife has been taken seriously ill.

4344   My wife says if I don't chuck golf, she'll leave me.
       I say — hard luck!
       Ye-es . . I'll miss her.

4345   You think so much of your old golf game that you don't even
       remember when we were married.
       Of course, I do, my dear; it was the day I sank that thirty-foot
       putt.

4346   Well, how do you like my game?
       I suppose it's all right, but I still prefer golf.

4347   Golf is the game that has turned the cows out of the pasture
       and let the bull in.

4348   He made a perfect thirty-six on the golf course today.
       Nine holes?
       No, Fifth Avenue model.

4349   He never swears when he makes a bum golf shot, but wherever
       he spits, the grass never grows again.

RELATED SUBJECTS
Exercise 382-400
Health (Good) 605-614
Club 3580
Athlete 4319-4323

BASEBALL

4350   She: Oh, look, we have a man on every base.
He: That's nothing, so has the other side.

4351   The radio announcer was transmitting a play-by-play account of the World Series game. At an exciting moment he yelled out: "He swang at it!"
Seventeen sets in Boston burned out.

RELATED SUBJECTS
Games 3604-3613
Sports 4319-4505

FOOTBALL

4352   I'll never forget the time I played there with Lock College.
You mean Yale.
What a game!
What position did you play?
In the first half I was left . . .
End?
Left *out*. In the second half I was back . . .
You were back in?
No, away back.

4353   What position did your cousin play on the football team?
He was back.
Back?
Yeah, he was a drawback.

4354   He played half-back on the team and way back on his studies.

4355   What is a pigskin used for?
To hold the pig together.

4356   How is it you haven't gone in for football?
If those men want to wallow in the mud, let them clean themselves up.
What has mud got to do with football?
They wanted to put me on the scrub team.

4357   (After football game)
       Where'd all these grapes 'round here come from?
       Them's not grapes — them's eyeballs.

4358   (To fat man) What do you do on the team?
       I blow up the footballs.

4359   Man kicks paper bag — says: It's the All-American in me.

4360   Were you a quarterback on the varsity?
       No, I was a nickel back on the bottle.

4361   Watch the game. A defensive player just tackled the right end.
       Ho, I know a better way to win this game than that.
       How?
       Just tackle the player in the ribs.

4362   Have you ever had any football experience?
       Well, not exactly, although I was hit by a truck and two sedans
           this summer.

4363   Your brother enjoys playing football?
       No, but he wants seats to the games after he graduates.

4364   How did the college get such a bad name?
       More men reported for football than were enrolled in school.

4365   Oh, that fellow with the ball is too young for this game.
       Too young? What do you mean?
       Why, don't you see — he's under six.

4366   Do you know anything about football?
       'Most everything. But I am never able to discover who is this
           fellow "Rah" they're always cheering. And another thing I
           can't understand is why half the boys playing win the game.

4367   Why did they stop that man when he was running with the ball?
       You know, the object of the game is to make a goal. He was
           on the other side.
       I don't see why they have to knock him down to tell him about
           it. Everyone makes mistakes.

4368   Then I got the ball and I started down the field. We needed a
           touchdown to win — I ran and ran — forty yards, sixty yards
           — over the goal line and fell on the ground.
       So you won the game and were a hero?
       No, in my excitement to cross the line I lost the ball.

4369   I knew you were on the football team — on account of your
           mustache.
       How could you tell by my mustache?
       I could see the first down on your upper lip.

4370   My nephew has given up his job in a watermelon store and gone on the college team. Every time he passes the football on, he sits down and plugs it to see if it's ripe.

4371   I thought he was a football player when I heard he'd been penalized for passing two bad ones — but then I found it wasn't a football — he was passing out bad checks.

4372   Son returns home from college — great success at football. Old mother has washed and worked hard to send him to college so he can be the best interferer and tackle ever known in the football world.
   Mother: Son, I've worked hard to achieve this end. I wanted you to be the best interferer and tackler in the world.
   Son: But why, mother?
   Mother: Well, with your ability to run interference and tackle, the bargain basements are going to see some of the best Christmas shopping they've ever seen.

4373   I don't see how football players ever get clean!
   Silly, what do you suppose the scrub teams are for?

4374   Football players must be contortionists. They're always going around their own ends.

4375   Are those fifty cent seats far from the scene of action?
   No, not very far, and besides, they're right across the street from a radio store that will broadcast the game.

4376   I'd like a ticket to a football game.
   Yes, ma'am. Which game?
   Oh, one that'll have a thrilling play in the last two minutes.

4377   My brother made a ninety-eight yard run in the big game.
   He did? That's great!
   Yeah, but he didn't catch the man ahead of him.

4378   The Sing Sing football team wants to play the West Point team.
   I wonder why Sing Sing wants to play the army.
   They probably want to prove the pen is mightier than the sword.

4379   Football Coach (to Players): And remember that football develops individuality, initiative, and leadership. Now, get in there and do exactly as I tell you.

RELATED SUBJECTS
Games 3604-3613
Athlete 4319-4323
School 4885-5894
College 5059-5096

FISHING

4380   I went to Fishermen's Wharf — I like the mackerel fine, but I didn't like the smelt.
You don't know your grammar.
You don't know the Fishermen's Wharf either.

4381   Where have you been — hunting?
I've been fishing.
How could you fish with that shotgun?
They were flying fish.
Were they biting today?
If they were, they were biting each other.

4382   What sort of fish is smelt?
Any of 'em, my boy, any of 'em.

4383   I saw your brother fishing in the mud. What's the idea?
Well, his coat fell in and . . .
He can't wear it any more.
I know, but his lunch was in the pocket.

4384   Fishing?
No, just drowning worms.

4385   Father, what is the biggest fish you ever caught?
You had better go and ask your mother. I've forgotten what I told her.

4386   What kind of fish are they?
Jelly fish.
What flavor?

4387   Gosh, I'd hate to be a fish.
Why?
Why, then I'd have to live in schools all my life.

4388   Why does a fish swim backwards?
To keep the water out of his eyes.

4389   Aristocratic Fish: His ancestors swam under the Mayflower.

4390   Do you like codfish balls
I dunno; I never attended any.

4391   Give me a sentence with the word "vermin" in it.
Before I go fishin' I go vermin'.

4392   There's a package of fish here, ma'am, marked C.O.D.
Send it right back. I never learned how to fix cod.

4393   I heard you went fishing this afternoon. How did you come out?
I got plenty of left shoes, but the right shoes didn't seem to be biting at all.

4394   In that country fish is so plentiful — they use it as a medium of
       exchange.
       They use fish as a medium of exchange?
       That's right.
       They must have a messy time playing with slot machines.

4395   I learned something interesting about whales. The small ones
       don't spout out as much water as the larger ones.
       Oh, yes, they are just young squirts.

4396   What do you do when you get a bite?
       Scratch it.
       What a fisherman you must be!

4397   Diner: Do you serve crabs here?
       Waiter: We serve any one — sit down!

4398   Do you know the best place to find clams?
       No. Where?
       On a plate.

4399   I tell you it was that long. I never saw such a fish!
       I believe you.

4400   I've been fishing.
       How could you go fishing? The river is frozen over with ice.
       I know — but I cut a hole in the ice — hold a watch over the
       hole, and when the fish come up to see what time it is I hit
       them over the head.

4401   First Pelican: Pretty good fish you have there.
       Second Pelican: Well, it fills the bill.

4402   You've been watching me for three hours. Why don't you try
       fishing yourself?
       I ain't got the patience.

4403   Is this fellow McFall all right to take on a fishing trip?
       Is he? Say, besides doing the cooking, he'll think up fishing
       stories for the whole bunch.

4404   Last summer I caught a bass that long — but I threw it back.
       Why throw it back? Sounds foolish!
       Well, I had my hook baited for sunfish.

4405   I know a swell place to go fishing.
       Where?
       Well, you know that old farm just outside the city limits?
       Yes.
       Well, about five miles down the road, there's a place marked
       "Private." You go through the gate — it has a sign on it:
       "Keep out — Trespassers will be prosecuted." Then east of

that there is a sign that says: "Positively no fishing."
What about it?
That's the place.

4406 If the fish aren't happy to be caught, why do they wag their tails at me when I pull them out of the water?

4407 (Man fishing for hours without a bite)
Little Boy: Oh, do let me see you catch a fish.
Mother: Now, don't you catch a fish for him until he says Please.

4408 Let me hear you say fish without closing your mouth.
Herring.

4409 Can any little boy tell me what a fish net is made of?
A lot of little holes tied together with strings.

4410 I don't like the looks of that codfish.
Well, if you want looks, why don't you buy a goldfish?

4411 I wonder why lobsters are red.
If you were in a glass case without any clothes, you'd be red, too.

4412 Do fish perspire?
Of course, nut. Whadda you think makes the sea salty?

4413 You don't mean to tell me that fishes are musical?
Certainly. Did you never hear of the piano tuna?

RELATED SUBJECTS
Exaggeration 1507-1517
Lying 1540-1564
Boast 2285-2304
Mosquitoes 3801-3805
Vacation 3965-3970
Food 4825-4878

WORM

4414 It probably took a thousand silk worms to make that dress.
Isn't it wonderful what they can train some worms to do?

4415 Mae West paid a visit to the zoo and all the animals would turn and stare as she passed.
You mean, even the animals turned to watch her?
Sure, when Mae West walks along, even a worm will turn.

4416 You know a worm will turn. Well, you can tell if it's a lady worm because when a lady worm turns she doesn't stick out her hand.

4417 Is your husband a bookworm?
No — just an ordinary one.

4418 Some day the worm will turn.
      But what's the idea in turning? It's the same on both ends,
        isn't it?

RELATED SUBJECTS
Garden 3761-3767

SHARK

4419 You just finished making a trip to the South Sea Islands.
      Yeah — and what a spot. The whole island is surrounded by man-
        eating sharks. Every time I'd go out swimming there'd be
        thousands of them around me and . . .
      Hey — wait a minute. Don't tell me you'd go out and swim
        around with man-eating sharks?
      Sure, I would — they never bother me.
      How come?
      I have a tattoo on my chest that protects me.
      Don't give me that. What is it you've got tattooed on your chest
        then?
      "Nixon was innocent" — and not even a shark would swallow
        that.

4420 I saw a man-eating shark at the aquarium.
      That's nothing; I saw a man eating herring in the park.

4421 Can I buy a live shark here?
      Gosh, lady, what do you want with a live shark?
      A neighbor's cat has been eating my goldfish and I want to teach
        him a lesson.

4422 First Shark: What's that funny two-legged thing that just fell
        in the water?
      Second Shark: I dunno, but I'll bite.

HUNTING

4423 A big lion made a rush at me. I didn't want to kill him, so I
        took a stick and hit him on the tail.
      And that was the end of the lion?

4424 I shaved every morning.
      You mean to tell me you shaved while you were hunting?
      Yeah, I had a lot of close shaves.

4425   I went hunting — and shot a raccoon.
Was it a big one?
Was it a big one? I found two college boys in it.

4426   I went lion hunting with a club.
Hunting lions with a club? Weren't you afraid?
No, there were about two hundred members in the club.

4427   What are you doing with that rifle?
I'm hunting for elephants.
But there are no elephants around here.
If there were, I wouldn't have to hunt for them, would I?

4428   Say, boy, did you see a fox run by here?
Yes, sir.
How long ago?
It'll be a year next Christmas.

4429   Why was he arrested?
For shooting quail.
Doesn't he know quail isn't in season?
Well, when it is in season, the quail aren't around, and there are
   lots of them when it isn't the season. If the quail don't obey
   the rule, he won't either.

4430   The city man went to the country to do a bit of hunting. A
   country acquaintance provided the dogs to accompany the
   hunter. The hunter sallied forth only to return in about an
   hour.
Country Friend: Well, why are you back so soon?
Hunter: I'm after more dogs.
Country Friend: More dogs! Those were good dogs I gave you.
Hunter: I know, but I've shot all those dogs already.

4431   I went hunting the other day and the dogs got in the way of a
   skunk. Finally, they gave up the chase.
Did they lose the scent?
They gave up the skunk, but I don't think they will ever lose
   the scent.

4432   Never shoot a duck standing. You must shoot a duck on the
   wing.
Can't I shoot him on the leg?
Yes, but you have to shoot him on the wing.
How can I shoot him on the leg and shoot him on the wing?
Just remember to wing a duck on the wing and everything will
   be rosy.
I know the game — Wing 'round the rosy.

4433   How can you tell the difference between ducks and geese?
       A duck goes quack quack and a goose goes honk honk. Now, if
          you were hunting and a flock of birds came into sight and
          went honk honk, what would you do?
       I'd step aside and let them pass.

4434   You need a decoy when hunting ducks.
       What's a decoy?
       It's like a duck, acts like a duck and still isn't a duck.
       Now, I'll ask one.

4435   He's a big dame hunter.

4436   Suppose you saw a lion — what steps would you take if he were
          coming towards you?
       Long ones.
       You know you're liable to run into an elephant over in Borneo.
          Have you got a gun?
       Of course, I got a gun.
       But does it shoot elephants?
       No, it shoots bullets.

4437   You're going hunting?
       Yes.
       But where are your pants?
       That's what I'm hunting for.

4438   Once I shot a buck.
       You did?
       Yeah, then I shot two bucks, then I shot three bucks and then I
          shot five bucks.
       Then what happened?
       Somebody hollered "Cheese it the cops" — and I dropped the
          dice and ran.

4439   Son, do you like steeple chasing?
       I don't know . . . I never chased any.

4440   How do you know you hit that duck?
       I shot him in the foot and in the head at the same time.
       How could you possibly hit him in the foot and head at the
          same time?
       He was scratching his head.

4441   The last time I went hunting for wild turkey, I didn't get any.
       You went on a wild goose hunt?
       No, a turkey chase. I only saw one turkey, and he was a duck.
       What do you mean?
       I threw a rock at him and made him duck.

4442 While we were hunting a big animal passed by me.
Reindeer?
No, it just poured, darling.

4443 There, Jack, I'm sure I hit that one.
Well, the rabbit certainly did seem to go faster after you shot
at him.

4444 I shot this tiger in India. It was a case of me or the tiger.
Well, the tiger certainly makes the better rug.

4445 Look at the lion's tracks.
You can't fool me — lions don't run on tracks — street cars run
on tracks.

4446 Have any luck hunting lions in Africa?
Yes, I didn't meet one.

4447 Gus, are all the rest of the boys out of the woods yet?
Yes.
All six of them?
Yes, all six of them.
And they're all safe?
Yep, they're all safe.
Then I've shot a deer.

4448 I just crept out and shot the brute in my pajamas.
But, Colonel, how did the elephant get into your pajamas?

4449 If an elephant charges you, let him have both barrels at once.
And the gun, too, so far as I'm concerned.

4450 Here's a telegram from Frank in Africa. He says he is sending us
some lions' tails.
Lions' tails? What are you talking about?
Well, read it yourself. It says quite clearly: Just captured two
lions. Sending details by mail.

4451 While we were hunting, I could have shot a bear.
Why didn't you?
I didn't like the look on his face — he wouldn't have made a
good rug.

4452 How can hunters locate game in the woods?
I don't know — how?
By listening to the bark of the trees.

4453 You are accused of shooting squirrels out of season. Have you
any plea?
Yes, your Honor. Self-defense.

GUN

4454 My father always carries a young horse pistol with him.
A young horse pistol?
Yeah — a colt.

4455 Here is a nice pistol, lady. It shoots nine times.
Say, what do you think I am — a polygamist?

4456 He pointed his gun at me.
Did he shoot?
He couldn't. I had my finger over the hole.

4457 Have you got a gun?
Of course, I've a gun.
Is it a good gun? What does it shoot?
Bullets, silly.

4458 Mother went down to buy a revolver.
Did your father tell her what kind to get?
No, he doesn't even know she's going to shoot him.

4459 Now, take this rifle and find out how to use it.
Tell me one thing. Is it true that the harder I pull the trigger
the farther the bullet will go?

4460 Wake up, John, wake up! There's a burglar in the house.
Well, I've no revolver. You go and look daggers at him.

4461 Did you hear? Joe shot himself twice, cleaning his gun.
Oh? Seriously?
Well, the first wound proved to be fatal, but the second one
wasn't so bad.

HORSE RACING

4462 I had a chance to make a cleanup — a chance to make a lot of
money on the horse race. I put a dollar on her head and a
dollar on her tail — bound to win no matter how she came in.

4463   The other day I picked a horse that I thought could win in
        a walk.
        And did it?
        The other horses double-crossed it and outran him.

4464   I'm betting on a horse that's starting 20 to 1. And I can't lose.
        What do you mean, you can't lose?
        I can't lose. The horse is starting 20 to 1, and the race don't
        start until one.

4465   I bet on a horse once.
        Did he win?
        No, I think he just ran out of curiosity!
        What do you mean — out of curiosity?
        The only reason he was in the race was to see if the other horses
        had tails.

4466   I put everything I owned on that horse you told me to bet on —
        and he lost.
        Lost! Why, he could have won in a walk.
        No — he tried that.

4467   Why don't you back horses?
        I backed a horse one time and lost fifteen dollars.
        How was that?
        I backed him into a store window.

4468   I put a two dollar bill on a horse once.
        What happened?
        The wind blew it off.

4469   What became of the horses since automobiles came out?
        If you played the races — you'd know without asking.

4470   Animals are superior to human beings. There are thirty horses
        in a race and fifty thousand people go to see it, but put thirty
        people in a race and not one horse would go to see it.

4471   Last week he won a race — he was head and head with another
        horse.
        If he was head and head with the other horse, how did he win
        the race?
        In order to finish right, he stuck out his tongue.

4472   I'd like to sell you a horse.
        If I did buy a horse, I'd only race him.
        Well, you'd beat this horse.

4473   Were you lucky at the races yesterday?
        I should think I was. I found a dollar after the last race, so I
        didn't have to walk home.

4474   What happens to horses you follow, Albert?
Oh, they usually follow the other horses.

4475   Is it wrong to bet on the horses?
It is the way I do.

4476   I lost fifty dollars on that tip you gave me for the horse race.
You told me that horse could win in a walk and he finished
last.
He could have won in a walk, but it was a running race.

4477   An inside tip meant a lot of money to me at yesterday's race.
It did?
Yeah, I got a tip my wife was there and I arrived in time to
stop her from making any bets.

4478   Horses can sleep standing up.
Yeah, but why do they wait until I've placed a bet on them to
do it?

4479   We're going to have Pete, the jockey, say a few words to you.
I never knew . . . I never knew . . .
I never knew anything filled with hay could be so hard.

4480   Girl: (at horse race) Come on anybody! Come on anybody!
Man: There is no horse named "Anybody."
Girl: I know. I bet on them all.

RELATED SUBJECTS
Dishonesty 2500-2502
Horse 3845-3854
Gambling 4500-4505
Money 5457-5479

DOG RACING

4481   I went to the dog races last night and I bet on a dog called
Wise Guy.
How did you make out?
He lost. He went all right up to the middle of the race, then he
stopped, turned right back to where he started from.
What happened to him?
He found out the rabbit he was chasing was a dummy.

4482   I've got a new dog — a dachshund — I entered him in the races
last Saturday.
How did he make out?
It was a circular track and he overtook himself.

RELATED SUBJECTS
Dog 3696-3740
Fleas 3778-3789

HORSEBACK RIDING

4483 Why didn't you ride in the Bridle Path?
I thought that was only for newly married couples.

4484 Do you think I could be a good horseman?
Well, you could at least look like part of the horse.
What part of the horse?
You'd do all right as that part under the mane, you horse's neck.

4485 Have you a riding habit?
No, I haven't been riding long enough to get the habit.

4486 I went horseback riding today.
Well, sit down and tell me about it.
I can't.
You mean, you can't tell me about the ride?
No, I can't sit down.

4487 Do you prefer an English saddle or a Western?
What's the difference?
The Western saddle has a horn.
I don't think I'll need the horn. I don't intend to ride in heavy
traffic.

4488 You're a wonderful horseman. I never thought you could stay
on that horse.
I just had to.
Why?
My pants were caught under the saddle.

4489 I was horseback riding yesterday and from the after effects I
think I'll learn to ride side saddle.
Why do that?
It saves a little place where you can sit down the next day.

4490 How come I didn't see you out on the bridle path this morning?
You know that mare I've been riding?
Yes.
Well, she had a Charlie horse.
Oh, I'll bet it's cute.

4491 That horse has never had anyone on him.
I've never been on a horse — so we start off even.

4492 They tell me when I'm in the saddle I'm a part of the horse.
Yeah, but they didn't tell you what part.

4493 I saw you riding a horse this morning. You were sitting on the
horse backwards. You were riding the wrong way.
How do you know which way I was going?

4494   That was a beautiful horse you were riding Sunday, but why
did you have that piece of iron tied to her tail?
Well, I felt sorry for her. She kept switching the flies off with
her tail. So I tied the iron on her tail so she could kill 'em and
then they couldn't come back to bite her.

RELATED SUBJECTS
Exercise 382-400
Horse 3845-3854

PRIZEFIGHT

4495   Boxer: Have I done him any damage?
Disgusted Second: No, but keep swinging. The draft might give
him a cold.

4496   What are you putting in your glove?
My good luck piece — my horseshoe.

4497   If you find you're losing the fight just start singing and we'll call
it off.
Well, if I'm out of tune, you'll know he knocked me flat.

4498   Don't be frightened — I'll not hit you with both hands.
You won't?
No, I'll only hit you with one hand. I'll need the other to hold
you up.

4499   Stop those punches!
You don't see them getting by me, do you?

RELATED SUBJECTS
Exercise 382-400
Ears 498-505
Stupidity 1337-1381
Sports 4319-4505

GAMBLING

4500   Do you gamble for money?
No, but my opponents do.

4501   I'm positively through with gambling forever.
Forever? I don't believe it.
Is that so? I'll bet you five dollars I'll quit.

4502   Do you know the biggest gambler that ever lived?
No — who?
Lady Godiva was the biggest — she put all she had on one horse.

4503   How did he die?
He passed away during a card game.
What did he die of?
Five aces.

4504   Let's go and play some poker.
No, thank you. I don't play the game.
I was under the impression you played poker.
I was under that impression myself — once.

4505   You don't even know where you are! I'll wager you twenty
dollars you're not even here and I'll prove it.
All right, go ahead.
You're not in St. Louis?
No, I'm not in St. Louis.
And you're not in Chicago?
No, I'm not in Chicago.
Well, if you're not in St. Louis or Chicago, you must be some
place else, and if you're some place else you can't be here. (Other
guy snatches money)
I didn't lose — give me back my money.
Whadda-yuh mean?
You took the money right out of my hand.
I did not.
You did.
Listen, you said I wasn't here — I was some place else. And if I
was some place else I couldn't be here. And if I couldn't be
here, how could I take your twenty dollars?

RELATED SUBJECTS
Drinking 2055-2140
Dishonesty 2500-2502
Hospitality 3564-3660
Boat 4174-4200
Airplane 4208-4217
Train 4218-4242
Luck 5588
Sports 4319-4505

ENTERTAINMENT

THEATRE

4506   I only saw one act and I left.
Why didn't you see act two?
The program said, act two same as act one.

4507   How's business?
The opening night nobody came; the next night it fell off a little.

4508   Oh, Phil, it says: Entire Balcony $2.50.
       What of it?
       Let's get it so we can be all alone.

4509   Last night I saw the fastest leg-show in town.
       So you took in a burlesque performance, eh?
       No, the six-day bicycle race.

4510   So you went to a great topless nightclub.
       Yes, thank goodness. My wife had to wait until we got home to
         hit the ceiling.

4511   I saw the first act, but not the second.
       Why not?
       I couldn't wait that long. It said on the program — second act
         two years later.

4512   Aren't the acoustics fine?
       You bet. I'll have to congratulate 'em before I leave.

RELATED SUBJECTS
Writer 1612-1642
Applause 4586-4590

ADMISSION

4513   The cheek of that conductor. He glared at me as if I hadn't
         paid my fare.
       And what did you do?
       I glared right back as if I had.

RELATED SUBJECTS
Ticket 4243-4246
Money 5457-5479

ACTOR

4514   I hear your brother has been in the movies.
       Yeah, but he had to quit on account of an accident.
       What happened?
       He was catching a custard pie on the face and some one had
         slipped a horseshoe in it.

4515   In that death scene of mine, I moved them all to tears.
       Yeah, they knew you were only playing dead.

4516   I'll never forget the first performance I gave. Was I bad!
       Who told you you were bad?
       A little bird.
       A little bird?
       Don't you get it?
       No.
       Well, I got it.

4517   I've been watching them shoot pictures in Hollywood.
       What do you think about the movies?
       I've decided the world would be a better place if they'd shoot
          less pictures and more actors.

4518   Did you see him in Hamlet?
       Yes. He played the king as though he expected somebody to
          trump him.

4519   What is your brother's profession?
       He's a vegetarian.
       A vegetarian isn't a profession.
       He's an actor, and only eats vegetables because the audience
          doesn't throw meat at him. But he lives in hopes.

4520   I knew an actor once who took his bows before the play even
          began.
       Why did he do that?
       He wanted to be sure there was somebody there.

4521   I have an important part in a play.
       Oh — are you the leading man?
       Well, not exactly. You see when the play begins, I'm the man
          who opens the door for the leading man.
       That's not so important.
       No? Say, if I wasn't there to open the door, how would the
          leading man get on the stage — and where'd your show be?

4522   Which of your roles did the audience like best?
       Romeo and Juliet. I was Romeo. I slipped and fell off the
          balcony.
       That was embarrassing. I suppose your audience was disap-
          pointed?
       You know they were disappointed because I was able to get up
          and continue.

4523   Do you know how to make up?
       Sure. I just kiss my girl and say I'm sorry.

4524   I gave a moving performance. Everyone was moved . . .
       Yeah — towards the nearest exit.

4525   Sampson and Delilah put on the first successful vaudeville show.
       How's that?
       Their act brought the house down!

4526   I was given a hand when I entered.
       Yes, and you were given the bird when you left.

4527   He's such a ham he belongs between two pieces of bread.

4528   (Romeo and Juliet)
       Kiss me, Romeo, and I'll go home.
       I can't.
       Please kiss me, Romeo, and I'll go home.
       No, I'm sorry — but I can't.
       Oh, Romeo, please — please kiss me and I'll go home.
       Voice: (from audience) Kiss her — go on and kiss her and
       we'll all go home.

4529   How did you like me in that show? I think I did good consid-
       ering I was shot in the first act.
       You did swell — the only thing wrong with the show was you
       should have been shot before the curtain went up.

4530   Once I was a famous actor. I did an Oriental act and all during
       the act I burned incense.
       I heard you did a punk act.

4531   They wanted to put me on after the monkey act. I refused to
       go on.
       I know why you wouldn't go on. You were afraid the audience
       would think it was an encore.

4532   Don't stand too near the footlights — they're hot and your corns
       might pop.

4533   Dad, what is an actor?
       An actor? My son, an actor is a man who can walk to the side
       of a stage, peer into the wings filled with theatrical props,
       dirt and dust, other actors, stagehands, old clothes, and other
       claptrap and say: What a lovely view there is from this win-
       dow.

4534   By Jove, he's wonderful. The way he displays affection toward
       the leading lady, eh?
       Yes — pretty good — but you know he's been married to her
       for eighteen years.
       What? Really married! Gosh — what an actor.

4535   Why aren't you people working in pictures?
       On account of sinus trouble.

Sinus trouble?
Yeah, nobody will sinus. (sign us)

4536   Good news! I've booked your performing pigeons for a six weeks'
       tour.
       Too late — I've eaten the act.

4537   Yes, my friends, usually my audiences are glued to their seats.
       What a quaint way of keeping them there.

4538   Casting Director: What experience have you had?
       Applicant: I was the fellow that called up on the telephone in
       the third act of our senior play.

4539   My sister's practicing to be an actress.
       She is?
       Yeah, and so far she's learned how to sleep until eleven o'clock
       in the morning.

4540   In my last show I was a lady killer.
       You a lady killer? In what show did you play that part?
       Bluebeard.

4541   How did you like our jokes?
       I can't see anything funny in them.
       Oh, well, you'll probably catch on after a while and laugh.
       No, I laughed at 'em twenty years ago.

4542   I think your gags are very good.
       Most of them have come across.
       Yeah, on the Mayflower.

4543   Dear Radio Star: Before you came on the air, I was hungry.
       After hearing you, I'm absolutely fed up.

4544   If you'd take all the Hollywood extras and put them end to
       end, they'd reach for a sandwich.

4545   Do you think they got that joke about the medals?
       I think so, it is a good joke.
       It always was.

4546   I'm very old-fashioned.
       You're old-fashioned?
       Yeah. Sometimes I find myself telling jokes my grandfather told.

4547   A lot of people listen to you!
       Sure — on the air. Why, I've even gotten fan mail from coal
       miners. As a matter of fact, radio reception is better under-
       ground.
       Goodness! Will I have to listen to you after I die!

4548 You're lucky. With this broadcast you reach millions of people
and they can't reach you.
Well, they can't reach you, either.

4549 Do you think I had better put more fire into my jokes?
No, put your jokes in the fire.

4550 So you didn't like my jokes.
No, they were terrible.
Oh, I don't know about that — I threw a bunch of them in the
furnace and the fire roared.

4551 I can't think of any jokes. I've got millions of them. Salesmen
jokes — Irish jokes . . .
Know anything about bugs or fleas?
Got millions of them . . .
You're telling me.

4552 Why not tell a joke?
I suppose I might as well.
Yeah — you've got to start some time.

4553 It must be an awful job making up jokes.
You'll have to ask someone who makes them up. I used to but
now I get them out of a book.
Why did you quit making them up?
I wanted to hear the audience laugh once in a while.

4554 She has the leading part in a theatre.
Star?
No — head usher.

4555 How many jokes have I had since I've been on the air?
Ten — all told.

4556 Have you had any experience on the air?
Yeah, I fell out of a balloon once.

4557 If you heard something funny on this program what would you
think?
I'd think somebody else was on the show.

4558 This joke ought to be good — I've had it in my head for ten
years.
Sort of aged in the wood, eh?

4559 If all the actors in Hollywood were laid end to end it would
probably be because they're making scenes for a prison picture.

4560 Fireman: Jump, lady, jump! We'll catch you in the net.
Actor: I'll do nothing of the sort. Tell the director to send my
double here at once.

4561   Do you know that your rooster is dead?
Dead. What happened to him?
He couldn't swallow that last joke you told.
I get it — joked to death!

4562   Now, here is where you jump off the cliff.
Yeah, but suppose I get injured or killed?
Oh, that's all right. It's the last scene in the picture.

RELATED SUBJECTS
Impersonation 1863-1868
Egotism 2305-2319
Radio 4598-4610

CHORUS GIRL

4563   The boys are pretty nervous tonight — they were held up by
stage robbers last night.
Is that so?
Yeah, they took a couple of chorus girls to dinner.

4564   A chorus girl gets her education by stages — a college girl by
degrees.

4565   I hear you took those chorus girls out to dinner. What did they
eat?
Soup, salad, fish, chicken, dessert and coffee.
What did you have?
Heart failure.

RELATED SUBJECTS
Description of People 263-303
Legs 433-439
Music 1747-1752
Dancing 3584-3603
Beauty 4725-4735

MAGICIAN

4566   We had a magician for dinner last night. When we served him
some stewed rabbit, he tasted it and left the table immediately.
Father said it was very unusual.

What was so unusual about that?

That really is unusual, because it's probably the first time on record that a rabbit made a magician disappear.

4567 Nurse: There! (She hands startled magician a bouncing baby boy) Let's see you make a bunny out of that!

RELATED SUBJECTS
Rabbit 3861-3862
Circus 4611-4613

MASTER OF CEREMONY

4568 Who called that master of ceremonies a monkey?
Who called that monkey a master of ceremonies?

4569 I want to be a massacre of ceremonies.
You mean a master of ceremonies.
No, I want to be a massacre of ceremonies — I wants to kill 'em.

4570 When you were a baby I knew you were going to be a master of ceremonies.
Why?
You talked for hours and hours and said nothing.

RELATED SUBJECTS   Actor 4514-4585
Names of People 939-1017 Applause 4586-4590
Humor 2365-2380   Radio 4598-4610

MOVIE STARS

4571 Where have you been all afternoon?
I saw a picture called "Henry the 16th."
You mean "Henry the 8th." Where did you get that sixteenth stuff?
I sat through it twice.

4572 How you been doing out in Hollywood?
Fine, just fine. I appeared in "The Dirty Dozen" and I'm signed up to play the Fool in "King Lear."
Type-casting, I suppose.

4573 Fan: Excuse me. Aren't you Robert Redford?
Actor: Yes, I am.
Fan: I thought so — you look so much like him!

4574 Do you know that without advertising, Clark Gable couldn't have become the great American lover?
How did he advertise?
Just by mouth to mouth advertising.

4575 Tell me, the movie you made — does it have an unhappy ending?
It may have the week after it opens.

4576   Look who is coming up the walk — that beautiful star, Lupe Velez. And who's that with her?
Weismuller in a striped suit — (Music starts) Hear their theme song, "The Tarzan's Stripes Forever."

4577   How many film stars can you name who have never been in a divorce court?
Well — there was Rin-Tin-Tin.

4578   It will be a great publicity stunt. We've got it all arranged. Pete Jones, the greatest Western star in the world, will ride down the avenue. All you have to do is pay thirty-five dollars for the rental of the horse.
It ain't that I'm kicking about — the money's nothing — but how do I know he can ride?

4579   Do you know why Greta Garbo vacations in Texas?
No, why?
Because it's the Lone Star State, silly.

4580   If I make you a star you must lead a life of strict decorum.
But can't my understudy do that?

4581   Don't you think that movie star is improving?
Yes, she's marrying a better grade of man every year.

4582   (Mae West descriptive adjectives) Old and Shaky! — Fair and Warmer! — So long, Chills and Fever! — Fat and Forty! — Hello, Bread and Butter! — Hello, Dark and Handsome! — Small and Shaggy! — Small and Rancid!

4583   Yesterday I took my brother for a ride on a roller coaster. He must have been drunk because as we were going up and down on the roller coaster, he said: Goodness, we're running over Mae West.

4584   I won't let my girl go to the movies because every time she sees Robert Redford it takes her three or four days to get used to me again.

4585   I sat through that picture show three times last night.
Why, I heard it was terrible!
That's just it! It was so lousy I had to sit through it three times to get my money's worth.

RELATED SUBJECTS
Egotism 2305-2319
Clothing 3391-3502
Autograph 4591-4593
Beauty 4725-4735

Worm 4415
Actor 4517; 4544
Famous People 5031

APPLAUSE

4586 When you left the stage I heard the audience went wild with applause.
That's because they knew I wasn't coming back any more.

4587 They presented me with the house — a brick at a time.

4588 Why do you keep applauding such a poor play?
To keep awake.

4589 You received a tremendous ovation; they're still clapping — what did you say?
I told them I would not go on with my act until they quieted down.

4590 Fran was just awful in the play today!
She says they applauded only half as good as yesterday.
Yeah, everyone clapped with only one hand.

RELATED SUBJECTS
Speech 5111-5123

AUTOGRAPH

4591 I've got to go and get the Armless Man's autograph before he puts on his shoes and stockings.

4592 Could I have your autograph?
But this is a blank check.
Sure, on plain paper I can get anybody's signature.
But if I fill it out you can fill out the check for any amount.
You ain't that rich.

4593 But I've signed your book before.
Yes, sir, but when I get ten of yours I can swap them for one of Elizabeth Taylor.

RELATED SUBJECTS
Actor 4514-4585
Famous People 5029-5042

SHAKESPEARE

4594 Why, don't you know that's a quotation from Shakespeare?
Shakespeare is immortal.
What do I care about his sex life?

4595 I suppose you read Shakespeare.
Oh, yes, I read all of his stuff as soon as it comes out.

4596   What did Juliet say when she met Romeo in the balcony?
       Couldn't you get seats in the orchestra?

4597   If Shakespeare were here today, he would be looked on as a
       remarkable man.
       Yes, he'd be more than three hundred years old.

                              RELATED SUBJECTS
                              Theatre 4506-4512
                              Actor 4514-4585
                              Radio 4598-4610
       RADIO

4598   My little brother is so dumb, that when the TV went on the
       blink, he said: I don't care. I'll just go in and watch the radio.

4599   I was listening to the President on the radio the other night. He
       seems perfectly familiar with the questions of the day.
       Yeah? Too bad he didn't know any of the answers!

4600   You'll never make a radio announcer.
       Why not?
       I heard every word you said.

4601   You can get anything on this radio.
       There are two things I can't get on my radio.
       What are they?
       The last two payments.

4602   Hello! Is this the City Gas Works?
       No, this is a radio station.
       Well, I didn't miss it very far, did I?

4603   We washed the network this afternoon and can't do anything
       with it.

4604   The radio has added five thousand words to our vocabulary —
       not including those used when the thing won't work.

4605   Turn on the radio.
       (Talk issues forth in Pig Latin)
       What is that?
       Pig Latin. They're broadcasting a message to the road hogs.

4606   Two minutes B.C.
       Two minutes B.C.?
       Yeah — two minutes before commercial.

4607   Radio announcers should start off the morning broadcast with:
       Who the hell left the radio on all night?

4608 (Loud shots)
What happened?
He's just been knifed!
Knifed? I heard three shots.
Sure — you can't hear a knife over the radio.

4609 They used to believe that the radio would replace the newspaper,
but it never happened.
No, you can't housebreak a dog on a radio.

4610 Please, Tommy, turn off the radio. That lady announcer with
the rasping voice ought to be kept off the air!
But mother, it isn't the radio — it's Mrs. Jones to see you.

RELATED SUBJECTS
Writer 1612-1642
Music 1747-1752
Humor 2365-2380
Actor 4514-4585

CIRCUS

4611 What kind of a circus is this?
Just like you.
What do you mean, just like me?
It's a freak circus.

4612 I have found a new circus act — the friendship of a lion and
a goat.
But doesn't that cause trouble? Don't they quarrel sometimes?
Oh, yes, they have their little quarrels, but then we buy a new
goat.

4613 I could only get two bags of peanuts.
How come?
The man was looking.

RELATED SUBJECTS
Admission 4513
Animals (Wild) 4640-4668

FREAKS

4614   (Big commotion)
What's the matter?
It's Stella, the fat woman. Her husband has eloped.
What of it? I can't take his place.
She won't stop crying. The last time she had a crying fit, a
couple of midgets were drowned.

4615   How did Madam Torso lose the lower part of her body?
Well, one night before retiring she started cutting her corns.
She got one of her absentminded spells and the first thing she
knew she'd cut her corns up to here. (Indicating)

4616   (Bearded lady explaining how she got that way.)
When I was a baby my mother mistook the hair tonic for paregoric, and the hair has come out like the old Harry ever since.

4617   What's the commotion over by the side show tent?
The fire-eater just drank some whisky straight and is burning up.

4618   I'm going to join a circus.
What are you going to do in a circus?
I'm going to be a midget.
You're too big for a midget.
That's the idea. I'll be the biggest midget in the world.

4619   How did he lose his arms?
He was eating pigs' feet and ate right up to his elbow before
he knew it was his own arms.

4620   That half-man, half-woman mumbles constantly.
Yes, she's always talking to himself.

RELATED SUBJECTS
Description of People 263-303
Fat People 348-370
Thin People 401-404

HUMAN SKELETON

4621   The human skeleton won't eat anything but olives.
He won't eat anything but olives?
No. Tonight he ate so many olives for dinner that he looked like
a string of beads.

RELATED SUBJECTS
Thin People 401-404

INDIA RUBBER MAN

4622   I have the India Rubber Man in my circus.
Has he ever been in jail?
No, he's never done a stretch in jail. My India Rubber man is
a bona fide rubber man — he was born in Czechoslovakia.
Oh, a rubber check.

4623   The India Rubber Man is very moody. He sat there at the table
and wouldn't eat a bite on account of his new set of teeth —
he just couldn't eat.
Why didn't you tell him to snap out of it?

4624   Circus Manager: Well, now what's wrong?
India Rubber Man: Every time the strong man writes a letter
he uses me to rub out the mistakes.

4625   A deafening report is followed by a groan. The circus hands run
from all directions. Had a tent stay snapped or a cage fallen
over? Perhaps someone had been shot. A crowd quickly
gathered in a far corner of the tent. A form lay prostrate and
silent on the ground. The India Rubber Man had had a
blowout.

4626   I see your girl friend was out with the India Rubber Man last
night.
What — that bounder?

4627   What's become of the India Rubber man?
Oh, he's gone up to Sing Sing for a stretch.

SWORD SWALLOWER

4628   What do you think of the Sword Swallower?
My uncle wanted to become a Sword Swallower.
How did he make out?
Not very good — every time he started to swallow a sword he'd
get the hiccups.

4629   The Sword Swallower is on a diet — just eating pins.

4630   The Sword Swallower is on a diet.
What's he eating?
Hasn't had anything but pen knives for a week.

4631   What did the Sword Swallower say when she picked up the
clown's foot by mistake?
My, but that tastes flat!

TATTOOED MAN

4632 (Telling how he happened to be tattooed)
I like to sleep late, but the wife and kids bothered me — wanted me to read the funny papers to them. So I had all the funnies tattooed on my body — now I can sleep late and the wife and kids don't bother me. (Proudly) I did it for the wife and kids.

4633 The tattooed lady went on a leave of absence.
Why — what happened?
She had a face-lift and now she has to redo her feet.

4634 My brother won his fight last night.
Why, I didn't know he was such a good fighter.
He isn't such a good fighter — but he had a lot of pictures tattooed on his chest and his opponent got so interested in the pictures he forgot to fight.

4635 I know a man that has the map of North America tattooed on his chest. He has such a large chest expansion — when he expands, Mexico joins the Union.

4636 Excuse me, do those tattoo marks on you wash off?
I can't say, lady, I never tried it.

4637 I learned today that our tattooed sailor friend had sued the osteopath.
What for?
He claims the osteopath threw all of his pictures out of focus.

4638 They just discovered how jig-saw puzzles originated.
How did they originate?
Putting a tattooed man together after a train wreck.

CONTORTIONIST
SEE:
Old Maid 2572
Football 4374

FLAGPOLE SITTER

4639 My uncle tried to be a flagpole sitter, too, but had to give it up.
Why was that?
He was always slipping down to halfmast.

ANIMALS (Wild)

4640   Didn't I tell you when a lion wagged his tail, he was friendly?
        He was roaring and wagging his tail at the same time.
        Well, what's that got to do with it?
        I didn't know which end to believe.

4641   What is it that Elks have no other animals have?
        Parades.

4642   And while we were hunting wild animals, we saw a man-eating
           tiger.
        Well, some people will eat anything.

4643   What's the most high-hat animal you know?
        A skunk — he's unapproachable.

4644   I wonder what all the lions, elephants and wild beasts did B.C.
        You wonder what all the wild beasts did B.C. What's B.C.?
        Before Circuses.

4645   Did you enjoy the animals?
        You know that fellow who has the lion act and those lionesses?
        Those what?
        Lionesses? You know what a lioness is, don't you?
        Yes — the way you cook potatoes.

4646   The bad weather gave the giraffe a terrible cold.
        Oh, and what could be worse than a giraffe with a cold?
        An Ubanga savage with chapped lips.

4647   What kind of animals do they have at the North Pole?
        Reindeer.
        Now, I'm not talking about the weather, and don't get familiar
           with me.

4648   What was that animal that ran by?
        That was a gnu.
        Where did you ever see a gnu before — in a zoo?
        No, in a crossword puzzle.

4649   "Mother," cried Mary, as she rushed into the house. "Henry
           wants the Listerine. He's just caught the cutest little black
           and white animal, but he thinks it's got halitosis."

4650   My uncle used to be with the circus. He was a doctor. He doc-
           tored all the wild animals.
        How did he treat the lions?
        With the utmost respect.

4651   Does the giraffe get a sore throat if he gets wet feet?
       Yes, but not until the next week.

4652   Is that a man eating lion?
       Yes, lady, but we're short of men this week, so all he gets is
       beef.

4653   You know reindeer developed horns to save their heads from
          bumps.
       Yeah? I thought the reindeer developed horns to make hat stands.

RELATED SUBJECTS
Hunting 4423-4453
Circus 4611-4613

ELEPHANT

4654   Do you allow elephants on this train?
       Yes, but you have to check their trunks.

4655   You know Molly, the elephant, is very kind-hearted. The other
          day in the parade she stepped on a bird and looking down
          noticed that the bird was a mother and realized the bird had
          a nest someplace with a little baby bird in it.
       And what did she do?
       She went up and sat on the bird to keep it warm.

4656   I'm afraid to go to the circus. I'm afraid to meet that elephant
          I gave the peanuts to.
       Why, elephants love peanuts.
       Yeah, but these peanuts had worms in them.

4657   The elephants got drunk. They were so drunk they went down
          to the public library and tried to rent themselves out as
          book-ends.

4658   Gee, the elephant must be dumb.
       What makes you say that?
       His head is so full of ivory it even sticks out.

4659   The elephants got drunk. They were so drunk they kept seeing
          pink Frank Bucks.

4660   Now, tell me, Bobby, where is the elephant found?
       The elephant, teacher, is such a large animal it's scarcely ever lost.

4661 Mama, why do elephants have such big trunks?
Well, they have to come all the way from India, dear.

4662 Did you see that elephant?
Yes, and I feel so sorry — he has to stand up all the time.
Is that so?
Yeah. He gets confused between his trunk and his tail — he can't tell which end to sit on.

4663 I saw you walking an elephant down the street. How do you manage to lead an animal like that?
It's not so hard — you just tie a rope on him; find out which way he wants to go and then hang on.

RELATED SUBJECTS
Memory 1576-1591
Circus 4611-4613
Zoo 4673

KANGAROO

4664 Why is that kangaroo crying?
Her little son ran away and left her holding the bag.

4665 A kangaroo has a back pocket in the front.
That's called a pouch. Don't you know what a pouch is?
Sure. Every night I sit on the pouch in a rocking chair.

4666 I heard he just got arrested for sticking his fingers in the kangaroo's cage.
He was a pickpocket.

4667 Papa wants to put zippers on kangaroos.
What's his idea?
To make brief cases for the big game hunters.

4668 1st Kangaroo: Anabelle, where's the baby?
2nd Kangaroo: My goodness, I've been robbed.

ANIMAL TRAINER

4669 Are you the celebrated lion tamer?
No, I only comb the lions and clean their teeth.

4670 What! A little squib like you a wild animal trainer?
My small size is the secret of my success. The lions are waiting for me to grow a little larger.

4671 My father is an animal trainer.
Can you do any tricks?

4672 What makes you think he is conceited?
His head is so swelled up, he can't get it in the lion's mouth.
Why, he's so conceited he does all his crossword puzzles with
his fountain pen.

RELATED SUBJECTS
Circus 4611-4613

ZOO

4673 That big brown bear at the zoo just had a little baby bear,
and they want us to write a story about it.
Tell them we'll send over the cub reporter.

RELATED SUBJECTS
Circus 4611-4613
Animals (Wild) 4640-4668

BARBER SHOP

BARBER

4674 Is it true that you gave the barber a dollar tip?
Yeah.
He cut you four or five times and put pieces of paper over the
cuts. Why give him a dollar tip?
Any time a man can be a barber, a butcher and a paper hanger
all at the same time, he is worth a dollar.

4675 Are you the man who cut my hair the last time?
I don't think so. I've only been here six months.

4676 Like the man said to the barber who was shaving him: My face
is in your hands.

4677 (After being shaved, man asks for a drink of water)
Are you thirsty?
No, I want to see if my face still holds water.

4678 Your hair needs cutting badly, sir.
No, it doesn't. It needs to be cut nicely. You cut it badly the
last time.

4679 Why did you make those cuts on his chin while you were shaving
him?
I was going with his niece to the dance tonight and that cut is
to let her know I can't see her tonight.

4680 Barber: Trim?
Customer: Oh, think so? Well, I have been working out at the Y lately.

4681 Hair cut, sir?
No — throat, please.

4682   Haven't I shaved you before, sir?
        No, I got that scar in France.

4683   (Barber using clippers on lady's neck)
        Lady: Is my neck so dirty you have to use the vacuum cleaner?

4684   Barber: Do you want it cut short?
        Customer: Yes, I really wish you'd keep quiet for a few minutes.

4685   (Man enters barber shop and takes off toupee)
        Man: I want a shampoo and hair cut and I'll be back in a half
            hour.

4686   You want your beard trimmed?
        No, just cut a hole in it.
        I get it — for ventilation.
        No, my wife wants to see the tie she gave me for Christmas.

4687   Are you good at your work? I'm particular about the way my
            hair is cut.
        Well, if you like, I'll do one side of your head first so that you
            can see for yourself.

4688   Shall I go over your face twice?
        Yes, if there's any left.

4689   What happened to you? Your face is all cut up.
        I went to a barber college to be shaved and one of the students
            failed in his examination on me.

4690   Why did you drop that hot towel on his face?
        You don't think I was going to burn my fingers, do you?

                            RELATED SUBJECTS
                            Male (the) 912-924
                            Gossip 1518-1537

HAIR

4691   I saw my friend Professor Einstein today.
        How did you find Einstein?
        I just pushed his hair back and there he was.

4692   How does that man keep his pompadour so perfect?
        He was scared stiff once and his hair stood on end.

4693   She said your hair was dyed.
        It's false.
        That's what I told her.

4694   That hair oil you gave me is no good.
        I didn't give you hair oil — I gave you glue by mistake.
        No wonder I can't get my hat off.

4695   Why are you wearing your hair over your eyes?
       I want to start this program off with a bang.

4696   Kid: Mama, why hasn't papa any hair?
       Mother: Because he thinks so much, dear.
       Kid: Why have you so much, mama?
       Mother: Because — go away and do your lessons.

4697   Wife: I've got you this bottle of hair tonic, darling.
       Husband: But my hair is all right.
       Wife: I know, but I want you to give it to your typist at the
       office — her hair is coming out rather badly.

4698   There is a teacher who gets in my hair—what shall I do?
       Comb, brush and cut hair regularly — wash thoroughly with
       water and Head and Shoulders, three times a week—after that
       you'll not be bothered.

4699   Who is that fellow with the long hair?
       He's a fellow from Yale.
       Oh, I've often heard of those Yale locks.

RELATED SUBJECTS
Age 45-107
Description of People 263-303
Beauty 4725-4735
Blondes 4736-4737

BALD-HEADED

4700   My hair is coming out — what shall I get to keep it in?
       A paper bag.

4701   Do you give a guarantee with this hair restorer?
       Guarantee, sir! Why, we give a comb.

4702   He isn't bald — he just has a tall face.

4703   Have any of your childhood hopes been realized?
       Yes. When mother used to pull my hair, I wished that I didn't
       have any.

4704   Papa, are you growing taller all the time?
       No, my child, why do you ask?
       'Cause the top of your head is poking up through your hair.

4705   This tonic will grow hair on a billiard ball.
       Who wants hair on a billiard ball?

4706   I took my girl to the restaurant and she stuck her fork into a
       bald-headed man's head thinking that it was a honey dew
       melon.

RELATED SUBJECTS
Description of People 263-303

WIG

4707   I have a date with my sweetheart and she doesn't know I wear
       a wig.
       For heaven's sake — keep it under your hat.

4708   He sewed sleeves on his father's toupee and wore it for a rac-
       coon coat.

4709   Have you no respect for this old grey toupee?

4710   Why don't you get yourself a toupee?
       A what?
       A toupee — a toupee . . .
       Shucks, I can't even drive a car.

4711   Had a tough time raising this mustache.
       Well, crops are bad everywhere this year.

4712   How did you happen to grow a mustache?
       Well, since my wife's gotten to wearing man's pants, I had to
       grow a mustache to let people know which was the man at
       our house.

4713   George's mustache made me laugh.
       Yeah — it tickled me, too.

4714   How come your uncle shaved off his walrus mustache?
       He had to do it. Everywhere he went, people would throw fish
       at him.

4715   Have you any mustache brushes?
       I'm sorry, we're out of those, sir, but we have some nice eyebrow
       brushes, which I'm sure would serve your purpose.

4716   You make me laugh with that football mustache of yours.
       What do you mean — football mustache?
       Eleven on each side.

4717   Why are you looking in the mirror so long?
       I'm counting my mustache.

4718   What's that on your upper lip?
        A mustache.
        No, it isn't — it's hair.

4719   How did you come to have such a long beard?
        My brother left home ten years ago with the razor.

4720   He spilled rum on his whiskers and in lighting his cigarette his
            whiskers caught on fire.
        What did he do then?
        Oh, he just fiddled with his whiskers while rum burned.

                        RELATED SUBJECTS
                        Face 217-262
                        Description of People 263-303

SHAVING

4721   Wait a minute — did you shave?
        Of course, I shaved.
        Next time, stand a little closer to the razor.

4722   After my uncle shaved yesterday he used flour instead of talcum
            powder.
        Why did he do that?
        I don't know, but when he gets hot now, he breaks out in
            biscuits.

4723   Why were you late?
        I was shaving and talked myself into a shampoo and a massage.

4724   Do you always shave outside? (To man shaving outside a tent)
        Certainly! Do you think I'm fur-lined?

                        RELATED SUBJECTS
                        Face 217-262
                        Gossip 1518-1537

BEAUTY SHOP

BEAUTY

4725   Are you going to the stag party tonight?
        You bet.
        Will your wife let you out?
        Every night at seven thirty my wife puts a beauty pack on
            her face, soaks her feet in beauty mud and puts beauty mud
            on her hands.
        So what?
        About nine o'clock she won't be able to move. I mixed cement
            with the mud.

4726   My wife put some beauty clay on her face and left it on six
      months.
      Why did she leave it on that long?
      She thought she looked better with the mud on.

4727   What tense is "I am beautiful"?
      Past.

4728   Tell me, pretty maiden, why are your cheeks so red?
      'Cause!
      'Cause why?
      Cause-metic.

4729   I read that women of this country last year spent thirty nine
      million dollars on cosmetics to make them beautiful.
      They sure don't look it.
      You're not supposed to know about beauty secrets.
      How can they expect to keep it secret when they dab it on in
      public?

4730   Who was that ugly looking woman with you?
      That's my fiancee and I want you to know that beauty is only
      skin deep.
      You'd better take her home and skin her then.

4731   I just got back from the beauty parlor. I was there three hours.
      Too bad that you stayed so long and then didn't get waited on.

4732   My gal's so dumb she won't buy cold cream unless it's packed
      in ice.

4733   She's as pretty as a picture.
      Yeah — and I'd like to hang her.

4734   She has that School Girl Complexion.
      Yes — Night School.

4735   I've just come from the beauty parlor.
      Too bad they were closed.

RELATED SUBJECTS
Face 217-262
Plastic Surgeon 318-324
Female (the) 925-938
Gossip 1518-1537

Flirting 2780
Proposal 2808
Iceman 3548
Vacation 3969

BLONDES

4736 Do you think she's a natural blonde or a bleached blonde?
I think she's a suicide blonde, if you ask me.
What kind is that?
Dyed by her own hand.

4737 I see she's let her hair go dark again.
Yes, she's gone off the gold standard.

R<small>ELATED</small> S<small>UBJECTS</small>
Hair 4691-4699

RESTAURANT

PROPRIETOR

4738 Manager: Now, girls — I want you all to look your best today.
Add a little dab of powder to your cheeks and take a bit more
care with your hair.
Waitress: What's on — something special?
Manager: No, the beef's tough.

4739 This was a very high class restaurant. They made gravy in all
colors to match any shade of vest.

4740 It's twelve o'clock — you can take care of the restaurant. I'm
going out to eat.
Don't you eat lunch here?
Do you think I'm crazy?

4741 Where are you going to eat?
Let's eat up the street.
Aw, no, I don't like asphalt.

4742 My uncle was in the restaurant business two weeks, but he had
to move.
What did he move for?
All the dishes were dirty.

4743 He opened a restaurant one day, and only one thing kept him
from bankruptcy.
What was that?
Hash!

4744 Why don't you jump in a creek?
A what?

Don't you know what a creek is?
A creek is a man who runs a restaurant.

4745   I went into a restaurant and hung up my coat. I put a sign on
        it. This coat belongs to a champion fighter — I'll be back.
        So what?
        When I went to get my coat, it was gone and there was a note
        that said: Taken by a champion sprinter and I won't be back.

4746   I went to a restaurant — that one across the street. You can
        eat dirt cheap.
        Who wants to eat dirt?

4747   We haven't had a complaint in twenty-five years.
        No wonder. The customers all starve to death before they are
        served.

4748   Come on, let's go into this restaurant.
        Will you carry me, because if you carry me I know you'll marry
        me, because I heard my sister say that her husband picked her
        up in front of a restaurant.

RELATED SUBJECTS
Businessman 5309-5321

WAITER
4749   Father, I can't eat this soup.
        Waiter, bring my son another soup.
        Father, I can't eat this soup, either.
        Waiter, bring this young man some other soup.
        Father, still I can't eat this soup.
        Well, why the deuce can't you?
        Father, I have no spoon.

4750   Remember when you were carving fowl? It slipped and fell into
        the captain's lap.
        Well, it wasn't the first time he had chicken in his lap.

4751   During dinner you spilled soup on the Admiral's head.
        But the Admiral didn't mind — it was Navy Bean soup.

4752   Waiter: Would you mind settling your bill, sir? We're closing
        now.
        Man: But hang it all, I haven't been served yet.
        Waiter: Well, in that case, there'll be only the cover charge.

4753 Are you the waiter who took my order?
Yes, sir.
H'm, still looking well, I see. How're your grandchildren?

4754 Waiter: Spoon, miss?
Boy Friend: Say, whose party is this?

4755 Don't order onions here. You have a date after supper.
Waiter: That's okay — when I give him the bill it will take
his breath away.

4756 You had an argument with the waitress last night — what was
the trouble?
I asked her what she had and she said: I have stewed kidneys,
boiled tongue, fried calves' brains and pigs' feet. So I said:
Don't tell me your troubles, sister. Give me a chicken pie and
go see your doctor.

4757 Have you ordered, sir?
Yes, but if you don't mind, I would like to make it an entreaty
instead.

4758 Waiter, this plate is wet.
That's your soup, sir.

4759 Customer: You served me twice as much yesterday.
Waiter: Where were you sitting?
Customer: Over there by the window.
Waiter: Oh, that was for advertising.

4760 Where's the menu?
Down the hall, three doors to the left.

4761 What's your hurry?
I just happened to remember there is a waiter's strike. I want
to tell my Uncle.
Doesn't he know about it?
He's been sitting in a restaurant since last Friday.
Waiting for some one to pick up his check?
No, waiting for the waiter to bring the cream for his coffee.

4762 Do you charge for bread?
No.
Do you charge for gravy?
No.
I'll take bread and gravy.

4763 Why does this chicken have a leg missing, waiter?
It was in a fight, sir.
Well, take it back then and bring me the winner.

4764 Bacon and eggs, waiter. The eggs not too hard and the bacon rather crisp. Buttered toast without too much butter, and iced tea without too much tea.
Yes, sir. Is there any special design you would like on the dishes?

4765 I want some raw oysters. They must not be too large or too small; not too salty and not too soft. They must be cold and I'm in a hurry for them.
Yes, Sir. Will you have 'em with or without pearls, sir?

4766 Have you any lobsters?
I'll call the chef.
I don't want him. I'm not a cannibal!

4767 I can't eat this ox-tail soup. The tail is still wagging.
Of course, our tails come from contented oxen.

4768 I'll have some Spimoni Vermatelli.
Where do you see that?
On the menu.
That's the name of the owner of this restaurant.

4769 And, waiter, bring me the same steak I had last night. I couldn't have hurt it in the least.

4770 Will you have pie, sir?
Is it customary?
No, it's apple.

4771 There's soap in this food.
That's all right. It's to wash the food down.

4772 The customer was busy sawing on the steak he had ordered and was having a difficult time.
Waiter: Is it tough?
Customer: (Exhausted) When I order beef and get horse, I don't care. But next time, take the harness off before you start serving.

4773 Have you any caviar?
No, but I can give you a plate of tapioca and some dark glasses and you'll never know the difference.

4774 Why do you bring me tea? I ordered coffee.
You should have gotten up earlier. The coffee is completely exhausted.
I'm not surprised at all. It was very weak for several days.

4775 What is your order, sir?
A demi-tasse, please.
And yours, miss?
I'll take the same thing he did and a cup of coffee.

4776   Diner: Waiter, what are those black specks in my milk?
       Waiter: I don't know, unless those are the vitamins they're
         talking so much about.

4777   Two minute eggs, sir? I thought you always wanted them
         three minutes.
       I know, but I've decided to sleep a little longer mornings.

4778   Waiter, this soup is cold. Bring me some that's hot.
       What do you want me to do? Burn my thumb?

4779   A man was eating alphabet soup. He had eaten eight bowls
         when the waiter said: How many bowls of alphabet soup
         are you going to eat?
       Man: I'm going to keep on eating this soup until I come to a
         period.

4780   No, I won't have any mushrooms, waiter. I was nearly poisoned
         by them last week.
       Is that really so, sir? Then I've won my bet with the cook.

4781   Did you say you wanted those eggs turned over?
       Yeah, to the Museum of Natural History.

4782   That ain't no sandwich. There ain't nothing in it.
       Sure it is. It's a Western sandwich — two hunks of bread with
         wide open spaces in between.

4783   My brother went into a restaurant and ordered everything he
         could see on the menu and the waiter gave him a check for
         twenty-five dollars. My brother said: What is it for? You asked
         me if I would like to have the food and I said yes, so I don't
         think I should pay for it.
       The waiter called the manager and when he heard about my
         brother he said: That's a very good trick. Then he offered my
         brother two dollars if he would go across the street to his rival
         and do the same thing. My brother said: Sorry, I can't do that.
         Your business rival gave me five dollars to come in here.

4784   Waiter, the portions seem to have got a lot smaller lately.
       Just an optical illusion, sir. Now that the restaurant has been
         enlarged, they look smaller . . . that's all.

4785   Steak or hamburger?
       What's the difference?
       One day.

4786   Waiter, just look at this piece of chicken; it is nothing but
         skin and bone.
       Yes, sir. D'you want the feathers, too?

4787 Customer: I haven't come to any ham in this sandwich yet.
Waiter: Try another bite.
Customer: (Taking huge mouthful) Nope, none yet.
Waiter: Hmmmm! You must have gone right past it.

4788 Customers get my goat when they order frankfurters.
Yeah — it tastes more like your cat to me.

4789 Waiter, I'll have one big pork chop with French fried potatoes
and I'll have the chop lean.
Yes, madam, which way?

4790 This soup isn't fit for a pig!
I'll take it back, sir, and bring you some that is.

4791 Diner: Do you call that a large portion?
Waiter: Yes, sir. You have no idea how small a large portion
may be nowadays, sir.

4792 If that's bouillon, I'm an idiot.
That's right, sir. It is bouillon.

4793 Man: (Holding up thin piece of meat) And did you cut this
piece of meat?
She: (Proudly) With my own itsy bitsy hands!
Man: You almost missed it.

4794 I was in a little accident and it was all a case of mistaken
identity.
A case of mistaken identity? Tell me about it.
Well, I took my girl friend out to dinner last night and we
goes in a swell restaurant. We walks in and orders a big
meal, and no sooner started to eat than my girl found a bug
in her soup!
That was terrible — what did she do?
She yelled: Waiter, remove this insect!
Well?
And he threw me down two flights of stairs.

4795 Soup, sir?
No, please. I just had my suit cleaned.

RELATED SUBJECTS
Conduct 1802-1862
Tip 4274-4276
Food 4825-4878
Table Manners 4881-4883

4851; 4852; 4854; 4855;
4856; 4857; 4862
Oysters 4874; 4875

CHEF

4796   De chef at de Green Parrot has been cookin' fo' twenty yeahs.
Ought t' be almos' done by now.

4797   Go see if the chef has pigs' feet.
I can't tell, he's got his shoes on.

COOKING

4798   She's a good cook, huh?
Yes, she can go in a delicatessen and buy a meal with her eyes
closed.

4799   How do you like this cake?
Fine. Did you buy it yourself?

4800   How would you like to come up to my house tomorrow night
and I'll cook you a dandy dinner?
I'l come up.
And after the dinner I'll drive you home.
No, the dinner will drive me home.

4801   How did you like that cake I baked for you?
It was terrible.
That's funny. The cook book said it was delicious.

4802   The way my wife cooks chickens — they sure tickle your palate.
Is your wife a good cook?
Terrible. She's awful lazy, too.
How is it — you say your wife isn't a good cook, but when
she cooks chicken she tickles your palate?
She don't take half the feathers off of 'em.

4803   It looks like a storm, you had better stay for dinner.
Oh, thanks, but I don't think it's bad enough for that.

4804   I want to learn how to cook and bake.
How does it happen you take the sudden notion to cook?
I got a letter from a boy friend of mine in prison and he wants
me to bake him a hacksaw pie.

4805   You know one time after we were married, I wanted to be
real nice and coy with him. That afternoon I saw a beautiful
mink coat down at the fur store and I kind of wanted it. So
I cooked him a grand dinner and after dinner I said to him:
What will I get if I keep baking pies for you?

And what did he say?
You'll get my life insurance.

4806 I almost baked a cake for my brother that is in the pen.
      And why didn't you?
      I couldn't remember if you put in a file and saw after the
      flour or before the eggs.

4807 Does your husband kick about his meals?
      No, what he kicks about is having to get them.

4808 Have you the firmness of character that enables a person to go
      on and do his duty in the face of ingratitude and criticism
      and heartless ridicule?
      I ought to have. I cooked for a camping party last year.

4809 The dinner was delicious. You must have an old family cook.
      Yes, indeed. She's been with us ten or twelve meals.

4810 I made this pudding all by myself.
      Splendid! But who helped you lift it out of the oven?

4811 It seems to me, my dear, that these pancakes are rather heavy.
      Then I'm afraid you're a poor judge, for the cook book says
      they're light and feathery.

4812 I'll bet you didn't eat all that cake I baked for you.
      I had to, I couldn't break off a piece.

4813 So you are taking a domestic science course?
      Yes, I want to be able to pick out the right things when I go
      into a delicatessen store.

4814 What are these?
      Biscuits. I made them myself.
      All right; you eat them yourself.

4815 It was a good cake but it defied the laws of gravity.
      How?
      It was heavy as lead, but wouldn't go down.

4816 Did you make that split pea soup for dinner?
      I've started it, but we can't have it till tomorrow. It's taken
      me all day to split the peas.

4817 I made a cherry pie for dinner because this is Washington's
      birthday.
      Well, bring me a hatchet so I can cut it.

4818 The two best things I cook are meat loaf and apple dumplings.
      Well, which is this?

4819   What kind of cake is that?
        It's marble cake. Want a piece?
        No, I'll just take it for granite.

4820   She made pies when you were in the kindergarten.
        That must have been the one she served me today.

4821   Is the steak ready now, dear?
        I'm sorry I'm so long, George, but it looked hopeless grilled,
        and it doesn't look much better fried, but if you'll be patient
        a little longer, I'll see what boiling does for it.

4822   Oh, look, a button in the salad.
        I suppose it fell off while the salad was dressing.

4823   What's this honey?
        Lucifer cake, dear.
        I thought you said you were going to make angel cake.
        I was, but it fell.

4824   Uncle Si and Aunt Mirandy were visiting their relatives in the
        city and witnessed an electric toaster and coffee pot being used
        on the table.
        "Well, I swan" — exclaimed Uncle Si. "You folks make fun
        of us eatin' in the kitchen, but I can't see that that's any worse
        than cookin' in the dinin' room."

                              RELATED SUBJECTS
                              Cow 3810-3838
                              Chicken 3872-3901
                              Grocery Store 5438-5448
                              Butcher Shop 5449-5453

FOOD

4825   Evolution: One man's meat is another man's croquette.

4826   I eat 'most everything — that is everything but blackberry pie.
        You don't like blackberry pie?
        No — the seeds get under my upper plate.

4827   Why don't you eat at the hotel?
        I think it's pretty tough paying fifteen dollars for a steak.
        And it's pretty tough if you only pay five dollars.

4828   What are you having?
        Calves' brains and ox-tail soup.
        That's a way of making ends meet.

4829   Take away this alphabet soup!
        Why, what's the matter?
        Those letters are spelling a nasty word.

4830 What could be worse than eating hash in a restaurant where you don't know what goes into it?
I know what could be worse — eating it at home where you do know what does go into it.

4831 How was this steak cooked?
Smothered in onions.
Well, it died hard.

4832 Why have you got your hand in the alphabet soup?
I'm groping for words.

4833 Will you have pie or ice cream?
Neither, thank you. I'll have an a la mode.

4834 What are we eating tonight?
Everything — everything that you're wild about.
Oh, we're having hash, huh?

4835 Will you join me in a bowl of soup?
Do you think there'd be room for both of us?

4836 What's your favorite dish?
A clean one.

4837 Affectionate pie: The crusts are stuck on each other.

4838 How do you keep the smell of onions off your breath?
Well, it's a long story. First, I peel carefully, then slice them with perfect precision; pepper and salt sufficiently to taste — then add a little vinegar and a few drops of salad oil — and then I throw them away.

4839 What have you got to eat? What's the best dish you have here?
The blonde, just behind you, sir.

4840 Did you read where in Alaska they have no food and they have to cut up their shoes and make soup out of them?
Hush! The cook may hear you and we'll have goulash soup and filet of sole hash for dinner.

4841 Looks like rain today, doesn't it?
Yes, but it smells like coffee.

4842 Do you feel like a cup of tea?
Of course not. Do I look like one?

4843 I ordered Swiss cheese and they brought me Limburger. No draft ventilation.

4844 The butter was so hard, the knife slipped and I buttered the bread up to my elbow.

4845   What do you think you're going to get for breakfast that begins
       with an N?
       N'egg?
       Nothing.

4846   How would you like a tomato and cucumber salad, without
       cucumbers?
       Fine.
       Sorry, we're out of cucumbers — wouldn't you rather have it
       without tomatoes?

4847   Is the steak tough?
       Yeah, but I've managed to bend the gravy.

4848   I had some of that dollar coffee.
       Dollar coffee?
       Yes, good to the last drop.

4849   These are times we must save money and make every nickel
       count.
       That's the reason I bought three loaves of bread today.
       Three loaves of bread? I haven't read in the newspapers where
       there has been a raise in bread.
       I don't know anything about the papers, but I saw a sign in the
       window that sure did say it.
       What'd the sign say?
       It said: Raisin bread tomorrow.

4850   Friends may come and friends may go, and very often sever,
       but the soup that mother makes from a dime's worth of
       bones . . . goes on forever and ever.

4851   We've got thousands of things to eat.
       What are they?
       Beans.

4852   What will you have with tea? I suggest a lemon.
       I'll say you do.

4853   I'll take a steak with potatoes lyonnaise.
       That's not potatoes — that's a lion's wife.

4854   Bring me some miscellaneous food.
       What?
       Miscellaneous — miscellaneous! Don't you know what mis-
       cellaneous is?
       No, but I know most all the food they cook here is a mess.

4855   How do you like your coffee?
       Half and half.

What do you mean — half and half?
Half in my cup and half in my saucer.

4856 This butter is so strong it could walk around the table and
say hello to the coffee.
Well, if it does the coffee is too weak to answer.

4857 This fish is not too fresh, Tony.
No, sir. Justa right.

4858 (Having been served the wing of the chicken)
Mother, can't I have another piece? This is nothing but hinges.

4859 Who invented the hole in the doughnut?
Oh, some fresh air fiend, I suppose.

4860 In Alaska, it's so cold that they serve soup in sieves.

The first sandwich was made in the seventeenth century.
Replicas of this are exhibited in glass cases in all railway
stations.

4861 Fresh, lady? Why, this fish breathed its last just as you came
in the door.
And what a breath it had!

4862 What on earth is this broth made from, waiter? Surely it
isn't chicken broth?
Well, sir, it's chicken broth in its infancy. It's made out of the
water the eggs were boiled in.

4863 What did you have for lunch?
Three guesses.
No wonder you are so hungry.

4864 Did your aunt enjoy her dinner?
Well, I guess she did — because two weeks later she wasn't
hungry yet.

4865 Johnny, can you tell me what a waffle is?
Yes'm, it's a pancake with a non-skid tread.

4866 How do the foreign dishes compare with American ones?
Oh, they break just as easily.

4867 Why don't you finish your alphabet soup? There's a few letters
left in your plate.
I know, but they spell spinach.

4868 Judge: What do you mean selling the unsuspecting public horse
meat?

Man: It wasn't all horse meat — I mixed it half and half. Half horse and half rabbit.

Judge: How many rabbits to one horse?

Man: One rabbit, your Honor, to one horse.

4869 Why, you can make bread out of potatoes.

That's nothing, women make monkeys out of men.

> RELATED SUBJECTS
> Flies 3790-3800
> Cow 3810-3838
> Chicken 3872-3901
> Fishing 4380-4413
> Waiter 4749-4795
> Table Manners 4881-4883
> Grocery Store 5438-5448
> Butcher Shop 5449-5453

BANANA
SEE:

Accident 654

Inventor 1788

Patriotism 2475

CHEESE

4870 Why do they put so many holes in Swiss Cheese when it's the Limburger that really needs the ventilation?

GRAPEFRUIT

4871 "Grapefruit Good for the Teeth," says one newspaper. But it's also an eye tonic.

4872 Which do you think has the bigger grapefruit? Florida or California?

What's the difference? A grapefruit's only idea in living is to squirt in your eye.

OYSTER

4873 I've just been reading the private life of an oyster.
Private life of an oyster? There's no such thing.
You never can tell what goes on inside of that shell.

4874 Waiter, these are very small oysters.
Yes, sir.
And they don't appear to be very fresh.
Then it's lucky they're small, ain't it, sir?

4875 Waiter: You sometimes find a pearl in an oyster stew.
Customer: I'm looking for oysters.

4876 Said the oyster, just about to be consumed by the preacher:
I've always been religious but I never thought I'd enter the clergy.

4877 Don't you know what an oyster is?
No — what is it?
A fish that's built like a nut.

SPAGHETTI

4878 Diet specialists now tell us that spaghetti is the best all-around food. All around what, is our question.

VEGETARIAN

4879 Buy a hot dog, sir?
No, I'm a vegetarian.
Well, what is this guy?
I often wonder.

4880 They are vegetarians. You know what a vegetarian is?
Sure, a horse doctor.
That's a veterinarian.
A veterinarian? I know what that is.
What is it?
A man who was once a soldier.

TABLE MANNERS

4881   Does he eat too much?
No, he eats too fast.
Well, why doesn't he get wise to himself and take it easy?
He can't — you see the poor guy's an iron worker.
So what?
So from force of habit he always bolts his food down.

4882   Why do you eat your dessert first?
My stomach's upset.

4883   This is the twelfth time you've been to the refreshment buffet.
Oh, that's all right. I tell everybody I'm getting something for
you.

RELATED SUBJECTS
Conduct 1802-1862
Home 3197-3205
Food 4825-4878

SECTION II

EDUCATIONAL SYSTEMS

CORRESPONDENCE SCHOOL

4884   How do you play hooky from the correspondence school?
I send them an empty envelope.

SCHOOL

4885   My aunt went to Boarding School.
I suppose she came home with high honors?
No, she came home with chronic indigestion.
Sounds like a Finishing School.
It nearly finished her all right.

4886   I don't believe you ever went to school.
I certainly did. I went to an Immoral School.

What kind of a school is that?
That's a school that has no principal and no class.

4887 When you went to school, didn't you learn the three R's?
Yeah — Rah! Rah! Rah!

4888 Well, Bobby, and how do you like school?
When it's closed.

4889 Papa, vat is science?
My, how could you be so dumb! Science is dose things vat says:
No Smoking.

4890 If you study real hard, you'll be a marvel.
I'd rather not study and stay like I am.

4891 Do you like school, Tommy?
Golly, missus! If it wasn't for school we wouldn't get any
holidays.

4892 Dad, you are a lucky man.
How is that?
You won't have to buy me any school books this year. I have
been left in the same class.

4893 Tell me the truth now. Who did your home exercise?
Father.
Quite alone?
No, I helped him with it.

4894 What did you learn in school today, Clarence?
How to whisper without moving my lips.

RELATED SUBJECTS
Absentmindedness 1297-1319
Smartness 1332-1336
Stupidity 1337-1381
Illiteracy 1390-1398
Conduct 1802-1862
Punishment 2521-2524

ALPHABET

4895 Do you know your alphabet?
Yes.
Well, what comes after the "G"?
Whizz!
That's right — and after "Whizz"?
Bang!

4896   What letter in the alphabet is drunk?
        I'll bite. Which one is it?
        The wobble-you!

4897   Now, Billy, what letter in the alphabet comes before "J"?
        I dunno.
        What have I on both sides of my nose?
        Freckles.

4898   I'll bet you don't know the alphabet.
        B — L — X — U — Y.
        Where did you ever learn an alphabet like that?
        When I was having my eyes tested.

RELATED SUBJECTS
Abbreviations 4955-4960

ARITHMETIC

4899   Here's a problem in arithmetic. If I laid four eggs over there,
        and four eggs over here, how many eggs would I have?
        I don't think you can do it, teacher.

4900   Are you good at additions?
        Am I good at addition? I added this account up ten times —
        here are the ten different answers.

4901   Here are four apples—now .tell me: how would you divide the
        four apples among five children?
        I'd make applesauce.

4902   If a man had four horses and only three stalls, how would he
        get the four horses into the three stalls?
        He'd make horseradish.

4903   One time I won a prize in arithmetic. The teacher asked us
        what was 2 x 20 and I said 34.
        You know that was wrong — 2 x 20 is 40.
        I was closer to it than anyone in the class.

4904   I'll give you some problems in arithmetic to see what you're
        capable of doing. How much is six and four?
        That's about eleven, ain't it?
        Six and four are ten.
        Six and four couldn't be ten, because five and five are ten.

4905   If you had four chickens on Friday and one chicken on Satur-
        day, how many chickens would you have?
        I would have seven chickens.
        You're crazy — four and one are five.
        But I have two already.

4906   Take thirteen from twenty. What's the difference?
        That's what I say — what's the difference?

4907   What would your father have to pay if he owed four hundred
            dollars to the grocer, five-hundred forty dollars rent, and
            thirty-eight dollars to the milkman?
        Nothing—he'd move!

4908   Johnny, how much is three times three?
        Nine.
        That's pretty good.
        Pretty good — say, it's perfect.

4909   Johnny, if your father earned three hundred dollars a week and
            gave your mother half, what would she have?
        Heart failure.

4910   Did your father help you with this sum?
        No, I got it wrong myself.

4911   (Explaining problem to dumb guy)
        Boy: Now, suppose you borrowed ten dollars from me . . .
        Dumb guy: Yah — to make it harder, suppose you borrowed
            ten bucks from me.

4912   He can only count to nine.
        Why?
        He lost the middle finger on his left hand.

4913   Put two and two together and the result is always what?
        Bridge.

4914   If I tear a piece of paper into four pieces, what do I get?
        Quarters.
        And if I divide it into eight?
        Eighths.
        And if I divide it into eight thousand parts?
        Confetti.
        (Switch: Substitute steak for paper and the answer is ham-
            burger.)

4915   Mum, do you know how to get the cubic contents of a barrel?
        No, ask your father.

4916   Aren't you ashamed of yourself? You've been learning for three
            years and you can only count up to ten. What will you do in
            life if you go on like that?
        I'll be a referee at boxing matches.

4917   Johnny, if your father could save twenty dollars a week for thirty
            weeks, what would he have?

A stereo, a new suit, and a set of golf clubs.

4918 If you had five apples and now you only have two apples, what
would I have taken?
An awful chance on getting your eye blacked.

4919 How many fingers have you?
Ten.
And if you lost four — what would be the result?
I wouldn't have to take music lessons.

4920 What's all this?
Those are my Mae West problems.
Mae West problems?
Yeah — I done 'em wrong.

4921 Find the greatest common denominator.
Great heavens — is that thing lost again?

RELATED SUBJECTS
Smartness 1332-1336

SPELLING

4922 I want to put in a person to person call to Mike Zanda — Zanda!
ZANDA! No — Z ... a ... b ... c ... d ... e ... f ... g ... h ... i ... j ... k ...
l ... m ... n ... o ... p ... q ... r ... s ... t ... u ... v ... w ... x ... y ... Z
like in Zilch.

4923 I couldn't learn to spell.
Why not?
My teacher was always changing the words.

4924 So your sister got fired?
Yeah — but she was going to leave anyway. Her boss is so
conceited — he thinks the words can only be spelled his way.

4925 It took you five weeks to learn to spell stovepipe and now I'll
bet you can't spell it.
I sure can. S ... t ... o ... v ... e s ... q ... u ... i ... d ... g ... e ... t ... y
w ... i ... d ... g ... e ... t ... y p ... i ... p ... e.
What's that squidgety widgety for?
That's for the elbows.

4926 You know I am writing a letter to my boy friend and I want
to know how to spell "sense".
Well, which sense do you mean?
Well, I said I haven't seen you sense Thursday.

4927 Johnnie — you mispelled most of the words in your composition.
Yes'm — I'm going to be a dialect writer.

4928 Now, if I write n-e-w on the blackboard, what does that spell?
New.
Now, I'll put a "k" in front of it and what have we?
Canoe.

4929 Spell the word neighbor.
N-e-i-g-h-b-o-r.
That's right. Now, Tommy, can you tell me what a neighbor
is?
It's a woman that borrows things

RELATED SUBJECTS
Definitions of Words 4978-4991
Pronunciation 4992

WRITING

4930 I want to buy a pencil.
Hard or soft?
Hard, it's for a stiff exam.

4931 Is there anything you can do better than anyone else?
Yes, sir, read my own handwriting.

4932 Really, Johnny, your handwriting is terrible. You must learn
to write better.
Well, if I did you'd be finding fault with my spelling.

4933 I just bought a nickel eraser.
Oh, I should think a rubber one would be much better.
RELATED SUBJECTS
School 4885-4894

ENGLISH

4934 Lay down, pup — lay down. Good doggie — lay down, I say.
You'll have to say "lie down" — that's a Boston Terrier.

4935 Is it correct to say: You have et?
No, it's wrong.
Why is it wrong to say: You have et?
Because I ain't et yet.

4936 Are you going to the movies after the program tonight?
No, I ain't going.
What grammar! You should say: I'm not going, they're not

going, he is not going, she is not going. Get the idea?
Sure — nobody ain't going.

4937 Did you study your history?
      Naw, I ain't had no time for nothin' but my English.

4938 Name a collective noun.
      Ash can.

4939 What does a dash before a sentence is finished mean?
      I know a guy that tried that and it meant five more years at
      hard labor.

4940 Can't you understand English?
      Can't you speak it?

4941 What makes his talk so funny?
      His English is broken.
      Don't look at me — I didn't break it.
      He's a linguist.
      He is what?
      He is a linguist. He speaks several languages.
      So do I.
      I'll try you out. Parlez-vous francais?
      I don't get you.
      I said, do you speak French?
      Oh, sure — sure! Why didn't you say so the first time?

4942 That sergeant of mine ought to be hung!
      Not hung, my boy, hanged.
      Hung, I say; hanging is too good for him.

4943 Who was that lady I seen you with last night?
      My, such bad English.

4944 William, construct a sentence using the word "archaic."
      We can't have archaic and eat it, too.

4945 All right, now we'll make up sentences using the word "beans."
      1st: My father grows beans.
      2nd: My mother cooks beans.
      3rd: We are all human beans.

4946 Where are you all going?
      Why do you talk like that? Why don't you talk like the rest
      of the people do in New York?
      Well, it took me forty years to learn to say "you all" and I've
      only been in New York six months and you can't expect me
      to learn to say "youse guys" in that length of time.

4947 Correct this sentence: It was me that spilt the ink.
      It wasn't me that spilt the ink.

4948   They say him and her's gonna get married.
Don't say him and her, say her and him. Always put ladies first.

4949   What is the opposite of sorrow?
Joy.
And the opposite of misery?
Happiness.
And what is the opposite of woe?
Giddap!

4950   Professor: This essay on our dog is, word for word, the same as your brother's.
Student: Yes, sir, it's the same dog.

4951   Do you come from Boston?
Certainly not! I'm talking this way because I cut my mouth on a bottle.

4952   Now, class, what do we mean by plural?
By plural we mean it's the same thing, only more of it.

4953   Tommy, what is a synonym?
A synonym is a word you use when you can't spell the other one. one.

4954   Mason Dixie line is the division between "you all" and "youse guys."

RELATED SUBJECTS
Nationalities 1059-1101
Stupidity 1337-1381
Children 3326-3333
Definitions of Words 4978-4991
Pronunciation 4992
Stenographer 5322-5329

ABBREVIATIONS

4955   My son just received his B.A.
I suppose now he'll be looking for a Ph.D.
No, now he's looking for a J-O-B.

4956   I've got my business manager here. Mr. Doakes C.P.N.
You mean C.P.A. Certified Public Accountant.
No — C.P.N. Constant Pain in the Neck.

4957   You should have written S.W.A.K. — sealed with a kiss — on
       the back of the envelope. You did seal it with a kiss, didn't
       you?
       No — with a little mucilage.

4958   What's she trying for at college — an M.A.?
       No — an M.R.S.

4959   He went to college and received an M.A. and a B.A. but his
       P.A. still supports him.

4960   This is the year 1980 A.D.
       A.D.?
       Yeah, All Day.

RELATED SUBJECTS
Alphabet 4895-4898

BOOKS

4961   Do you know the deepest book ever written?
       Sure — Twenty Leagues Under the Sea.

4962   Did you ever read Tolstoi's "Goodbye"?
       I didn't even know he was leaving.

4963   I brought this book back; mother says it isn't fit for me to read.
       I think your mother must be mistaken.
       Oh, no, she isn't. I've read it all through.

4964   I'm reading a story but I don't like the ending.
       How do you like the beginning?
       Oh, I haven't come to that yet.
       You must read backwards.
       I'll be glad to. Who wrote it?

4965   Have you read "Freckles"?
       No, ma'am — mine are the brown kind.

4966   Do you agree with the philosophy of Bacon?
       Only when it's crisp.

4967   This woman Salome must have been mean.
       Yes?

I'll say so. The literary critic says: In the final analysis it was Salome that made Oscar Wilde.

4968 Do you know the Spell of the Yukon?
Of course, Y-U-K-O-N.

4969 You know that pet bookworm I have? You won't see him for some time. He left yesterday. He is taking a two-year trip through *"Gone With the Wind."*

4970 Is this a free translation?
No, sir. The book will cost you two dollars.

4971 Do you know Poe's Raven?
No, what's he mad about?

4972 I love to browse in a library.
High browse or low browse?

4973 Can I see that book I had last week?
I guess so. Was it fascinating?
No, but it's got my girl friend's telephone number in it.

4974 Whatcher been doin' this evenin'?
Reading "Ben Hur."
Oh, readin' racy literature nowadays.

4975 Did ya ever read *Alice in Wonderland?*
When was it published?
Long before ya was born.
That accounts for it escapin' me.

4976 I want some good current literature.
Here are some books on electric lighting.

4977 Do you read Poe?
Naw — I read pretty good.

RELATED SUBJECTS
Writer 1612-1642
Shakespeare 4594-4597

DEFINITIONS OF WORDS

4978 That would put me in jeopardy. Don't you know what jeopardy means?
Sure — my uncle is one — a jeopardy sheriff.

4979 Why don't you go straight home?
What?
I said — go straight home. You know what straight means?
Sure — without gingerale.

4980　Don't under-rate yourself. I hope you know what under-rate is?
　　　Sure, seven.

4981　Don't you know what an operetta is?
　　　Don't be silly. An operetta is a girl who works for the telephone company.

4982　I guess 'most all their trouble is caused because they're opposites.
　　　Opposites? Have you made a study of opposites?
　　　You bet I have.
　　　What's your definition of an absolute opposite?
　　　You drinking a horse's neck.

4983　You go ahead and recite and I'll get apoplexy.
　　　I'll recite first and then get him.
　　　Apoplexy isn't a man.
　　　Then get her.

4984　Don't you know the difference between ammonia and pneumonia?
　　　Sure, one comes in bottles and the other in chests.

4985　Have you put the little sailors on the table yet?
　　　Little sailors?
　　　Yeah, the goblets.

4986　You are wearing me down until I'm skin and bones—a regular skeleton.
　　　What is a skeleton?
　　　A skeleton is a person with the inside out and the outside off.

4987　We'd better do something to remedy the status quo.
　　　What's status quo?
　　　That is the Latin for the mess we's in.

4988　Hey, Clarence, wot does Riviera mean?
　　　Reeveera? Why, that's foreign for "river" — haven't you ever heard of the Muddyrainian Rivera?

4989　Have you ever heard of the Sesquicentennial?
　　　No, what's the name of it?
　　　What?
　　　What did you say?
　　　I didn't say anything.
　　　Oh, I didn't hear you.

4990　What's an innocent bystander?
　　　A person so simple-minded he doesn't know enough to get out of the way.

4991　Can you tell me the meaning of the word "unaware"?
　　　Unaware is what you put on first and take off last.

RELATED SUBJECTS
English 4934-4954

PRONUNCIATION

4992   You went to California last summer, didn't you?

Yeah. On my way back I stopped off at San-Jew-wan.

No — it is San Juan — the "J" is pronounced like an "H". You understand?

You'll have to give me a little time to get that. You see I was only there two months — Hune and Huly.

RELATED SUBJECTS
English 4934-4954
Speech 5111-5123
Attorney 5235-5244

PUNCTUATION

4993   I was a stenographer, but I couldn't work for my boss any more.

Why not?

Because my boss wanted a period after every sentence.

Well, your boss was right.

Yes, but he wanted a recreation period.

4994   How would you punctuate this sentence? Mary went swimming and lost her bathing suit.

Kid: I'd make a dash after Mary.

4995   What is your rule for punctuating?

I set as long as I can hold my breath and then put in a comma;

when I yawn I put in a semicolon, and when I want a chew of tobacco I make a paragraph.

RELATED SUBJECTS
School 4885-4894
English 4934-4954
Letter 5161-5172
Stenographer 5322-5329

FOREIGN LANGUAGES

4996 Can you read Chinese?
Only when it's printed in English.

4997 I took Pete and his girl friend to dinner the other night. They laughed and laughed when I spoke to the waiter in French — but they didn't know I told him to give Pete the check.

4998 Mr. Twirp, what do you know about French syntax?
Gosh, I didn't know they had to pay for their fun.

4999 Sign seen in store window: English spoken — American understood.

5000 He speaks French like a native.
Yes, like a native American.

5001 Number language:
Anything perfect — 100
Not so good — zero
Half right — 50
Divorce — 2 divided by 1.
Married life — 10 (Wife's one and he's nothing)

5002 So I wrote my sister Jessica — Dadica and Momica went to visit Aunt Lizzica. Uncle Samica is buying a new machinica but he doesn't know whether to buy a Fordica or a Chevica. The old cowica had a calfica and he was going to name it Bessica but changed it to Jimica because it was a bullica. Hope you are well. Your brother, Billica.

RELATED SUBJECTS
Nationalities 1059-1101
Foreign Cities 3990-3999
School 4885-4894
Pronunciation 4992
College 5059-5096

GEOGRAPHY

5003 Where are the Andes?
I don't know; if you'd put things where they belong, you'd be able to find 'em.

5004 Tommy, tell me where Mexico is.
It's on page ten of the joggerfy.

5005 What shape is the earth?
I dunno.
Well, what kind of earrings does your girl wear?
Square ones.
No, I mean the ones she wears on Sunday.
Round.
Then, what shape is the earth?
Square on week days — and round on Sundays.

5006 When is a desert like a dessert?
When it's baked Alaska.

5007 Where is the capitol of the United States?
All over the world.

5008 Were you born in Texas?
No, I wasn't.
Well, you look like you were. I can tell. You've got Texas teeth.
Texas teeth?
Yeah, you know, wide open spaces.

5009 You know, they are so smart in Paris that even the little kids speak French!

5010 You don't even know the shape of the earth.
I do, it's square.
No, it's round.
Well, my brother says he's traveled to the four corners of the earth.

5011 Can you tell me how California is bounded?
It's bounded on the west by movie stars; on the bottom by oil; on the north by sun; on the top by sundown; on the south by Tia Juana and on the east by Maine.

5012 Can you tell me what shape the world is?
Well, it's in pretty bad shape just now.

5013 What shape is the earth?
Well, I've decided it isn't round or flat — it's crooked.

5014   Hey, who discovered America?
Ohio.
Ohio — you're crazy — it was Columbus.
Yes, sir, I know. But I didn't think it necessary to mention the gentleman's first name, sir.

RELATED SUBJECTS
Indian 1146-1154
Foreign Cities 3990-3999
Famous Places 4000-4015
School 4885-4894
Cities 5558-5562

HISTORY

5015   What was the greatest comeback in history?
Napoleon's retreat from Moscow.

5016   Do you know what happened to Pompeii?
Sure — he died of an eruption.

5017   Haven't you ever heard of the fall of Rome?
No, but I remember hearing something drop.

5018   My brother swallowed my history book. Now he has hiccups all the time.
That shows history repeats itsef.

5019   I'll find out what you know about history. Who were the Puritans?
Huh?
Who were the Puritans? Who were the people who were punished in stocks?
The small investors.

5020   Can you tell me what the former ruler of Russia was called?
Tsar.
Correct. And what was his wife called?
Tsarina.
Right. What were the Tsar's children called?
Tsardines!

5021   What is an emperor?
I don't know.
An emperor is a ruler.
Oh, sure, I used to carry an emperor to school with me.

5022   What part of the body is the fray?
What part of the body is the fray? What are you talking about?

Well, right here in this history book it says — the general was shot in the thick of the fray.

5023 Weren't you stretchin' a point when you told that story about Lee's surrender at Appomattox, you know when you said Grant was dressed in his underwear?
No — and I kin prove I'm right about it. Listen to this: Here is what it says in the history book. At the time of Lee's surrender, the Confederate General wore a brand new uniform, while General Grant was dressed in a very old Union suit.

5024 Now, what did Caesar exclaim when Brutus stabbed him?
Ouch!

5025 What did they teach you at school today, sonny?
Oh, teacher told us all about Columbus who went two thousand miles on a galleon.
She did, did she? Well, don't believe all she tells you about those foreign cars, my boy.

5026 What makes you think Atlas was a bad man?
The book says that he held up the whole world.

RELATED SUBJECTS
Indian 1146-1154
Foreign Cities 3990-3999
Famous Places 4000-4015
School 4885-4894
Famous People 5029-5049

PLYMOUTH ROCK

5027 The first thing the Pilgrims did was to land on Plymouth Rock.
Why should the Pilgrims be so hard hearted? What had the Plymouth Rock ever done to them that they should land on it?

5028 Where did the Pilgrims land?
On Plymouth Rock.
That was a terrible way to start out.
What do you mean?
Being on the rocks from the beginning.

FAMOUS PEOPLE

5029 They were playing the andante movement.
I didn't even know she could dance, this Aunt Dante of yours.
Have you any idea what andante movement is?
Sure — she's an Italian lady and her father was an Italian Poet.

He wrote a famous poem.
You mean Dante's Inferno?
He's where?
Not where. Dante's Inferno.
I didn't know that — when did he leave?
He's been dead over a hundred years.
Is that so? I didn't even know he was sick.

5030   Have you ever read Bacon?
No — but I've eaten it.
No — I mean Bacon, the author — he was a great author.
Oh yeah — I knew Bacon very well — why, we used . . .
You knew Bacon? Say, Bacon is dead over two hundred years . . .
Is that so? My, how time flies.

5031   Mrs. Brown: Whatever happened to Charlie Chaplin?
Mr. Brown: He died awhile back, dear. Didn't you know?
Mrs. Brown: No, I never heard. Poor soul; so he's dead?
Mr. Brown: Yes, dear, dead and buried.
Mrs. Brown: And buried, too! Oh, mercy! Its even worse than I
     thought!

5032   Do you know who Patrick Henry was and what he did?
Sure. He's the fellow that started the gimmies.
The gimmies?
Yeah — he said: Gimme liberty or gimme death.

5033   Have you seen the Mickey Rooney doll?
The Mickey Rooney doll?
Yeah, wind it up and it gets married.

5034   Venus de Milo wore the first sleeveless gown.
Why did she do it?

5035   Who's the hottest ham in show business today?
Miss Piggy, of course.

5036   Why have people given up other creeds and followed the Hare
     Krishnas?
I guess because they would like to start life with a new sheet.

5037   Al Capone must have been one of the strongest men who ever
     lived. They say he liked to hold up banks.

5038   Paul Revere: (Shouting at window) Husband at home?
Lady: Yes.
Paul Revere: Tell him the British are coming. (Shouting at an-
     other window) Husband at home?
Lady: No.
Paul Revere: To hell with the British.

5039   Paul Revere: Awake, the British are coming! Awake, the British
        are coming! To arms! To arms! To arms!
        Woman: (Yelling out of window) Well, that's nothing to yell
        about and wake up the whole neighborhood — every one has
        two arms!

5040   What did Franklin say when he discovered electricity in light-
        ning?
        Nothing, he was too shocked.

5041   What is the best thing you know about James Madison?
        His wife Dolly. I think she makes the best cakes in the world.

5042   He doesn't even know when George Washington was born.
        Washington was born in Virginia in 1732.
        I saw that in a book, but I thought it was the phone number.

RELATED SUBJECTS
Nobility 1134-1135
Society 1136-1144
Autograph 4591-4593
Geography 5003-5014
History 5015-5026

EXAMINATION

5043   I must caution you about your son. I caught him cheating in
        his botany examination. He had seven flowers in his button-
        hole and a quantity of pollen up his sleeve. Tomorrow we have
        an anatomy examination and if I catch him with a nudist
        under his coat, he will be expelled.

5044   Give for one year the number of tons of coal shipped out of
        the United States.
        Fourteen ninety-two — none.

5045   How did you get along in your examinations?
        I got 100.
        What did you get 100 in?
        I got 50 in arithmetic and 50 in spelling.

5046   I got discouraged — I failed in everything but geography.
        How was that?
        I didn't take geography.

5047   What is the date, please?
        Never mind the date. The examination is more important.
        Well, sir, I wanted to have something right on my paper.

5048   When better exams are made — they won't be passed.

5049   Student: Did you give me my grades in round numbers?
        Professor: Yes — I gave you zero.

5050   Did you pass your exam?
        Well, it was like this — you see. . . .
        Shake! Neither did I.

5051   Whatcha been doing?
        Taking part in a guessing contest.
        But I thought you had an exam in math.
        I did.

5052   Professor: Why the quotation marks all over this paper?
        Student: Courtesy to the man on my right, professor.

5053   How did you come to mark this man's paper 101%. Don't you
            know that nothing can be more perfect than 100%?
        Yeah — but this man answered one question we didn't ask.

5054   Did you pass your finals?
        And how.
        Were they easy?
        Dunno . . . ask Jim.

5055   I would have passed my examination but for one thing.
        What was that?
        The little boy that always sits back of me was sick.
        SEE ALSO
        Writing (Hand) 4930

GRADUATION

5056   I got to go to the gymnasium to get graduated.
        You're going to graduate in the gymnasium? That's a funny
            place.
        Well, it says here on the card: Come to the exercises.

5057   But you graduated from college, why do you want to go back
          and take a post-graduate course?
       Because I've got three bottles of gin left.

5058   I won't graduate from college this year.
       Why not?
       I didn't go.

> RELATED SUBJECTS
> Children 3326-3333
> Gift 3943-3962
> School 4885-4894
> College 5059-5096

COLLEGE

5059   So you managed to escape from college?
       Yeah, I'm a fugitive from a brain gang.

5060   Did you ever attend college?
       Yes.
       Did you matriculate?
       What?
       I say, did you matriculate?
       No, I chewed and smoked a little, but maybe some of the other
          boys matriculated.

5061   Would you like to buy a magazine?
       What's the idea?
       I'm working my brother's way through college.

5062   What is meant by "college bred"?
       College bred means a wad of dough, with plenty of crust and
          a lot of crumbs gathered together for a good loaf.

5063   Where did your brother go to college?
       He went to Oxford.
       Oxford? Say Oxford has turned out men of culture, class —
          repute, fame . . .
       He was good too in his way.
       In his way? What way?
       In his dumb way. . . .

5064   I have a brother in Penn State.
       What a small world this is! I have a brother in State Pen, too.

5065   He wants to be a college man, so he put hair tonic on his slicker,
          trying to make a raccoon coat out of it.

5066   What is your son studying in college?
       Languages.
       Languages? I thought he was taking medicine.

Well, I got a bill that said: Twenty dollars for French; Fifty dollars for Spanish; and Two hundred dollars for Scotch.

5067 When you were in college what did you go in for?
Because it was raining.

5068 Incidentally, what was the by-word — what was your college yell?
Lend me five bucks.

5069 I'll let you know I got a letter at college.
I know — a letter from the dean saying you'd better settle down and study or they'd kick you out.

5070 Are you a student?
No, I just go to college here.

5071 You can always pick a college man out of any crowd.
Yes, too bad they are so untidy.

5072 The newcomer placed his hand on the shoulder of the convict before him and began the rhythmic lockstep back to jail. He leaned forward a little and whispered to the tired convict ahead: Is this all there is to this rock splitting job?
Ain't fourteen hours a day of it enough?
Nothing to it.
Seven days a week of it! Bad food — lousy beds . . .
It's heaven!
Say, where the hell did you come from?
I . . . I was a college professor.

5073 Well, I see you went to a fraternity.
Oh, no. I just sat on a stove by mistake.

5074 George comes from a very poor family.
Why, they sent him to the University, didn't they?
Yes, that's how they got so poor.

5075 Letter from daughter at college: I realize, mother, that daddy is paying a lot to keep me at school and that I must try and learn something. I am taking up contract bridge.

5076 Was your father a college man?
Yes, but we never mention it. The college he went to had a rotten football team.

5077 I'm taking three courses in college: French, Spanish and Algebra.
Let me hear you say good evening in Algebra.

5078   I was a four letter man in college.
       A four letter man?
       Yeah.
       I know — d-u-m-b.

5079   I'm a college graduate and I'd like to know what I should do
         to make my living in this world.
       Just marry the first girl you find that has a steady job.

5080   What's your boy going to be when he finishes his education?
       An octogenarian, I think.

5081   Where have you been for the last four years?
       At college taking medicine.
       And did you finally get well?

5082   What is your son taking in college?
       Oh, he's taking all I've got.

5083   Yes, it's a great college — it's a college that makes a man proud
         of having thought some of going there.

5084   Some professors feel the reason the modern student doesn't burn
         the midnight oil as he used to is that he doesn't get in soon
         enough.

5085   Did your son get what was coming to him at college?
       Well, they gave him a black sheepskin

5086   What's the enrollment of your college?
       Four hundred with and two hundred without.
       With and without what?
       Football players.

5087   My brother didn't have a college education. He was thrown out
         of Smith.
       Why, Smith is only for women.
       That's why he was thrown out.

5088   I'm going to enter the diplomatic service.
       Domestic or foreign?
       Neither. I'm going to be president of a University.

5089   Are you a college boy?
       No. Couldn't get in where I wanted to.
       What did you try for?
       Wellesley.

5090   I got a letter from the college that says our Nellie's been stealin'.
       What?
       Says she's takin' home economics.

5091   Has your son's college education proved of any real value?
       Yes, indeed, it has entirely cured his mother of bragging about
       him.

5092   Well, son, now that you're a grad what are you going to do?
       I'm going to talk to you about the good old days.

5093   How old is Professor Greene?
       Pretty old. They say he used to teach Shakespeare.

5094   What did your son learn at college?
       Well — he hadn't been home a week before he showed me how
       to open bottles with a half dollar.

5095   What is the professor's research work?
       It consists principally of hunting for his spectacles.

5096   By the time the average college boy of today succeeds in accumu-
       lating the horsehide, the pigskin, the coonskin and finally the
       sheepskin, poor father hasn't much hide left either.

RELATED SUBJECTS
Absentmindedness 1297-1319
Love 2595-2640
Sports 4319-4505
School 4885-4894
Abbreviations 4955-4960

RACCOON COAT

5097   Your little boy is pulling all the fur off your raccoon coat.
       Take the coat away from him.
       I did but he keeps crying.
       Then give him the cat.

RELATED SUBJECTS
Flirtation 2779-2784
Furs 3505-3515
Moth 3516-3524

DEGREE

5098 Sure, mum, I've got three degrees. One from Harvard, one from
      Princeton and the third degree from the police.

RELATED SUBJECTS
Graduation 5056-5058

SECTION III

GOVERNMENT

POLITICS

POLITICIAN

5099 Here, have some candy. It's political taffy.
      Political taffy? Why do you call it that?
      Because it has lots of pull.

5100 (Man wearing three hats)
      What's the idea?
      You know I've decided to become a politician.
      What are you wearing three hats for?
      A politician has one hat to cover his head, another he tosses in
      the ring and one hat he talks through.

5101 Fellow citizens, I have fought for our country. I have often had
      no bed but the battlefield, and no canopy but the sky. I have
      marched over the frozen ground till every step has been
      marked with blood.
      (Listener) By golly, I'll be darned if you haven't done enough for
      your country. Go home and rest. I'll vote for the other fellow.

5102 How did the audience receive your campaign speech when you
      told them you had never bought a vote?
      A few cheered, but the majority seemed to lose interest.

5103 I thought he was a politician.
      He was until his laugh failed

5104 My uncle's a politician.
      What is he running for?
      They just looked up his record and he's running for a train.

5105 The other party has been robbing you for ten years, now give us
      a chance.

5106   Hello there, Judgie, old boy, old boy.
Don't get so familiar — the election is over.

5107   Politician: Hey, you, get me three well-sharpened pencils and a couple dozen sheets of paper. I've got to make a list of all the promises I must forget when I'm safely elected.

5108   My father was a great Western politician in his day.
What did he run for?
The border.

5109   Politician: I don't like anyone who uses the hammer all the time.
2nd Politician: Didn't you say you wanted me to help you keep your platform in good shape?

5110   I've got a perfect news story.
A man bit a dog!
Naw, a bull threw a Congressman.

> RELATED SUBJECTS
> Dishonesty 2500-2502
> Election 5124-5130
> Money 5457-5479

SPEECH

5111   If all the people who sit through after-dinner speeches were lined up three feet apart, they would stretch.

5112   And now that he was finished, and the facts were before them, there existed a vast silence, as of the far places of the earth. It was a silence pregnant with possibilities; anything might be born of a calm such as that. But strange to say, absolutely nothing happened. They were all asleep.

5113   He made an unusually good after-dinner speech.
What did he say?
He said: Waiter, give me the check.

5114   Did you ever speak before a big audience?
Yes.
What did you say?
Not guilty.

5115   You are a fine after-dinner speaker. People wouldn't be able to eat if they heard you before dinner.

5116   An after-dinner speaker gushed on and on. Deacon Miller nodded and presently rested his head on the tablecloth. The chairman reached over and bumped him lightly on the head with his gavel.
Deacon Miller: Hit me harder — I can still hear him.

5117   Greatest after-dinner speaker in the world is the one who says: Well, boys, this is on me.

5118   Speaker: There are so many ribald interruptions I can scarcely hear myself speaking.
Man: Cheer up, Guv'nor — you ain't missin' much.

5119   Speaker: Gentleman, lend me your ears.
Man (in audience): You can have mine, and thank heaven I can't hear without 'em.

5120   (Speaker getting tired of being interrupted)
Speaker: We seem to have a great many fools here tonight. Wouldn't it be advisable to hear one at a time?
Man (in audience): Yes. Get on with your speech.

5121   Wake that fellow next to you, will you?
Better do it yourself; you put him to sleep.

5122   Have you ever addressed the public?
Oh, yeah, I've addressed thousands of people in Madison Square Garden.
What did you say?
Pop corn — peanuts — soda pop!

5123   Speaker: I want land reform . . . I want housing reform . . . I want educational reform . . . I want. . . .
Listener: Chloroform.

RELATED SUBJECTS
Toast 2440-2442
Congratulation 2443-2444
Proverbs 2543-2546
Applause 4586-4590
Definitions of Words 4978-4991
Pronunciation 4992

ELECTION

5124   Hey, that election is crooked.
        How come?
        Why, I went into the voting booth and saw Jim and Roy stuffing
            the ballot box.
        When did you see that?
        The third time I went in to vote.

5125   He makes money on election day. He is sort of a taxidermist.
        What is that?
        He stuffs the ballot boxes.

5126   But why are you going to the North Pole?
        They told me if I wanted to vote I'd have to go to the poles.

5127   The mayor stole the last election.
        No, he didn't.
        He did, too.
        No, he paid spot cash for it.

5128   You are charged with voting three times. What have you got
            to say about it?
        Then I've been gypped. They only paid me for once.

5129   How did the election come out in your district?
        Oh, crooked politics beat us. We were fixing to offer one dollar
            for votes and the other side came along and offered two
            dollars. It was certainly a terrible blow to reform.

5130   What is a suffragette?
        A being who has ceased to be a lady and is no gentleman.

SEE ALSO   RELATED SUBJECTS
Honesty 2494   Honesty 2490-2499
Politician 5106   Politician 5099-5110
                           Policeman 5225-5228
                           Judge 5245-5250

PRESIDENT

SEE:
Age 62   Ambition 1874
Nose 539   Wolf-at-door 3312
Female (the) 935   College 5088

DEPARTMENTS

MILITARY

NAVY

5131   Sailor: I've been following the water for sixteen years.
        Woman: (looking him over) You look like you never caught
            up with it.

RELATED SUBJECTS
Army 5134-5147
War 5148-5152

OFFICER

5132 I served in the army in the world war.
Tell me, did you get a commission?
Naw, just a straight salary.

5133 You say your brother's an officer: What rank?
Just plain rank.

RELATED SUBJECTS
Detective 4277-4279
Policeman 5225-5228

ARMY

5134 Private, why did you salute that refrigerator?
Because it was General Electric.
And that jeep?
Because it was General Motors.

5135 I hear your uncle got kicked out of the army. Is that true?
Yes, he got kicked out of the army for taking a furlong.
You mean furlough, don't you?
No, he went too far and stayed too long.

5136 What are the Army and Navy for?
For? The Army and Navy forever.

5137 My brother went two years to West Point — he's a half soldier.
That's nothing. My brother's a wholesaler.

5138 The fellow I was with last night fought with Pershing.
What about?

5139 I'm a West Pointer.
You look like an Irish Setter to me.

5140 Private: Sarge, when you're shot, how do you know you're not
    dead?
Sarge: Two ways: if you are hungry and your feet are cold.
Private: How does that prove anything?
Sarge: Well, if you're hungry, then you know you're not in
    heaven, and if your feet are cold, you know you're not in the
    other place.

5141   I heard you were courtmartialed in the army.
       Yes, I started that alphabet habit long before Roosevelt.
       The alphabet habit? What did you do?
       I was A.W.O.L.
       And what was the verdict?
       J.A.I.L.

5142   I understand in the thick of the battle they found you running
          back to safety.
       Oh, no, I wasn't running back to safety. I was just backin' up
          to get a good runnin' start to charge!

5143   Soldier: Shall I mark time with my feet, sir?
       Lieutenant: (sarcastically) Did you ever hear of marking time
          with your hands?
       Soldier: Yes, sir. Clocks do it.

5144   Once, while we were engaged in battle, the enemy got closer
          and closer and all of a sudden one of the enemy was right
          in front of me and he stuck a gun right in my chest and
          pulled the trigger.
       Wait a minute. The bullet would have gone through your heart
          and killed you.
       I know it — but I was so scared — my heart was in my mouth
          when he fired.

5145   Once when I was on sentry duty, when the enemy opened up
          with all them shells and machine guns, I formed a line.
       What? One man form a line?
       Yes, sir, I formed a bee-line for the rear.

5146   I was in the service, too.
       Was you ever wounded?
       No, fortunately I escaped without a scratch!
       So did I — them "cooties" never did bother me!

5147   When I was in the army, we studied cootie arithmetic.
       Cootie arithmetic — what have cooties to do with arithmetic?
       Well, they added to our troubles, subtracted from our pleas-
          ures, divided our attention and oh how they multiplied.

                                          RELATED SUBJECTS
                                          Gun 4454-4461

WAR

5148 I wonder why they are always having revolutions in South America.
I don't know—from what I've seen, it's just for the newsreels.

5149 —How do you feel about the draft—It leaves me cold.

5150 Were you in the late war?
Yeah, I was two years late.

5151 Son: Father, how do wars begin?
Father: Well, suppose America quarreled with England, and . . .
Mother: But England and America must not quarrel.
Father: I know — but I'm taking a hypothetical instance.
Mother: You are misleading the child.
Father: No, I'm not . . .
Mother: Yes, you are . . .
Father: I tell you I am not! It's outrageous . . .
Son: All right, Dad. Don't get excited. I think I know how
wars begin.

5152 Now that my brother joined up, the war will be over soon. He's
never held a job for more than two weeks in his life!

RELATED SUBJECTS
Courage 2320-2339
Fear 2340-2347
Patriotism 2475-2478
Gun 4454-4461

SPY

5153 Oh, mother, when is father coming home?
Your father is a brave man in the Secret Service.
What's he doing in the Secret Service?
He's a spy.
Who is he spying for?
Ah, that's the secret.

5154 I came here on a great mission — a secret mission.
What is it?
I don't know — it's so secret they didn't tell me.

5155 Are you a Russian spy?
No — I'm a mincepie.
You've gotta lot of crust.

RELATED SUBJECTS
Secret 1565-1575

MEDAL

5156 I was very successful during the war; I decorated myself with
medals.
Boy! What brass!

5157 See this medal — I got it from the police department.
      Is it gold or bronze?
      Neither — it's a police medal.

5158 I won several decorations in the war. Once a young lady came
      up to me and said: "Oh, Captain Zilch, did you kill any of
      the enemy during the war?" So I told her yes, and do you
      know she asked me which hand I used, and I told her my
      right hand, and then you'll never guess what she did.
      No, what?
      Why, that beautiful young lady grabbed my hand and covered
      it with kisses.
      You sure are an idiot.
      Why so?
      Why didn't you tell her you bit them to death?

5159 He was to get a medal for bravery but they couldn't give it to
      him.
      Why not?
      He was so ugly they couldn't find a French General who would
      kiss him.

                              RELATED SUBJECTS
                              Courage 2320-2339
                              Navy 5131
                              Army 5134-5147
                              War 5148-5152

PEACE PARLEY

5160 I'm going to a peace parley.
      What is a peace parley?
      A parley is a parrot—and a parrot is a bird—and a peace parley
      is where all the nations get together and give each other the
      bird.

WAR DEBT

SEE: Proverbs 2543
Nationalities 1085   Bills 3286
                                 Shark 4419

POST OFFICE

LETTER

5161 What's that peculiar odor I smell around this post office?
      Probably the dead letters.

5162 She is so dumb she has spent the day looking for a round mail
      box so she can post circular letters.

5163   Why was your letter so damp?
       Postage due, I guess.

5164   Hey, did you see the letter sail through the window? There
          comes another letter. Where are they coming from?
       It's the air mail.

5165   My brother sent me Fifty Dollars but I couldn't use the money
       because it said on the envelope "return in five days."

5166   (Reading letter — panting for breath)
       Why are you panting?
       She writes so fast and I'm such a slow reader.

5167   Care to buy a nice letter opener, sir?
       Don't need one. I'm married.

5168   So Hilda's broken it off with Bobby. I wonder if she still keeps
          his lovely letters.
       No. As a matter of fact, they're keeping her now.

5169   Dear, you've got a special delivery letter at home marked: Pri-
          vate and personal.
       What did it say?

5170   Irate Woman: Have you been reading all my mail, sir?
       Postman: No, ma'am — only the letters.

5171   Young man: Any letters for me today?
       Postman: No.
       Young man: That's very strange.
       Postman: Nothing so strange about it. You haven't answered
          her last letter.

5172   What does P.S. at the end of a letter mean?
       Please settle.

RELATED SUBJECTS
Love Making 2641-2719
Breach of Promise 3055-3056
Attorney 5235-5244
Businessman 5309-5321
Stenographer 5322-5329

LEGISLATION

LAWS

5173   My brother's interested in law.
       Did he study law?

No, but he got a lot of inside information. He always went
with a policeman. They made him a member of their lodge.
They liked him so well they gave him the third degree.
The third degree? That means he had to answer a lot of
questions.
Yeah. He must have answered them all right because they kept
him at their clubhouse for ninety days.

5174   How do you manage to keep crime down in your city?
Oh, whenever we find we can't keep people from gambling,
murdering and killing, we just pass a law legalizing it.

RELATED SUBJECTS
Policeman 5225-5228
Attorney 5235-5244
Judge 5245-5250

5175   Husband: I have no complaints with legislation to give equal
rights to women.
Wife: But they say that it won't stop with jobs, and eventually
men and women will even be sharing public showers!
Husband: Like I said, no complaints.

5176   Man, it's a bummer! It's a bummer how they haven't legalized
pot.
There's only one way to get it passed.
And how's that, man?
Take it to the the highest court, man!

5177   I don't know what happened to this country! What has happened
to good old American Law and Order? Today, admitted
lawbreakers get pardoned and are set free. Convicted
criminals get short sentences and are out pushing their books
and making a mint selling their stories to the movies.
And how does one get away with it?
Just get elected, son, just get elected.

CRIMINALS

THIEF

5178   You're arrested for kidnapping.
Listen, I'm no kidnapper. I'll admit I steal overcoats.
Yeah, and yesterday you stole one with a man in it.

5179 I heard your brother got put in jail again.
Yeah. All on account of taking a little piece of glass.
They couldn't put him in jail for just taking a piece of glass.
This piece of glass turned out to be a diamond.

5180 Are you guilty of stealing the horse?
Can a duck swim?
Don't change the subject.

5181 How do you earn your living? Do you pick pockets?
No, sir. I take 'em as they come.

5182 I have an uncle that hates police alarms.
Why?
He claims it interferes with his work.

5183 My cousin is learning to steal.
Learning to steal — but why?
So he can follow in his father's fingerprints.

5184 Some one took my car this morning.
Why not tell the sheriff?
I can't. He is the one who took it.

5185 They put my brother in jail for stealing, but it wasn't his fault.
Oh, it wasn't his fault?
No, how did he know the woman didn't mean what she said?
What did the woman say?
Well, my brother was helping her house clean and she gave him
a rug and told him to beat it.

5186 Do you think I'd stoop to steal two dollars out of your pants?
No, the pants were hanging up.

5187 Ah, Miss Sticky Fingers, tell me when did you discover you
had taking ways?
I don't know — I guess it is hereditary. My father was a
kleptomaniac.
I see — and you're following in your father's fingerprints?

5188 Say, where'd you get that fur robe?
I just took it out of that car across the street as a joke.
Well, that's carrying a joke too far. Now, you can tell the joke
to the Judge.

5189 Suppose a policeman should come in.
Be nonchalant — say: Police to meet you!

5190 You are accused of entering a piano store and stealing a piano.
What have you to say?
I did it in a moment of weakness.

I suppose if you had been feeling strong, you'd have stolen the First National Bank.

5191   I say, old fellow, why on earth are you washing your spoon in your finger bowl?
Do you think I want to get egg all over my pocket?

5192   Just what good have you done for humanity?
Well, I've kept three or four detectives working regularly.

5193   I once stole money.
Where did you steal it from?
A bank.
How much did you steal?
A half dollar.
What bank was it?
My little baby son's.

5194   Your Honor, I was quietly attending to my own business and this officer arrested me.
That's strange. What is your business?
I'm a burglar. I was robbing a house.
How did you come to rob the house?
I can't tell you. It's a trade secret. But don't punish me too severely, Judge, I was down and out.
You may be down but not out. Thirty days!

5195   Yesterday, a burglar got in the house.
Did he get anything?
I'll say. My wife thought I was coming home late.

5196   What does your husband do?
He's interested in up-lift business.
Up-lift business?
Yeah, he goes around and says: Stick 'em up.

5197   What were you doing breaking into a cigar store?
I was only trying to get a ten cent cigar.
Why did you break open the cash register?
I was only trying to put the dime in it.

5198   Wife: I think there's a burglar in the house.
Husband: Well, let him alone. He'll find out his mistake himself.

5199   And you didn't hear the burglar?
No, as a matter of fact, we were eating our soup . . .
Then, of course, none of you heard anything.

5200   Policeman to suspicious stranger caught at midnight in a store:
What are you doing in this store?
Man: Can't you see, I'm taking stock.

5201   (Burglar's wife being cross-examined by the District Attorney.
        Attorney: Madam, you are the wife of this prisoner?
        Woman: Yes.
        Attorney: You knew he was a burglar when you married him?
        Woman: Yes.
        Attorney: May I ask how you came to marry such an individual?
        Woman: You may. You see I was getting old and had to choose
            between a burglar and a lawyer!

5202   (Man being held up by two burglars)
        Burglar: Excuse me, sir. I wonder if you could oblige me with
            the loan of a penny?
        Man: 'Why — er — yes, I think so. But may I ask for what
            purpose you require it?
        Burglar: Oh, certainly, sir. My mate and I wish to toss the
            coin to decide our little argument as to which of us shall
            have your watch, and which your wallet.

5203   Victim: But my watch isn't a good one. Its value is only senti-
            mental.
        Burglar: That doesn't matter — I'm sentimental.

5204   You've committed six burglaries in a week.
        That's right. If every one worked as hard as I do we'd be on
            the road to prosperity.

5205   Can I sell you a burglar alarm?
        No, but if you've got anything that will keep my wife from
            waking up when one visits us, trot it out.

5206   Lawyer: Well, my man, so you want me to defend you? Have you
            any money?
        Man: No, but I got a 1979 Ford car.
        Lawyer: Well, you can raise some money on that. Now, let's
            see — just what do they accuse you of stealing?
        Man: A 1979 Ford car.

5207   Where were you on the night this man was murdered at ten
            o'clock?
        I was on the corner of Tenth and Main holding up the drug
            store.

5208   My brother was a little unfortunate in business. First, he opened
            a grocery store and that failed; then he opened a shoe store
            and that failed — and then he opened a bank and although
            he was successful he had to give it up. He couldn't open any
            more banks.
        Why not — was it overwork?
        No — they sent him up the river for six months.

5209   You know, I missed a knife and fork after the dinner party I
          gave last night.
          You're not insinuating I stole your knife and fork?
          No, I know you don't use them.

5210   I understand your uncle is finally taking a step to cure himself
          of stealing?
          Yeah — the lockstep.

5211   Well, my man, and what do you do when you are out of prison?
          In the spring I picks peas, in summer I picks fruit, in the autumn
             I picks hops, and in winter I picks pockets.
          And what happens then?
          Then I comes in here and picks rocks.

5212   Judge: This robbery was consummated in an adroit and skillful
          manner.
          Prisoner: Come now, your Honor. No flattery, please.

5213   So you robbed the cash register in the grocery store because you
          were starving?
          Yes, sir!
          Why didn't you take something to eat?
          Because I'm a proud man, Judge, and I make it a rule to pay
             for everything I eat.

5214   So they caught you with this bundle of silverware. Whom did you
          plunder?
          Two college dorms, your Honor.
          Call up the downtown hotels and distribute this stuff.

RELATED SUBJECTS
Dishonesty 2500-2502
Detective 4277-4279
Gun 4454-4461
Policeman 5225-5228
Arrest 5229-5230
Trial 5251-5275
Penitentiary 5283-5298

BLACKMAILER

5215   Just one moment, pardner, can you spare a fellow a dime?
       What brought you to this state?
       You'd not believe it, sir! But the tabloid newspapers ruined
          my business. Why, sir, I was once a successful blackmailer.

> RELATED SUBJECTS
> Detective 4277-4279
> Gun 4454-4461
> Policeman 5225-5228

KIDNAPPER

5216   Do you mean I'm going to be held here for ransom?
       I should say not. Let Ransom get his own women.

5217   Madam, we shall hold you until your husband ransoms you.
       Oh, dear, I wish now I'd treated John a little better.

5218   Your wife was kidnapped while she was on the links today.
       Ye gods! And she had my best clubs with her!

> RELATED SUBJECTS
> Detective 4277-4279
> Gun 4454-4461
> Policeman 5225-5228
> Penitentiary 5283-5298

MURDERER

5219   How long is your uncle in for?
       Two months.
       What did he do?
       Killed his wife.
       And they only gave him two months?
       Yes, then they're going to hang him.

5220   She shot her husband.
       That so? What did she get?
       Page one, the *Daily News*.

5221   Officer, where do I go to apologize for shooting my husband?

5222   (The judge gazed with horrified wonder at the accused mur-
          derer)
       Judge: Do you mean to tell me that you killed this poor old
          woman for the paltry sum of three dollars?
       Murderer: Well, you know how it is, yer Honor, t'ree smackers
          here and t'ree smackers dere — it soon counts up.

5223   You say you've a perfect answer to this wife murder charge?
          What is it?
       She wasn't my wife.

5224   He got a life sentence for murder and six months extra for
        carrying concealed weapons.

RELATED SUBJECTS
Death 124-145
Detective 4277-4279
Gun 4454-4461
Policeman 5225-5228
Arrest 5229-5230
Trial 5251-5275
Hanging 5299-5308

LAW ENFORCEMENT

POLICEMAN

5225   My brother has a new job.
        Yes — what doing?
        He's connected with the Police Department.
        Police Department? How?
        Only by a pair of handcuffs.

5226   He will make a wonderful policeman. He can fall asleep any-
        where.

5227   How to get a cop when you need one: Write your representative
        in Congress. He will forward your letter to the district
        assemblyman — if he is on good terms with the commissioner
        he'll have the commissioner appoint a member of your family
        as a cop and you'll have a cop in the family all the time.

5228   Judge: Why didn't you seize the thief when you found him?
        Policeman: How could I? I had my club in one hand and my
        revolver in the other.

RELATED SUBJECTS
Accidents 615-709
Pedestrian 4029-4037
Automobile 4042-4146
Gun 4454-4461
Officer 5132-5133
Criminals 5178-5224

ARREST

5229   He had a job in a bank but he had to quit it.
        Why, because he needed a rest?
        No, because he didn't want to get arrested.

5230　Sergeant at police station to habitual criminal: What! you back again?

Man: Yes, sir. Any letters?

> Related Subjects
> Criminals 5178-5224
> Trial 5251-5275

REWARD

5231　Good morning, ma'am — did you offer a reward for the return of your little dog?

Yes, did you find my little dog?

No, not yet, ma'am — but as I was just going in search of him I thought you might let me have a little of the reward on account.

> Related Subjects
> Criminals 5178-5224
> Opportunity 5585-5587

STOOL PIGEON

5232　A little bird told me.

It must have been a stool pigeon.

> Related Subjects
> Criminals 5178-5224
> Policeman 5225-5228
> Arrest 5229-5230

THIRD DEGREE

5233　You say the third degree didn't bother you a bit.

No, not at all.

Didn't they fire questions at you rapidly? Didn't they ask where you were at certain hours of the day and night? Didn't they ask for explanations?

Yes.

Didn't they strike you in an endeavor to eke out a confession? Didn't they tell you that you couldn't drink or smoke until you told the truth? Didn't they threaten you?

Yes, they did all that.

And still you say it didn't bother you a bit. Are you inhuman?

No, I was just used to it. My wife's been doing that for years.

> Related Subjects
> Criminals 5178-5224
> Policeman 5225-5228

ALIBI

5234   It would be better if you could prove an alibi. Did anyone see
          you at the time of the crime?
          Fortunately — no!

RELATED SUBJECTS
Lying 1540-1564
Criminals 5178-5224
Attorney 5235-5244
Trial 5251-5275

CONFESSION

SEE:
Nationalities 1092

Church 2529
Unfaithfulness 3064
Thief 5193

COURT PROCEDURE

ATTORNEY

5235   I'm a tailor in a lawyer's office.
          A tailor in a lawyer's office?
          Yes — I press suits.

5236   I'm looking for a criminal lawyer. Have you one here?
          Well, we think we have, but we can't prove it on him.

5237   What is a lawyer?
          A lawyer is a man who gets two other men to strip for a fight
          and then takes their clothes.

5238   And how's lawyer Jones doing, Doctor?
          Poor fellow, he's lying at death's door.
          That's grit for ye; at death's door, an' still lying.

5239   Don't talk to me about lawyers, my dear. I've had so much
          trouble over the property that I sometimes wish my husband
          hadn't died!

5240   Lawyer: (Handing check for $100 to client who had been
          awarded $500) There's the balance after deducting my fee.
          What are you thinking of? Aren't you satisfied?
          Client: I was just wondering who got hit by the car, you or me?

5241   I'm going to be a lawyer like my uncle. He's a good lawyer —
          he gets a lot of people out of jail.
          He must be good.
          I'm going down to visit him now.
          At his office?
          No, at the jail. I've got to try to get *him* out.

5242   Are you a lawyer?
          Yes.

Well, something terrible has happened to me.
Tell me all about it.
I was walking along with my friend, David, and David said:
Somebody is following us, and I asked: Who is it? And David
   said: I don't know. And then a man came up and handed me
   this big piece of paper.
Affidavit?
No, he was after me.

5243 Do you know what legal is?
Sure — the American National Bird.

5244 When I address the jury, I'll plead for clemency.
Nothing doing. Let Clemency get his own lawyer.

RELATED SUBJECTS
Last Will and Testament 200-207
Accidents 615-709
Advice 1978-1989
Divorce 3089-3105
Mortgage 3181-3183
Income Tax 3317-3323
Criminals 5178-5224
Stenographer 5322-5329

JUDGE

5245 Your Honor, the case rests.
I think I'll rest, too.

5246 Judge: How many times have you been up before me?
Prisoner: I don't know — I thought you were keeping score.

5247 You want to go in and say: Good morning, Judge. How do you
   feel?
Not me — I did that once and the Judge said: Fine — $10.

5248 Were you ever up before the Judge?
I don't know; what time does the Judge get up?

5249 I'm going to leave for court.
How did you happen to become a judge?
My brother was on the bench for years.
A real judge, eh?
No, he was a substitute for the New York Yanks.

5250 Judge: I'll fine you five dollars for breaking that glass window.
Man: Here's a ten dollar bill.
Judge: I have no change. I'll keep the ten dollars — go out
   and break another window.

TRIAL

5251   Have you anything to offer the court before sentence is passed
       upon you?
       No, yer honor; me lawyer took me last dollar.

5252   Prisoner, the jury finds you guilty.
       That's all right, Judge. I know you're too intelligent to be in-
       fluenced by what they say.

5253   Are you positive that the prisoner is the man who stole your
       car?
       Well, I was until you cross-examined me. Now I'm not sure
       whether I ever had a car at all.

5254   Lawyer: Don't you think you are straining a point in your
       explanation?
       Witness: Maybe I am, but you often have to strain things
       to make them clear.

5255   Foreman of Jury: Judge, this lady is suing this man for one
       thousand dollars for a kiss?
       Judge: Correct. You, gentlemen of the jury, are to decide if it
       was worth it.
       Foreman of Jury: That's the point. Could the jury have a
       sample?

5256   Guilty or not guilty?
       Not guilty.
       Have you ever been to prison before?
       No, this is the first time I have stolen anything.

5257   You say you have known this man all your life? Do you think
       he would be guilty of stealing this money?
       How much was it?

5258   Judge: Do you want a lawyer to defend you?
       Prisoner: Not particularly, sir.
       Judge: Well, what do you propose to do about the case?
       Prisoner: Oh, I'm quite willing to drop it as far as I'm con-
       cerned.

5259   Judge: Will you tell the jury all you know about the case?
Witness: Yes, if they can spare the time.

5260   Guilty or not guilty?
Well, I thought I was guilty, but I've been talking to my lawyer
and he's convinced me I'm not guilty.

5261   The Judge may give you a suspended sentence.
(Man cries) A suspended sentence?
Don't you know what will happen if you get a suspended
sentence?
Sure. They'll hang me.

5262   Mr. Doakes, take the stand.
Where do you want me to take it?

5263   What floor is this, your Honor?
The fifth floor.
I'm going upstairs.
What for?
I want to be tried in a higher court.

5264   Judge: Order, order, order in the court!
Prisoner: I'll take a ham sandwich on rye with beer.

5265   Guilty or not guilty?
Yeah.
What do you mean — yeah?
I'm guilty or I'm not guilty.

5266   At four o'clock on September 1st I took a bath.
September 1st wasn't Saturday.
Well, anybody can make mistakes.

5267   I understand that our friend Jim has six new lawsuits.
Is that so? He always was a classy dresser.

5268   Are you guilty or not guilty?
It seems to me that that is a mighty personal question.

5269   To Witness: Take the chair.
Witness: What for? I got plenty of furniture now.

5270   Guilty or not guilty?
I'm guilty. I'm wanted in four states.
Dismissed. You are not wanted here.
Can't I have ten days?
Not here. Go where you're wanted.

5271   Judge: Have you a lawyer?
Prisoner: No, but I have some good friends on the jury.

5272   Judge: You men are accused of robbing a bank. Twenty years
        each.
        Men: But we're innocent. We tell you, we're innocent.
        Clerk: The next case is the People vs. Tough Mug O'Malley
        — arrested for robbing a bank, with a machine gun.
        Judge: What have you to say for yourself?
        Man: Guilty.
        Judge: Discharged.
        First Men: Why is that? We told you we're innocent and
        we get twenty years — he says he's guilty and is discharged.
        Judge: It's for your own protection. Why should I put a con-
        fessed criminal in a jail with four innocent men?

5273   Judge: How do you plead?
        Plaintiff: I plead guilty and waive the hearing.
        Judge: What do you mean, waive the hearing?
        Plaintiff: I mean I don't want to hear any more about it.

5274   Judge: What terrible crime has this man committed?
        Attorney: He has done nothing. He was merely an innocent
        bystander when Tough Jim tried to kill a man and we are
        holding him as a witness.
        Judge: And where's Tough Jim?
        Attorney: Out on bail.

5275   Judge: Gentlemen of the jury, have you come to a decision?
        Foreman: We have, your Honor. The jury are all of the same
        mind — temporarily insane.

RELATED SUBJECTS
Criminals 5178-5224
Policeman 5225-5228
Arrest 5229-5230
Attorney 5235-5244

FINES—SENTENCES

5276   I hereby sentence you to ninety-nine years in the State Peniten-
        tiary. Have you anything to address to the court?
        Well, I guess you're pretty liberal with another man's time.

5277 Judge: I'm going to sentence you to ten years in the penitentiary. Have you anything to offer before sentence is pronounced? Man: Yes, your Honor, could you arrange it so I'd get my old number back? Then I won't have any trouble gettin' my mail.

5278 Judge: Thirty days or fifty dollars. Drunk: Better give me the fifty, Judge. That'll keep my wife from nagging me about where I was last night.

5279 You're going to be in jail a long time. Can I have an outside room? An outside room? Yeah — outside the jail.

5280 And now, my son, what do you think your sentence should be? I believe that it should be electrocution or life imprisonment, or both.

5281 Judge: You seem to always be getting drunk. Thirty days! Man: All right, Judge, I'll toss you — sixty days or nothing.

5282 Judge: And on top of the fifty dollar fine I'm going to give you thirty days. Prisoner laughs. Judge: Say, what are you laughing about? Prisoner: It just occurred to me that now I won't have to attend my wife's bridge party tomorrow night.

RELATED SUBJECTS
Punishment 2521-2524
Arrest 5229-5230
Money 5457-5479

PENITENTIARY

5283 (Visiting prisoner)
Visitor: I've brought you some books to help pass the time away.
Prisoner: That's great! What's the names?
Visitor: "The Great Outdoors" — "Vacation Guide" — and "The Open Country."
Prisoner: What? No travel books?

5284 Are you in jail for drinking?
No, how could a guy mistake a place like this for a saloon?

5285 How did you get out of jail?
I got the hives and scratched out.

5286 Prison walls do not a prison make; nor iron bars a cage.
      Well, if they don't then my uncle's been nuts to sit where he
      has for the last three years.

5287 How long are you in for?
      Fifteen years.
      Ah, well — here's another day nearly gone.

5288 Warden: I'm sorry. I find we have kept you here a week too
      long.
      Convict: That's all right, sir. Knock it off next time.

5289 What do you intend doing when you get out of prison?
      If I tell you, Chaplain, promise me you won't let on.

5290 I've got a kid brother in Sing Sing — he's a pickpocket.
      Just a freshman, eh?

5291 My brother's doing a stretch for shooting his wife. . . .
      My uncle is doing two years for bumping off his wife. Small
      world, isn't it?

5292 I suppose you tried to get in good with the warden?
      Of course. I says to him: Why, Warden, I'll do anything you
      say.
      And what did the Warden say?
      He said: Don't put yourself out.

5293 1st Convict: When I get out of this place I'm going to have
      a hot time, ain't you?
      2nd Convict: I don't know; I'm in for life.

5294 Don't cry because your boy friend's in the penitentiary — now
      he'll be able to pick out any trade and learn it.
      He'll be able to follow any trade he wants?
      Sure he will.
      That's great — it's just the opportunity he's been waiting for.
      What trade does he want to follow?
      He wants to be a sailor.

5295 My uncle is doing odd jobs for the government.
      What do you mean?
      Thirty, sixty and ninety days.
      How is he doing?
      Fine — a ten thousand dollar fine.

5296 Out with it, man. How did you effect your escape?
      Well, sir, me wife sent me a file concealed in a cake, and I'm
      not sure now whether I ate the cake and sawed me way out
      with the file, or ate the file and sawed me way out with the
      cake.

5297 He got ten years with two years off for good behavior, so he took the two years off after spending three days in jail.

5298 Where have you been? I haven't seen you for quite a while.
I've been away for ten days.
Ten days? What doing?
Ten days.

RELATED SUBJECTS
Punishment 2521-2524
Criminals 5178-5224
Policeman 5225-5228
Trial 5251-5275

HANGING

5299 Did I tell you about going up to the penitentiary to see my brother yesterday?
I thought they were supposed to hang him six months ago.
They said they would grant him one request, and he told them he wanted to sing a song before he died.
And then they hanged him?
No, he's still hanging.

5300 Guard: (to prisoner about to be electrocuted) Have you any last words?
Prisoner: Yeah, I'd like to offer my seat to a lady.

5301 A priest, visiting a man about to be hanged, asked: Do you believe in the Father, Son and the Holy Ghost?
Man: Here I am about to die and you ask me riddles!

5302 You mean they're going to hang me?
Yes, on Monday morning.
Can't you hang me on Saturday?
Why don't you want to hang on Monday?
Well, it seems like a terrible way to start the week.

5303   (Guards rushing man to hanging)
       Prisoner: What's your hurry? They ain't gonna be nothin'
       doin' until I get there.

5304   Murderer: (Pardoned) No noose is good noose!

5305   Did you see anybody while you were visiting your brother being
       executed?
       I saw one of the guards leading a man down that last mile.
       The prisoner said: If you take me in that execution room,
       I'll holler long and loud. And the guard said: You may holler
       loud, but not long.

5306   Oh, Judge, must my husband die on the gallows?
       Of course not, of course not, lady. All we do is tie the rope
       around his neck and shove him off. From then on it's entirely
       up to him.

5307   We're going to give you something you want for your last meal.
       All right, can I have some champagne?
       Sure. Any particular vintage?
       Yes—1998.

5308   So they didn't hang your brother after all? What happened?
       Well, you know they always give you whatever you want to
       eat for your last dinner.
       Yeah.
       My brother ordered roast duck, fried chicken, pork chops,
       strawberry pie, chocolate ice cream and French fried potatoes.
       And then the governor pardoned him?
       No, he died from indigestion.

                              RELATED SUBJECTS
                              Death 124-145
                              Punishment 2521-2524
                              Criminals 5178-5224
                              Trial 5251-5275

COMMERCE AND INDUSTRY

BUSINESSMAN

5309   My uncle runs a gasoline station and with every gallon of gas
       he gives away something free.
       He's losing money, isn't he?
       Yeah, but look at the business he's doing.

5310 My uncle owns ten gasoline stations and not one of them has
      a roof.
      What's the idea?
      No overhead.

5311 My brother has a job with a big company.
      Is it a reliable firm? Do they stand behind their products?
      No, they don't stand behind their products. They sell mules.

5312 Don't you know you can't sell life insurance without a license?
      I knew I wasn't selling any, but I didn't know the reason.

5313 What business did you say your uncle was in?
      He runs a clinic.
      He's a doctor at a clinic?
      Not that kind of clinic — a clinic and pressing joint.

5314 How's business?
      Terrible. Even the people who never pay have stopped buying.

5315 My uncle made all his money in crooked dough.
      That isn't a nice way to make a living.
      I'd like to know why not — he's a pretzel manufacturer.

5316 How's business?
      Not bad.
      That's good.

5317 Well, I sold you the business as a goin' concern. Wot's the
      grumble — it's gone, ain't it?

5318 What business are you in?
      The food business.
      What part?
      The eating part.

5319 How is business?
      It's looking up — it's flat on its back.

5320 But if you are selling these watches under cost price, where
      does your profit come in?
      We make our profit out of repairing them.

5321 Smith and Jones had competing businesses and resorted to outdo
      the other. When one slashed prices, the other did the same.
      Smith finally prayed and prayed, and the devil came and said:
      I will give you anthing you wish, but I warn you: what you
      wish, your competitor will have double!
      Okay, okay. Then I wish I could go blind in *one* eye!

STENOGRAPHER

5322 Before I can engage you, you will have to pass an intelligence
test.
Intelligence test? Why, the advertisement said you wanted a
stenographer.

5323 Why did your sister lose her job as a stenographer?
Her boss was so bowlegged she fell through his lap.

5324 You've been a stenographer for about all the big guys in this
building.
Yes, I guess I'm on my last lap now.

5325 Wife: I didn't like your stenographer, so I fired her.
Husband: What! Before you gave her a chance?
Wife: No, before giving you a chance.

5326 In my day I was a bird of a stenographer.
Yeah — a one fingered one. Sort of an underwood pecker.

5327 Can you write shorthand?
Yes, sir — but it takes me longer.

5328 Can you take dictation?
No, I've never been married.

5329 Employer: You came here with good testimonials, Miss Brown,
and do you mean to tell me you don't know the King's English?
Steno: Of course, I know it. Otherwise he wouldn't be King,
would he?

STOCK MARKET

5330 I had a seat on the curb but the street cleaner swept me off.

5331 He is a big man in the stock market.
I invest all my money in stocks.
What are you — a bull or a bear?
I'm a jackass.

5332 I have an Uncle working in Wall Street.
Is he rich?
He was once — use to have a corner on the market — but now
he has a market on the corner.

5333 Were you one of the many fooling with the stock market?
Not me, I was serious; the market did the fooling.

5334 How did Richleigh make all his money?
By judicious speculation and investment.
And how did Poorman lose all his money?
Gambling on the stock market.

5335 Get my broker, Miss Jones.
Yes, sir — stock or pawn?

5336 I hear your uncle lost his great wealth in Wall Street.
Yeah — he was standing on the corner and dropped his last
quarter into the sewer.

5337 I had an interesting interview with a stock salesman today.
I didn't know you were a farmer — are you buying pigs or
cattle?

5338 A woman made a killing in Wall Street today.
Stock operator?
No, she found her husband making love to his secretary.

STATISTICS

5339 Every time you breathe somebody dies.
Come on, I'm going to take you outside and blow in your face.

5340 Do you know that every other person who gets married is a
woman?
I'll bet the rest of them are men.

5341   Do you like candy, young lady?
Oh, sir, yes—indeed, I do, sir.
Thanks. I'm gathering statistics for Whitman's.

5342   I've just been reading some statistics here — every time I
breathe a man dies.
Gosh, man! Why don't you use Listerine?

5343   Five-sixths of the world's people live outside the United States
and struggle along without a slogan.

5344   When better records are made, somebody will break them.

5345   In New York there is a man run over every ten minutes.
What a man!

5346   We are taking a census of ultimate consumers. Are you one?
I used to be — but now I go without.

RELATED SUBJECTS
Businessman 5309-5321
Depression 5495-5499

NEWSPAPER

5347   Good morning, madam . . .
I'm sorry, but I never read magazines . . .
But . . .
No, I don't want to join any country clubs either. I belong to
several clubs now, and I am disgusted with them all. All the
women are cats, and besides I can't afford them.
I'm . . .
Yes, you probably are going to tell me that you want to recom-
mend your hosiery or Paris frocks. Well, I buy all my dresses
in the bargain basement. They're good enough for me, and
they're all I can afford right now.
Permanent . . .
Waves do not interest me in the least. No doubt your beauty
parlor is good, but when a woman is my age no beauty parlor
can do her much good. It's a waste of money.
Your house . . .
No, we don't need any repair work done. My husband used to
be a laboring man and is very handy around the house. Be-

sides, we don't want to spend any money on the house until
it's paid for. What are you writing there? Don't sign me up
for anything, because I won't take it.

I'm not, madam. I'm a reporter from the News and we're taking interviews from prominent club women for the society
page. Thank you very much. Good day!

Ohhhhhhh!

5348 I'm a reporter. I pry into the crevices of old mother earth for
your amusement. In other words, I dig up the dirt.

5349 See here, you've published an announcement of my death by
mistake. That's got to be retracted.

Well, we never contradict anything we print in our newspaper,
but I'll tell you what I'll do — I'll put you in the birth
column tomorrow and give you a fresh start.

5350 Extra! Extra! Extra paper!
All right, if you have an extra one, I'll take it. Thanks.

5351 Thursday I lost a gold watch which I valued very highly.
Immediately I inserted an ad in your lost-and-found column
and waited. Yesterday I went home and found the watch in
the pocket of another suit. God bless your paper!

5352 The Leader was the first paper to announce the death of Bob
Thomas and the first to deny the report as untrue. The Leader
is always first in everything.

5353 My little sister's baby ate a whole newspaper up.
What did you do — send for a doctor?
No, we just fed him a Literary Digest.

5354 Man (to newspaper boy on corner): Don't all those papers
make you tired, my boy?
Newsboy: Naw, I don't read 'em.

5355 Anything new in the paper today?
Oh, no, my dear, just the same old things only happening to
different people.

5356 Business is so good he has so many advertisements he has no
room for news hardly. Last week he had to write an apology
for leaving out part of the news. He couldn't get everything
in so right on the front page he put a little notice. It read:
On account of lack of space, Mrs. Murphy's chilblains and
the birth of nine children will be postponed until next week.

5357 Woman: I want to see your Beauty Editor.
Woman: Are you following her advice?
Woman: Yes, indeed, I am.

Man: Got confidence in it?
Woman: Yes, I have.
Man: Then, you don't want to see her.

RELATED SUBJECTS
Nobility 1134-1135
Society 1136-1144
Conversation 1501-1502
Gossip 1518-1537
Writer 1612-1642
Poet 1643-1652
Actor 4514-4585
Letter 5161-5172

ADVERTISING

5358   It is a short road that has no advertising signs.

5359   Do you find that advertising brings quick results?
I should say it does. Why, only the other day we advertised
for a night watchman, and that night the safe was robbed.

5360   Are you certain that advertisements in your paper bring results?
Absolutely. Why, the last time a man advertised a lost dog, the
dog walked in while the man was writing out the advertisement.

RELATED SUBJECTS
Writer 1612-1642
Radio 4598-4610
Businessman 5309-5321
Stores 5393-5402

TESTIMONIAL

5361   Will you be after?
After? I don't understand.
Will you be after?
What do you mean — after?
I'm going to endorse the Hi-Point Rheumatism medicine and
I've decided to be "before" and I want you to be "after."

RELATED SUBJECTS
Radio 4598-4610
Businessman 5309-5321

OCCUPATIONS

5362   My brother is working with five thousand men under him.
Where?
Mowing lawns in a cemetery.

5363   We'll start from the bottom and you can work up.
Not in my business.
Why not?
I'm a well digger.

5364   I'll make you manager.
What shall I manage?
Just manage to keep out of my way.

5365   Have you ever had any hobbies?
Let's see. I've had the rheumatism and hives, and mumps — but
I can't remember ever having hobbies.

5366   That man wanted me to go into the sausage business with him.
How does his proposition look to you?
Looks like a lot of bologna.

5367   My brother's got a new job. He's a bug electrician.
A bug electrician?
Yeah, he puts the bulbs in lightning bugs.

5368   My father has a job — he's a draft clerk in the Treasury.
A draft clerk?
Yeah, he opens and shuts the windows.

5369   My brother's got a job in an electric shop — he got hold of a
live wire.
What happened?
I don't know — but it's the only job he ever held on to.

5370   My husband peddles balloons wherever there's a parade in
town. What does your husband do?
He sells smoked glasses during the eclipse of the sun.

5371   What position did you hold in your last place?
I was a doer, sir.
A doer — what's that?
Well, sir, you see, when my employer wanted anything done
he would tell the cashier, the cashier would tell the bookkeeper,
the bookkeeper would tell the clerk and the clerk would tell
me.

And what would happen then?
Well, sir, as I hadn't anyone to tell it to, I'd do it.

5372   My brother Joe had a job working under Carter?
Under the president?
He takes care of the furnace in the White House.

5373   What are you by trade?
A poor man.
How's that?
I traded some oil stock for a butcher shop.

5374   Yes, and what's more, what I do for a living takes a lot of guts.
Are you a daredevil?
No, I string violins.

5375   So your uncle's an efficiency expert at the fire department?
Not any more.
What happened?
He put non-breakable glass in the fire alarm boxes.

5376   What do you work at?
At intervals.

NIGHT WATCHMAN

5377 I know a fellow who didn't go to bed for three years at night.
Impossible! How could a man stay up all night for three years?
     What was the matter with him?
He was a night watchman.

5378 What we want is a night watchman who will watch, alert and
ready for the slightest noise or indication of a burglar. Somebody who can sleep with one eye and both ears open and is
not afraid to tackle anything.
I see, sir. I'll send my wife around.

WINDOW WASHER

5379 My uncle broke his leg last week.
How did it happen?
He is a window washer and he was working on the fifth floor
when he stepped back to admire his work.

5380 My brother's got a job. He's a midget window cleaner.
What in the world is a midget window cleaner?
He goes around cleaning people's eye glasses.

CAPITAL AND LABOR

5381 What's capital and labor?
Well, suppose I loaned you two dollars, that's capital. When I try
to get it back, that's labor.

STRIKE

SEE:
Work 1917
Waiter 4761

INTERVIEW (re: Position)

5382 You know how to serve customers?
Yes, sir. I can serve 'em either way.
What do you mean — either way?
So they'll come back, or so they won't.

5383 And why did you leave your last position?
To be frank, sir, the wife of my employer objected to his flirting
with me.
Ah — um — er — well, I think that you may start tomorrow.

5384 Do I understand that you left your last job because you got tired
      of punching the clock?
      No, because I got tired of punching the boss.

5385 I may say I'm pretty smart. I've won several prizes in crossword
      and word picture competitions lately.
      Yes, but I want someone who can be smart during office hours.
      This was during office hours.

> RELATED SUBJECTS
> Ambition 1874-1893
> Work 1894-1944
> Businessman 5309-5321
> Occupations 5362-5380

REFERENCE

5386 Did your employer give you a reference?
      Yes, but it doesn't seem to be any good.
      What does he say?
      He said I was one of the best men his firm ever turned out.

5387 Letter of reference: The bearer of this letter has worked for me
      one week and I am satisfied.

> RELATED SUBJECTS
> Work 1894-1944
> Occupations 5362-5380

LATENESS

5388 My girl was furious with me.
      What's the matter?
      I was an hour late and she had been ready for at least fifteen
      minutes.

5389 How late were you for the party last night?
      Only about six drinks.

5390 Hello. Sorry I was late . . .
      What's your excuse this time, Sam?
      Well, I was called over to Lee's place to help out. One of his
      mules sprained a leg, so I made a splint for it. Then just as I
      was leavin' we found a sick calf, so I made a bed for him. And
      as if that wasn't enough, he's got two sick chickens and . . .
      An' I suppose you laid eggs for 'em?

5391 How many times have I told you to be on time?
      I don't know. I thought you were keeping score.

5392   What time is it?
      It's not one o'clock yet.
      Are you sure?
      Well, I've got to be back at the office by one o'clock and I'm not there yet.

RELATED SUBJECTS
Work 1894-1944
Laziness 1967-1977
Dates 2785-2791
School 4885-4894
Occupations 5362-5380

MARKETS

STORES (In General)

5393   I hear your store was robbed last night. Lose much?
      Some. But it would have been worse if the thugs had got in the night before. You see, yesterday I just finished marking down everything twenty percent.

5394   What do you mean by arguing with that customer? Don't you know our rule? The customer is always right.
      I know it. But he insisted that he was wrong.

5395   What are you going to do with that sugar?
      Oh, you can charge it.
      On what account?
      On account of not having any money with me.

5396   Gimme a dime's worth of asafetida. Dad wants you to charge it.
      All right; what's your name?
      Shermerhorn.
      Take it for nothin' . . . I ain't going to spell asafetida and Shermerhorn for no dime.

5397   Is this a second-hand store?
      Can't you see it's a second-hand store?
      Well, I want a second hand for my watch.

5398   Business is so rotten I'm disgusted.
      Why did you open this shop when you just failed in your last shop?
      I wanted to have a closing sale.

5399   Woman: (Talking over telephone) Send up a bale of hay.
      Merchant: Who's it for?
      Woman: The horse.

5400   Whaddya got in the shape of automobile tires?
      Funeral wreaths, life preservers, invalid cushions and doughnuts.

5401   I bought it at the fifteen cent store.
You mean, the five and ten.
Well, five and ten makes fifteen.

5402   Your opening sale has closed. What now?
Our closing sale opens.

RELATED SUBJECTS
Shopping 3540-3546
Advertising 5358-5360
Occupations 5362-5380
Money 5457-5479

SALESMAN

5403   What happened when that high pressure salesman called today?
Oh, I sold him father's old clothes and all the discarded furniture in the attic.

5404   Your uncle is a traveling man.
How can you tell?
I can tell by the bags under his eyes.

5405   I'm an independent salesman.
Yeah.
Yeah — I take orders from no one.

5406   To what do you owe your extraordinary success as a house to house salesman?
Well, when the woman of the house opens the door I always ask is yuh mother in, little girl?

5407   Salesman: Tell your mother that I am selling a good ant powder.
Child: We have only uncles at this house — and they don't use powder.

5408   So you're a salesman. What do you sell?
Knot holes.
Knot holes? Who to?
To the brewers. They use them to make bungholes for beer barrels.

5409   I hear you're working in a grocery store.
I was, but I got fired. You see the man told me to listen to his sales talk, so I listened. A lady came in and asked for tomatoes. The boss said: Lady, we have canned tomatoes with the flavor and fragrance fresh from the vine.
That's good salesmanship. You should have followed his talk.
I did. The first one came in and asked for canned pigs' feet. I said: Lady we have canned pigs' feet with the flavor and fragrance fresh from the pig-sty.

5410 You should never touch a live wire. It's dangerous.
Then why do they sell them?
Nobody sells live wires.
Certainly they do. I saw an ad in yesterday's paper and it said:
Wanted, a live wire salesman.

5411 Is your brother a good salesman?
Well, he got two orders today.
What for?
One to get out and the other to stay out.

5412 Is he a good salesman?
I'll say — he could sell the foothills a pair of shoes.

5413 Did you ever have any real exciting experiences while you were
a traveling salesman?
About twenty years ago — I was ordered out of a Wyoming town
by a notorious two-gun man who didn't like the cut of my
clothes.
Well, I suppose you lost no time in getting away?
No — I bought him a couple of drinks and sold him the suit.

5414 There is a salesman outside with a lady.
Tell him I'll take her.

5415 1st: Any business?
2nd: Well — yes. The wife gave me some orders this morning.

5416 I made some very valuable contacts today.
I didn't make any sales, either.

RELATED SUBJECTS
Work 1894-1944
Salary 3271-3280
Occupations 5362-5380

PROFIT

5417 I bought a dog for five dollars and I sold him. How much did I
lose?
You bought a dog for five dollars and you sold him and you want
to know how much you lost? Well, what did you sell him for?
For chewing up the furniture.

RELATED SUBJECTS
Shopping 3540-3546
Businessman 5309-5321
Money 5457-5479

DEPARTMENT STORE

5418   I want something to wear around the dormitory.
How large is your dormitory?

5419   Woman: Can you show me what you have in diamond bracelets?
Clerk: But madam! This is hardware.
Woman: Oh, don't worry! I haven't any sales resistance.

5420   How's your brother getting along with his new job?
Well, so far he's learned to sneer just right when he asks a man
if he wants to take his old hat home.

5421   I say, would you take that yellow tie with the pink spots out of
the window for me?
Certainly, sir. Pleased to take anything out of the window any
time, sir.
Thanks, awfully. The beastly thing bothers me every time I pass.

5422   The modest young lady approached a clerk in a department store
and asked to have him show her a teddy. He went over to the
lingerie department and held up a pair. The young lady blushed
furiously and said: Oh, no, sir, I want the kind my baby plays
with.

5423   I'd like to see something in silk stockings.
You men are all alike.

5424   Is the color fast?
Why don't you chase it and see?

5425   I want to buy a petticoat.
Yes, miss, period costumes on the third floor.

5426   When your father sent you for samples of cloth didn't he say
what color and material he wanted?
I don't think it matters. He wants them for pen wipers.

5427   Have you any pillow cases?
Yes, sir. What size?
I really don't know, but I wear a size seven hat.

5428   Thanks for showing me all these silks, but I'm not buying anything myself. I was just looking for a neighbor.
Do you think she could be in that one bolt of mauve that I didn't
show you?

5429   I have a brother who works in a department store. Yesterday he came home and said he was fired. He made a mistake and took a sign off a blouse counter and put it on the bath tub display. The sign read: How would you like to see your best girl in one of these for $9.99?

RELATED SUBJECTS
Furniture 3163-3170
Installment Plan 3171-3180
Bills 3281-3308
Clothing 3391-3502
Gift 3943-3962
Detective 4277-4279
Books 4961-4977
Businessman 5309-5321
Stores 5393-5402

DRUG STORE

5430   I want a bottle of iodine.
Sorry, but this is a drug store. Can't I interest you in an alarm clock, some nice leather goods, a few radio parts, or a toasted cheese sandwich?

5431   What's the matter with all your sponges?
Why, nothing's wrong with them — they're all good sponges.
I don't agree with you — they're all full of holes.

5432   A pharmacist is a man in a white coat who stands behind the soda fountain selling ten dollar watches in a drug store.

5433   Gimme a tablet.
What kind of a tablet?
A yellow one.
But what's the matter with you?
I want to write a letter.

5434   Do you know the duties of a drug store clerk?
Sure, I can make sandwiches, sell stamps and sell soda.

5435   He is a great druggist, isn't he?
He is — but don't you think he makes his chicken salad a little too salty?

5436   Man: I want a mustard plaster.
Druggist: We're out of mustard; but how about mayonnaise?

5437   Customer: Hear business is slack; how's it with you?
Druggist: Oh, the stamps are going fine.

GROCERY STORE

5438   Would you like some wax beans, ma'am?
Go away with your lousy imitations. I want real ones.

5439   Is that the head cheese over there?
No, ma'am, the boss ain't in.

5440   Customer: Five pounds of coffee, please.
Grocer: Yes, anything else today?
Customer: Well, if it isn't too heavy a package, I'll take it with me.
Grocer: Oh, no, it'll only weigh three or four pounds.

5441   How many pieces of that candy do I get for a dime?
Oh, two or three.
I'll take three, please.

5442   Woman: This milk—is it fresh?
Grocer: Is it fresh? Why, it's so fresh that just three hours ago it
was still grass!

5443   Sufferin' snakes! You sold the wrong eggs to that last woman.
How so?
You sold her some of that lot we dated September tenth and it's
only September 1st now.

5444   Gimme an all-day sucker.
Here you are.
Looks kind of small.
Yeah, the days are getting shorter.

5445   How much are your peaches?
Thirty cents each, lady.
I'll have one, please.
Givin' a party, lady?

5446   We have some very nice alligator pears this morning.
How silly — why, we don't even keep goldfish, mister.

5447   Customer: Three of those apples you sent me were rotten. I'll
bring them back.
Merchant: That's all right, you needn't bring them back. Your
word is just as good as the apples.

5448   Woman: Grocer! I want my money back! The coffee I bought
this morning tastes like mud!
Grocer: Of course, it does! It was just *ground* this morning!

BUTCHER SHOP

5449   How much do you pay?

Seventy dollars a week—but what can you do to make yourself useful around a butcher shop?

Anything.

Well, be specific. Can you dress a chicken?

Not on seventy dollars a week.

5450   Customer: Look here, butcher, you are giving me a big piece of bone. With meat as high as it is I don't want all that bone.

Butcher: I'm not giving it to you, mister, you're paying for it.

5451   And so you want a dollars' worth of dog bones, do you sonny?

Yes, sir. And please give me some with more meat on 'em this time. Pop couldn't get a good mouthful off the last bunch.

5452   (Over telephone)

Hello! This is Mrs. Jones. Will you send some nice cutlets right away?

I'm sorry, but we haven't any cutlets.

Well, then, a couple of nice lean pork chops.

We haven't any pork chops either, Mrs. Jones.

Oh, how provoking! Then a small sirloin steak will have to do.

We haven't any steak.

For heaven's sake! Aren't you Smith, the butcher?

No, I'm Smith, the florist.

Oh! Well, send me a dozen white lilies. My husband must be starved to death by now.

5453   Oh, Mrs. Nash, how about a nice turkey?

No, thanks, I prefer a goose.

SHOE STORE

5454   How much are your twenty dollar shoes?

Ten dollars a foot.

5455 The soles of my shoes are so thin I could step on a dime and tell whether it's heads or tails.

5456 Where is your father?
My father is at home.
How do you know?
I have his shoes on.

RELATED SUBJECTS
Feet 405-430
Businessman 5309-5321
Stores 5393-5402
Salesman 5403-5416
Money 5457-5479

FINANCE

MONEY

5457 Skunks are never broke.
How come?
They always carry scents.

5458 Say, will you change this quarter for me?
Sure! What do you want it changed for?
'Cause mother thinks it's a bad one.

5459 I'll never go out with another millionaire as long as I live.
What's the matter, are you tired of them?
No, I married one last night.

5460 Is your son mercenary?
No, I can't say he is. He doesn't seem to love money enough to work for it.

5461 How much money do you have on you tonight?
Well, between ninety-eight and a hundred dollars.
That's a lot of money.
Not such a lot — only two dollars.

5462 Why do you say he is financially embarrassed?
He's so shy in his payments.

5463 You wouldn't marry me for money, would you?
No, I wouldn't marry you for all the money in the world.

5464 Come on, let's go.
I can't. I just dropped a dime on the floor.
Why don't you pick it up?
I can't — you're standing on it.

5465 About the only business that makes money without advertising, is the Mint.

5466 Florida is certainly the land of palms.
All you see is palms — everybody has their hand out.

5467 This quarter's no good — it won't ring.
Whaddya want for two bits — chimes?

5468 Definition of money: Obsolete — no longer in use.

5469 I don't like the ring of this half dollar.
What do you want for fifty cents — a peal of bells?

5470 May I ask what happened to the sinking fund?
It sank.

5471 Did anyone lose a roll of bills around here with a rubber band
around them?
Yes, I did.
Well, I've found the rubber band.

5472 I'm sorry your husband is bankrupt.
Oh, yes, it has upset him so terribly that he's going to retire from
business and go abroad.

5473 I'm starting on my second million!
Your second million? You haven't got the first million.
Yeah — they always say making your second million is the easiest.

5474 I want to have my face put on some money.
I would be glad if I had my hands on some.

5475 Somebody slipped me a bad half dollar.
Maybe it isn't a bad half dollar — let me see it.
I can't — I bought this tie with it.

5476 When I first came to New York I had only a dollar in my pocket
with which to make a start.
How did you invest that dollar?
Used it to pay for a telegram home for more money.

5477 Can you change a dollar for me?
Almost. I can change sixty-five cents for it.

5478 My father lost money on everything my brother made.
What did your brother make?
Mistakes.

5479 Would you be happy if you had all the money you wanted?
I'd be happy if I had all the money my creditors wanted.

RELATED SUBJECTS
Insurance 208-216
Economy 1997-2030

Husband 3113-3115
Installment Plan 3171-3180
Family 3209-3217
Budget 3315-3316
Finance 5457-5537

WEALTH

5480 Ireland is the richest country in the world. Her capitol is always Dublin.

5481 One way to make money is to buy dirt cheap and sell in the highest market. What do you think of that system?
Well, I don't know. You see, I never bought dirt.

5482 He's so rich he can afford to use a toothpick in public.

5483 He's worth in the neighborhood of a million dollars, I've heard.
Good! That's my favorite neighborhood.

5484 I'm glad to find you as you are. Your great wealth hasn't changed you.
Well, it has changed me in one thing. I'm now eccentric where I used to be impolite, and delightfully witty where I used to be rude.

5485 That immensely wealthy fellow yonder started out with a shoe string.
That just shows his ability. Imagine being able to sell somebody one shoe string.

5486 Why do so many women carry their wealth around in their stocking?
Because they are entitled to bank their money where it draws the most interest.

RELATED SUBJECTS
Income Tax 3317-3323

Income Tax 3322
Golf 4337
Autograph 4592
Businessman 5315
Stock Market 5336

DONATION
SEE:
Musical Instruments 1762
Mother-in-law 3116

BANK

5487   What's the idea of overdrawing your checking account?
Oh, it's all right, dear. I just sent them a check to cover the
amount I overdrew.

5488   A woman went to the bank and asked for a new check book: I've
lost the one you gave me yesterday, but it doesn't matter. I
took the precaution of signing all the checks as soon as I got it,
so, of course, it won't be any use to anyone else.

5489   Where are we going to get that check of yours cashed, pal?
I couldn't say. I can't think of a single place where I'm unknown.

5490   Why does the moon go to the bank?
To change quarters.

5491   The bank has returned that check.
Isn't that splendid! What can we buy with it this time?

5492   Just got a notice from the bank saying I'm overdrawn.
Try some other bank — they can't all be overdrawn.

5493   Your bank account is overdrawn.
Well, maybe all my checks aren't in yet.

5494   What were you doing in that bank?
Starting an account.
Savings account?
No, spending account.

RELATED SUBJECTS
Economy 1997-2030
Marriage 2882-3051
Attorney 5236-5244
Businessman 5309-5321
Stock Market 5330-5338
Money 5457-5479

DEPRESSION

5495   What is your opinion of the recession?
        Recession? Say, people in California don't know what the word
        recession means. Things are ten times as tough in Arizona.
        What makes you think that?
        Well, I was down in Arizona last week on the desert and I heard
        a couple of snakes talking behind a rock. One snake said to the
        other: "If things don't pick up by next August—we won't have
        a spot to hiss in."

5496   Since the recession they've changed the sign: Keep off the
        grass—to Don't eat the grass!

5497   Well, old man, get through the hard times all right?
        Oh, so so.
        Still occupying that penthouse?
        Yes, I've managed somehow to keep a roof under my feet.

5498   If every one in America who says he hasn't a pot would buy one,
        the pottery business would pick up.

5499   Well, how has the recession affected you?
        Haven't felt it at all.
        You haven't? What have you been doing?
        I've been doing time for five years.

> RELATED SUBJECTS
> Salary 3271-3280
> Businessman 5309-5321
> Stock Market 5330-5338
> Statistics 5339-5346
> Finance 5457-5537

BROKE

5500   Hey, lend me a quarter, will ya?
        Say, if it cost five cents for a trip around the world, I couldn't
        get out of sight.

5501   Have you ever been in want?
        I don't know — what town's it near?

> RELATED SUBJECTS
> Money 5457-5479
> Bank 5487-5494
> Beggar 5518-5537

CHISELER

5502 The boy's no good — all he does is sponge off the old man's back.
Oh, sponging off the old man?

RELATED SUBJECTS
Boast 2285-2304
Dishonesty 2500-2502

LOAN

5503 You couldn't loan me ten dollars, could you?
No, but how did *you* know it?

5504 Hy, Bill. Didn't I borrow ten bucks from you yesterday?
Nope.
How careless of me. Could you give it to me now?

5505 Can you lend me a tenner for a month, old boy?
What does a month-old-boy want with a tenner?

5506 I'm looking for somebody to lend me five dollars.
Well, you've got a nice day for it.

5507 Loan me five dollars, will you?
No.
I was only fooling.
I wasn't.

5508 Let me take five till pay day, will you, old man?
Sure — here you are. By the way, where are you working now?
Nowhere.

5509 I think you're a nice kid. I've known you about five years. Could
you let me have five dollars?
I'm sorry — I couldn't.
Why?
Because I have known you for five years.

5510 Lend me five dollars, old man. I promise you, on the word of a
gentleman, to pay it back tomorrow.
Bring the gentleman around and let me see him.

5511 Mr. Jones — er — ah — that is — can — er — I will — will
you . . .
Why, yes, my boy, you may have her.
What's that? Have whom?
My daughter, of course. That's what you mean — you want to
marry her, don't you?
Why no — I just wanted to know if you could lend me five
dollars.
Certainly not! Why, I hardly know you.

5512　Send some money or we'll all go to the poorhouse Friday.
　　　　Wait until Saturday and I'll go with you.

5513　Smith has just refused to lend me a five spot. Did you think there
　　　　were such mean people in the world?
　　　　Yes, I'm another like that myself.

　　　　　　　　　　　　RELATED SUBJECTS
　　　　　　　　　　　　Friend 1037-1056
　　　　　　　　　　　　Businessman 5309-5321
　　　　　　　　　　　　Finance 5457-5537

PAWN BROKER

5514　What time is it?
　　　　What's the matter with that watch I gave you for your birthday?
　　　　　　Isn't it going?
　　　　Going? It's gone. I went to bed late last night and forgot to wind
　　　　　　the pawn ticket.

5515　My father has a three hundred dollar watch.
　　　　What is its movement?
　　　　To and from the pawn shop.

5516　What do you have there?
　　　　A pawn ticket.
　　　　Just one?
　　　　Yeah.
　　　　Oh, I wish you had two — then we could both go.

5517　What do those three balls in front of a pawn shop mean?
　　　　Two to one you'll never get it back.

　　　　　　　　　　　　RELATED SUBJECTS
　　　　　　　　　　　　Money 5457-5479
　　　　　　　　　　　　Broke 5500-5501

BEGGAR

5518　Are you content to spend your life walking 'round the country
　　　　　　begging?
　　　　No, lady. Many's the time I've wished for a car.

5519　Why do you beg, little boy, are you hungry?
　　　　No, but papa is thirsty.

5520　Tramp: The lidy next door 'as give me a piece of 'ome-made cake.
　　　　　　Won't you give me something, too?
　　　　Lady: Yes, I'd better give you a digestive tablet.

5521   I have seen better days, sir.
I suppose you have, but I have no time to discuss the weather with you now.

5522   Your neighbor just gave me a piece of pie. What are *you* going to give me?
A dose of bicarbonate of soda.

5523   Mister, will you give me a quarter for me sick wife?
No, I'm awfully sorry, old man, but I've got a wife.

5524   Could you give a poor fellow a bite?
I don't bite myself, but I'll call the dog.

5525   Here's a penny, my poor man. How did you become so destitute?
I was like you, mum — agivin' away vast sums to the poor and needy.

5526   Boss, will you give me a dime for a sandwich?
Let's see the sandwich.

5527   Have you money for a cup of coffee, mister?
No, but don't worry about me, I'll get along all right.

5528   Have you a good square meal for a hungry man, missus?
Yes, and he'll be home presently, so you'd better go.

5529   Housewife: You can earn your dinner if you'll chop up that pile of wood.
Tramp: Let me see the menu first.

5530   Why do you feed every tramp who comes along? They never do any work for you.
No, but it's quite a satisfaction to see a man eat a meal without finding fault with the cooking.

5531   Beggar: Lady, will you give me a quarter to get where me family is?
Lady: Certainly. Here's the quarter. Where is your family?
Beggar: At de movies.

5532   A tramp came to the door of a motherly old lady and said: I haven't eaten in three days.
Lady: That's no good. You must force yourself to eat.

5533   Lady, could you give me something to eat?
My good man, have you no work?
Kind lady, I am an artist.
What do you do in art?
I make house to house canvasses.

5534   Please, mum, could I have a dollar?
What for?
I want to start a bank account.

5535   I haven't much to eat in the house, but would you like some cake?
Yes.
Yes — what?
Yes, dear.

5536   Cook: Why, you're the same man I gave a piece of mince pie to
yesterday.
Tramp: Yus, but I 'ardly expected to find the same cook 'ere today.

5537   Have you a piece of cake, lady, to give a poor man who hasn't
had a bite to eat for two days?
Cake? Isn't bread good enough for you?
Ordinarily, yes, ma'am, but this is my birthday.

> RELATED SUBJECTS
> Ambition 1874-1893
> Money 5457-5479
> Broke 5500-5501

COMMUNICATION SYSTEMS (*Commercial*)
TELEPHONE

5538   Telephone Operator: You want Hollywood 1234? The line is
busy. But I could give you Hollywood 4321 or Gladstone 1234
— they are very nice numbers.

5539   Telephone Operator: It's a long distance from Washington.
Man: (Hangs up) It sure is. Anyone knows that.

5540   The President of the Telephone Company was aroused from his
slumbers by the ringing of the telephone.
President: Hello.
Voice: Are you an official of the telephone company?
President: Yes. What can I do for you?
Voice: Tell me how it feels to get out of bed at two o'clock to an-
swer a wrong number.

5541   Girl: (over telephone) Hello, mother? I just called to tell you I
won't be home.
Man: That phone is not connected, lady.
Girl: That's all right — my mother's not home.

5542   (Over telephone) What number is this?
       Voice: You ought to know — you called it.

5543   Is there any particular place where you want the telephone installed?
       No. I'll take my phone where I find it.

5544   (Phone rings.)
       What? No-no-not right now. Thanks for calling.
       Who was that?
       Oh, the operator. She said she got hold of a few *right* numbers, and thought I could use them.

5545   It costs seventy-five cents to talk to Bloomfield.
       Can't you make a special rate for listening? I want to call my wife.

5546   Hello, this is Pete.
       Hello, Pete — what's on your mind?
       I'm broke down in Los Angeles and I need a hundred dollars right away.
       There must be something wrong with the line. I can't hear you.
       I say, I want to borrow one hundred dollars.
       I can't hear a word you're saying.
       Operator: (coming on line) Hello! This is the operator. I can hear him very plainly.
       Then you give him the hundred dollars.

5547   How would you classify a telephone girl? Is hers a business or a profession?
       Neither. It's a calling.

5548   Please, sir, I think you're wanted on the 'phone.
       You think! What's the good of thinking?
       Well, sir, the voice at the other end said, "Hello, is that you, you old idiot?"

5549   I can remember when people thought the telephone was something impossible.
       It still is.

RELATED SUBJECTS
Radio 4598-4610
Businessman 5309-5321

TELEGRAM

5550   I wonder who this telegram is from.
       Western Union. I recognize the handwriting.

5551   Look what he sent me.
       A bale of wire!
       Yeah, I told him to send me a cable and that's what he sent.

5552   Why did you strike the telegraph operator?
       I gives him a telegram to send to my gal and he starts reading it
          — so I ups and gives him one.

5553   What's the big idea sending yourself as a telegram?
       Well, I forgot where your office was, so I sent for a telegraph mes-
          senger and sent myself as a telegram.
       But did you have to come collect?
       I wanted to make sure the boy would bring me in a hurry.

5554   Here's a telegram for you — collect ten dollars.
       Is it from a friend?
       No, can't be — I don't know a friend that knows ten dollars
          worth of words.

5555   Papa got a telegram!
       Bad news?
       Yes. It came collect — but he can't open it until later.
       Why not?
       It's a night letter.

5556   I want to send a telegram.
       To whom is the message going?
       My sister.
       Your sister? What's her name?
       What's her name? The same as mine.
       How do you spell it?
       Spell it any way you want to — you're supposed to know every-
          body's name and address.

5557   Clerk: (reading wire) Dear Joe I'm coming out to visit you stop
          business is swell regards from your brother Joe. That'll be five
          dollars.
       Man: Five dollars! Let me see it again (To himself) He knows
          he's my brother and he'll see me when I get there and he'll
          know I wouldn't be visiting him unless business is good. (to
          clerk) Just send my name . . . collect.

RELATED SUBJECTS
Radio 4598-4610
Businessman 5309-5321

CHAMBER OF COMMERCE

CITIES

5558   We're going to Pittsburgh.
What burgh?
Pittsburgh — pitts — pitts — you know what's in the middle of a peach.
Worms if it's a bad peach.

5559   Why do they always say Pittsburgh is smoky — is it because of the factories there?
No — it's the stogies the men smoke.

5560   What do they mean by the "City's pulse?"
Oh, I suppose it has something to do with the policemen's beats.

5561   It's a story about Mr. and Mrs. Cats of Suffern, New York.
Mr. and Mrs. Cats?
Yeah. Didn't you ever hear of the Suff'rin' Cats?

5562   Astoria, New York, is a nice place.
How do you know? Ever been there?
No, but it's a nice place. Children cry for Astoria.

RELATED SUBJECTS
Travel 3971-4246
Geography 5003-5014

POPULATION

5563   How many people live in your home town?
About two thousand, counting the cemetery.

RELATED SUBJECTS
Foreign Cities 3990-3999
Famous Places 4000-4015

CALIFORNIA

5564   It seems as though this year the usual unusual weather has been more unusual than usual.

5565   They tell me they got bullfrogs in the Los Angeles river seven years old that never learned to swim.

5566   And you mean to say that in California you have 365 days of sun-
       shine a year?
       Exactly so, sir, and that's a mighty conservative estimate.

RELATED SUBJECTS
Weather Bureau 5589-5596

FLORIDA
SEE:
Christmas 3921
Grapefruit 4872
Money 5466

TIME

THE HOUR
5567   I have a watch but it doesn't run.
       Why don't you throw it away?
       I should say not. It's right twice a day.

5568   The question of the hour: What time is it?

5569   (Two drunks were so tipsy that neither one could see a thing
       clearly.)
       1st: Hey, what time *is* it?
       2nd: (Thrusting out his watch) There it is.
       1st: (staring at the watch) So it is!

5570   Do you know how to beat time?
       No.
       Be a music teacher.

5571   I've had this watch for years — runs perfectly — never loses a
       minute — and . . .
       That's nothing. I dropped my watch into the Hudson River a
       year ago and it's been running ever since.
       What — the same watch?
       No the Hudson River.

5572   Two men were out playing poker and had completely lost track
       of the time.
       Pete: What time you got?
       Fred: 4:00 *A.M.*
       Frank: Wow! Guess your wife will hit the ceiling!
       Fred: Guess so. She's such a rotten shot.

5573   I'd like to buy an alarm clock. What I want is a clock that'll rouse
father without waking the whole family.
I don't know of any such alarm clock as that, but we keep just
the ordinary kind that will wake the whole family without dis-
turbing father.

5574   Oh pshaw! I left my watch upstairs.
Never mind, it'll run down.
No, it won't — there's a winding staircase.

5575   If a man smashed a clock, could he be accused of killing time?
Not if he could prove that the clock struck first.

RELATED SUBJECTS
Dates 2785-2791
School 4885-4894
Businessman 5309-5321
Lateness 5388-5392

CUCKOO CLOCKS

5576   (Cuckoo Clock cuckoos five times — then we hear three shots)
What's the idea shooting that cuckoo out of the clock?
Just killing time.

5577   How do you like my new cuckoo clock?
Fine.
(Bird comes out and cuckoos ten times)
But it's only nine o'clock. Why does the bird cuckoo ten times?
I don't know — unless it's because he's cuckoo.

DAYS

5578   What's the date today?
I don't know. Why don't you look at the newspaper you have in
your pocket?
That won't do any good. It's yesterday's paper.

5579   Which month has twenty-eight days?
All of them.

5580   How many days in February?
Thirty.

Thirty? What makes you say that?
Well, all I know is last February my old man got thirty days.

5581   What is it, Julia, that comes in like a lion and goes out like a lamb?
Father.

5582   Do you believe that opportunity knocks once at every man's door?
Pope? Good gracious! I thought it always came from the grocer.

RELATED SUBJECTS
Progress of World 5635-5636

SEASONS OF YEAR

5583   Aren't you going to summer in the country?
No, I'm going to simmer in the city.

5584   In the spring a young man's fancy turns to what the girls have
been thinking of all winter.

OPPORTUNITY

5585   Do you believe that opportunity knocks once at every man's door?
No, but on certain streets it will tap a couple of times on the
window.

5586   (Three knocks on door)
Who is there?
It is I, Opportunity!
Don't be silly — Opportunity only knocks once and you knocked
three times.

5587   Yes, Dad, I have a chance to embrace an opportunity.
Fine, son. I'm tellin' you — give it a good hug.

RELATED SUBJECTS
Ambition 1874-1893

LUCK

5588   Cheer up, Dame Fortune will come to your door one of these fine
days.
She'll have to knock then. Her daughter, Miss Fortune, has
wrecked the bell.

WEATHER

WEATHER BUREAU

5589 The way to forecast the weather is to cut an onion and carefully study the slices.
You mean, vegetables are weather prophets?
Yes. You chop up an onion, slice a tomato, take a cabbage and shred it — then mix thoroughly after adding some breeze.
What does that give you?
Cole slaw.
How about the weather?
You look in the newspaper.

5590 (Woman talking to weatherman) How about a shower tonight?
That's all right with me; if you need one — take one!

5591 There has never been a woman appointed to the Weather Bureau?
I wonder why.
The weather is changeable enough as it is.

5592 You should get a job in the Weather Bureau.
Why?
You're an expert on wind.

5593 Weather report from Mexico: Chili today and hot-tamale.

5594 My uncle was the weather man in our town and he predicted sunny weather for all the last few months. He had to leave town.
Why?
Because the weather didn't agree with him.

5595 I don't like this cold weather.
Oh, it's nothing.

What are you talking about? — It's zero.
Well, that's nothing.

5596   How do you suppose that weather prophet happens to hit all the
        rainy days for a whole year ahead?
        He has a simple, sure-fire system. He knows the dates of all the
        Sunday School picnics, circus days, baseball games and every-
        thing of that sort — and the rest is easy.

RELATED SUBJECTS
Nature 5637-5640

TEMPERATURE

5597   It was so hot we fed the chickens cracked ice to keep them from
        laying hard boiled eggs.

5598   Was it hot where you spent your vacation last summer?
        Terrible, and no trees! We took turns sitting in each other's shade.

5599   Which travels faster — heat or cold?
        Heat.
        What makes you think so?
        Because you catch cold.

5600   Do you know how to make anti-freeze, sir?
        Sure, hide her pajamas.

5601   If you're so cold, why don't you try a hot water bottle?
        I tried that.
        Didn't it work?
        I couldn't get my feet in the neck of the bottle.

5602   My feet are cold.
        Well, all you have to do is go to bed and have a brick at your feet.
        I tried that.
        Did you get the brick hot?
        Get it hot? It took all night just to get it warm.

5603   It's getting colder . . .
        Yeah — I woke up this morning and it was ten in my room.
        I couldn't sleep with that many in my room.
        Well, I'll admit it is a little hard — especially if you're the last
        one in and you have to sleep hanging on the edge.

5604   Shut the door, it's cold outside.
        Will that make it any warmer outside?

5605   You know how cold it was?
        Uh huh.
        I got in between so many blankets I had to put in a bookmark to
        show where I was.

5606   It is getting cold — the thermometer is falling.
        Prop it up until I can save up enough money to buy an overcoat.

5607   It was so cold the cutest snow man walked out of the yard and
        tried to get into our house.

5608   It was cold yesterday — so cold I could hardly stand it. You know
        the Statue of Abraham Lincoln in the park — the one with his
        hand on the little boy's head?
        Yeah. What about it?
        Well, it was so cold Abe had to take his hand off the little boy's
        head and put it in his pocket.

5609   My apartment is cold and I'm hot under the collar!
        Well, go back in your apartment and cool off.

5610   So cold, I'm stiff as a board.
        Don't blame it on the weather.

5611   It's so cold, I saw an icicle wearing ear muffs.

5612   It was so cold, he dropped a bottle of milk and a pound of sugar
        and he picked up the swellest tasting ice cream.

5613   Paper will keep you warm.
        Yeah — I remember a thirty day note that kept me in a sweat for
        a month.

                 RELATED SUBJECTS
                 Vacation 3965-3970
                 North Pole 4009

FOG

5614   London is the foggiest place in the world.
        Oh no, it's not. I've been in a place foggier than London.
        Where was it?
        I don't know where it was, it was so foggy.

                 RELATED SUBJECTS
                 Automobile 4042-4146
                 Weather Bureau 5589-5596

RAIN

5615   Wasn't that an awful storm a few days ago? On Long Island the snow was up to the roof tops — can you account for that?
No, it is too deep for me.

5616   Is it raining outside?
Did you ever see it raining inside?

5617   When it snowed there was more snow on our neighbor's yard than there was on ours.
How could that be?
Our neighbor has a larger yard.

5618   It's raining cats and dogs outside.
Yes, I just stepped into a poodle.

5619   Did the rain freshen things up?
My wife said the rain was too fresh. She no more than stepped out of the house when the rain started patting her on the back.

5620   What's the idea of showing up with those shin guards on? We're not playing hockey.
I know it, but when I came in it was raining cats and dogs.
So what?
I had to wade through a lot of poodles.

5621   Think it will rain this afternoon?
I wouldn't be surprised. I've got a new hat, a fresh shoe shine and I've just had my car washed.

5622   I know what snow is.
Well, what is it?
Popped hailstones.

5623   Can you think of anything worse than raining cats and dogs?
Yes, hailing taxis.

RELATED SUBJECTS
Nature 5637-5640

LIGHTNING

5624   When I was a kid our house was hit by a flash of electricity.
Flash of electricity? Don't you know the difference between electricity and lightning?
Yes, you don't have to pay anything for lightning.

RELATED SUBJECTS
Death 124-145
Fear 2340-2347
Weather Bureau 5589-5596

UMBRELLA

5625   Why are you carrying those three umbrellas?
One to forget in the train, one to leave in the restaurant and one in case it rains.
It's too late now. You're all wet anyway.

5626   My grandfather never uses an umbrella when it rains.
What does he do?
He just gets wet.

5627   I just saw six people under an umbrella and not one of them got wet.
How come?
It wasn't raining.

5628   Here's your umbrella, old man. I didn't know until today that I never returned it. I swiped a silk umbrella today so I don't need your old cotton one any longer. Besides, there's two ribs broken in it.

5629   Where did you get that umbrella?
It was a gift from sister.
You told me you hadn't any sisters.
I know — but that's what's engraved on the handle.

5630   Well, my dear, you will kindly observe that I have not left my umbrella behind in the church today.
No — the trouble is that you didn't take one with you. You'll find yours at home.

5631   Pardon me, but you're holding your umbrella so your legs are getting all wet.
I know, but my legs are forty years old and my hat is brand new.

> RELATED SUBJECTS
> Absentmindedness 1297-1319
> Forgetfulness 1609-1611
> Weather Bureau 5589-5596

WIND

5632   Last week a cyclone hit our house.
Did it hurt the house any?
I don't know — we haven't found it yet.

5633   The wind is blowing from the south.
How do you know it's a south wind?
I have a method of my own. I have a pole cat tied up in the center of town and the residents from the north are complaining.

5634   (Telling story)
It is a dark night and the wind is whistling through the air

like this (whistle: *Nothing Could Be Finer Than To Be In Carolina*)

How could the wind whistle *Nothing Could Be Finer Than To Be in Carolina?*

It's a southern wind.

RELATED SUBJECTS
Weather Bureau 5589-5596
Nature 5637-5640

WORLD

PROGRESS OF WORLD

5635   Twenty-five years ago when something whizzed by your head you knew some horse was feeling his oats. Nowadays when something whizzes by you — you know some jackass is feeling his rye.

5636   Times have changed. It used to take two sheep two years to produce material for the outfit of a well-dressed woman. Now a silkworm can do it on his Sunday afternoon off.

RELATED SUBJECTS
Geography 5003-5014
History 5015-5026
Depression 5495-5499
Opportunity 5585-5587
Luck 5588

NATURE

5637   Nature is wonderful! A million years ago she didn't know we were going to wear spectacles, yet look at the way she placed our ears.

5638   Why do they refer to Nature as a woman?
Because they can't find out how old it is.

5639   You seem to be filled with freshness!
I should be — I spent all morning in the park reveling with Dame Nature.
Oh, and *you* a married man!

5640   Nature is wonderful.
Yeah, I like nature — especially human nature — if it's beautiful girls.

RELATED SUBJECTS
Heaven 2555-2565
Farmer 3741-3760
Weather Bureau 5589-5596

INDEX